IF THEY WERE ALIVE TODAY

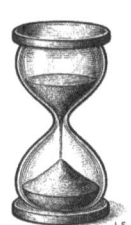

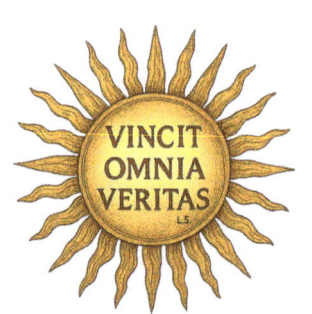

ᴼᴸᵒ LOCHLAINN SEABROOK WRITES IN THE FOLLOWING GENRES ᴼᴸᵒ

Adult	Men
Alternate History	Metaphysics
American Civil War	Military History
American History	Mysteries and Enigmas
American Politics	Mysticism
American South	Natural Health
Ancient History	Natural History
Anthropology	Onomastics
Apocrypha	Paleography
Biblical Exegesis	Paleontology
Biblical Hermeneutics	Paranormal
Biography	Patriarchy
Children	Philosophy
Christian Mysticism	Photography
Coffee Table	Pictorial
Comparative Mythology	Poetry
Comparative Religion	Politics
Cooking	Prehistory
Cryptozoology	Presidential History
Diet and Nutrition	Quiz
Education	Reference
Encyclopediology	Religion
Entertainment	Revolutionary Period
Ethnic Studies	Science
Etymology	Scripture
European History	Self-help
Evolutionary Biology	Spirituality
Exposés	Spiritualism
Family Histories	Sport Science
Film	Technology
Genealogy	Thanatology
Ghost Stories	Thealogy
Gospels	Theology
Health and Fitness	UFOlogy
Humor	Vexillology
Illustrations	Victorian Period
Law of Attraction	Western
Lexicography	Wildlife
Life After Death	Women
Matriarchy	World History

Mr. Seabrook does not author books for fame and glory, but for the love of writing and sharing his knowledge.

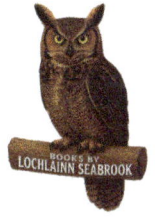

Be curious, not judgmental.

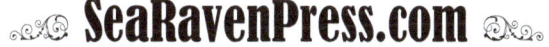

IF THEY WERE ALIVE TODAY

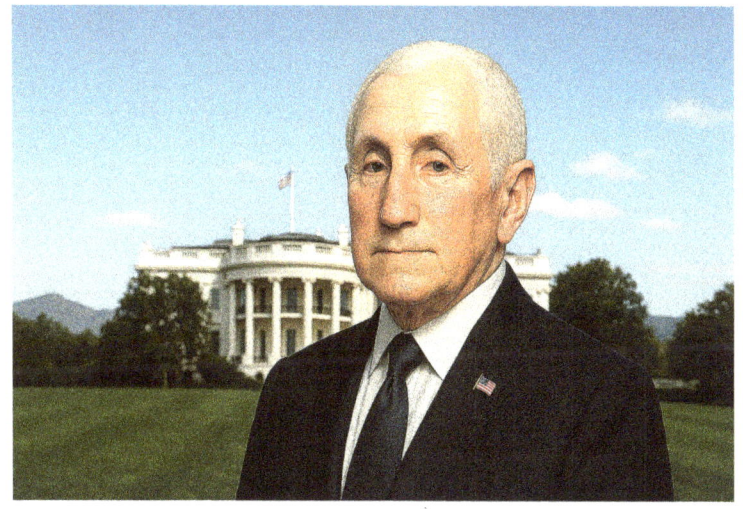

How Famous Historic Americans Might Look if They Lived in the 21st Century

LOCHLAINN SEABROOK
Bestselling Author, Award-Winning Historian, Acclaimed Artist

Diligently Researched and Generously Illustrated by the Author for the Elucidation of the Reader

2025

Sea Raven Press, Park County, Wyoming, USA

IF THEY WERE ALIVE TODAY

Published by
Sea Raven Press, LLC, founded 1995
Park County, Wyoming, USA
SeaRavenPress.com

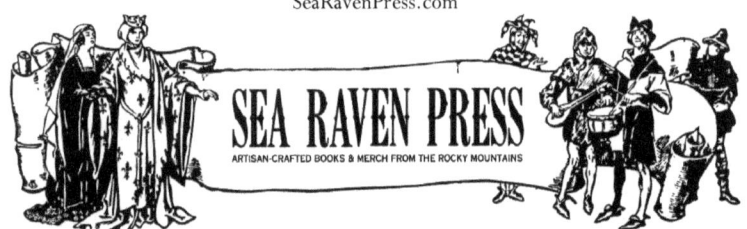

Copyright © all text, artwork, and illustrations Lochlainn Seabrook 2025
in accordance with U.S. and international copyright laws and regulations, as stated and protected under the Berne Union for the Protection of Literary and Artistic Property (Berne Convention), and the Universal Copyright Convention (the UCC). All rights reserved under the Pan-American and International Copyright Conventions.

PRINTING HISTORY
1st SRP paperback edition, 1st printing, July 2025 • ISBN: 978-1-955351-60-7
1st SRP hardcover edition, 1st printing, July 2025 • ISBN: 978-1-955351-61-4

ISBN: 978-1-955351-60-7 (paperback)
Library of Congress Control Number: 2025941931

This work is the copyrighted intellectual property of Lochlainn Seabrook and has been registered with the Copyright Office at the Library of Congress in Washington, D.C., USA. No part of this work (including text, covers, drawings, photos, illustrations, maps, images, diagrams, etc.), in whole or in part, may be used, reproduced, stored in a retrieval system, or transmitted, in any form or by any means now known or hereafter invented, without written permission from the publisher. The sale, duplication, hire, lending, copying, digitalization, or reproduction of this material, in any manner or form whatsoever, is also prohibited, and is a violation of federal, civil, and digital copyright law, which provides severe civil and criminal penalties for any violations.

If They Were Alive Today: How Famous Historic Americans Might Look if They Lived in the 21st Century, by Lochlainn Seabrook. Includes an introduction, illustrations, and bibliography.

ARTWORK
Front and back cover design and art, book design, layout, font selection, and interior art by Lochlainn Seabrook.
All images, pictures, photos, illustrations, image captions, graphic design, and graphic art copyright © Lochlainn Seabrook.
All images selected, placed, manipulated, cleaned, colored, tinted, and/or created by Lochlainn Seabrook.
Cover image: George Washington reimagined as a modern U.S. president.
All rights reserved.

All persons who approve of the authority and principles of Colonel Lochlainn Seabrook's literary work, and realize its benefits as a means of reeducating the world about facts left out of mainstream books, are hereby requested to avidly recommend his titles to others and to vigorously cooperate in extending their reach, scope, and influence around the globe.

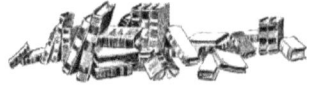

The views documented in this book concerning historic American figures are those of both the author and the publisher.

WRITTEN, DESIGNED, PUBLISHED, PRINTED, & MANUFACTURED IN THE UNITED STATES OF AMERICA

Dedication

To all my childhood heroes.

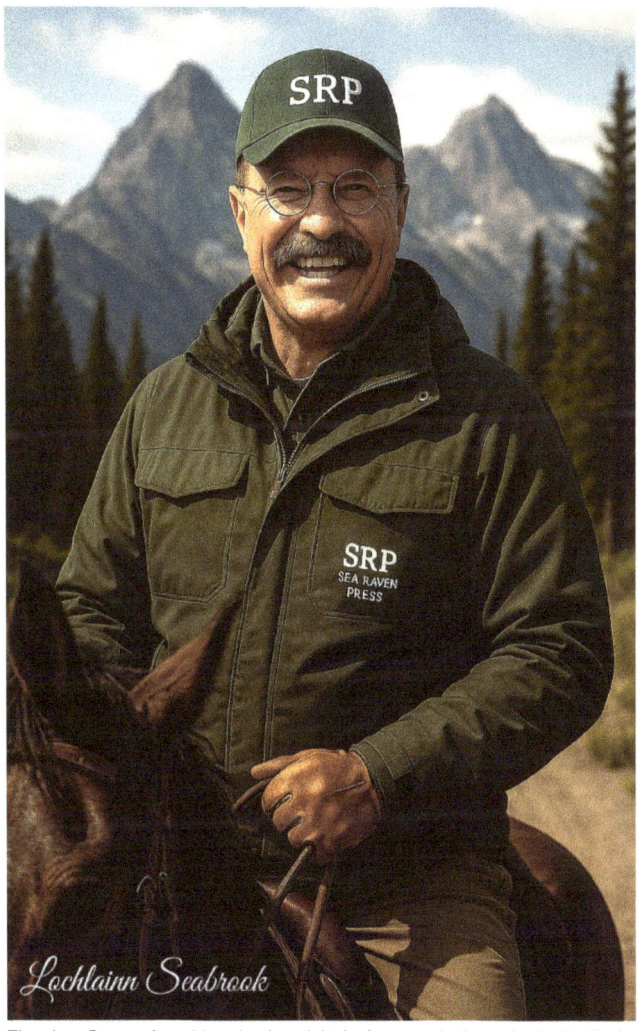

Theodore Roosevelt as I imagine he might look now enjoying a day in the Rocky Mountains. Copyright © Lochlainn Seabrook.

Epigraph

"A nation that does not remember what it was yesterday does not know what it is today."
Robert E. Lee

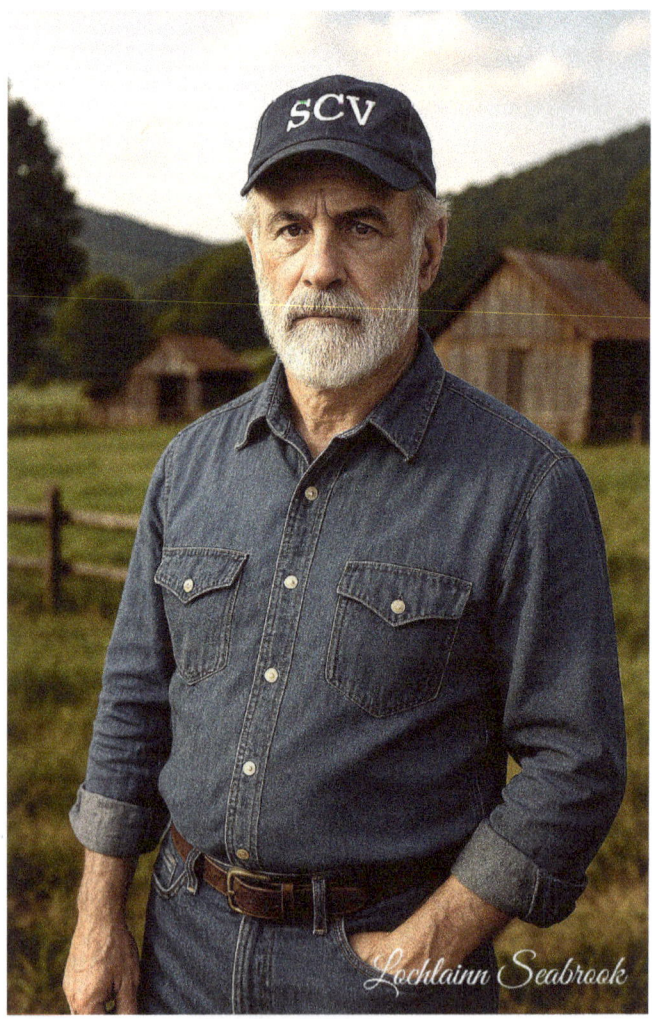

Robert E. Lee as I imagine he might look on his Virginia farm today. Copyright © Lochlainn Seabrook.

CONTENTS

Notes to the Reader, by Lochlainn Seabrook ~ page 11
Key to Individual Entries ~ page 12
Introduction, by Lochlainn Seabrook ~ page 13

ENTRIES: ALPHABETIZED

1: Adams, John ~ page 15
2: Alcott, Louisa May ~ page 19
3: Allen, Ethan ~ page 23
4: Audubon, John James ~ page 27
5: Beauregard, Pierre G. T. ~ page 31
6: Bell, Alexander Graham ~ page 35
7: Boone, Daniel ~ page 39
8: Boyd, Belle ~ page 43
9: Calhoun, John C. ~ page 47
10: Carson, Kit ~ page 51
11. Carver, George Washington ~ page 55
12. Chesnut, Mary Boykin ~ page 59
13. Cody, William Frederick ~ page 63
14. Crockett, David ~ page 67
15. Cumming, Kate ~ page 71
16. Custer, George Armstrong ~ page 75
17. Davis, Jefferson ~ page 78
18. Earhart, Amelia ~ page 83
19. Edison, Thomas ~ page 87
20. Einstein, Albert ~ page 91
21. Emerson, Ralph Waldo ~ page 95
22. Ford, Henry ~ page 99
23. Forrest, Nathan Bedford ~ page 103
24. Franklin, Benjamin ~ page 107
25. Geronimo ~ page 111
26. Gordon, John Brown ~ page 115

27. Greenhow, Rose O'Neal ❧ page 119
28. Hamilton, Alexander ❧ page 123
29. Hawthorne, Nathaniel ❧ page 127
30. Henry, Patrick ❧ page 131
31. Houston, Sam ❧ page 135
32. Jackson, Andrew ❧ page 139
33. Jackson, Thomas "Stonewall" ❧ page 143
34. Jefferson, Thomas ❧ page 147
35. Lee, Robert E. ❧ page 151
36. Lewis, Meriwether ❧ page 155
37. Lindbergh, Charles ❧ page 159
38. Longfellow, Henry Wadsworth ❧ page 163
39. Madison, James ❧ page 167
40. Muir, John ❧ page 171
41. Navarro, José Antonio ❧ page 175
42. Pierce, Franklin ❧ page 179
43. Poe, Edgar Allan ❧ page 183
44. Revere, Paul ❧ page 187
45. Roosevelt, Theodore ❧ page 191
46. Rutherford, Mildred Lewis ❧ page 195
47. Sitting Bull ❧ page 199
48. Tesla, Nikola ❧ page 203
49. Thoreau, Henry David ❧ page 207
50. Tompkins, Sally ❧ page 211
51. Twain, Mark ❧ page 215
52. Washington, Booker T. ❧ page 219
53. Washington, George ❧ page 223
54. Watie, Stand ❧ page 227
55. Whitman, Walt ❧ page 231
56. Whitney, Eli ❧ page 235

Bibliography ❧ page 239
Meet the Author-Illustrator ❧ page 249
Praise for the Author ❧ page 251
Our Connection to the Confederacy ❧ page 254
Learn More ❧ page 255

NOTES TO THE READER

"NOTHING IN THE PAST IS DEAD TO THE MAN WHO WOULD
LEARN HOW THE PRESENT CAME TO BE WHAT IT IS."
WILLIAM STUBBS, VICTORIAN ENGLISH HISTORIAN

HISTORICAL ACCURACY NOT GUARANTEED
☛ As this book is a pictorial featuring times, places, and people who, in many cases, existed long before the invention of photography, I have relied on creative vision and artistic license to fill in many of the blanks, so to speak. As a result, historical accuracy in my depictions is far from guaranteed.

It would be safest to regard the illustrations in my book as imaginary records, images that depict what I believe may be the closest we can come to envisioning noted historic Americans as they *might* look and dress today, not necessarily as they *would* look and dress today—which is precisely how I have worded my captions. Note that in particular military uniforms are not necessarily portrayed according to current mil-spec (military specification).

C.S. SOLDIERS AS U.S. SOLDIERS
☛ The irony of my portraying C.S. (Confederate) officers as modern day U.S. army officers has not been lost on me. However, today's U.S. army is the closest 21st-Century equivalent to the 19th-Century C.S. army. One must also consider the fact that a number of my Confederate generals, for example, Lee, Jackson, and Stuart, were all commissioned officers in the U.S. army before the War Between the States. In all actuality then, my transition is neither unrealistic or shocking. In either case, Confederate officers were among the most patriotic Americans who ever lived—as my voluminous writings on the history of the Confederacy have steadfastly demonstrated. Conclusion? If they were alive today there is no question that the three above named West Point graduates would have been commissioned officers in the U.S. army.

FOREIGN-BORN AMERICANS
☛ Some of my individuals (for instance, Hamilton, Tesla, Einstein, and Audubon), were not born in the United States. However, all eventually became naturalized loyal citizens, and are today thus considered all-American figures.

WHY WE LOVE THE OLD CONFEDERACY
☛ For those who are interested in why we here at Sea Raven Press write about and publish books on the Southern Confederacy, see page 254.

KEY TO INDIVIDUAL ENTRIES

in the order they appear on the first page of each entry

NAME: Birth name, or name most commonly known by.

DATES: Birth date and death date.

LOCATION: Place of birth.

BIOGRAPHICAL ATTRIBUTES: Occupations, beliefs, and traits that made him or her famous, or were unique to them.

FIRST IMAGE: Portrait of the individual as he or she originally looked during their actual lifetime, usually during their prime.

SECOND IMAGE: Usually best known or primary occupation, set in the 21st Century.

THIRD IMAGE: Usually least known or secondary occupation, set in the 21st Century.

FOURTH IMAGE: One of his or her favorite pastimes or hobbies, set in the 21st Century.

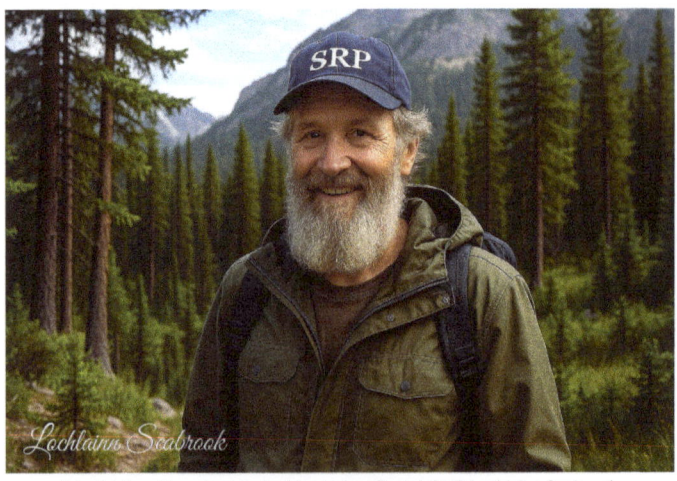

John Muir as I imagine him looking today. Copyright © Lochlainn Seabrook.

INTRODUCTION

WHO HAS NOT WONDERED how notable 17th-, 18th-, and 19th-Century Americans might look *If They Were Alive Today*? How would they dress? What hairstyle would they wear? What kind of work would they do? This, my first alternate history book, is my adventurous attempt to answer these questions.

But how to select only a few dozen individuals out of the many thousands of famous Americans who lived and died before the mid 20th Century? I chose those with whom I have something in common. Such commonalities include being consanguineously related, having lived in the same town they did, having worked at the same establishment they once worked at, and most importantly, having mentioned him or her in my literary works, or having even written entire books about them—among other affinities. In some cases they were simply childhood heroes, *beaux ideals* who filled my young mind with awe and reverence.

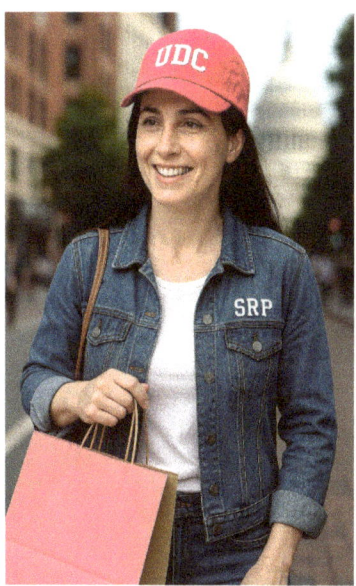

Rose O'Neal Greenhow as I imagine her appearing today. Copyright © Lochlainn Seabrook.

If They Were Alive Today is no mere fantastical collection of celebrated people from the past. It is a serious biographical work that is intended to both pay homage to and chronicle the memories and amazing accomplishments of these 56 exemplars. Thus, each entry, along with its accompanying three imaginary illustrations, was created with the utmost respect for each individual. More to the point, nothing is meant in any way to mock or impugn the life or character of these iconic men and women. Quite the opposite. For a variety of reasons I consider them legendary trailblazers, hence their appearance in my book.

Whether you personally admire the individuals I have selected for inclusion or not, it must be acknowledged that all made important, sometimes groundbreaking, even epoch-defining, contributions to our history, helping forge, shape, and mold our Confederate Republic—as President George Washington called the U.S.—into what is now modern day America.

This was a fascinating book to write. It is my hope that you will find it fascinating as well, and that you will discover some of your own favorite figures in the following pages. Authentic history is educational and enlightening. Alternate history is fun and thought provoking.

Lochlainn Seabrook
Park County, Wyoming, USA
July 2025

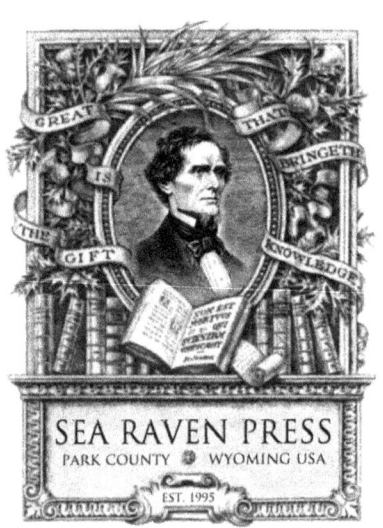

"Books invite all; they constrain none."
Hartley Burr Alexander (1873-1939)

JOHN ADAMS
1735-1836, Massachusetts

American Founding Father, first vice president of the U.S., second president of the U.S., public servant, lawyer, farmer, writer, husband of Abigail Adams.

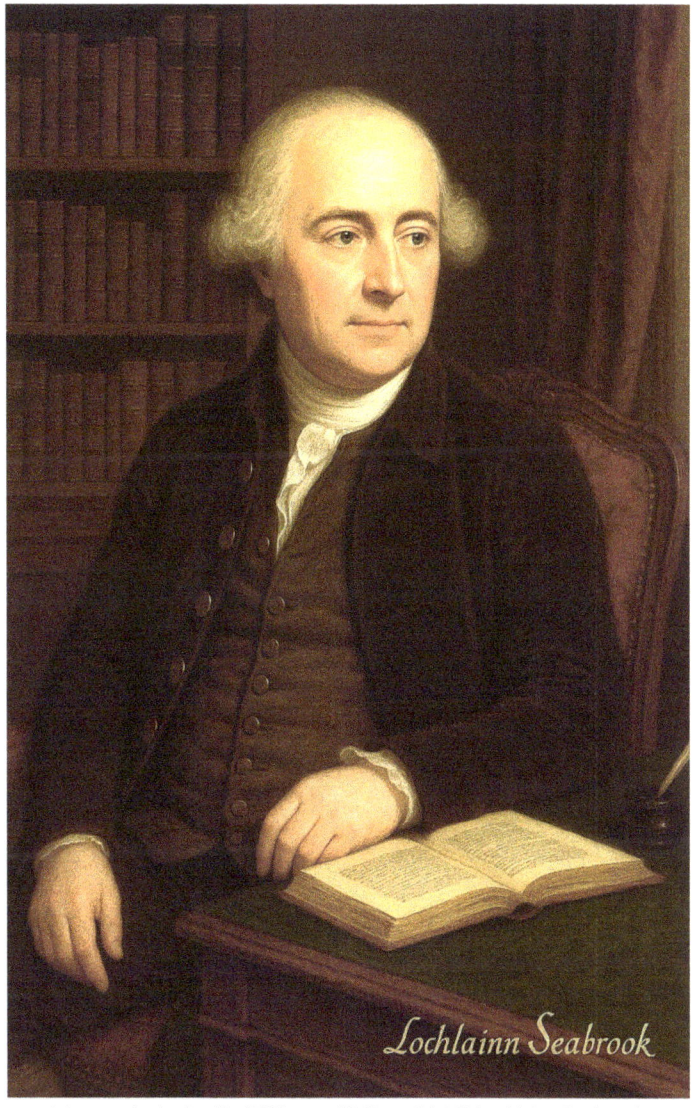

Adams as he looked in 1780, age 45. Copyright © Lochlainn Seabrook.

16 ∞ IF THEY WERE ALIVE TODAY

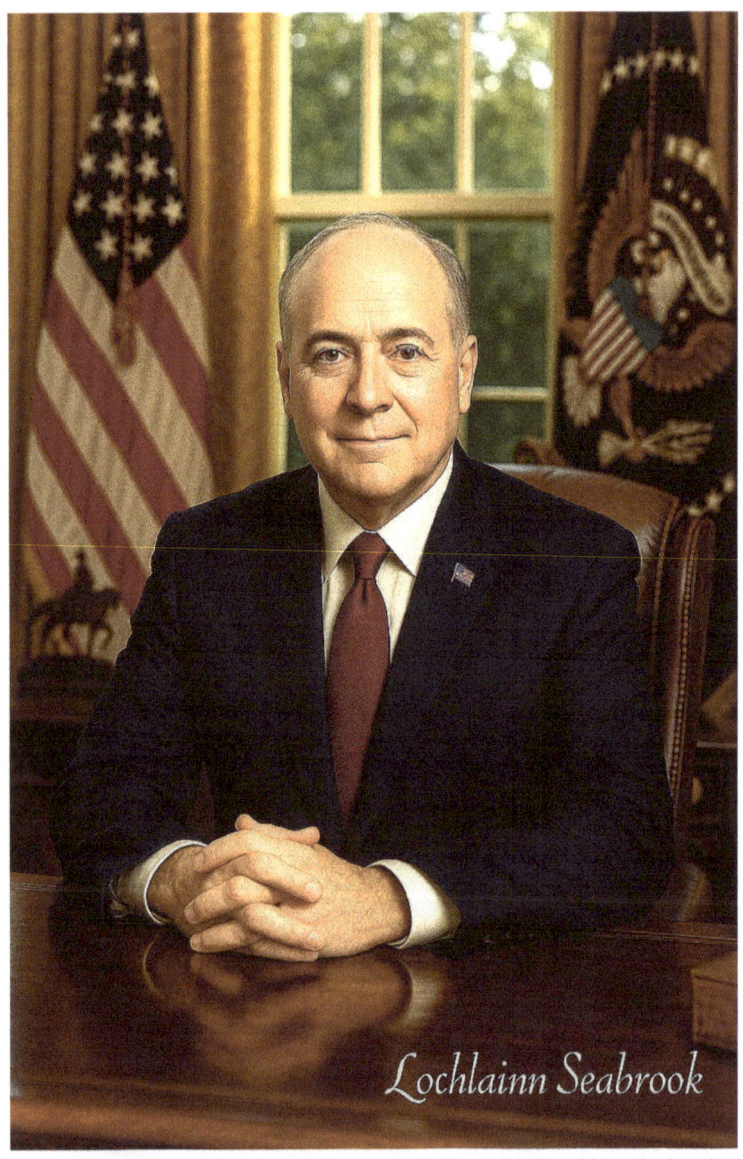

Adams as he might look today as U.S. president. Copyright © Lochlainn Seabrook.

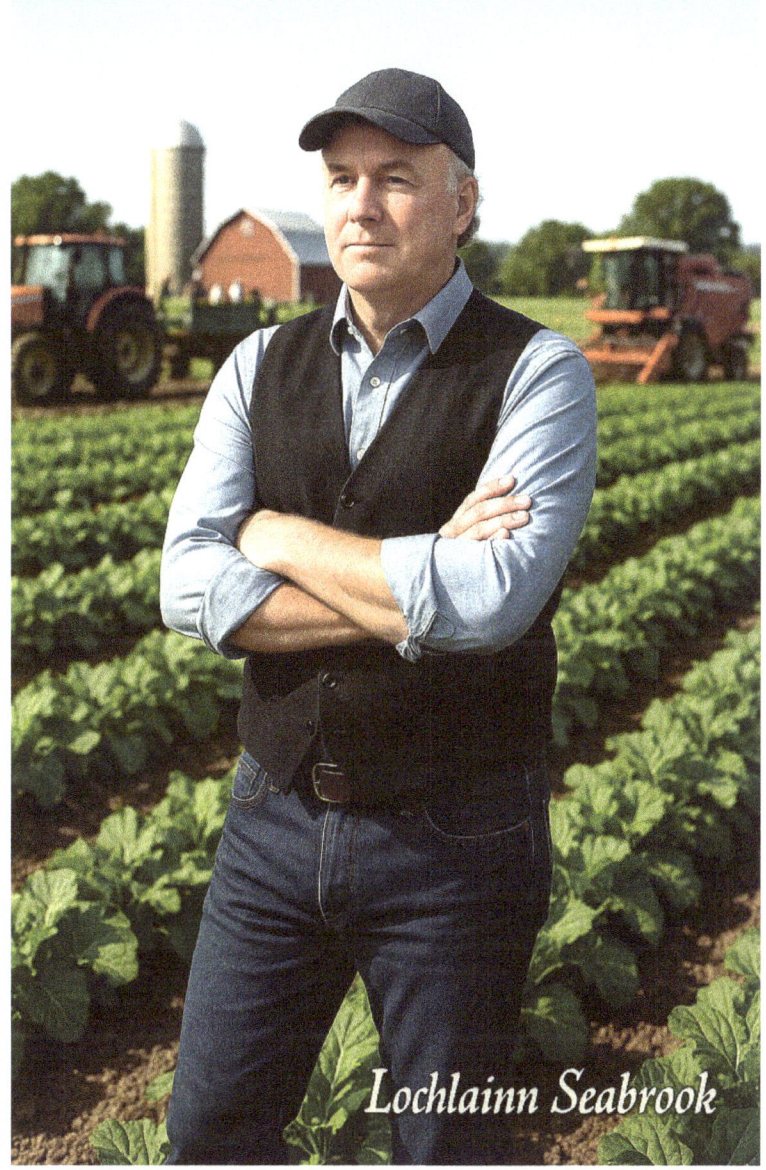

Adams as he might look today as a modern farmer overseeing his agricultural estate in Quincy, Massachusetts. Copyright © Lochlainn Seabrook.

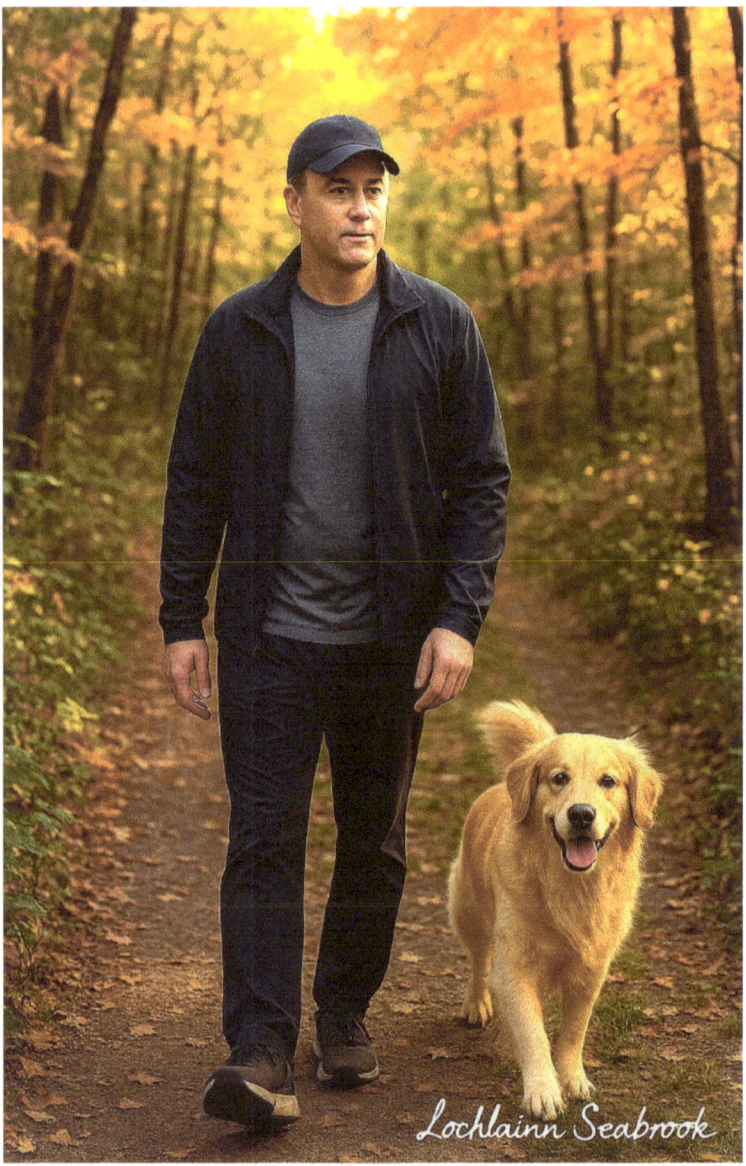

John Adams as he might look today engaging in one of his favorite pastimes: walking in the New England countryside. Copyright © Lochlainn Seabrook.

LOUISA MAY ALCOTT
1832-1888, Massachusetts

Socialist-leaning author, servant, seamstress, governess, nurse, teacher, daughter of transcendentalist-socialist Bronson Alcott.

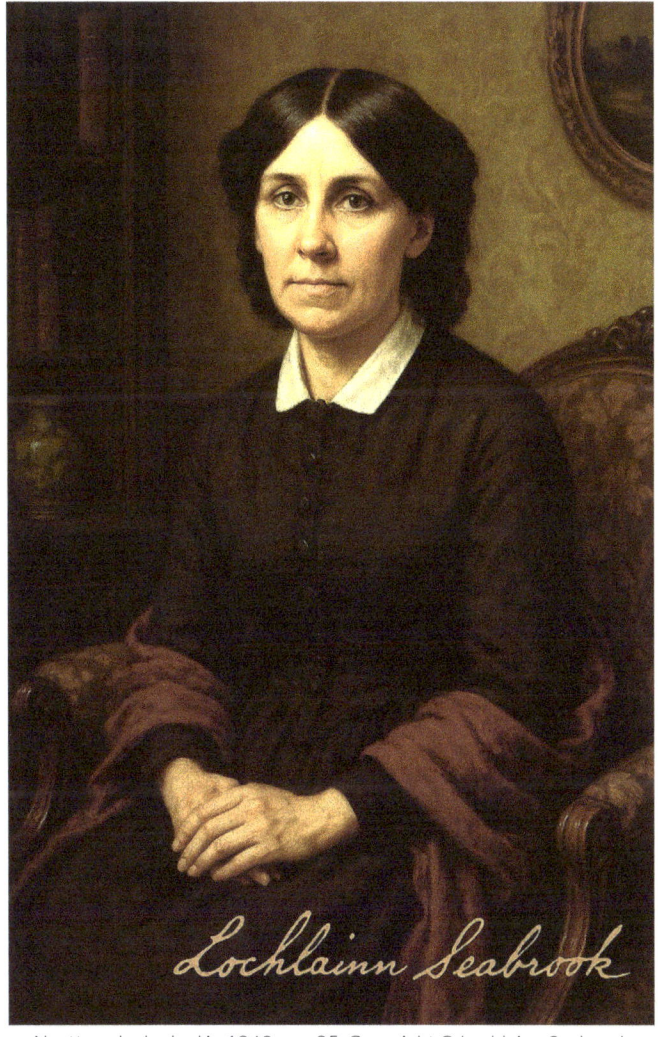

Alcott as she looked in 1868, age 35. Copyright © Lochlainn Seabrook.

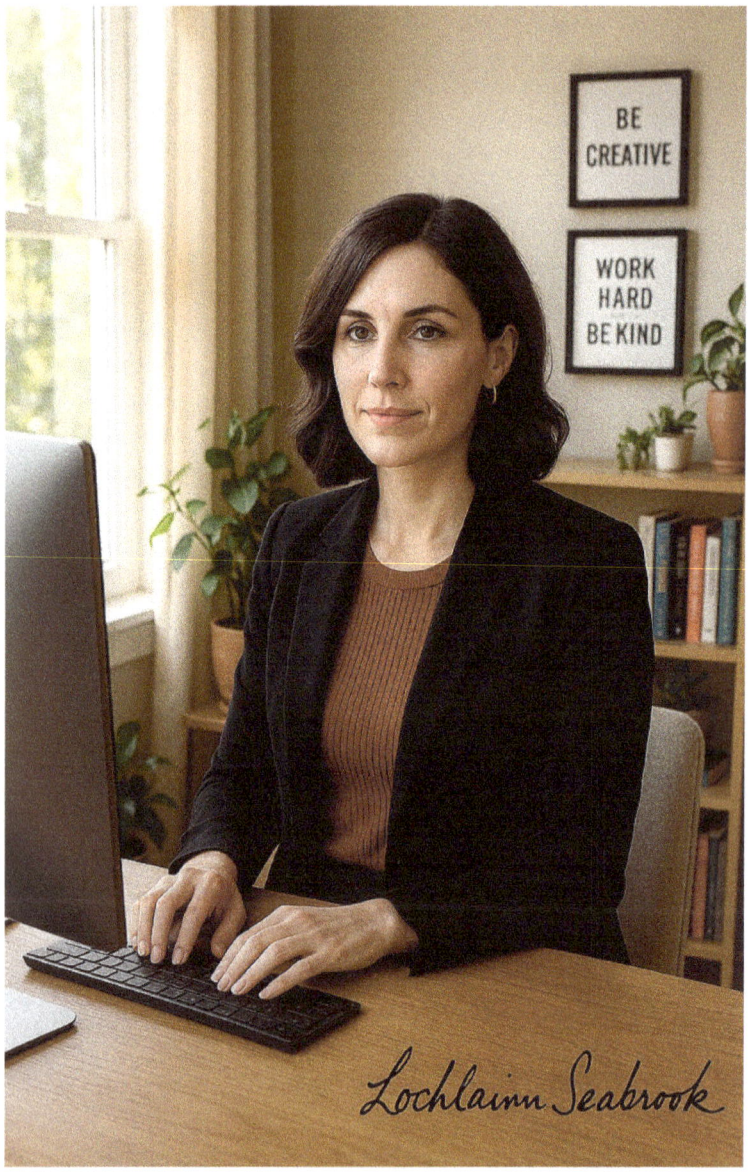

Alcott as she might look today as a modern author. Copyright © Lochlainn Seabrook.

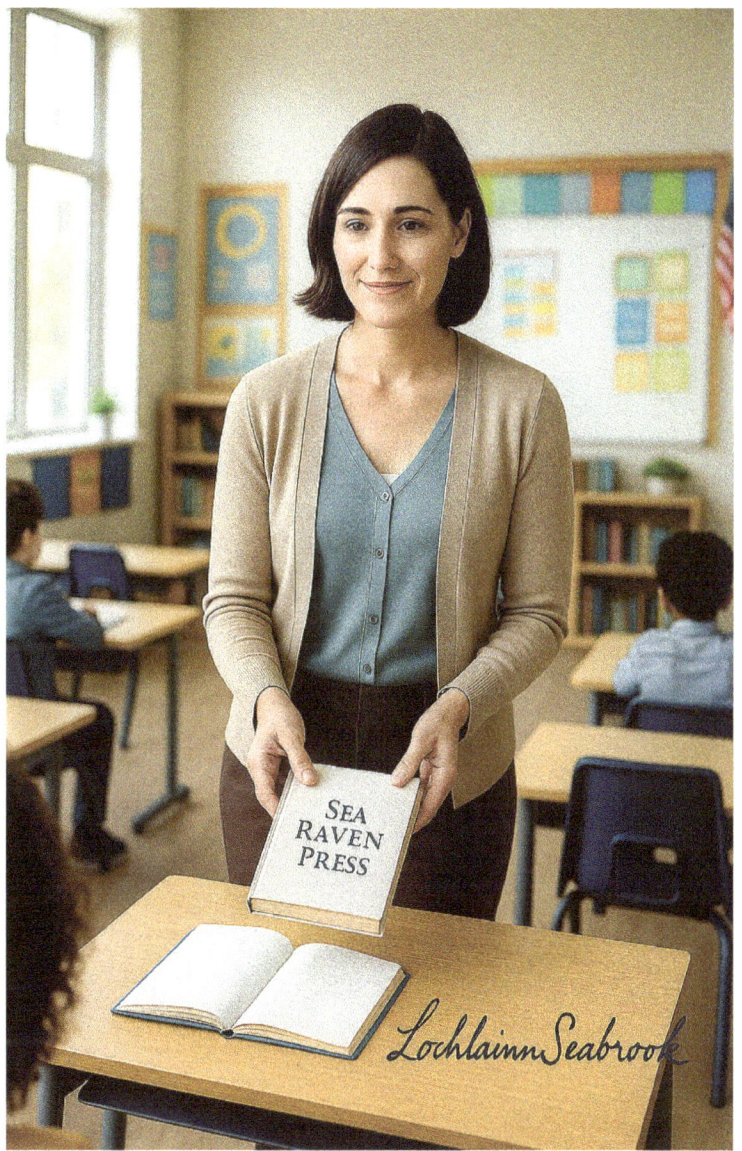

Alcott as she might look today as a school teacher. Copyright © Lochlainn Seabrook.

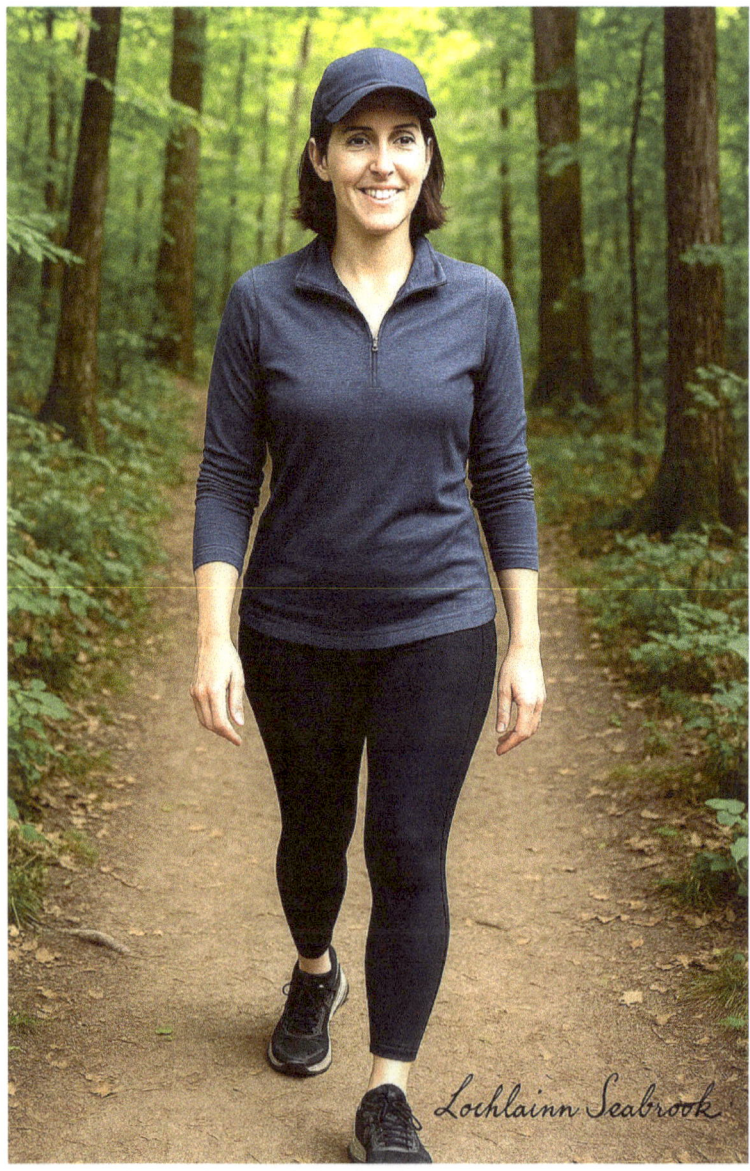

Louisa May Alcott as she might look today engaging in one of her favorite pastimes: nature-walking in the woods of Concord, Massachusetts. Copyright © Lochlainn Seabrook.

ETHAN ALLEN

1738-1789, Connecticut

American patriot, Revolutionary War soldier, militia leader, iron foundry operator, farmer, land speculator, author, deist.

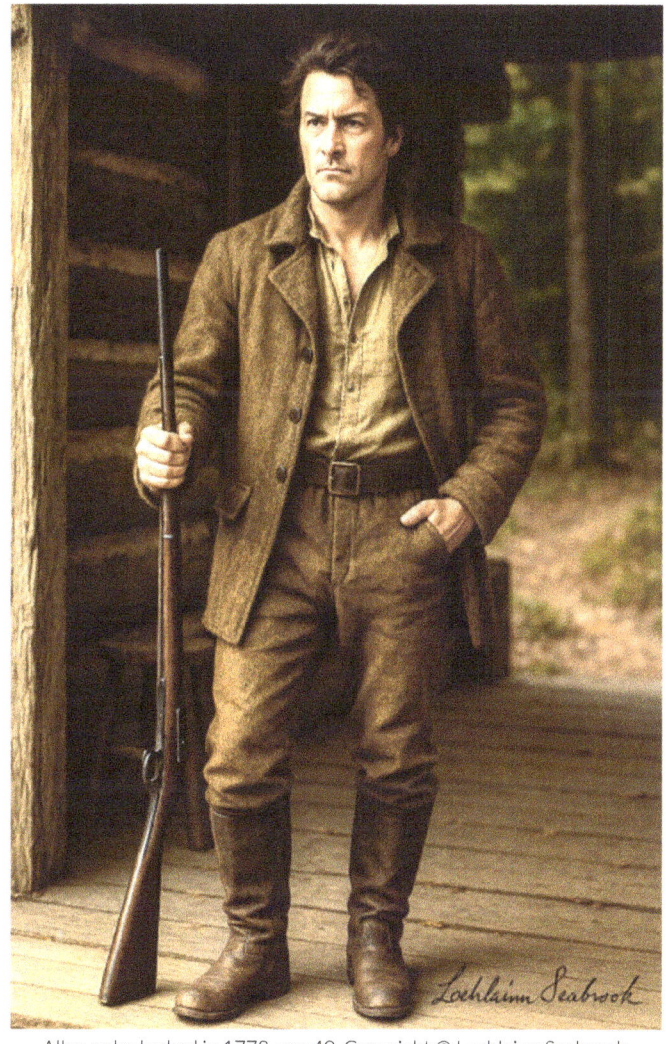

Allen as he looked in 1778, age 40. Copyright © Lochlainn Seabrook.

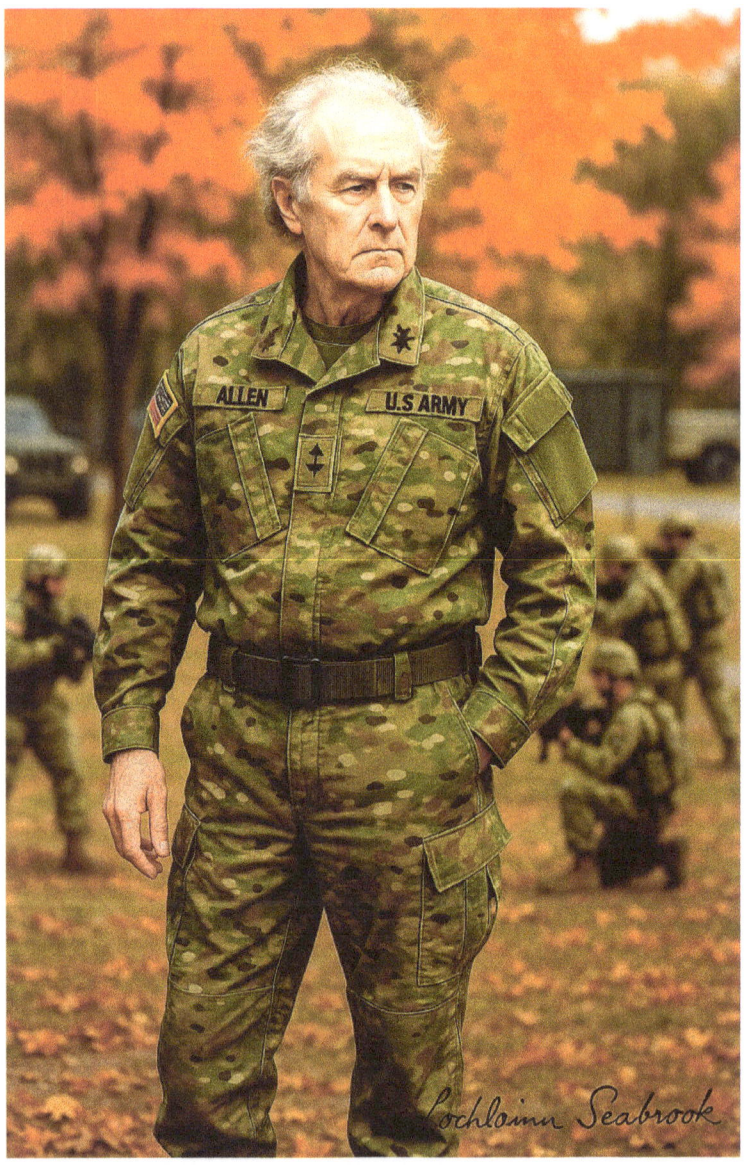

Allen as he might look today as a modern U.S. army colonel. Copyright © Lochlainn Seabrook.

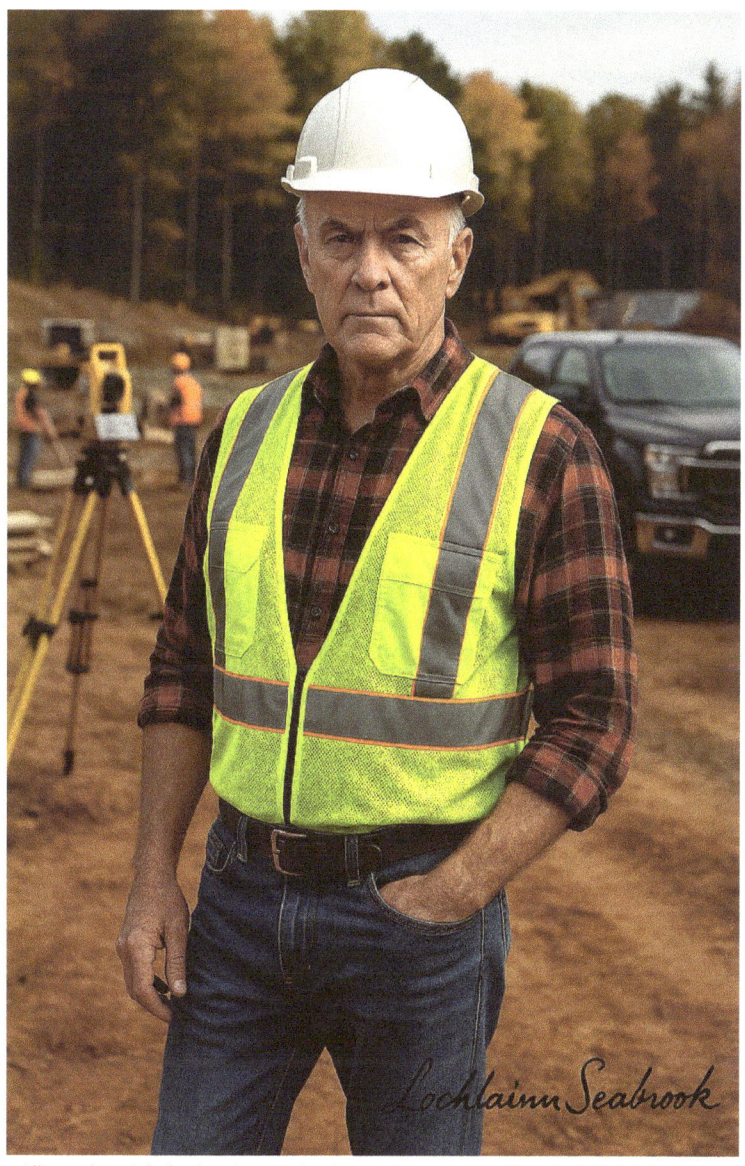

Allen as he might look today as a land speculator. Copyright © Lochlainn Seabrook.

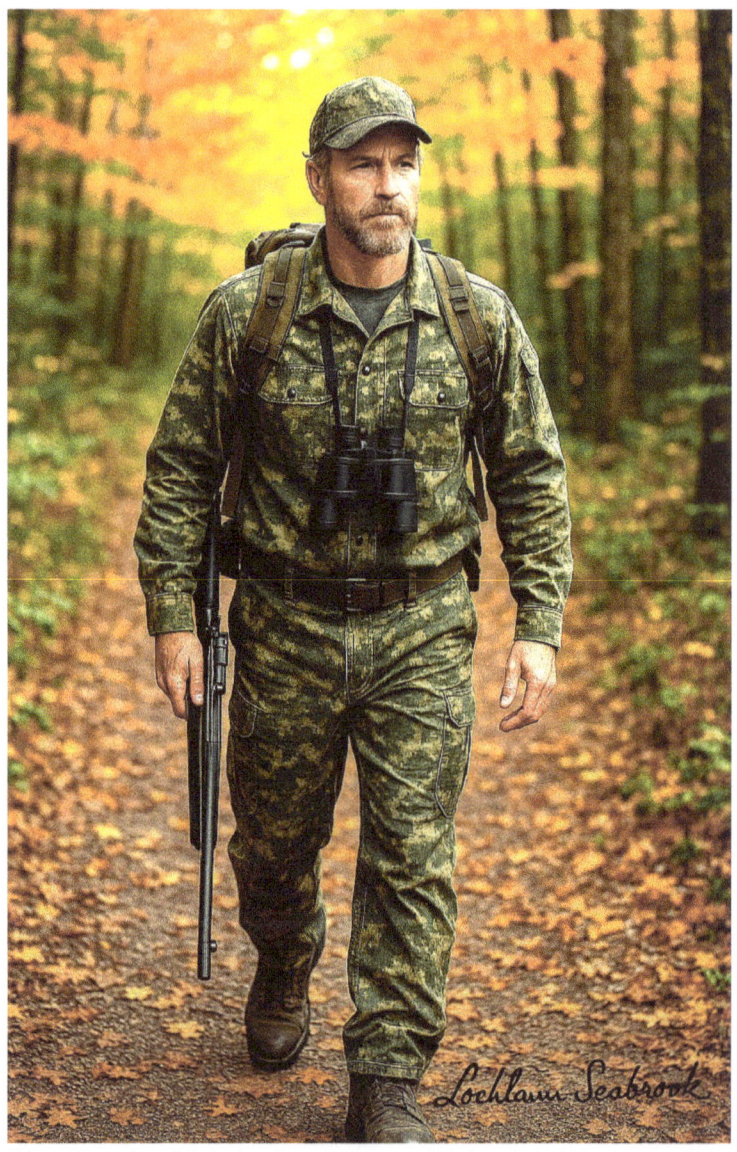

Ethan Allen as he might look today enjoying one of his favorite hobbies: hunting in the wilds of New England. Copyright © Lochlainn Seabrook.

JOHN JAMES AUDUBON
1785-1851, Haiti

Naturalist, ornithologist, painter, writer, lecturer, businessman, general store manager, mill owner, import and export trader.

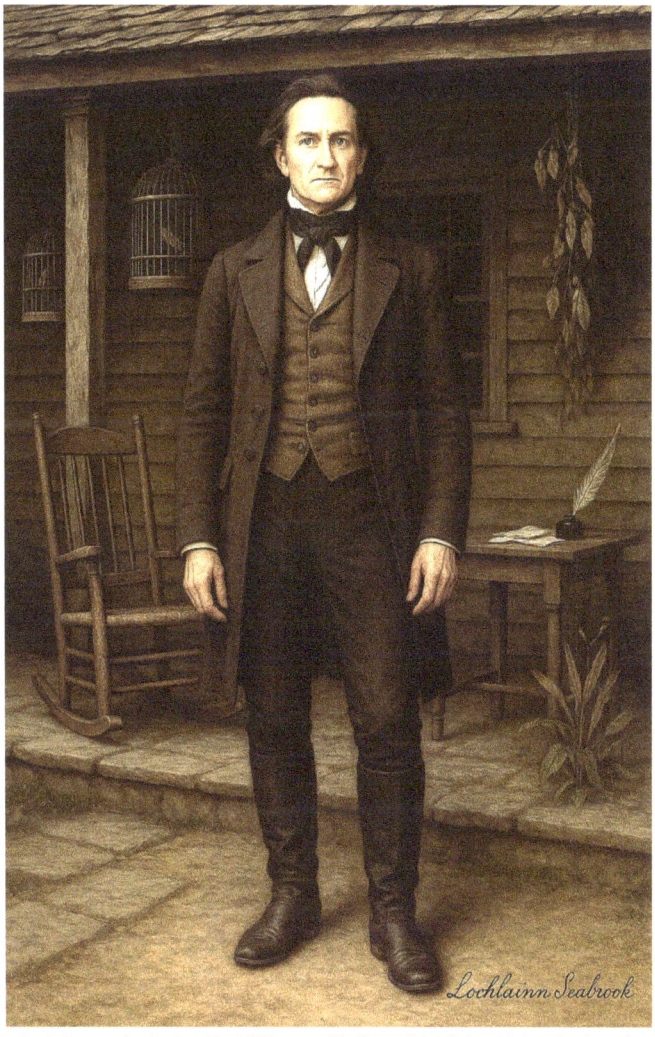

Audubon as he looked in 1830, age 45. Copyright © Lochlainn Seabrook.

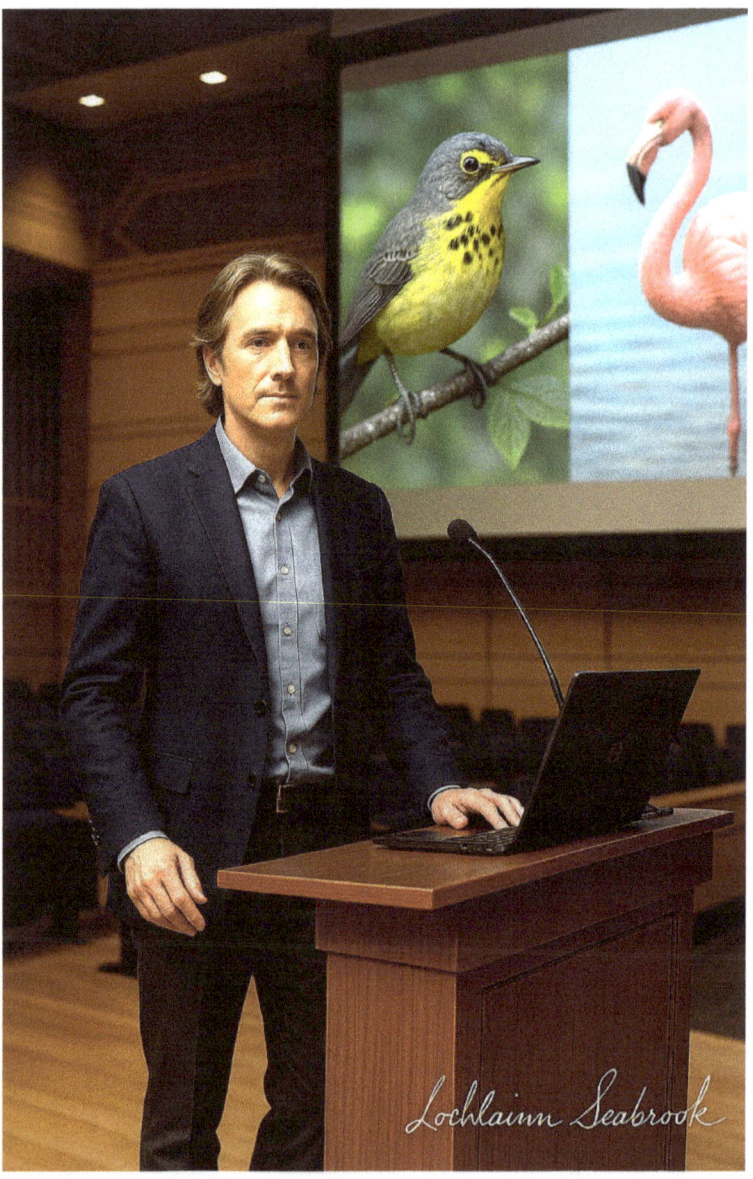

Audubon as he might look today as a respected ornithologist and nature artist and writer delivering a lecture at a New York university. Copyright © Lochlainn Seabrook.

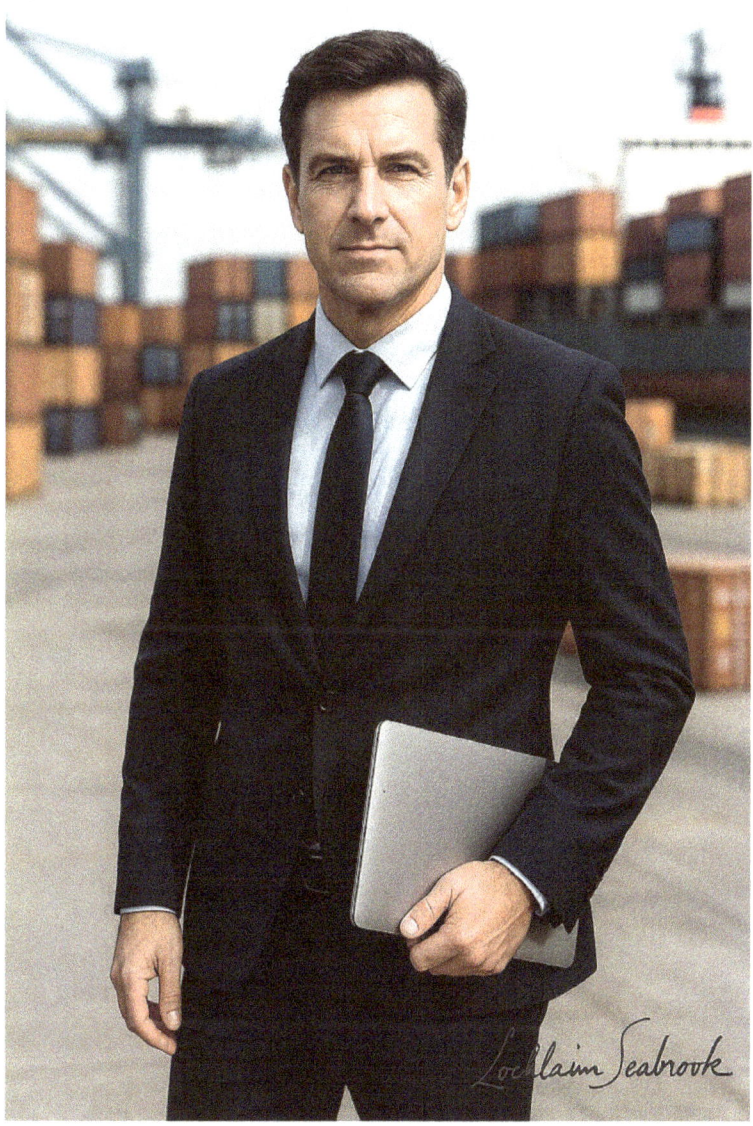

Audubon as he might look today as a 21st-Century import and export trader. Copyright © Lochlainn Seabrook.

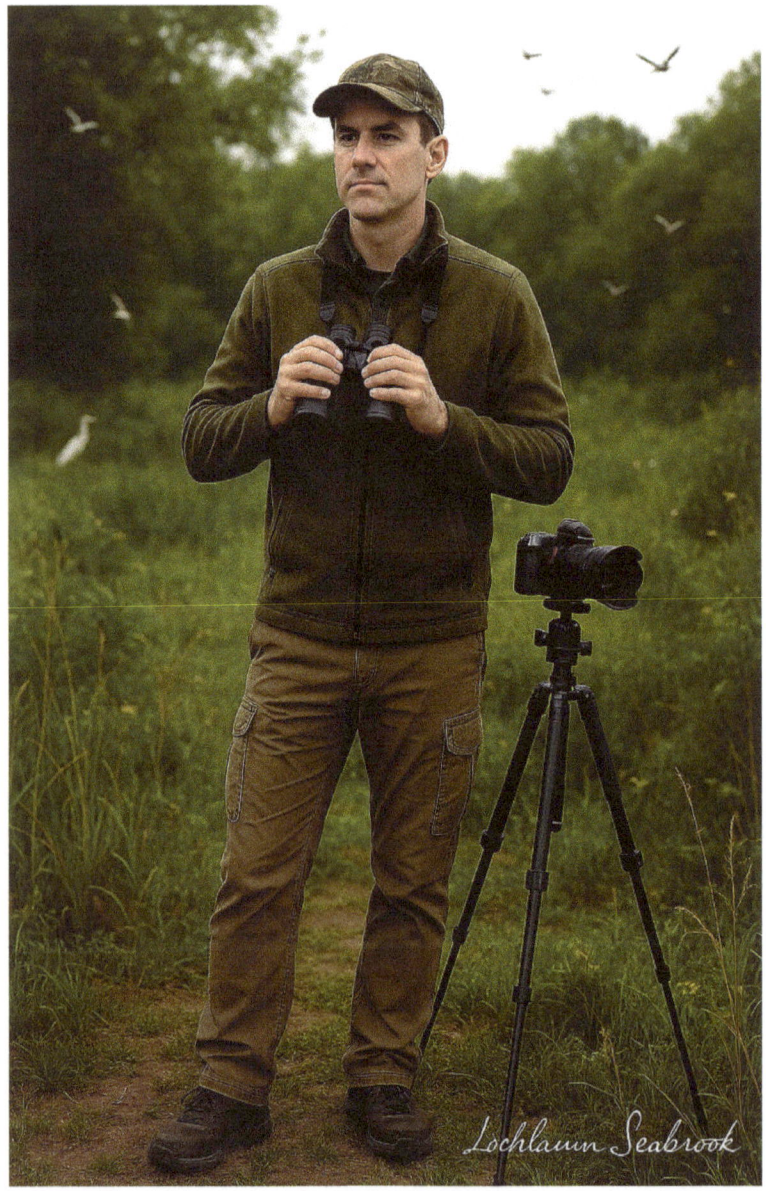

John James Audubon as he might look today engaging in one of his favorite hobbies: birdwatching in a Louisiana nature preserve. Copyright © Lochlainn Seabrook.

PIERRE G. T. BEAUREGARD
1818-1893, Louisiana

Career military officer, Mexican War soldier, Confederate general, railroad executive, civil engineer, conservative political activist.

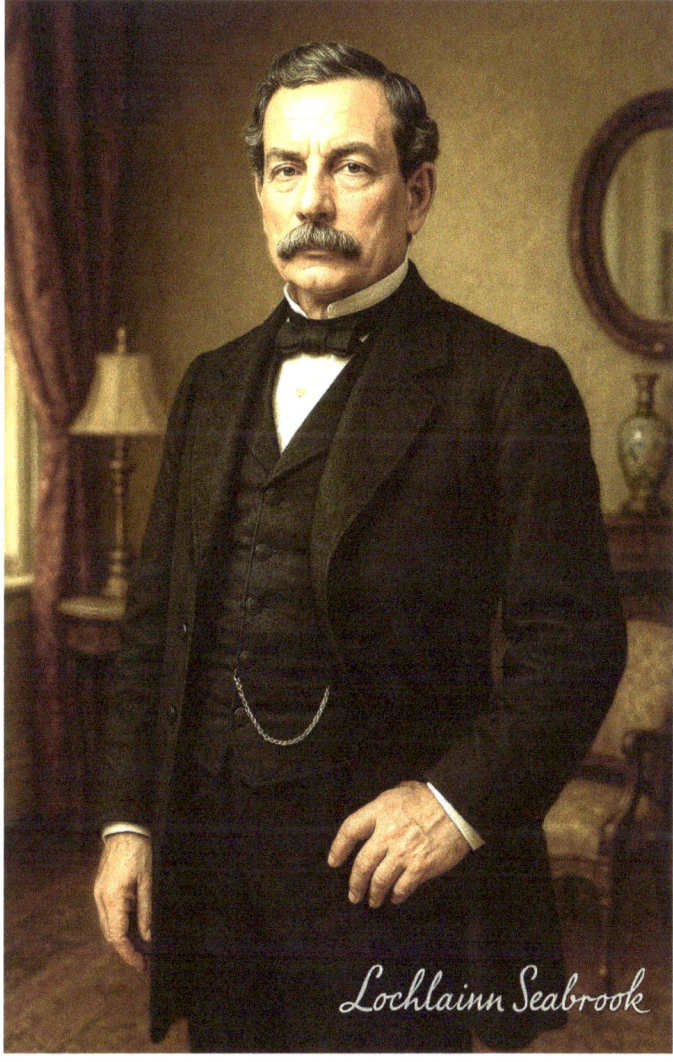

Beauregard as he looked in 1878, age 60. Copyright © Lochlainn Seabrook.

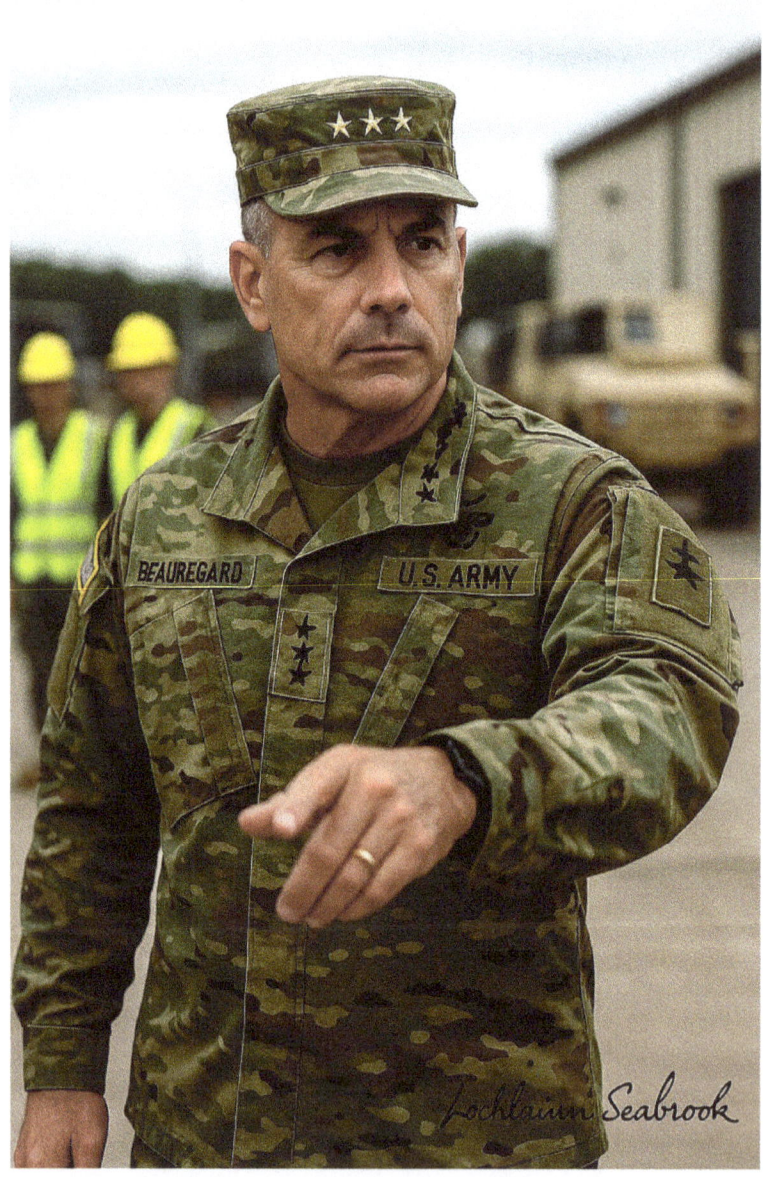

Beauregard as he might look today as a U.S. army general leading a group of engineers on a U.S. military base in Louisiana. Copyright © Lochlainn Seabrook.

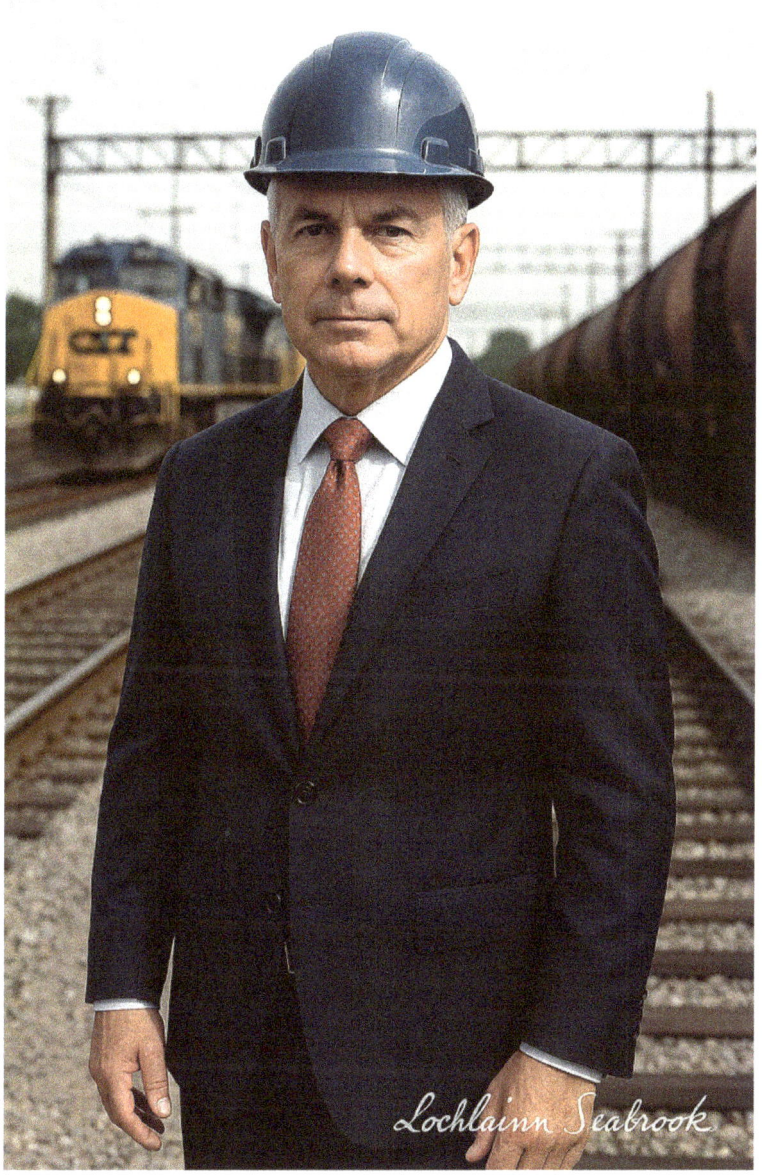

Beauregard as he might look today as a modern railroad executive. Copyright © Lochlainn Seabrook.

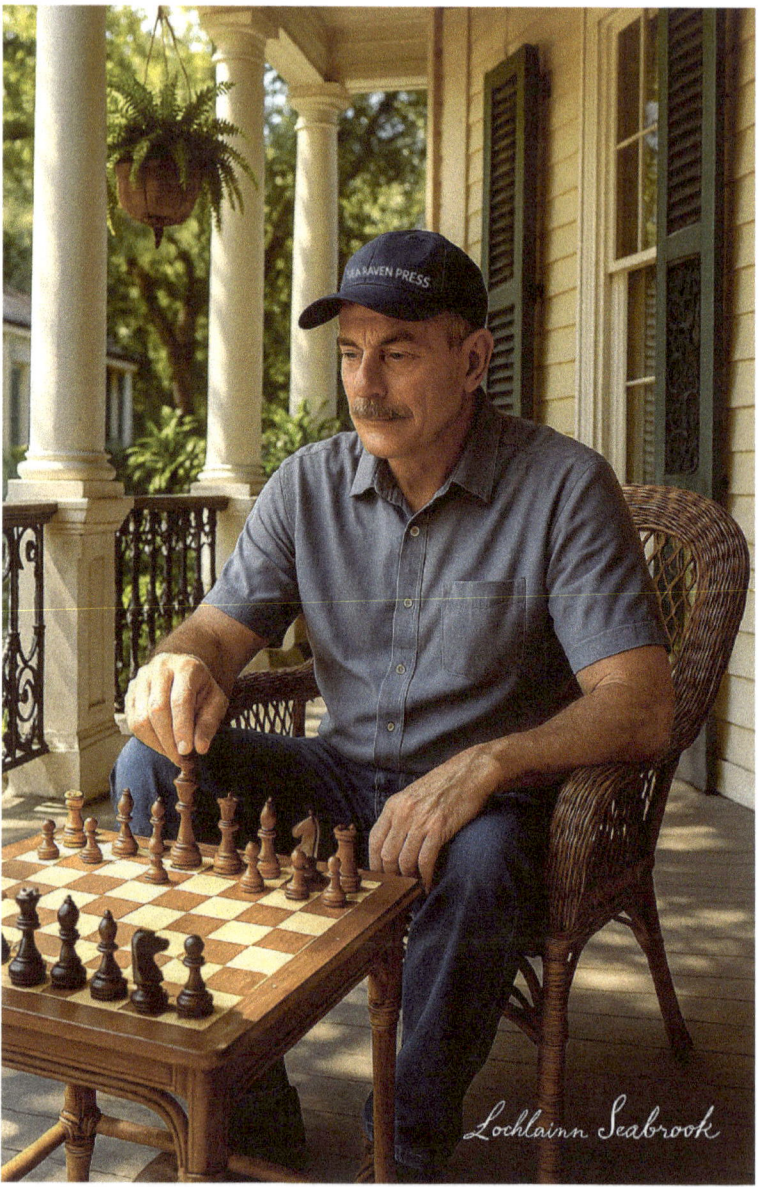

Pierre Gustave Toutant Beauregard as he might look today engaging in one of his favorite pastimes: chess. Copyright © Lochlainn Seabrook.

ALEXANDER GRAHAM BELL
1847-1922, Scotland

Inventor in hearing science, researcher, elocutionist, teacher of the deaf, businessman, speech therapist, educator, lecturer.

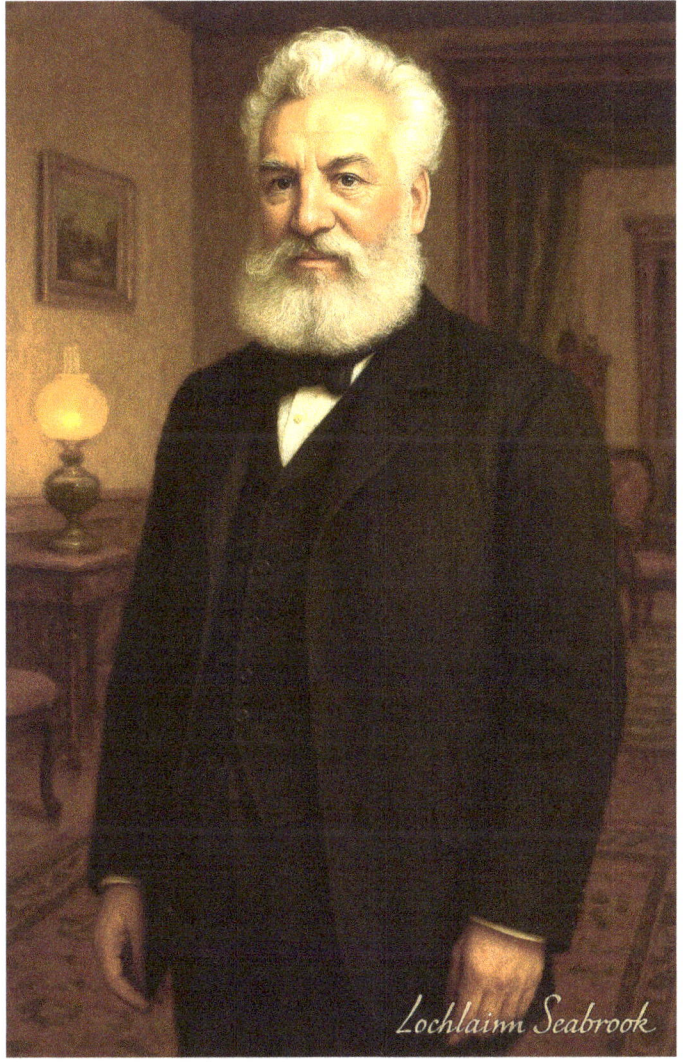

Bell as he looked in 1912, age 65. Copyright © Lochlainn Seabrook.

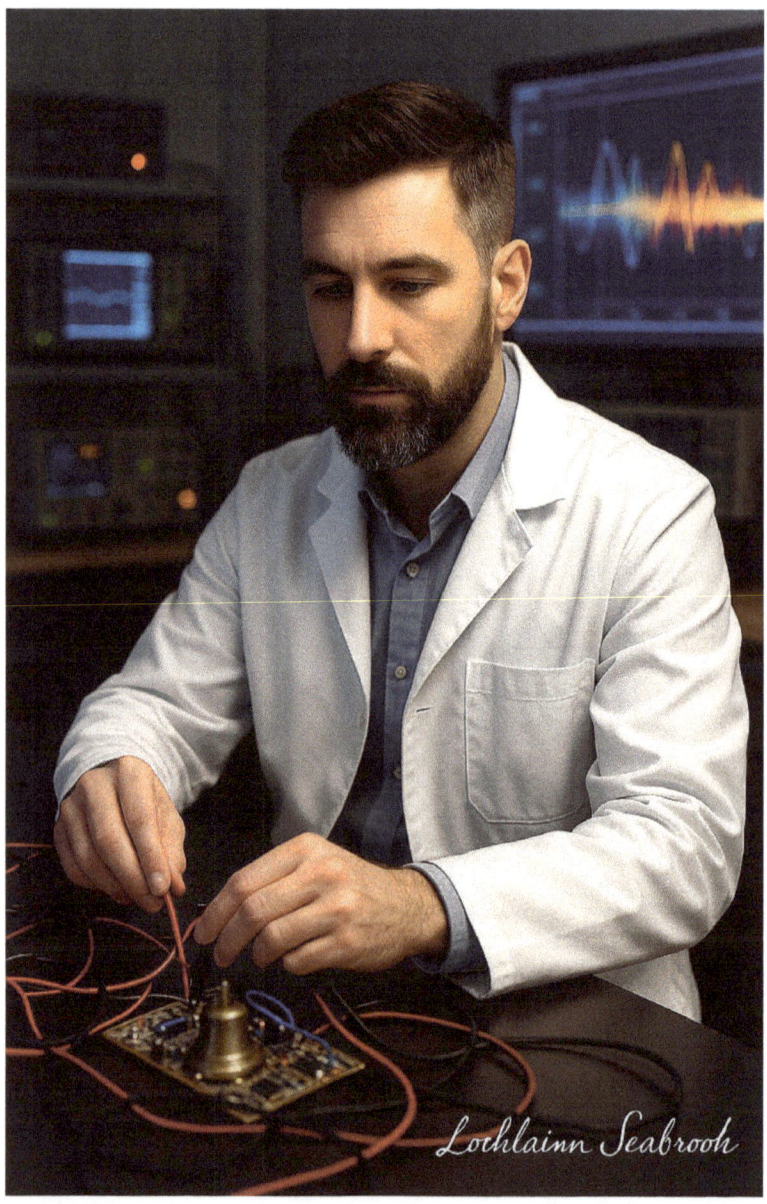

Bell as he might look today as an acoustic researcher. Copyright © Lochlainn Seabrook.

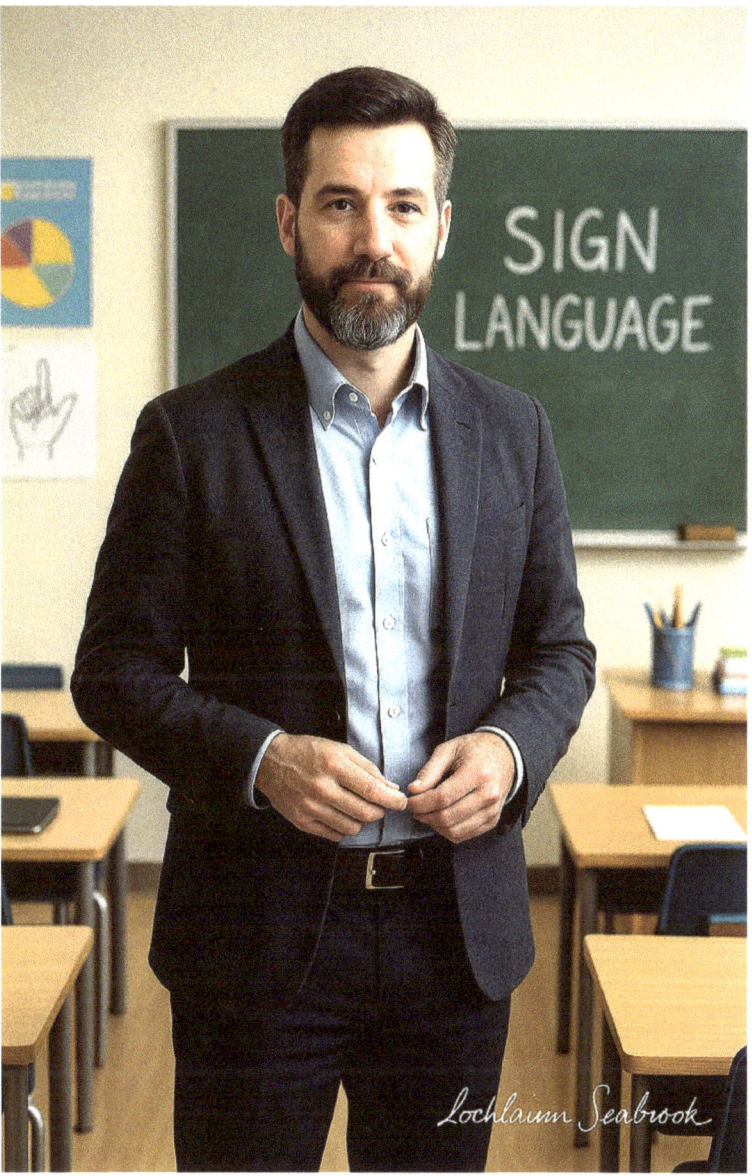

Bell as he might look today as a teacher of the deaf. Copyright © Lochlainn Seabrook.

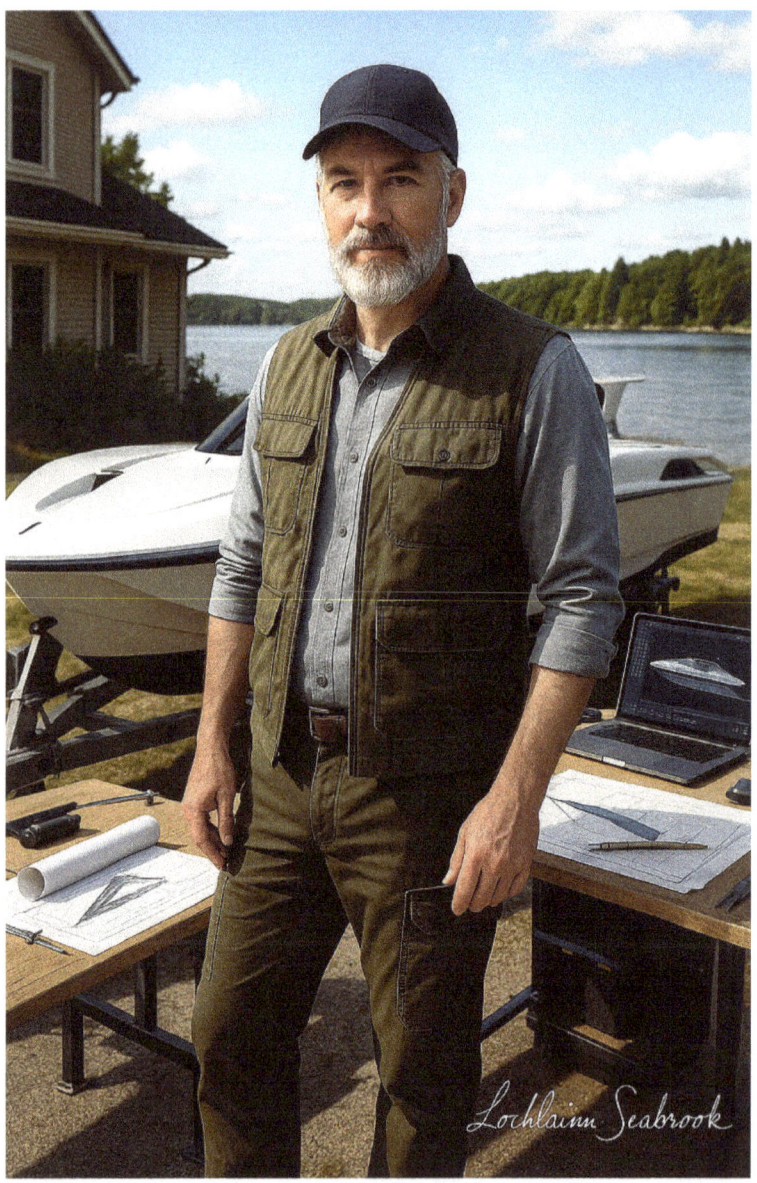

Alexander Graham Bell engaging in one of his favorite hobbies at his home in Canada: hydrodynamic research and boat design. Copyright © Lochlainn Seabrook.

DANIEL BOONE

1734-1820, Pennsylvania

Scout, fur trapper, fur trader, commercial hunter, military serviceman, farmer, blacksmith, teamster, land speculator, surveyor.

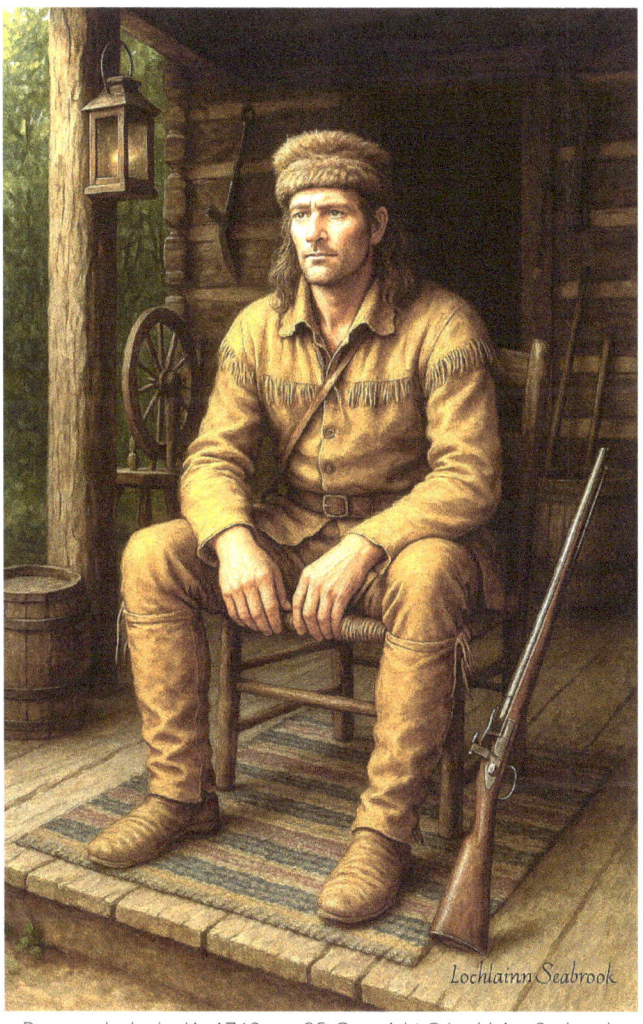

Boone as he looked in 1769, age 35. Copyright © Lochlainn Seabrook.

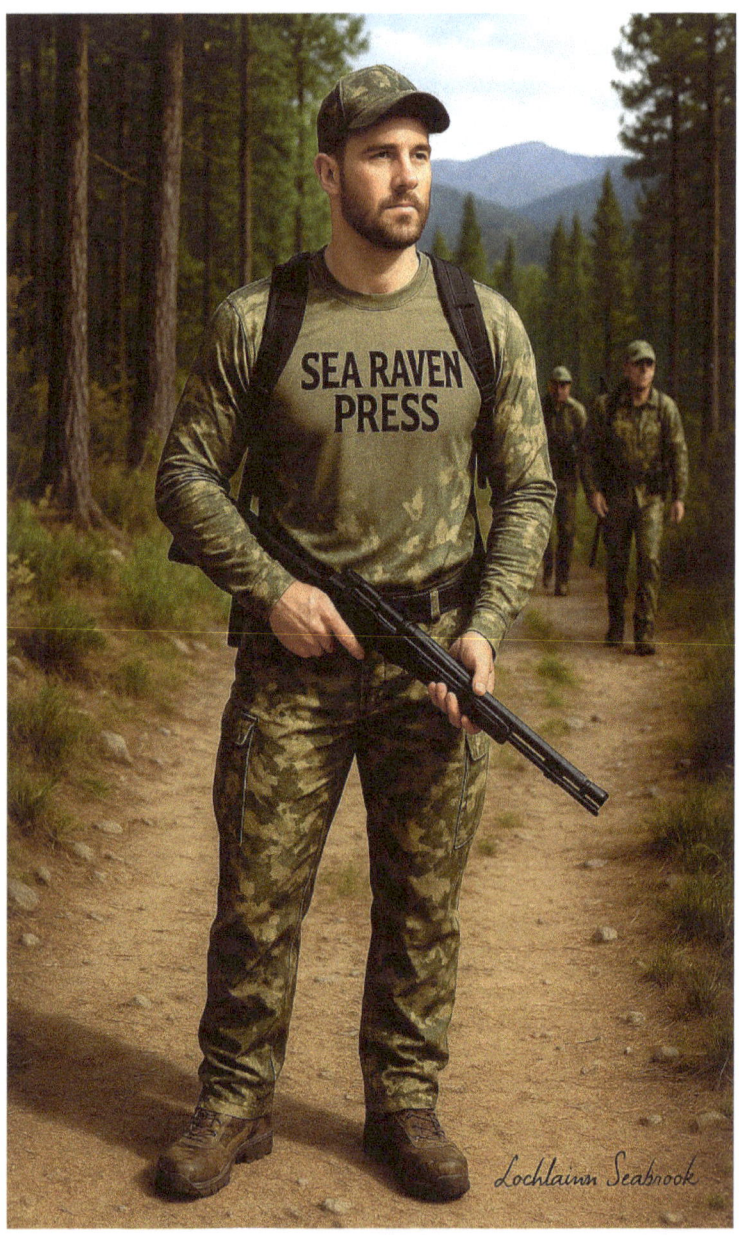

Boone as he might look today as a hunting guide, outfitter, and scout. Copyright © Lochlainn Seabrook.

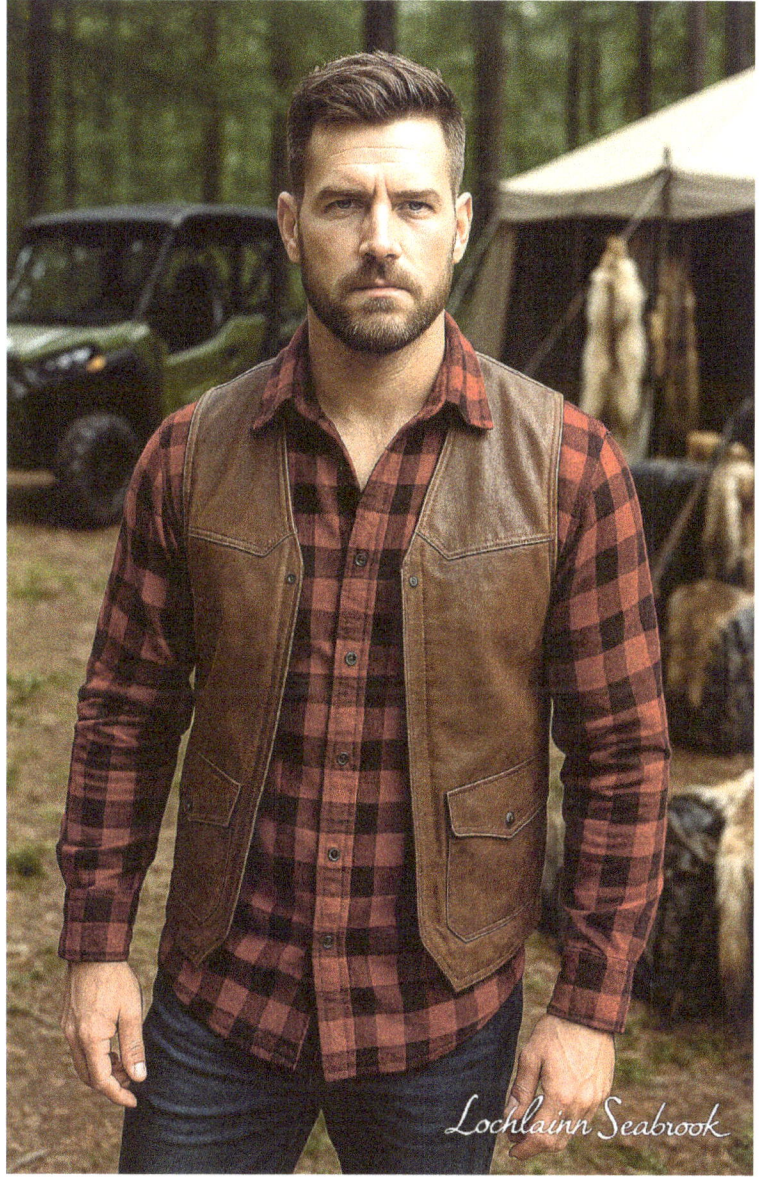

Boone as he might look today as a fur trader and trapper. Copyright © Lochlainn Seabrook.

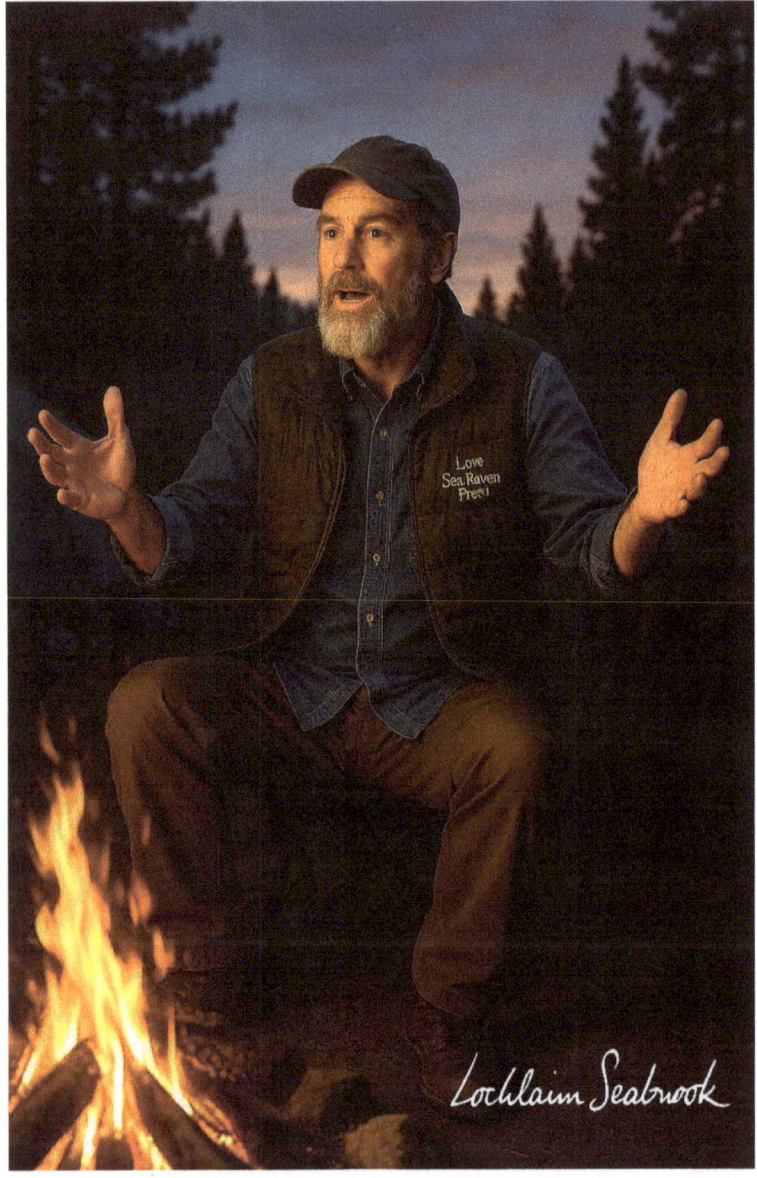

Daniel Boone as he might look today enjoying one of his favorite pastimes: storytelling. Copyright © Lochlainn Seabrook.

BELLE BOYD
1844-1900, Virginia

Well-to-do Southerner, Confederate spy, performing stage actress, public speaker, lecturer, author, storyteller.

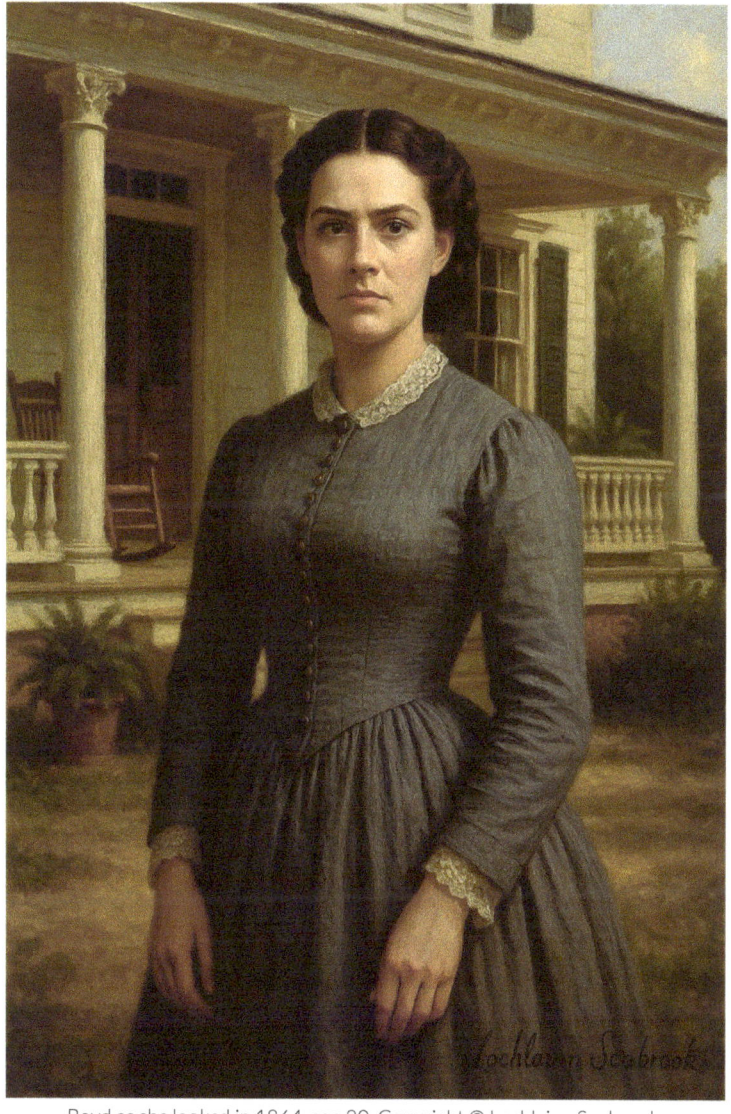

Boyd as she looked in 1864, age 20. Copyright © Lochlainn Seabrook.

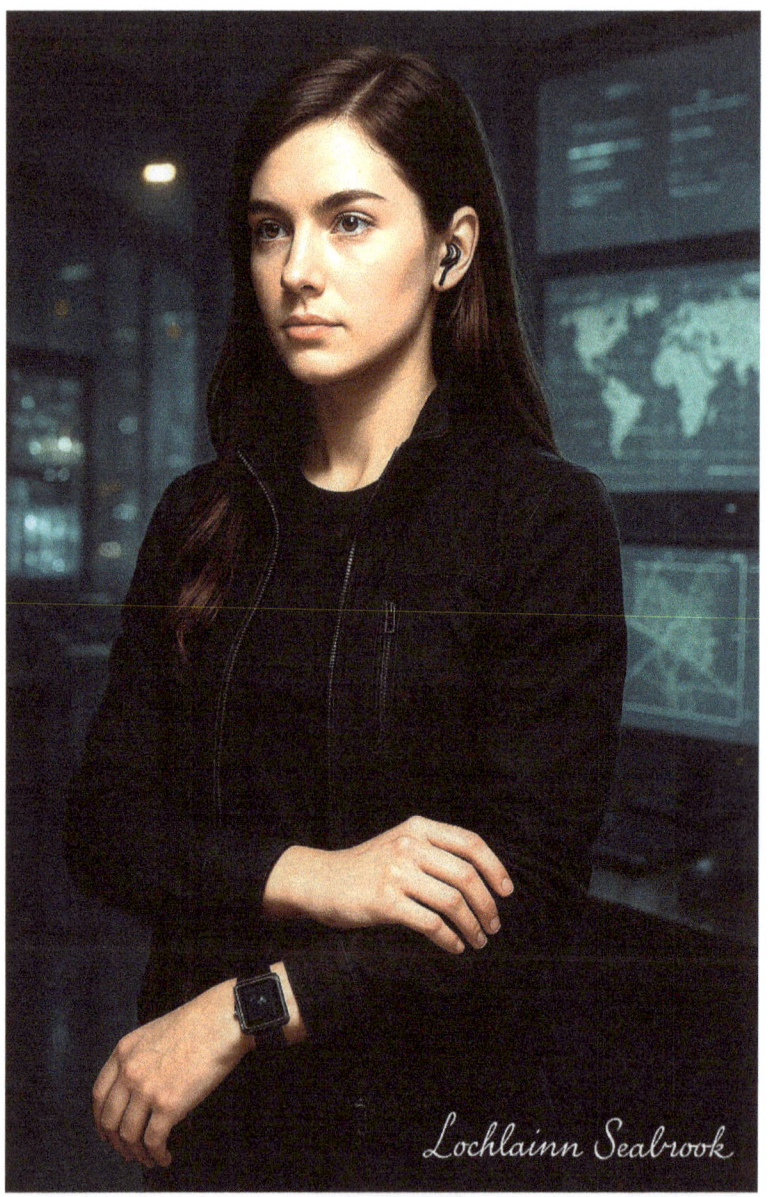

Boyd as she might look today working as a teenage spy. Copyright © Lochlainn Seabrook.

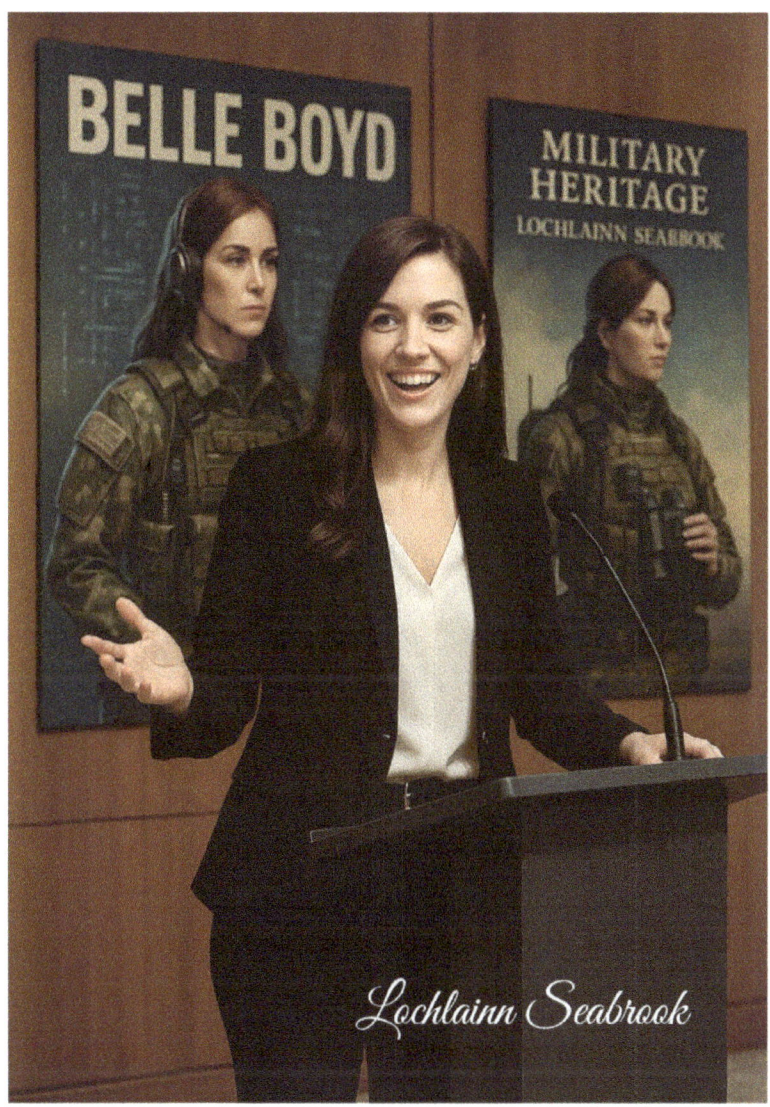

Boyd as she might look today working as a lecturer, story teller, and author, touring the country promoting her book detailing her career as an American spy. Copyright © Lochlainn Seabrook.

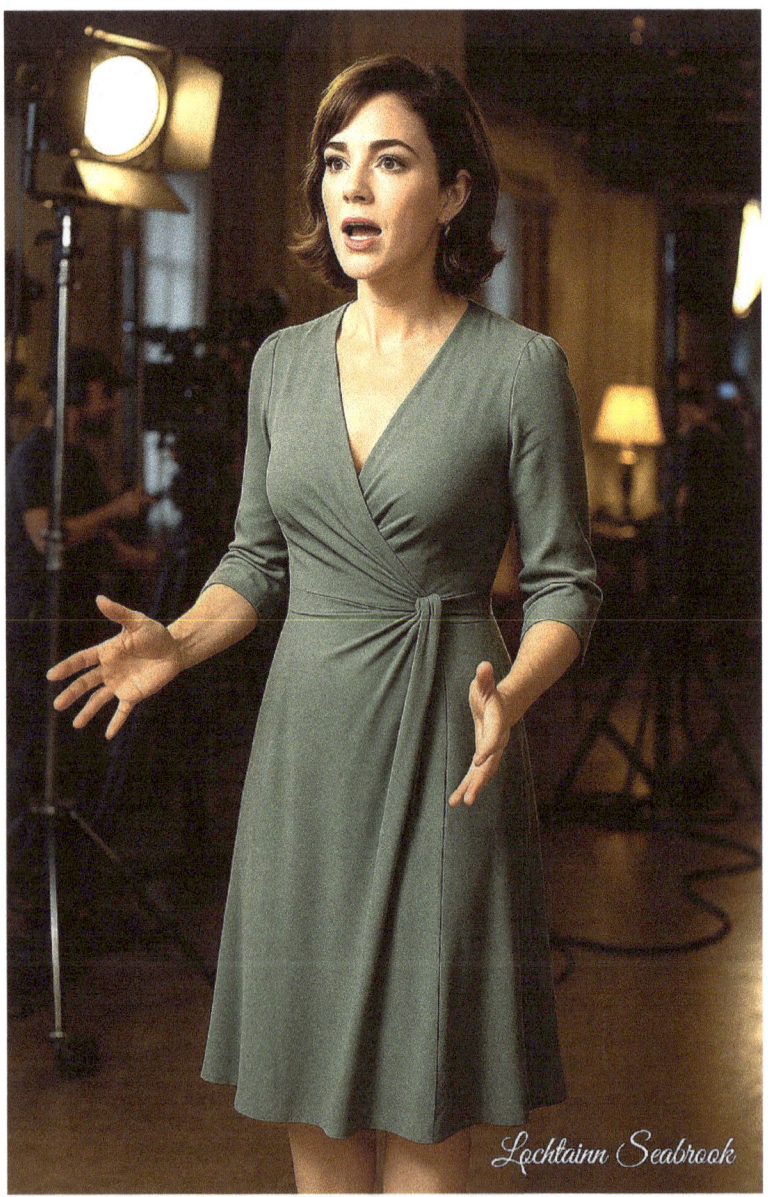

Maria Isabella "Belle" Boyd as she might look today engaging in one of her favorite pastimes: acting. Copyright © Lochlainn Seabrook.

JOHN C. CALHOUN

1782-1850, South Carolina

Conservative U.S. vice president, secretary of war, secretary of state, senator, U.S. representative, statesman, lawyer, planter.

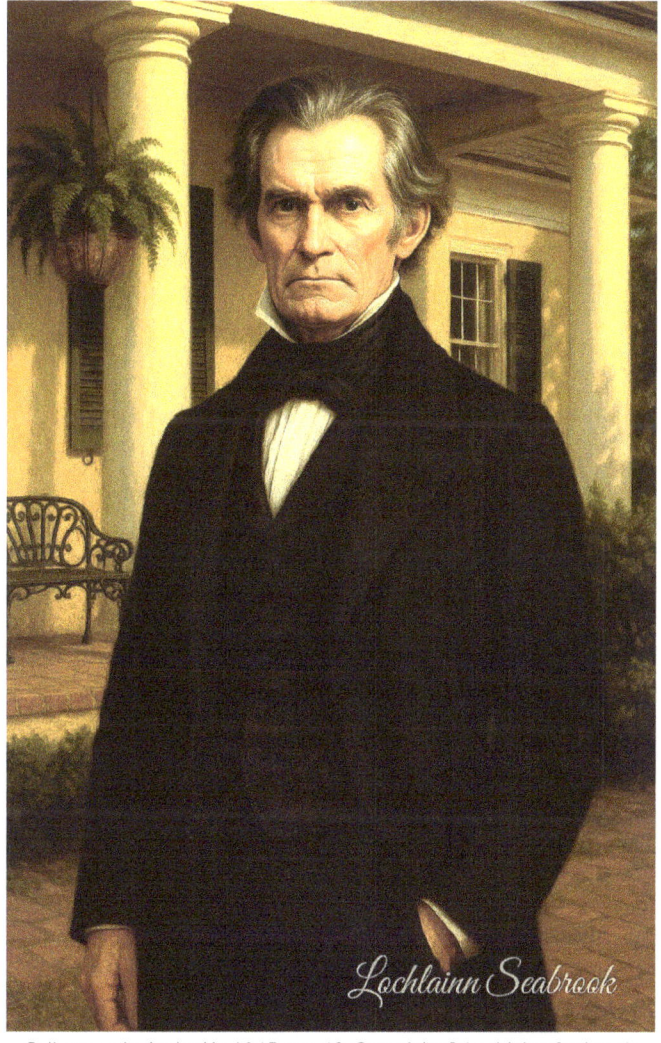

Calhoun as he looked in 1845, age 63. Copyright © Lochlainn Seabrook.

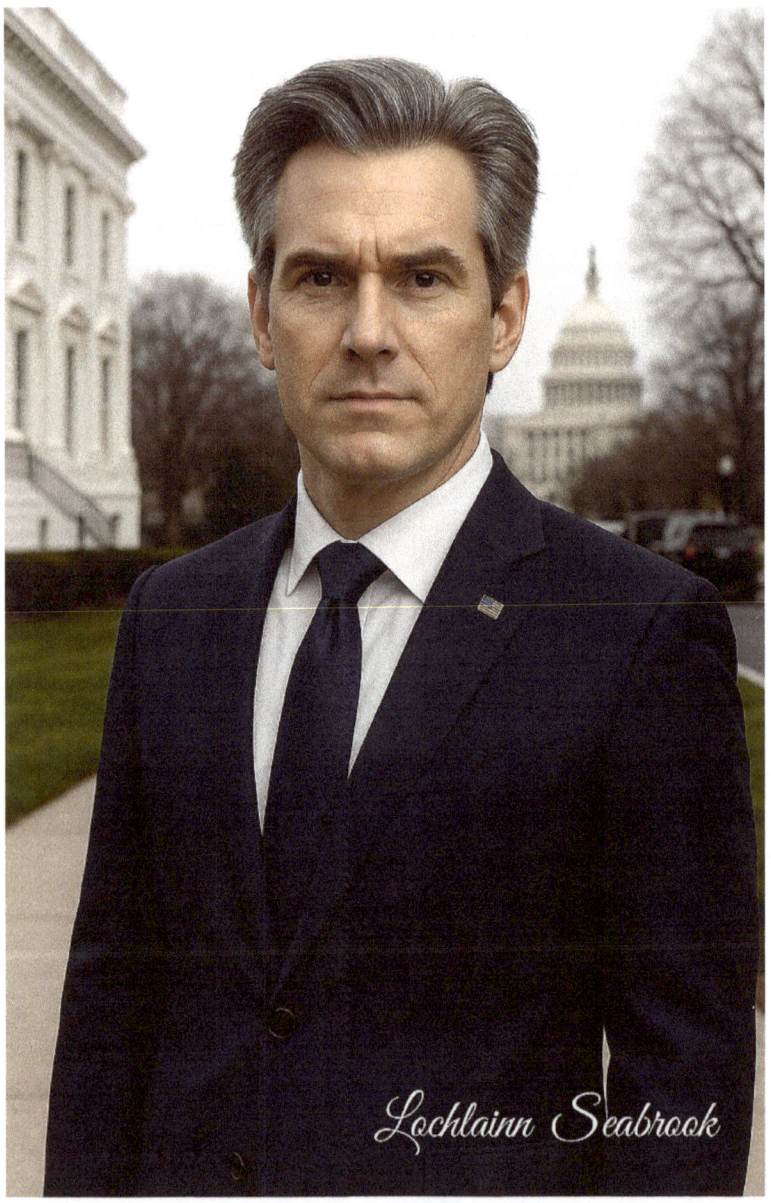

Calhoun as he might look today as a 44 year old U.S. vice president. Copyright © Lochlainn Seabrook.

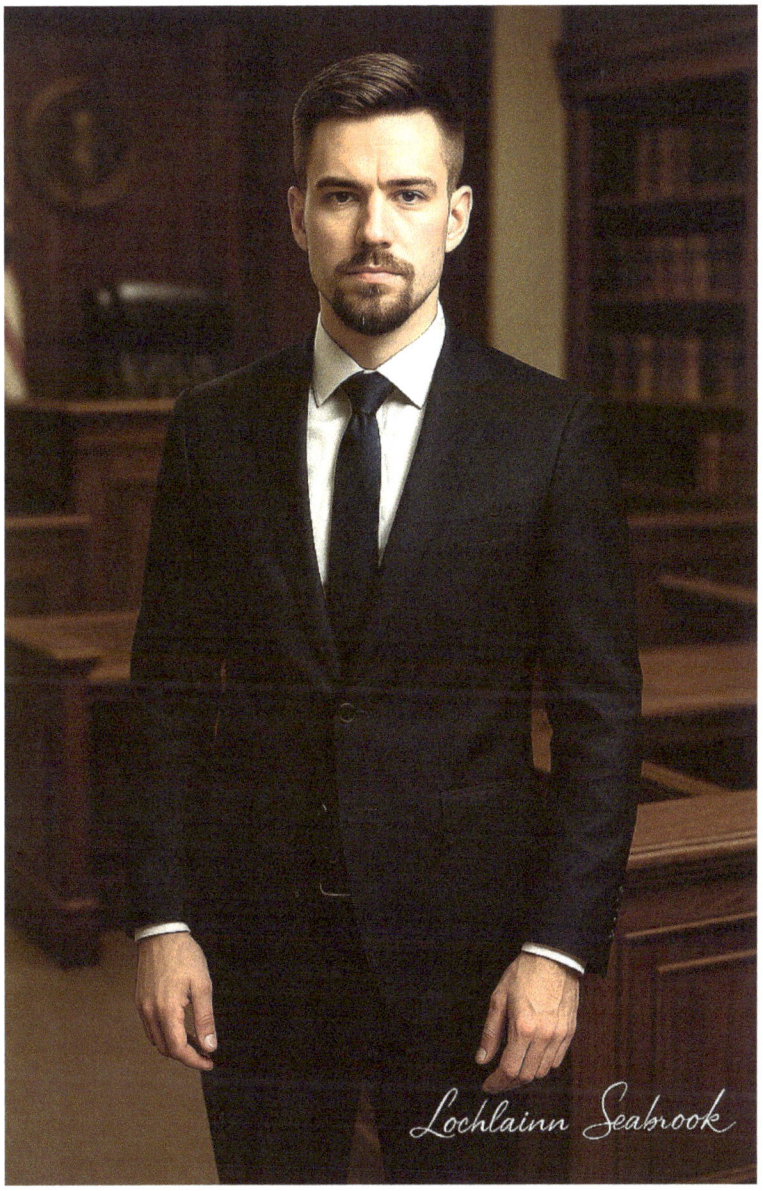

Calhoun as he might look today as a 25 year old lawyer. Copyright © Lochlainn Seabrook.

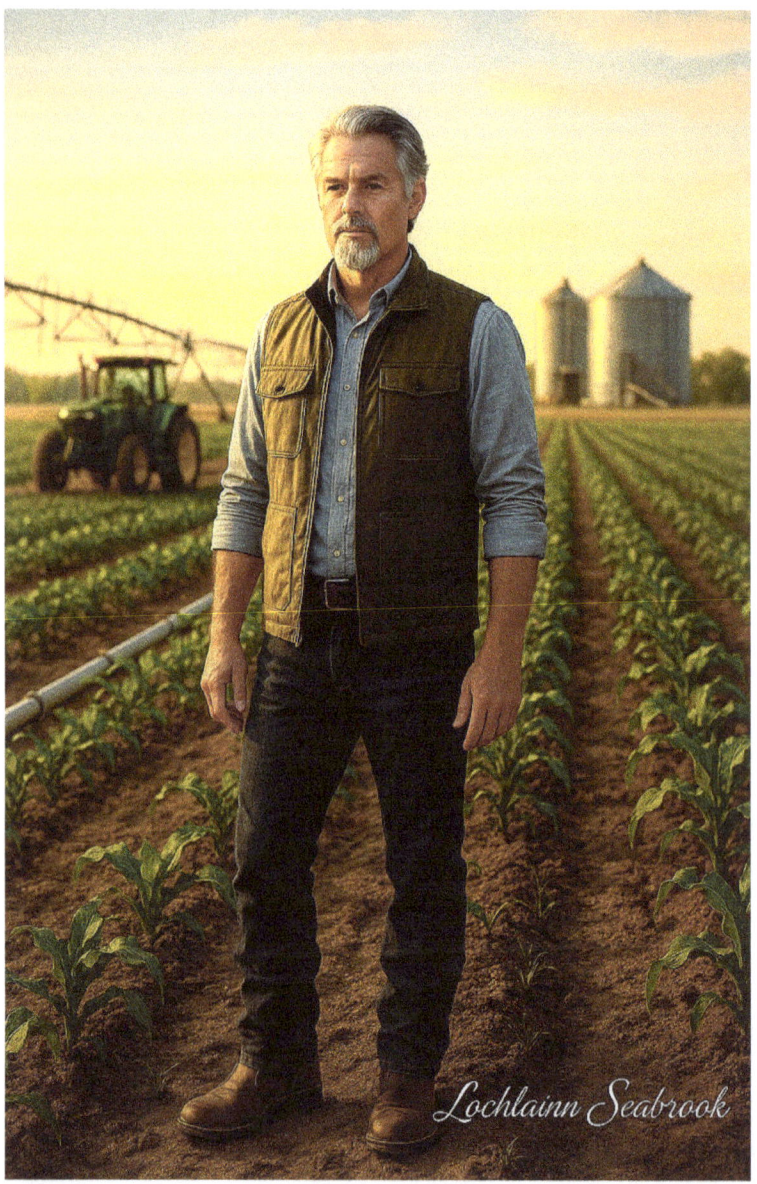

John Caldwell Calhoun as he might look today engaging in one of his favorite pastimes: agricultural innovation. Copyright © Lochlainn Seabrook.

KIT CARSON
1809-1868, Kentucky

Frontiersman, expedition guide, trapper, scout, explorer, soldier, military officer, Indian agent, saddlemaker, mountain man, fur trader, hunter.

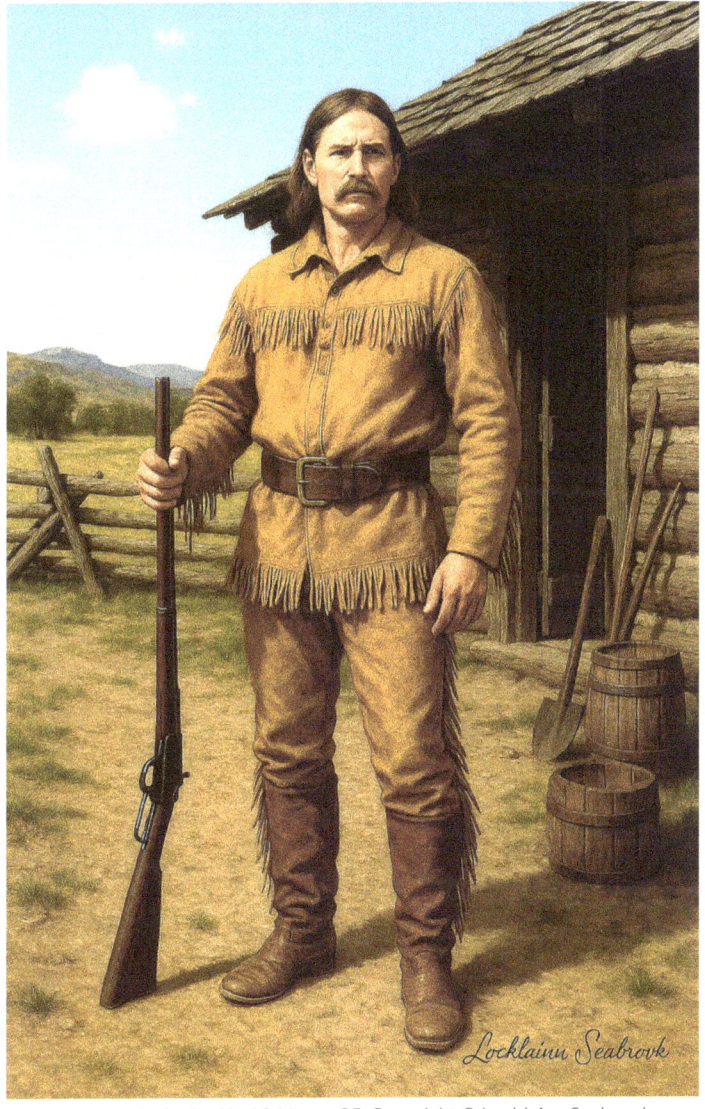

Carson as he looked in 1844, age 35. Copyright © Lochlainn Seabrook.

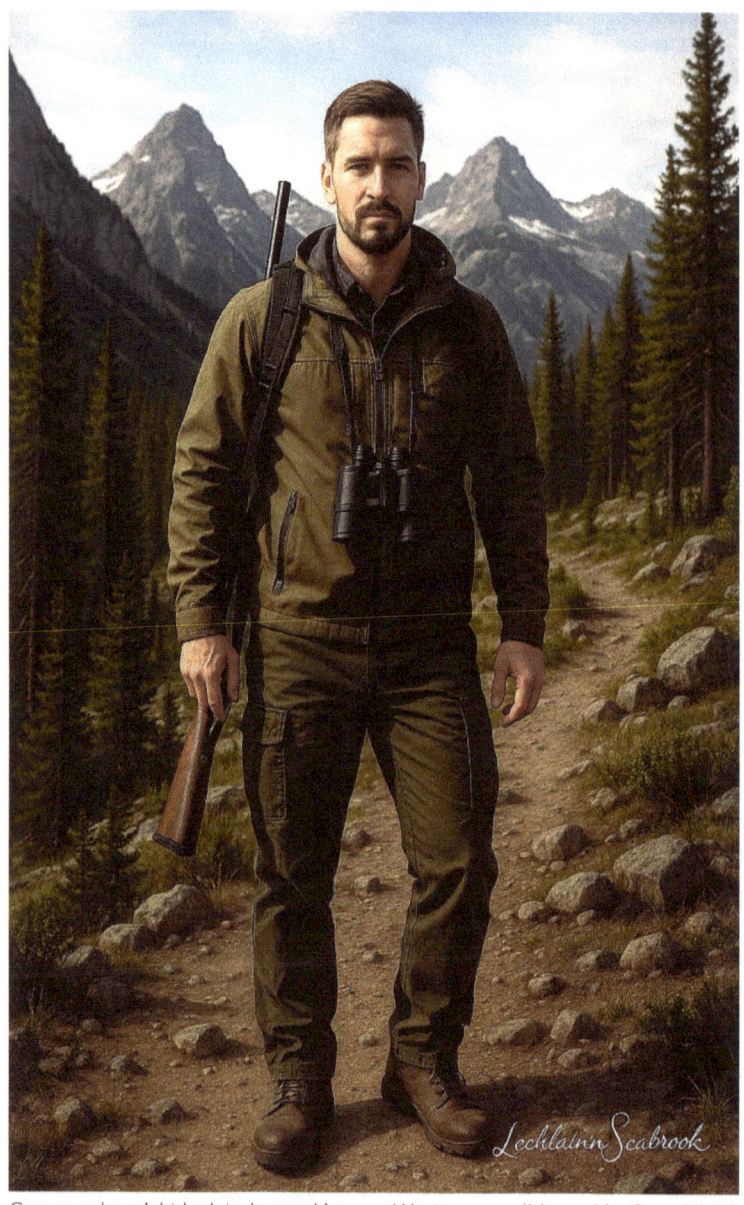

Carson as he might look today working as a Western expedition guide. Copyright © Lochlainn Seabrook.

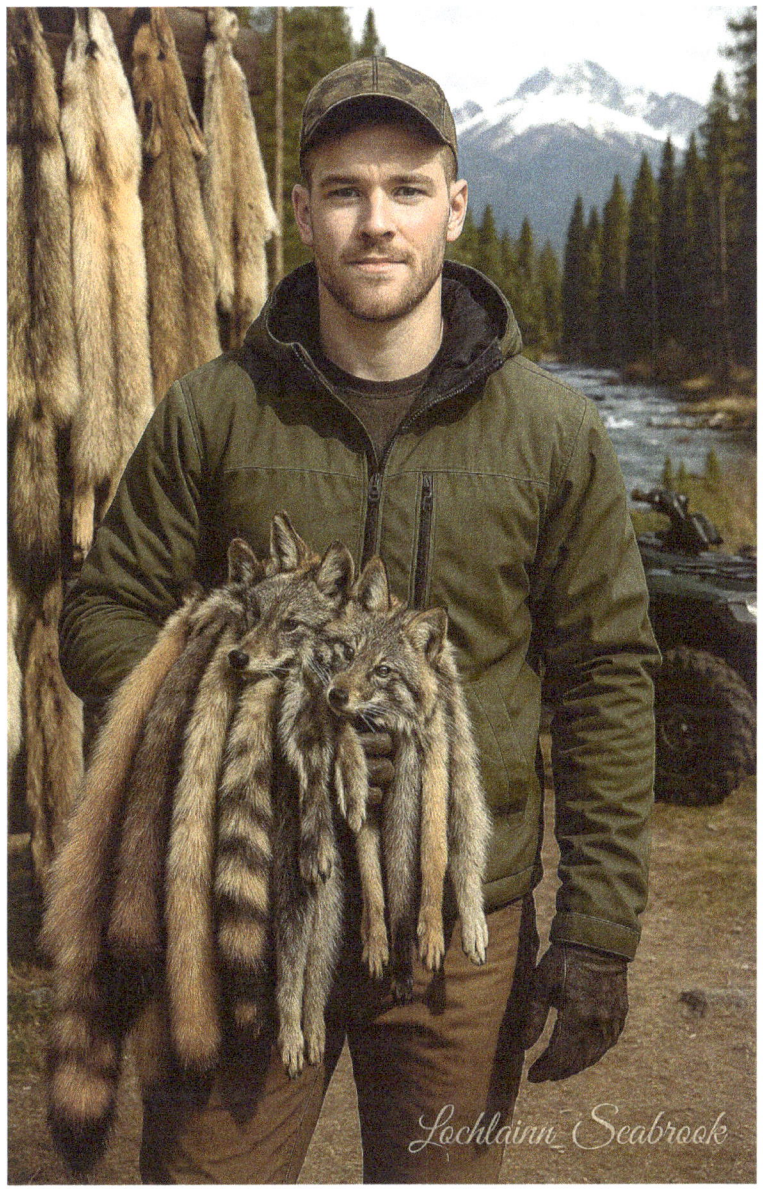

Carson as he might look today working as a young fur trapper. Copyright © Lochlainn Seabrook.

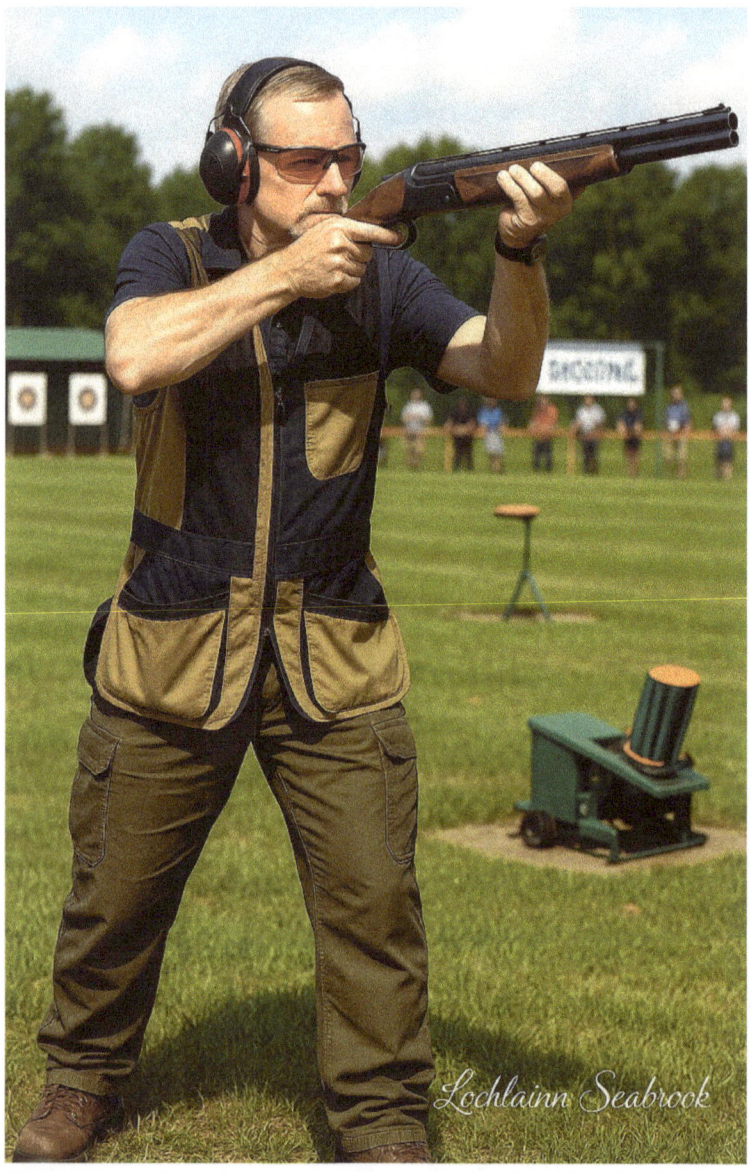

Kit Carson as he might look today engaging in one of his favorite hobbies: shooting sports. Copyright © Lochlainn Seabrook.

GEORGE WASHINGTON CARVER

c. 1864-1943, Missouri

Agricultural scientist, inventor, botanist, educator, organic and sustainable farming proponent, artist, farmhand, cook, tutor, laborer, ardent Christian, wholistic conservationist.

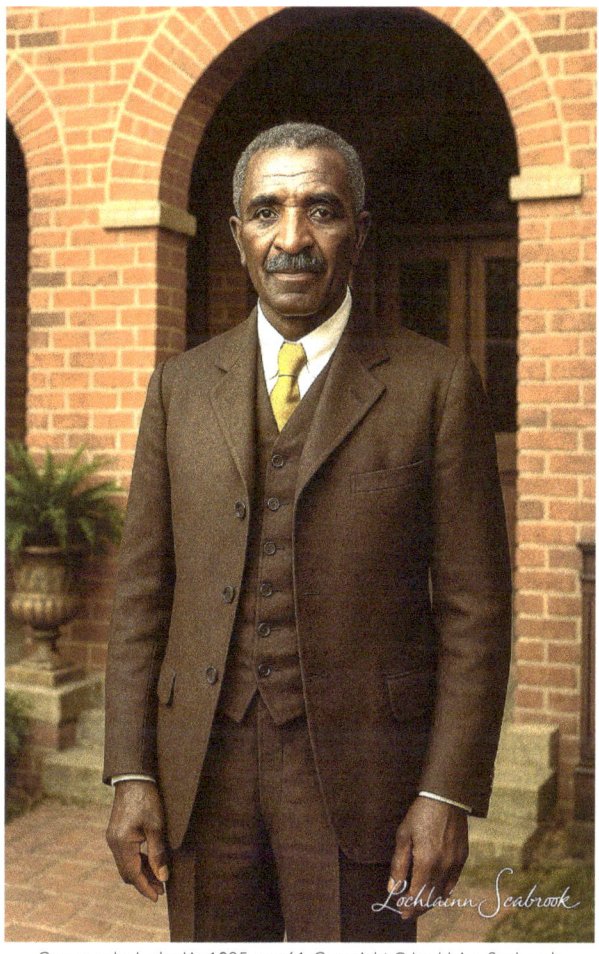

Carver as he looked in 1925, age 61. Copyright © Lochlainn Seabrook.

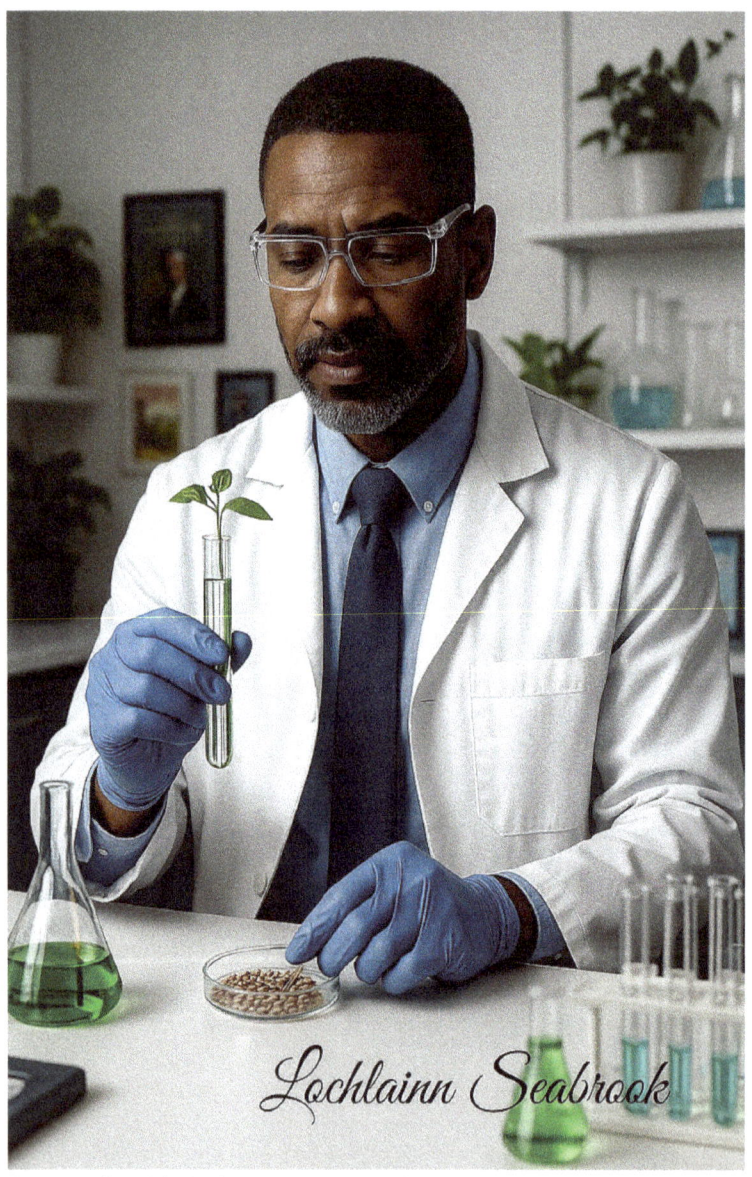

Carver as he might look today as an agricultural scientist. Copyright © Lochlainn Seabrook.

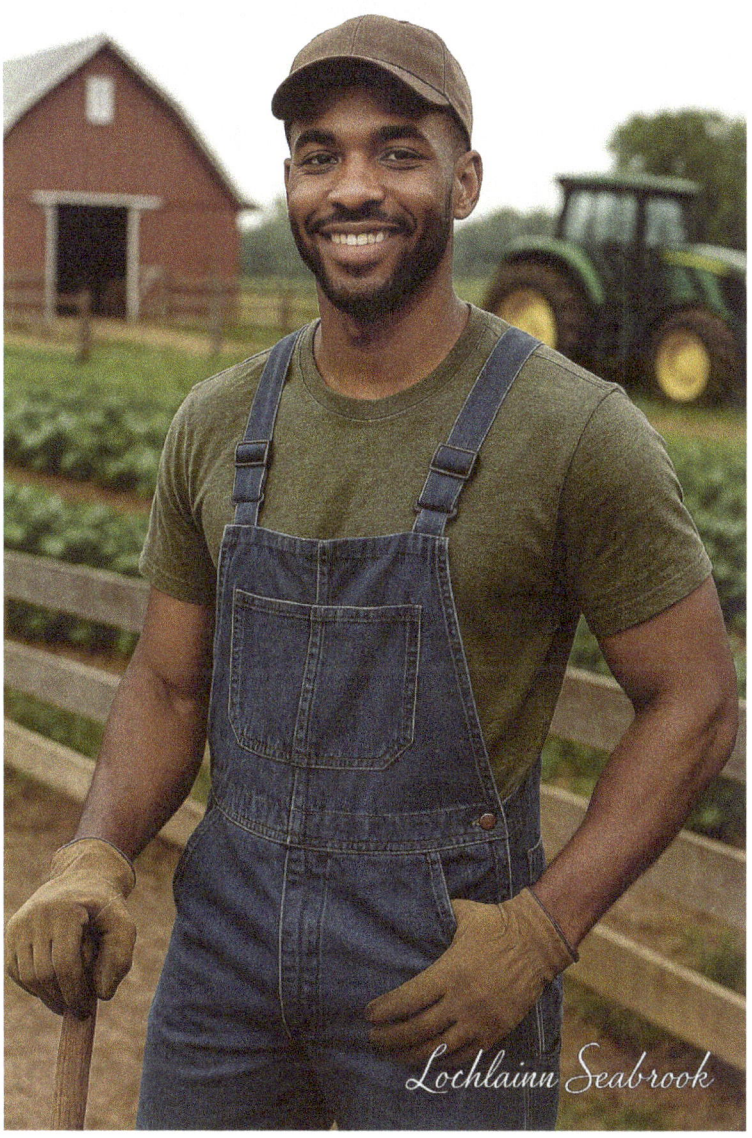

Carver as he might look today as a young farmhand. Copyright © Lochlainn Seabrook.

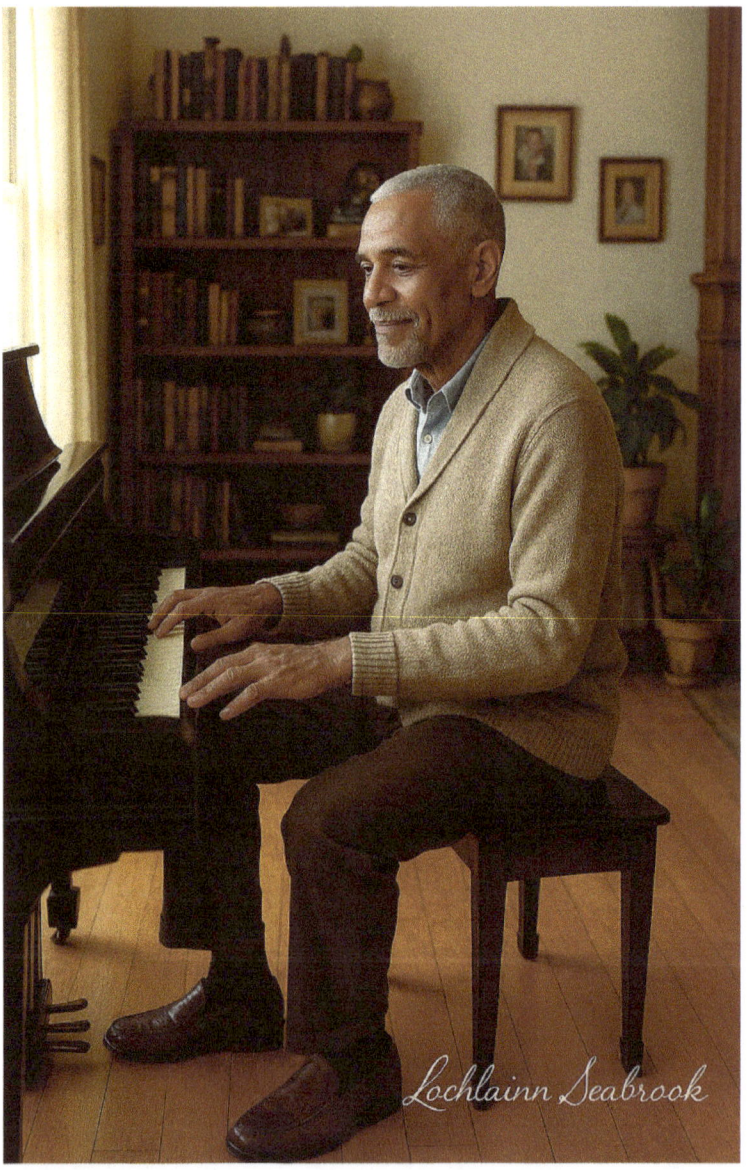

George Washington Carver as he might appear today enjoying one of his favorite hobbies: playing the piano. Copyright © Lochlainn Seabrook.

MARY BOYKIN CHESNUT

1823-1886, South Carolina

Conservative Southern aristocrat, socialite, author, diarist, intellectual, Confederate advocate and supporter, wife of U.S. senator and Confederate general James Chesnut Jr.

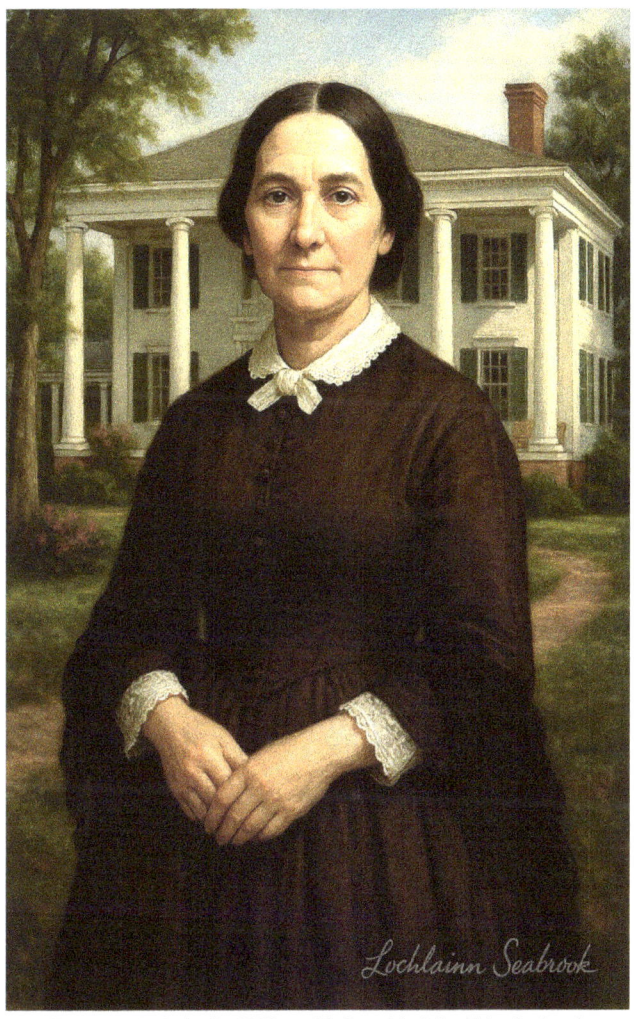

Chesnut as she looked in 1878, age 55. Copyright © Lochlainn Seabrook.

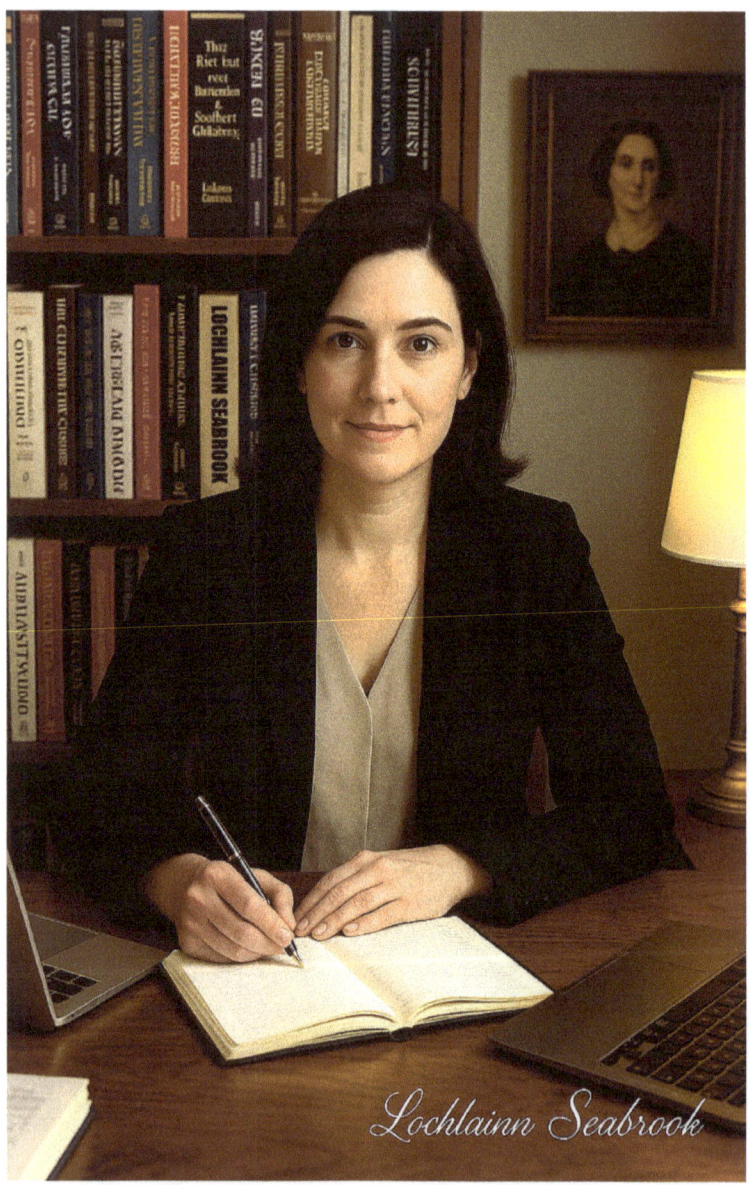

Chesnut as she might look today as a successful diarist-author. Copyright © Lochlainn Seabrook.

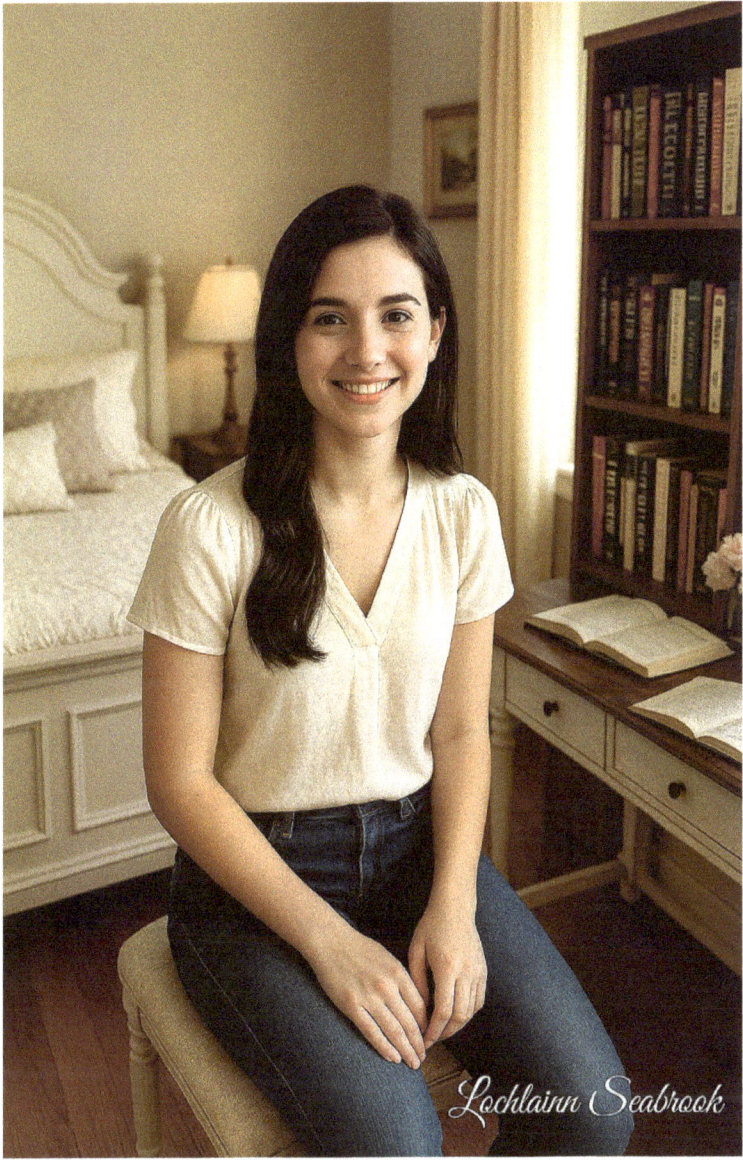

Chesnut as she might look as a modern day 16 year old Southern belle and debutante. Copyright © Lochlainn Seabrook.

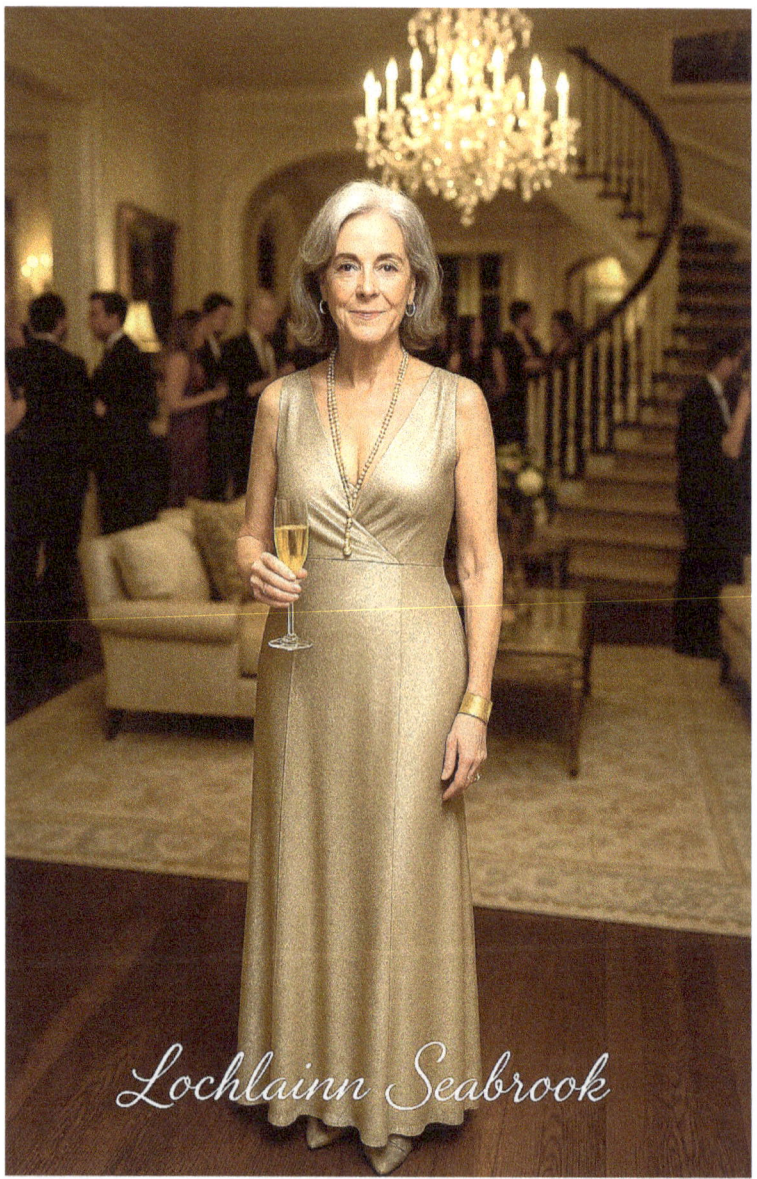

Socialite Mary Boykin Chesnut as she might look today engaging in one of her favorite pastimes: hosting a party in her home. Copyright © Lochlainn Seabrook.

WILLIAM "BUFFALO BILL" CODY

1846-1917, Iowa

Showman, businessman, entrepreneur, U.S. army scout, pony express rider, gold prospector, wagon train driver, stagecoach driver, buffalo hunter, civilian contractor for the U.S. army.

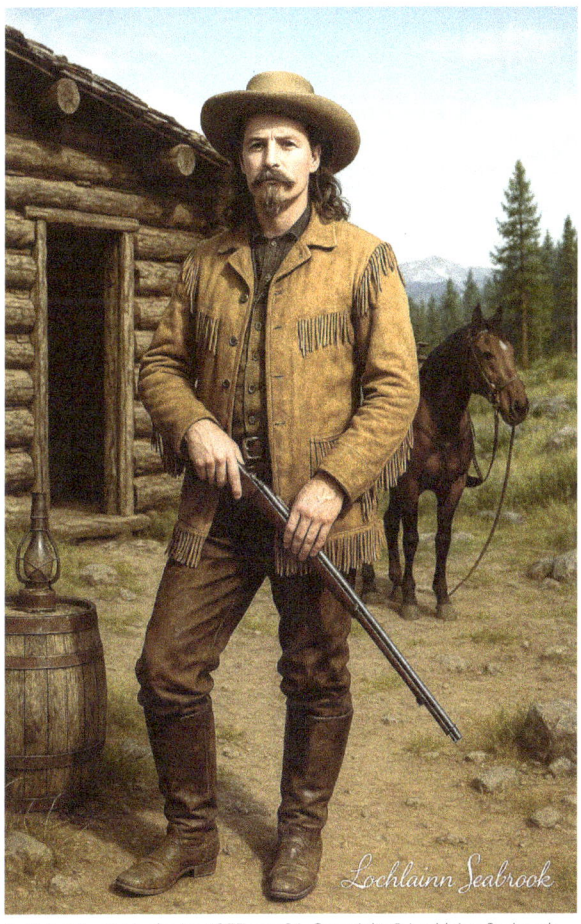

Buffalo Bill as he looked in 1877, age 31. Copyright © Lochlainn Seabrook.

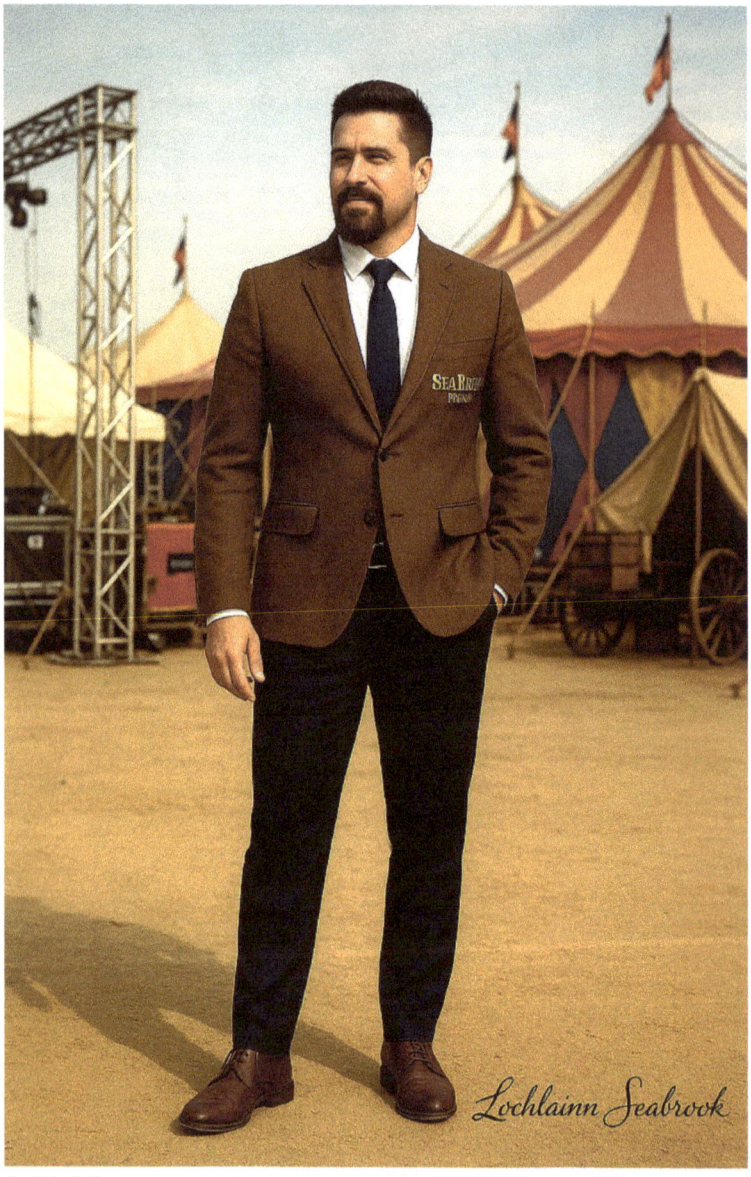

Buffalo Bill as he might look today as a successful showman, businessman, and owner of a live, traveling, theatrical, Western-themed roadshow. Copyright © Lochlainn Seabrook.

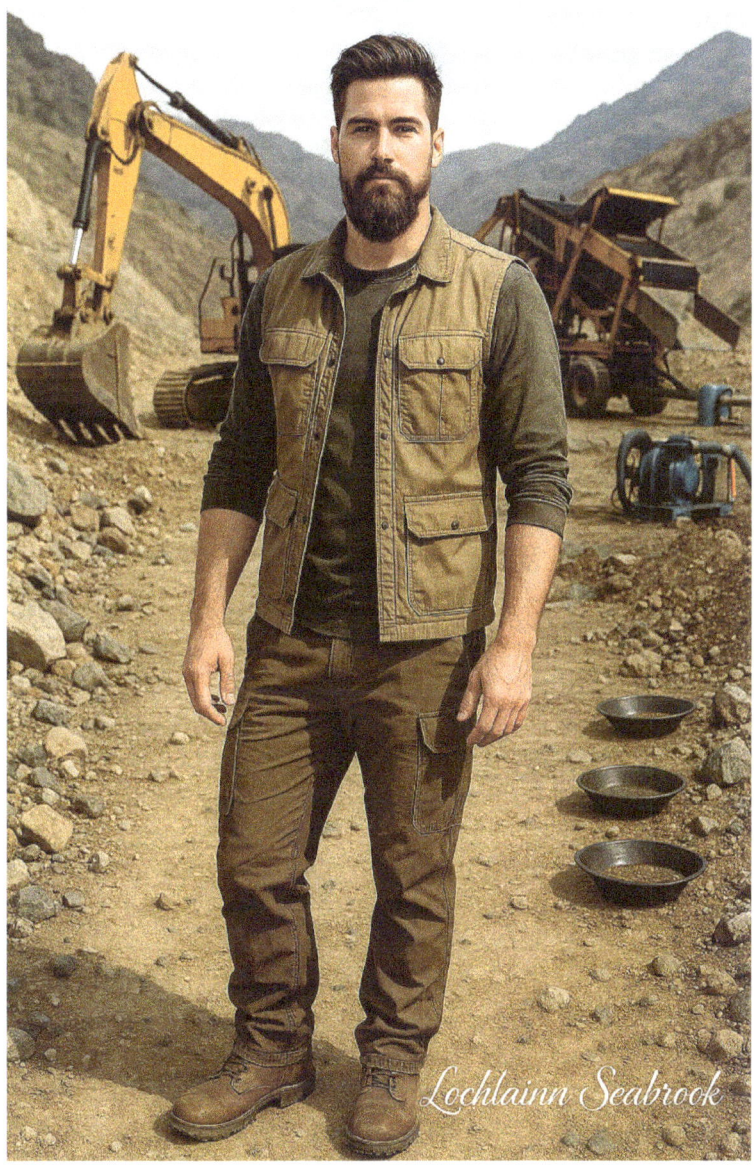

Buffalo Bill as he might look today working as a young gold prospector in Colorado. Copyright © Lochlainn Seabrook.

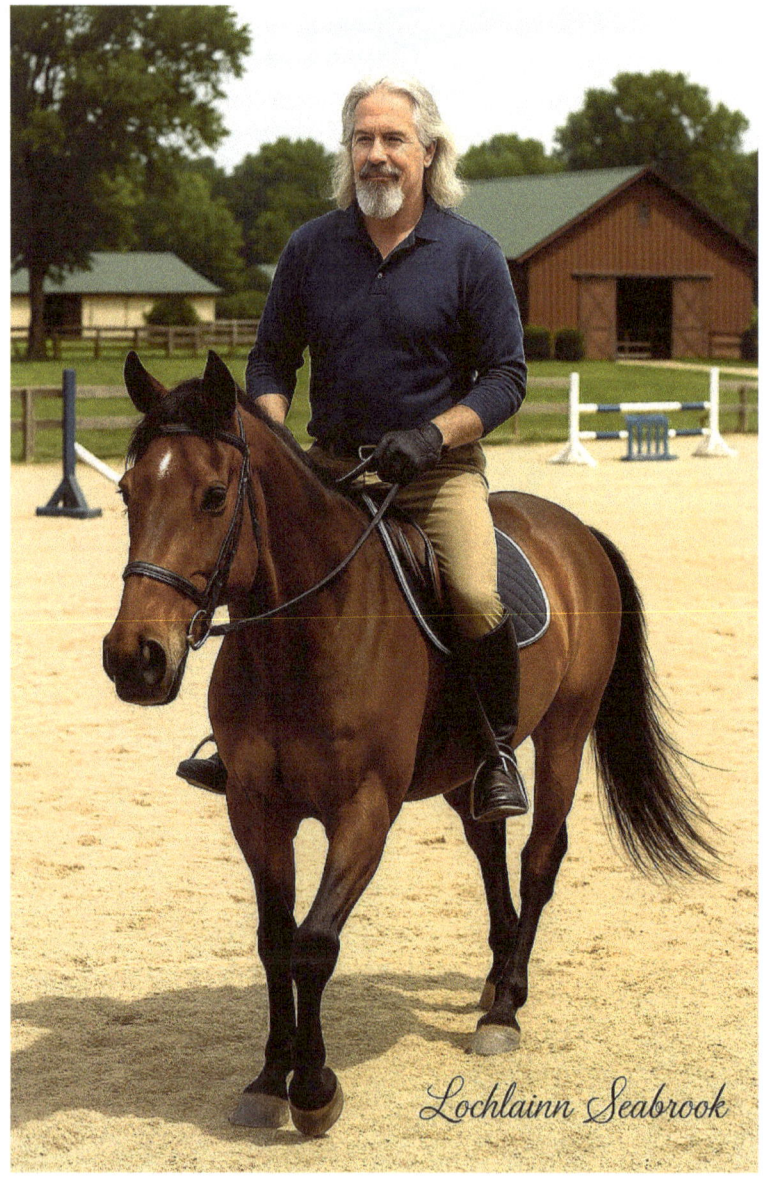

William Frederick "Buffalo Bill" Cody as he might look today engaging in one of his favorite pastimes: horseback riding. Copyright © Lochlainn Seabrook.

DAVID CROCKETT

1786-1836, North Carolina (later part of Tennessee)

Frontiersman, woodsman, hunter, fur trader, teamster, laborer, cattle herder, military scout, soldier, magistrate, state legislator, U.S. congressman.

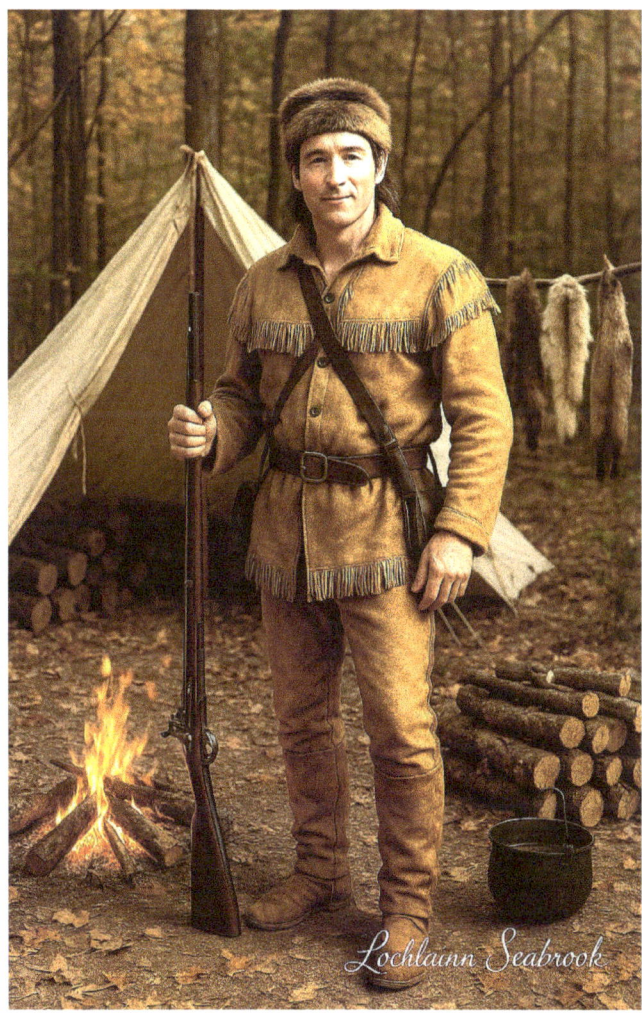

Crockett as he looked in 1816, age 30. Copyright © Lochlainn Seabrook.

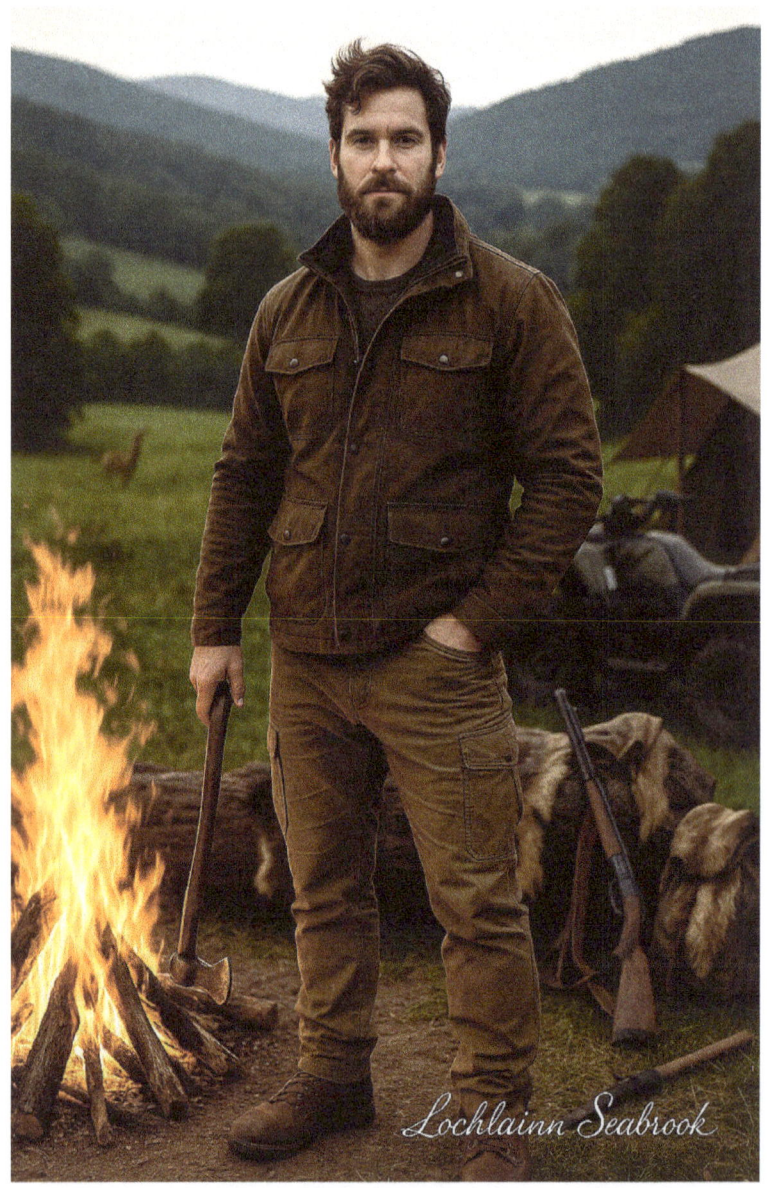

Crockett as he might look today as a popular mountain man in Colorado. Copyright © Lochlainn Seabrook.

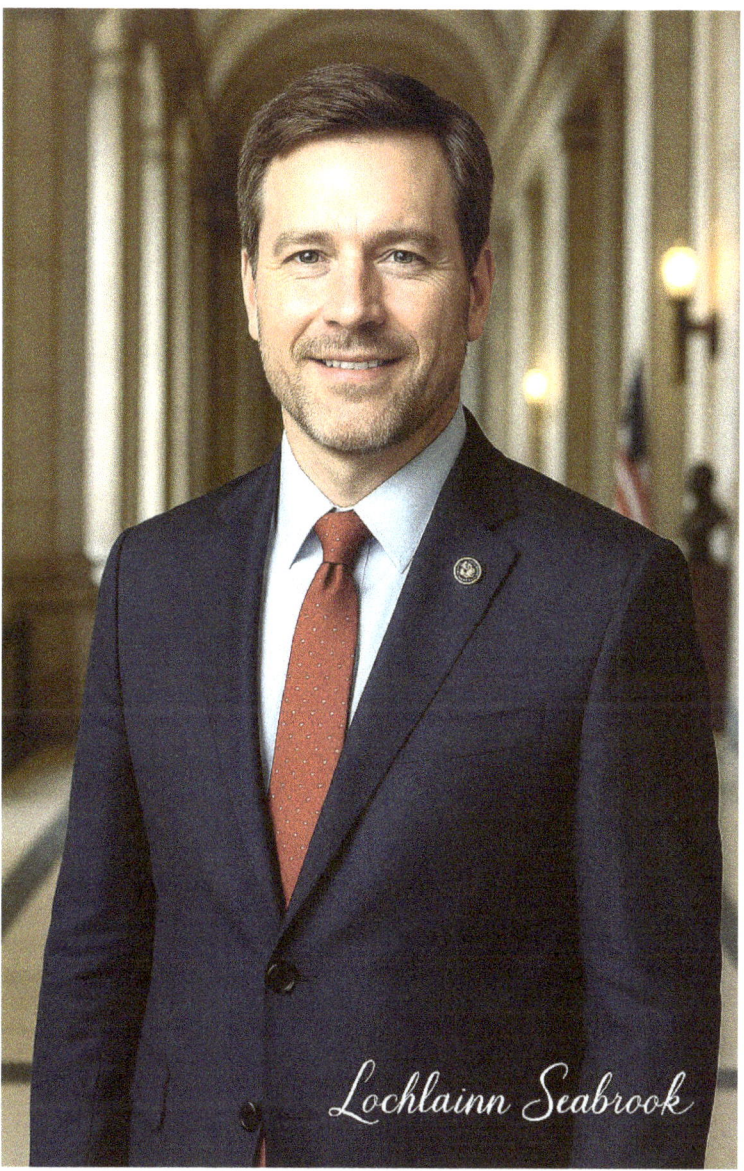

Crockett as he might look today serving as a Tennessee congressman. Copyright © Lochlainn Seabrook.

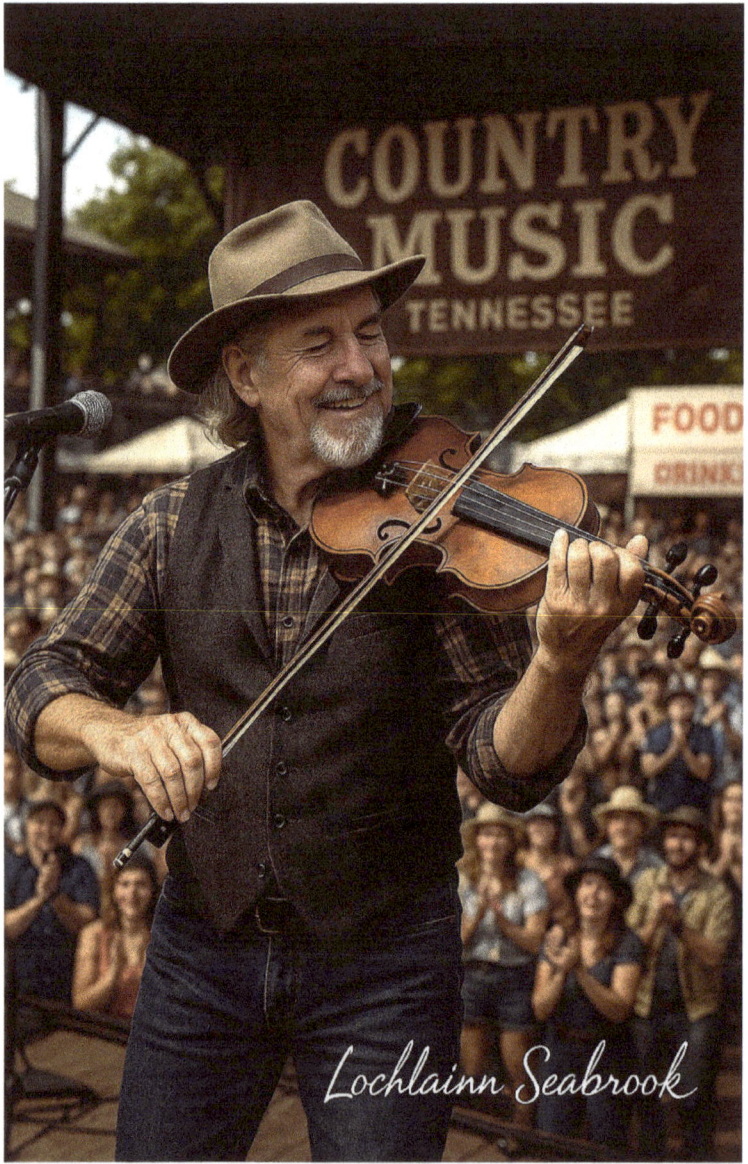

David "Davy" Crockett as he might look today engaging in one of his favorite hobbies: fiddle playing. Copyright © Lochlainn Seabrook.

KATE CUMMING

c. 1830-1909, Scotland

Confederate nurse, diarist, author, Confederate heritage advocate, Confederate veterans supporter, conservative Christian, humanitarian.

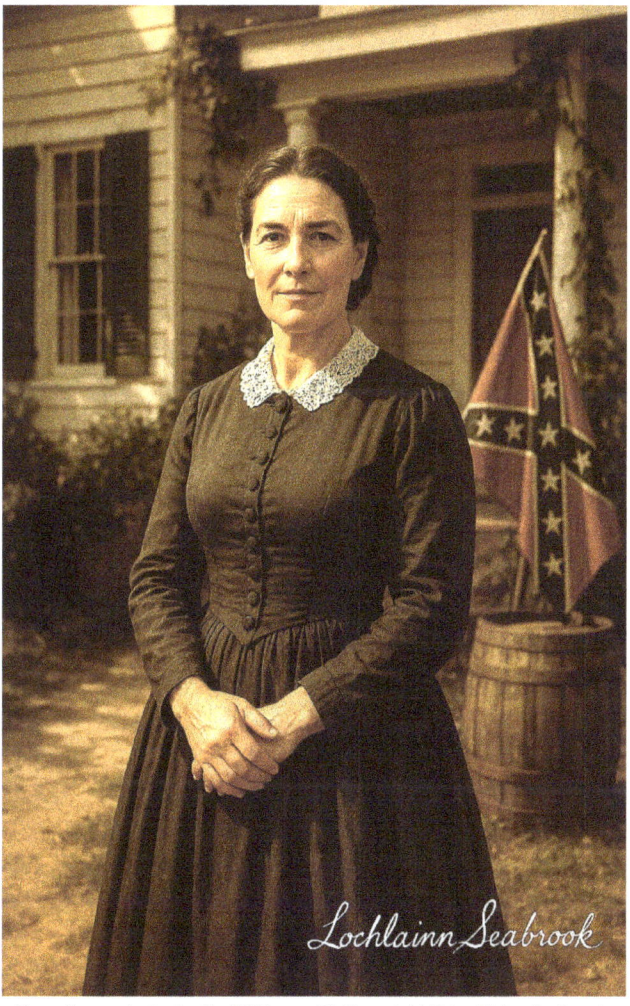

Cumming as she looked in 1881, age 51. Copyright © Lochlainn Seabrook.

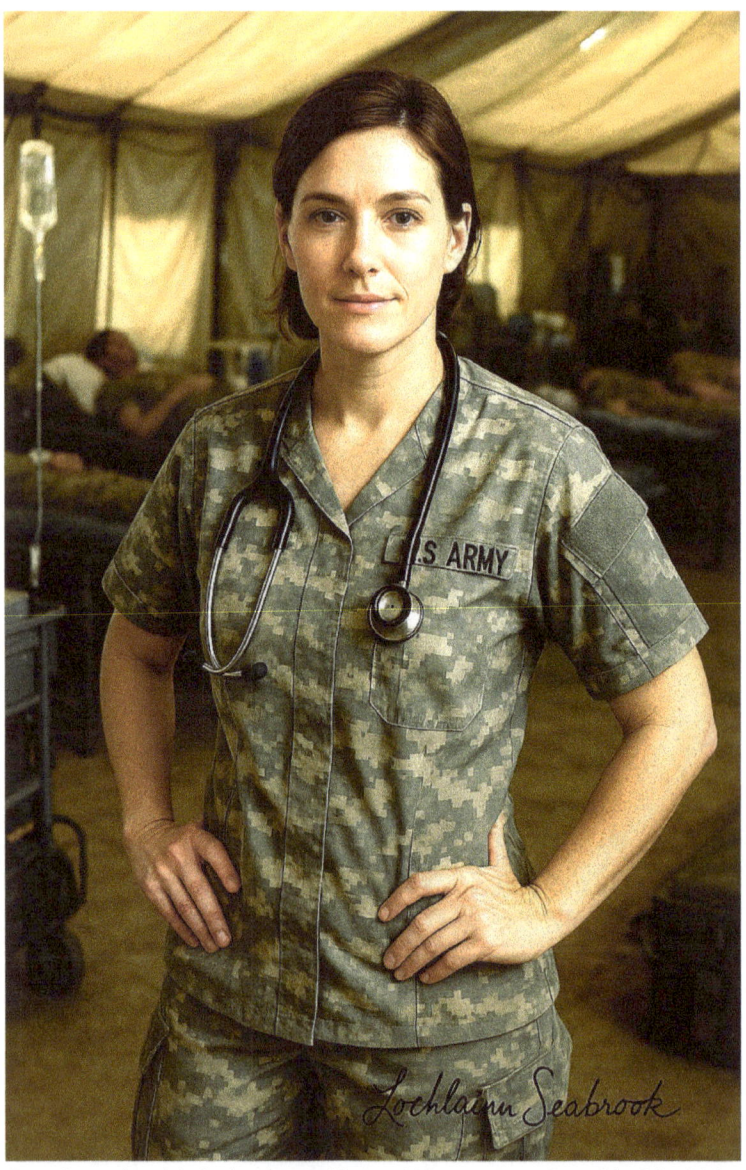

Cumming as she might look today working as a U.S. army nurse. Copyright © Lochlainn Seabrook.

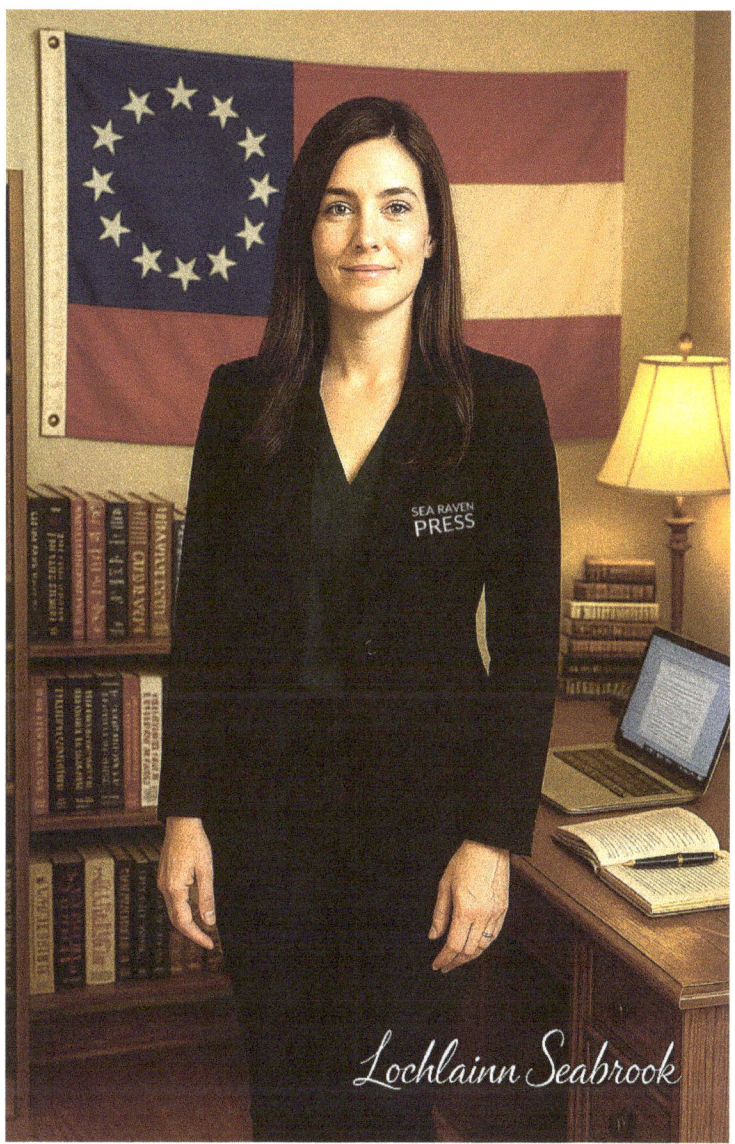

Cumming as she might look today as a pro-South, pro-Confederate author-diarist. Copyright © Lochlainn Seabrook.

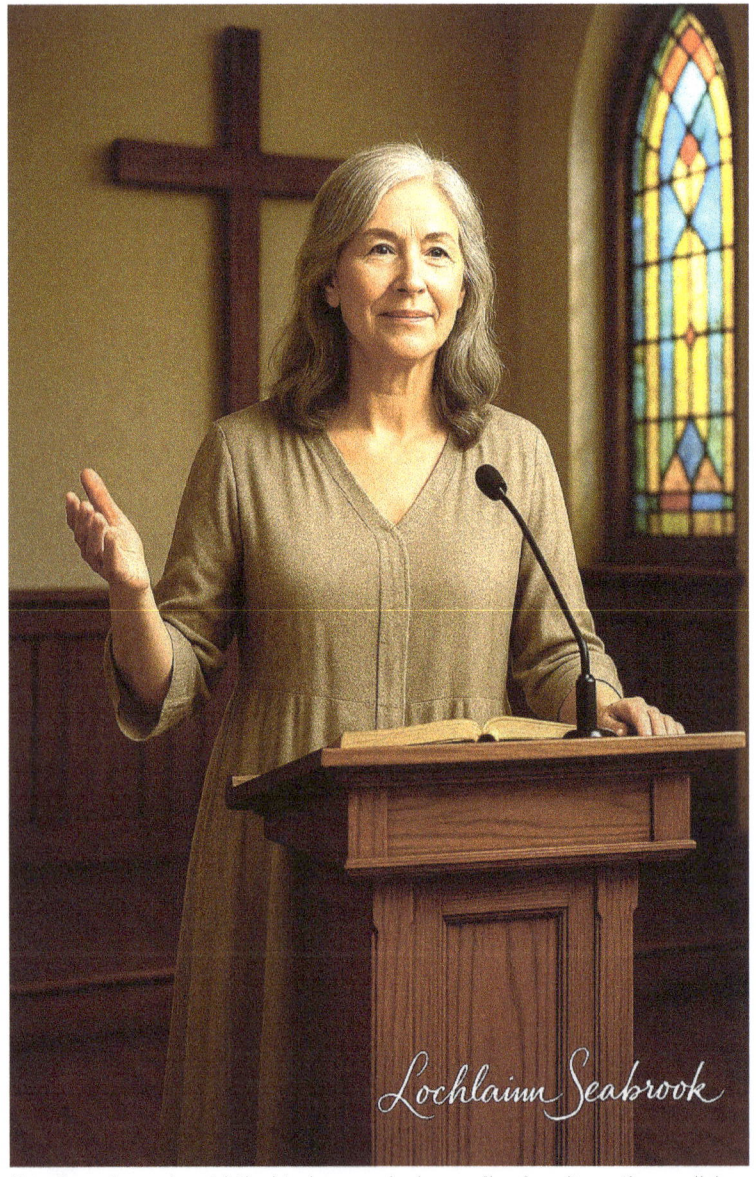

Kate Cumming as she might look today engaging in one of her favorite pastimes: religious devotion. Copyright © Lochlainn Seabrook.

GEORGE ARMSTRONG CUSTER

1839-1876, Ohio

U.S. army general, U.S. cavalry officer, West Point Military graduate, commanding U.S. officer at the Battle of Little Bighorn, author, teenage school teacher, horseman, fashionista.

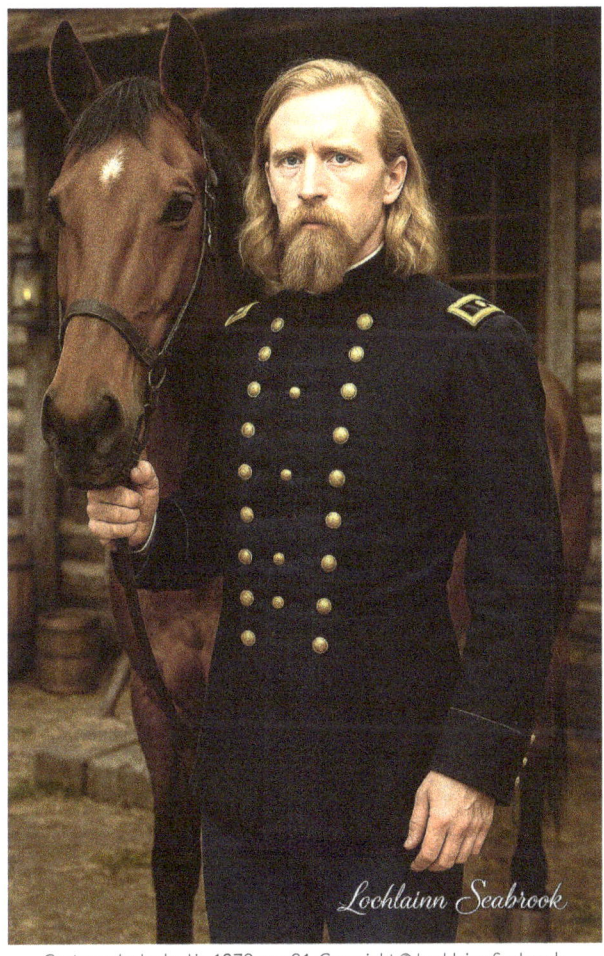

Custer as he looked in 1870, age 31. Copyright © Lochlainn Seabrook.

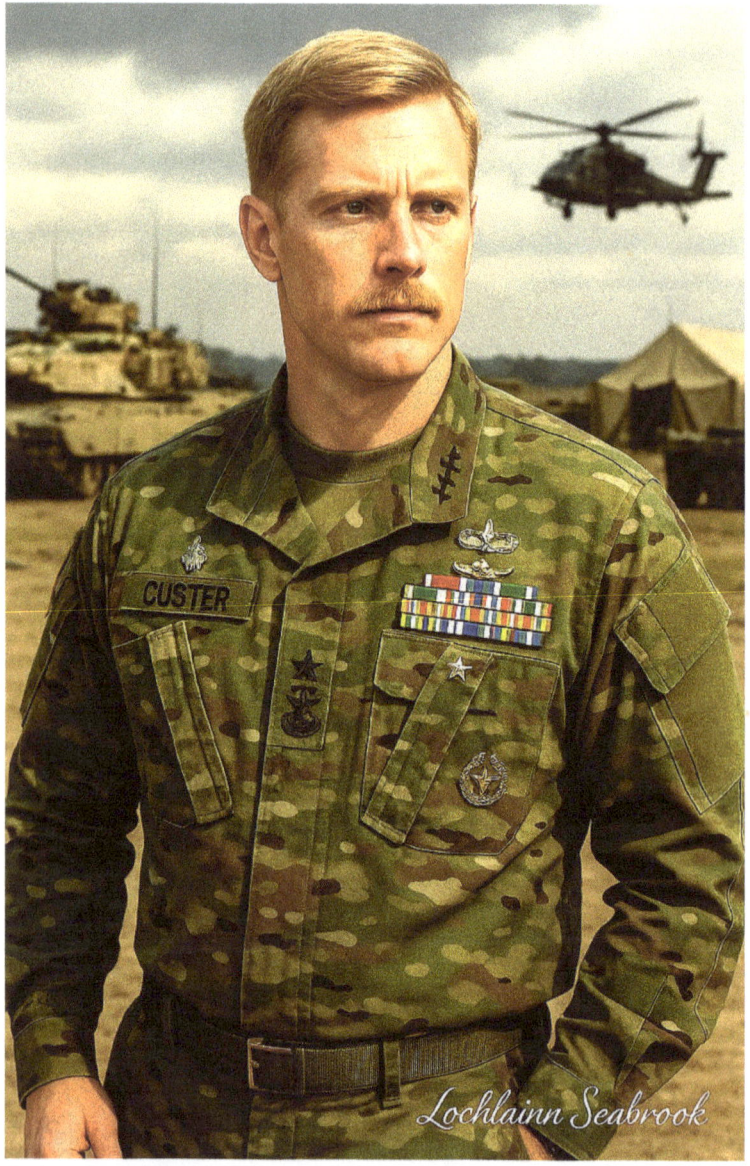

Custer as he might look today serving as a U.S. army general commanding the 1st Cavalry Division. Copyright © Lochlainn Seabrook.

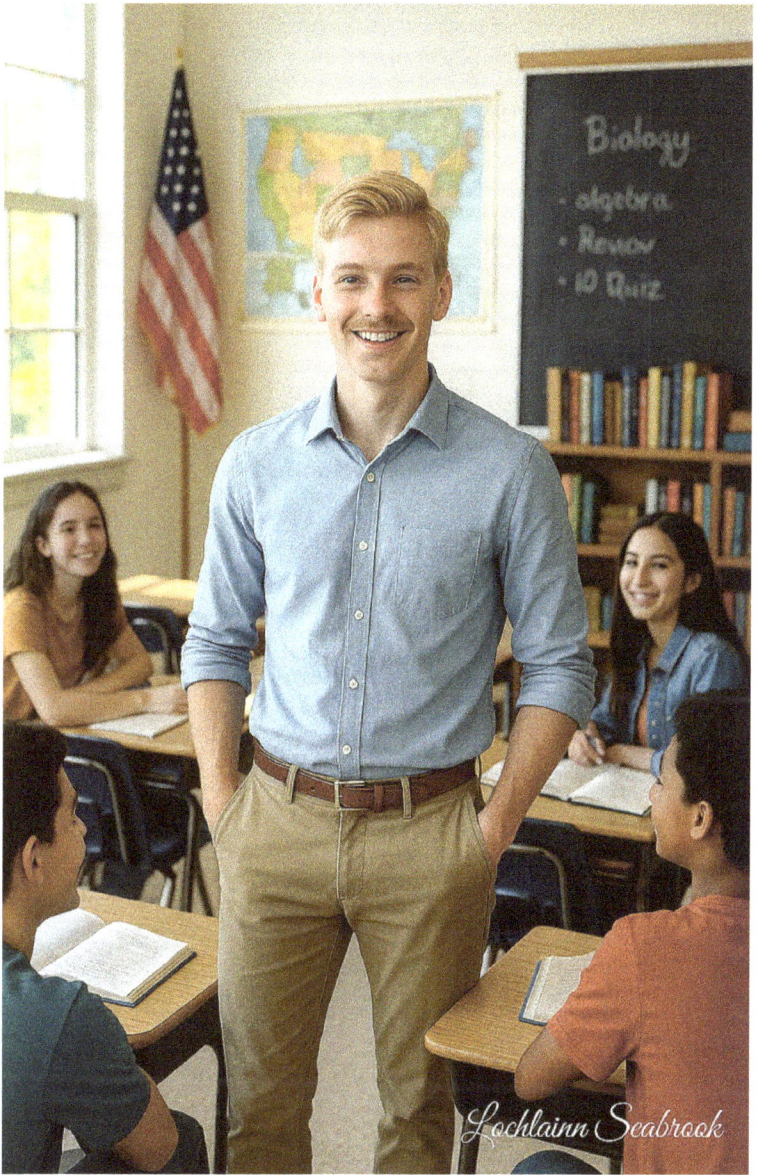

Custer as he might look today as a young schoolteacher. Copyright © Lochlainn Seabrook.

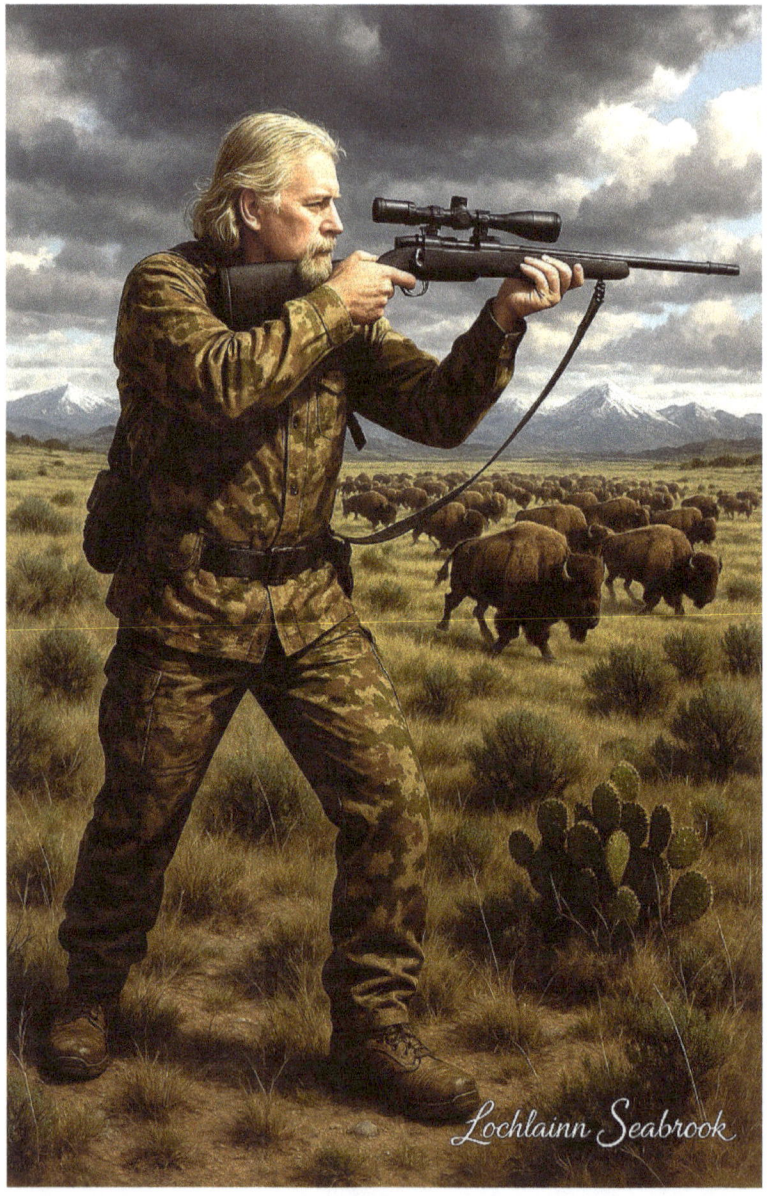

George Armstrong Custer as he might look today engaging in one of his favorite pastimes: bison hunting. Copyright © Lochlainn Seabrook.

JEFFERSON DAVIS

1808-1889, Kentucky

Conservative American statesman, U.S. representative, U.S. senator, U.S. secretary of war, U.S. military officer, C.S. president, Mexican-American war hero, West Point graduate, orator, political prisoner, historian, author, farmer, equestrian, husband of Sarah Knox Taylor and Varina Banks Howell.

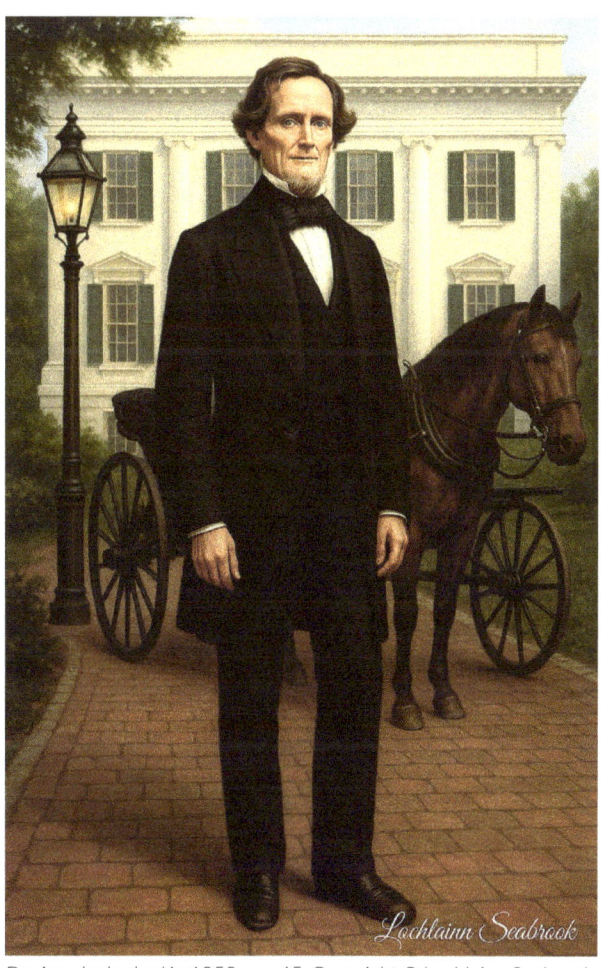

Davis as he looked in 1853, age 45. Copyright © Lochlainn Seabrook.

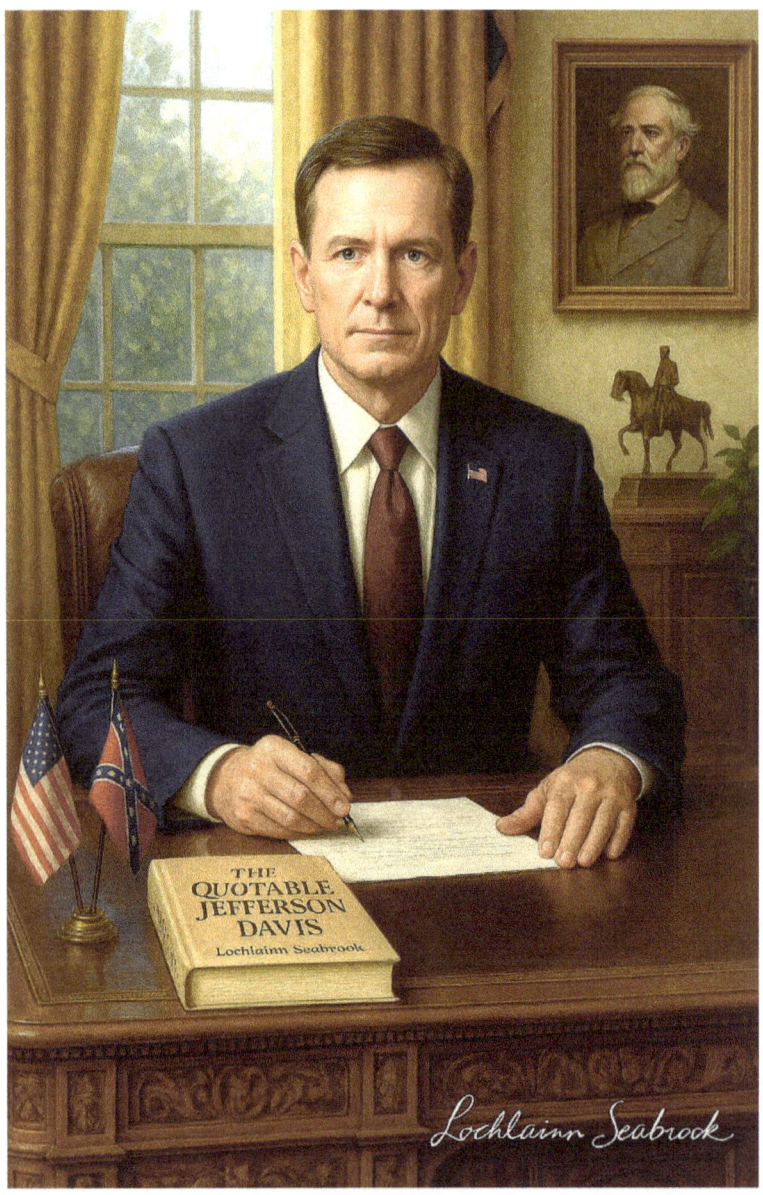

Davis as he might look today serving as president of the United States of America. Copyright © Lochlainn Seabrook.

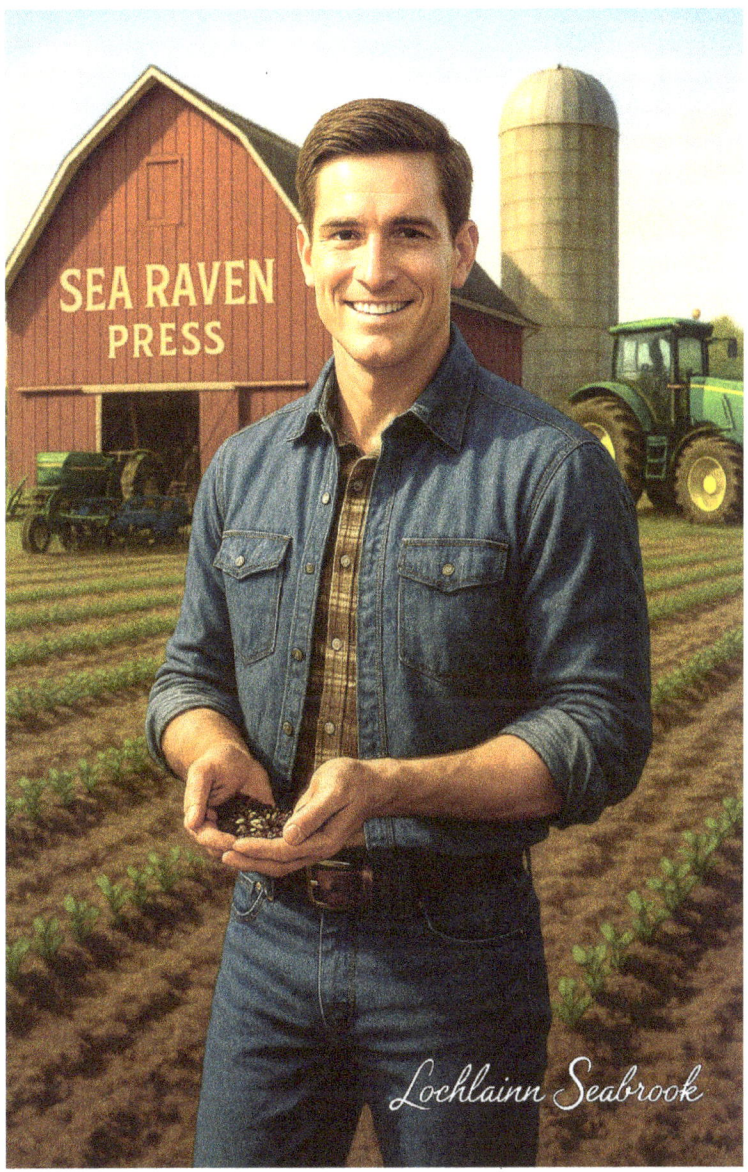

Davis as he might look today as a young wealthy Mississippi farm owner. Copyright © Lochlainn Seabrook.

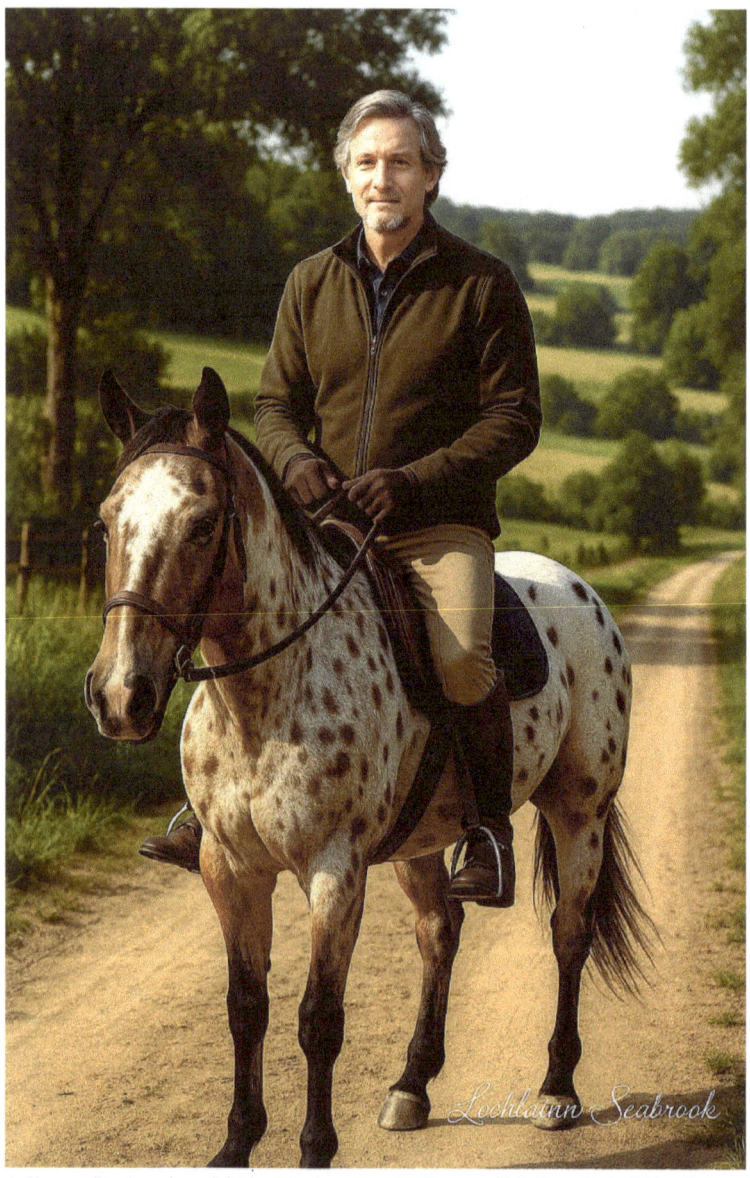

Jefferson Davis as he might look today engaging in one of his favorite hobbies: leisure horseback riding. Copyright © Lochlainn Seabrook.

AMELIA EARHART

1897-1939, Kansas

Aviator, record-breaking flight pioneer, author, lecturer and speaker, flight instructor, social worker, nurse's aid, file clerk, truck driver, photographer, women's rights advocate.

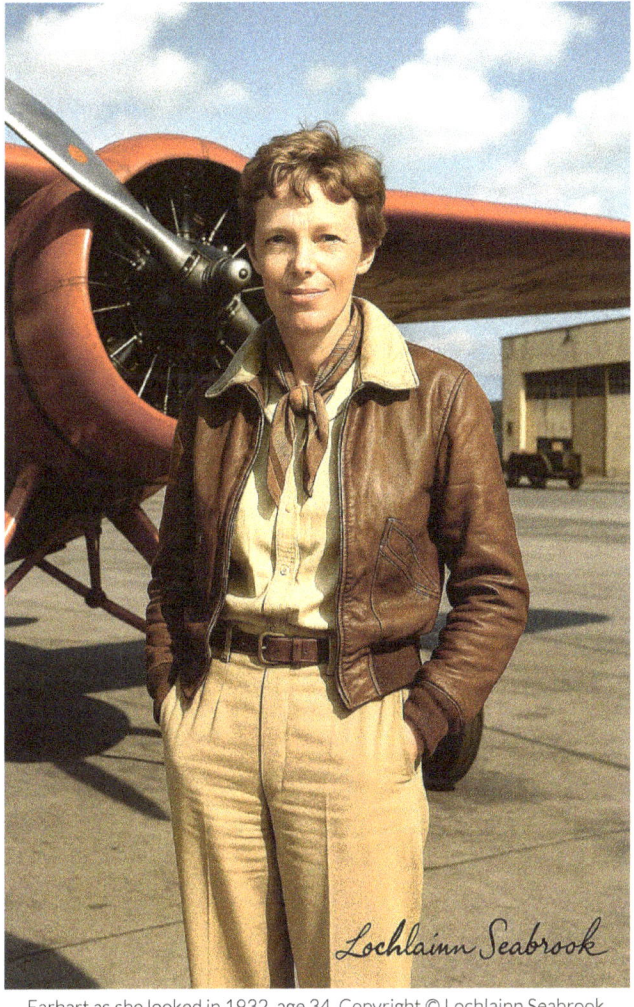

Earhart as she looked in 1932, age 34. Copyright © Lochlainn Seabrook.

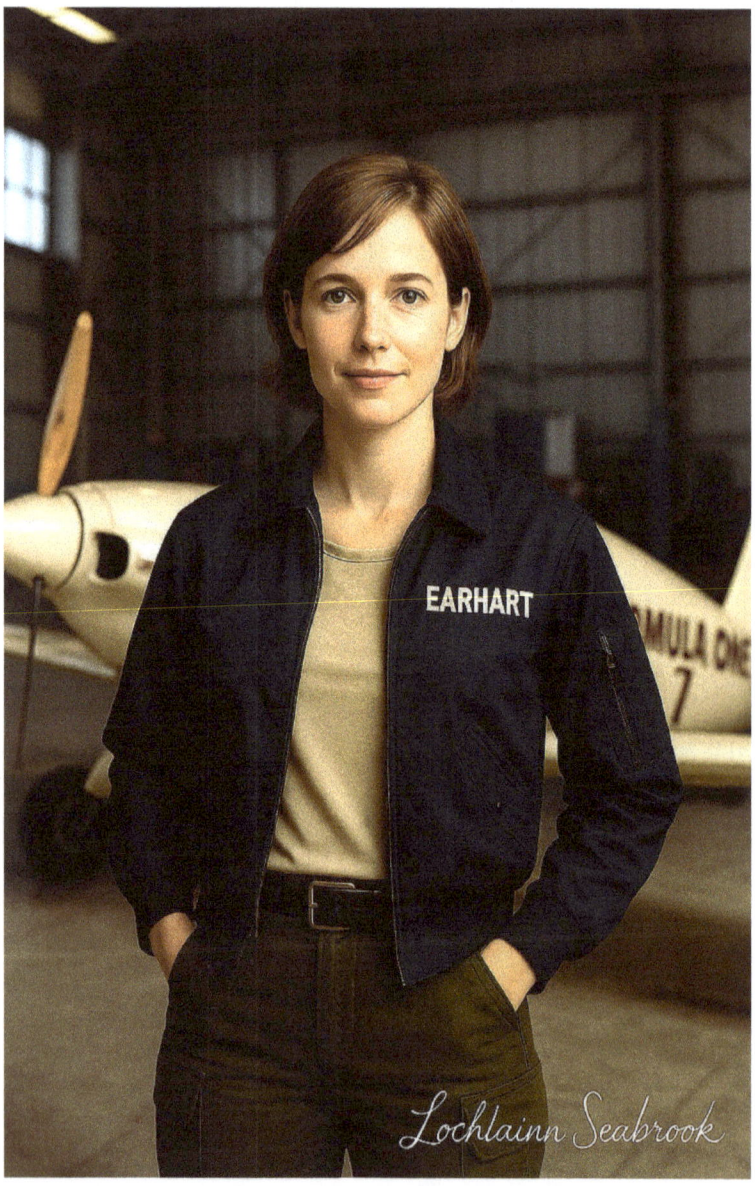

Earhart as she might look today as a young air racer. Copyright © Lochlainn Seabrook.

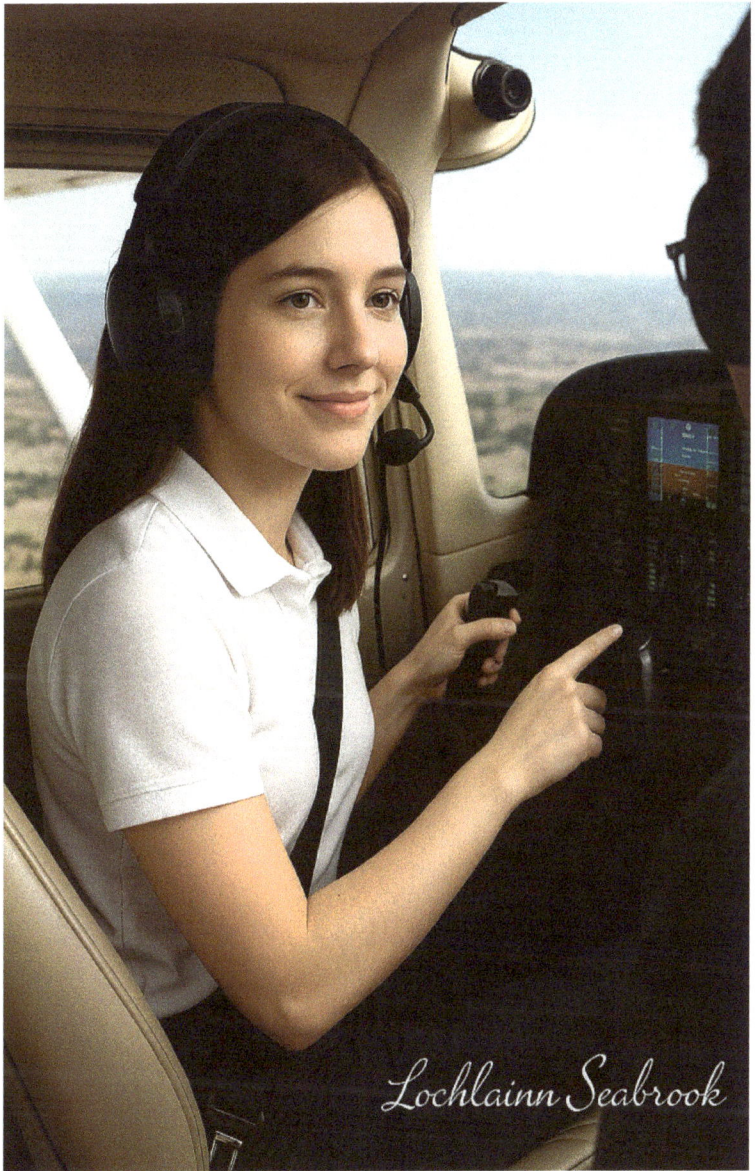

Earhart as she might appear today working as a young flight instructor in California. Copyright © Lochlainn Seabrook.

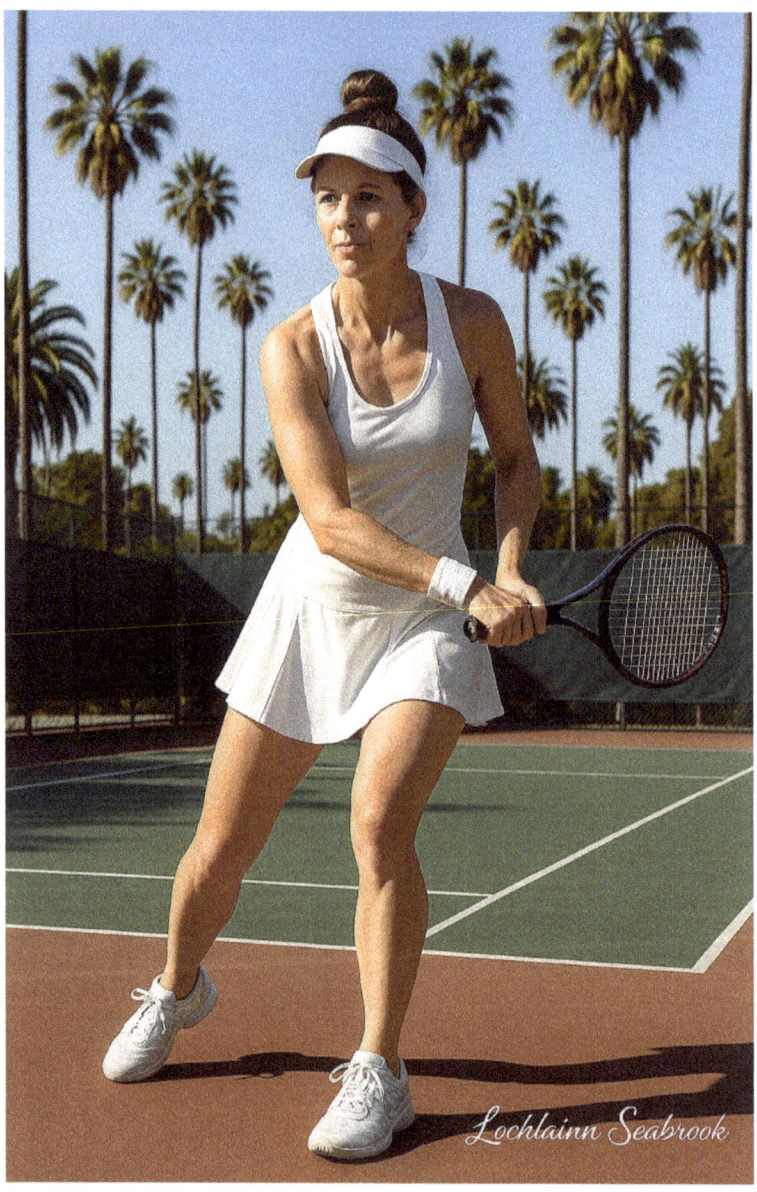

Amelia Mary Earhart as she might look today enjoying one of her favorite hobbies: tennis. Copyright © Lochlainn Seabrook.

THOMAS EDISON

1847-1931, Ohio

Industrialist, inventor, businessman, entrepreneur, motion picture pioneer, electronics tinkerer, telegrapher (telegraph operator), perfected the electric light bulb, invented the phonograph.

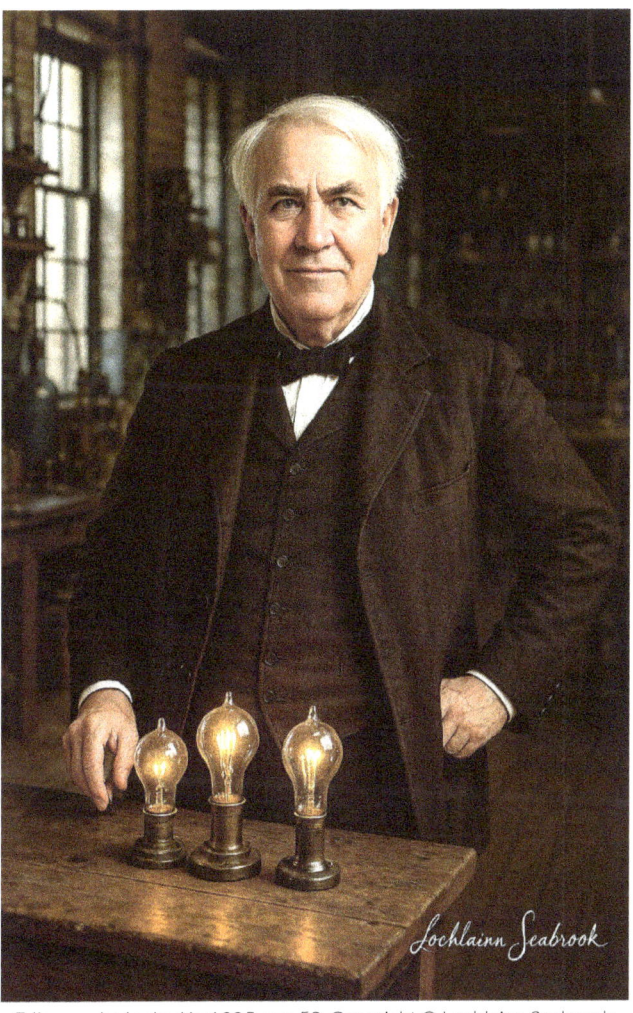

Edison as he looked in 1905, age 58. Copyright © Lochlainn Seabrook.

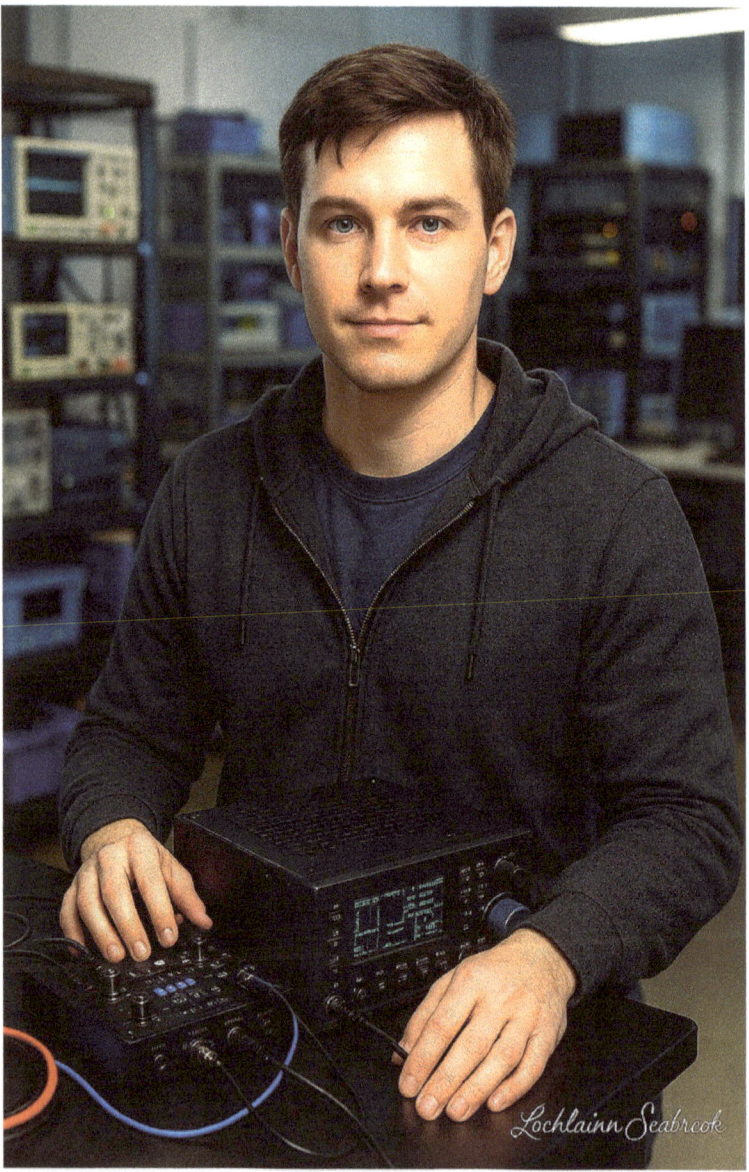

Edison as he might look today as a 21st-Century inventor and electronics innovator at the peak of his success and career. Copyright © Lochlainn Seabrook.

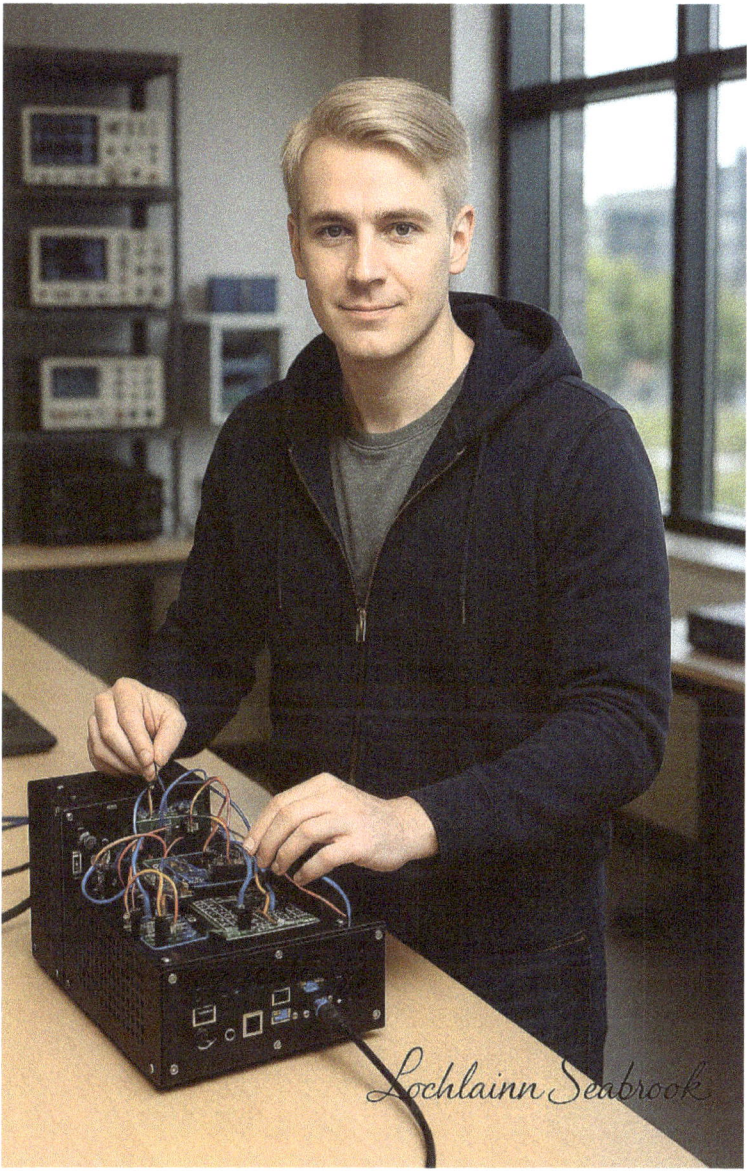

Edison as he might look today working for a company as a 20 year old IT specialist and network technician (the modern day equivalent of a mid 19th-Century telegrapher). Copyright © Lochlainn Seabrook.

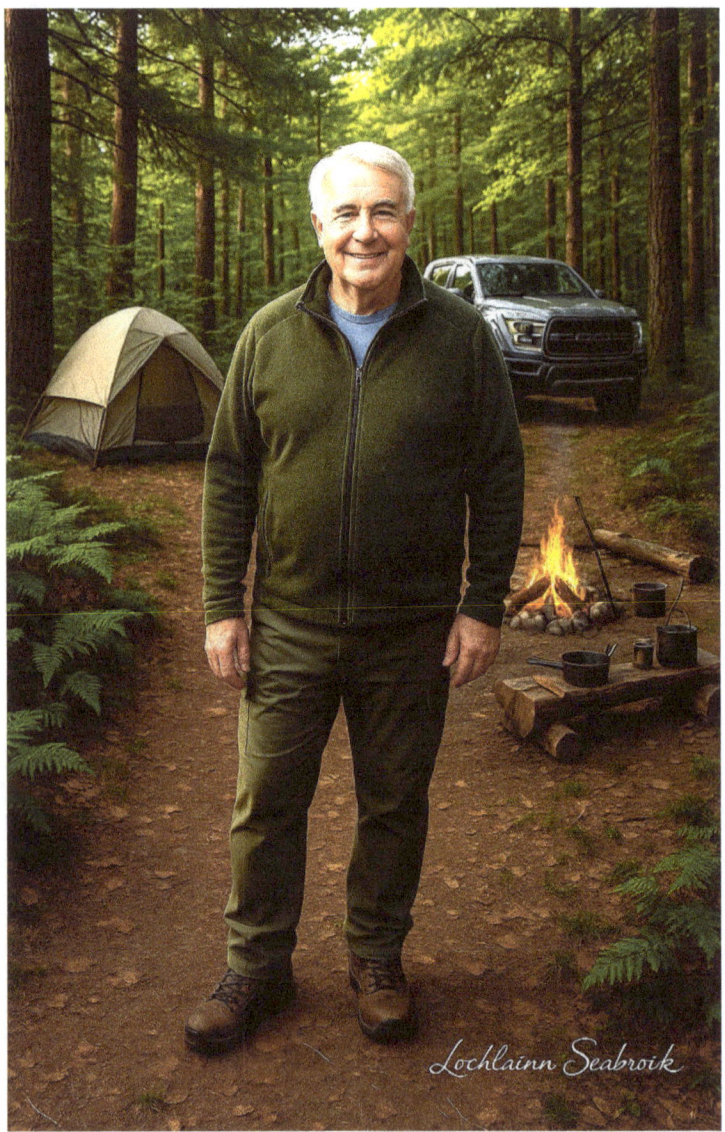

Thomas Alva Edison as he might look today as a 70 year old engaging in one of his favorite pastimes: camping with his friends Henry Ford, John Burroughs, and Harvey Firestone, in the Appalachian wilderness. Copyright © Lochlainn Seabrook.

ALBERT EINSTEIN

1879-1955, Germany

Theoretical physicist, research scientist, physics professor, inventor, intellectual, tutor, substitute teacher, high school teacher, author, writer, essayist, patent clerk and examiner, university lecturer, musician, humanitarian, civil rights activist, Zionist, pacifist, co-founder of the Hebrew University of Jerusalem.

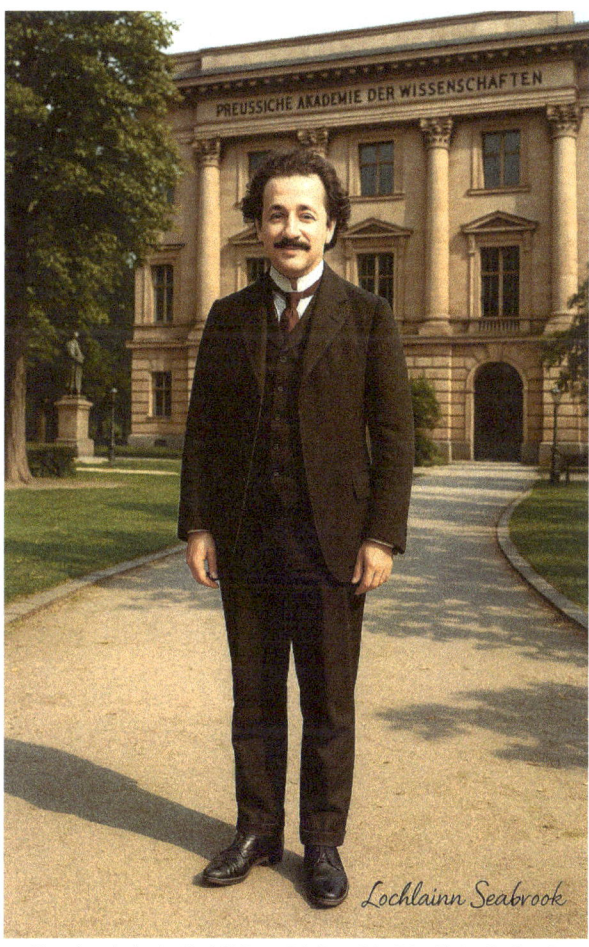

Einstein as he looked in 1915, age 36. Copyright © Lochlainn Seabrook.

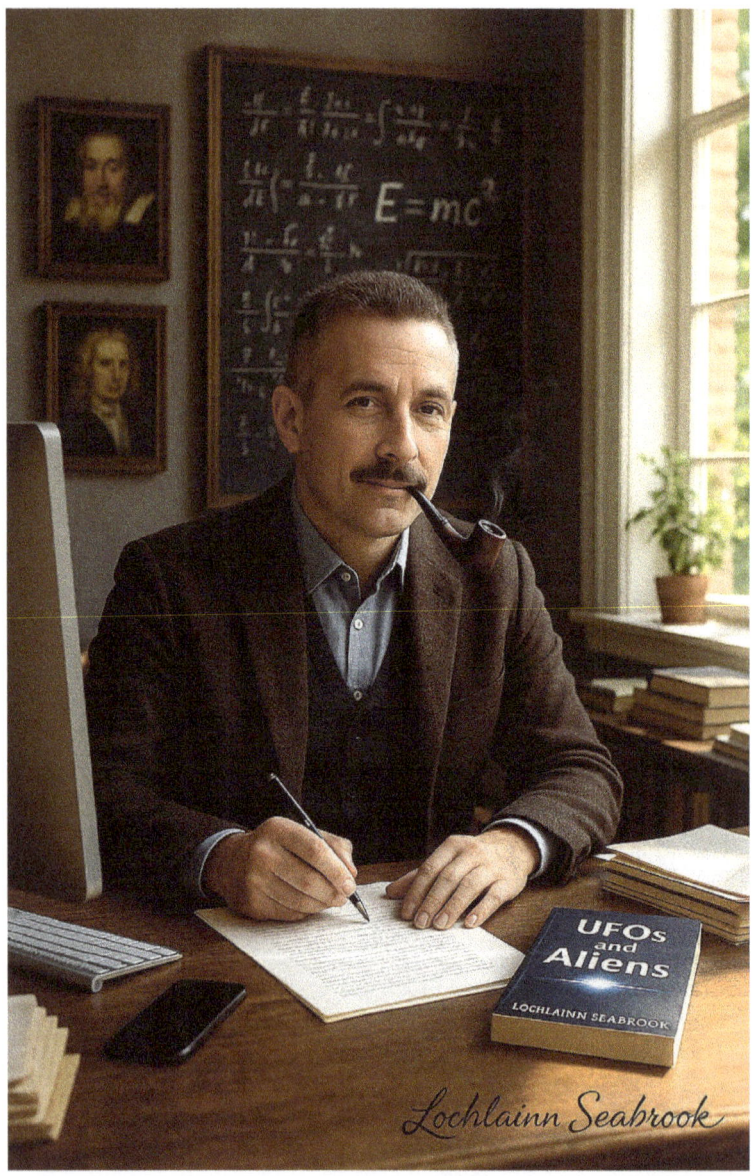

Einstein as he might look today as a noted 50 year old physicist and author. Copyright © Lochlainn Seabrook.

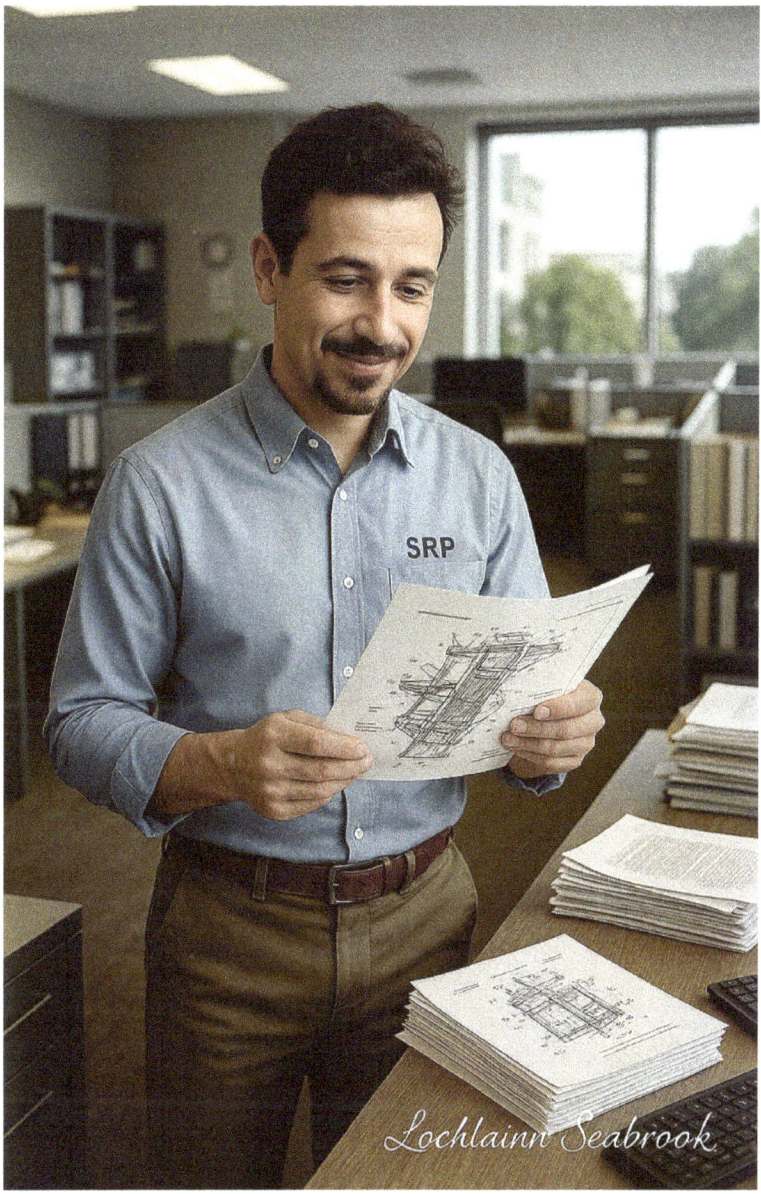

Einstein as he might look today as a 25 year old patent examiner at the United States Patent and Trademark Office in Washington, D.C. Copyright © Lochlainn Seabrook.

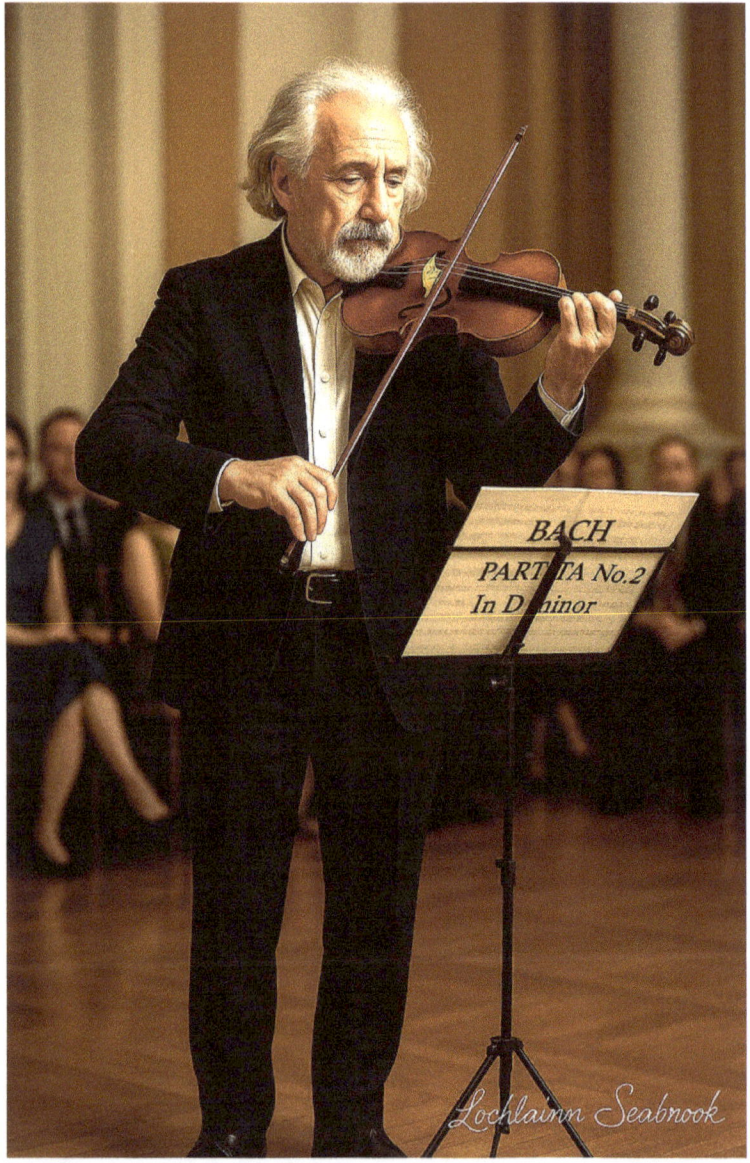

Albert Einstein as he might look today as a 71 year old enjoying one of his favorite hobbies: performing on his violin at social gatherings and fund raising events. Copyright © Lochlainn Seabrook.

RALPH WALDO EMERSON

1803-1882, Massachusetts

Author, essayist, lecturer, philosopher, poet, intellectual, Transcendentalist, Christian minister, schoolteacher, mystic, individualist, nonconformist.

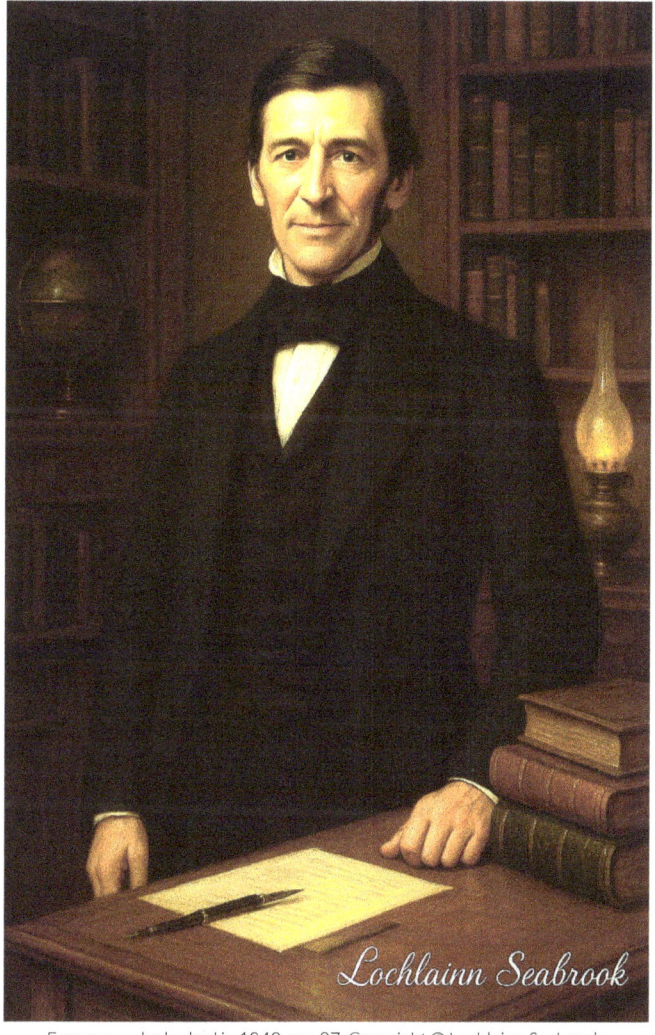

Emerson as he looked in 1840, age 37. Copyright © Lochlainn Seabrook.

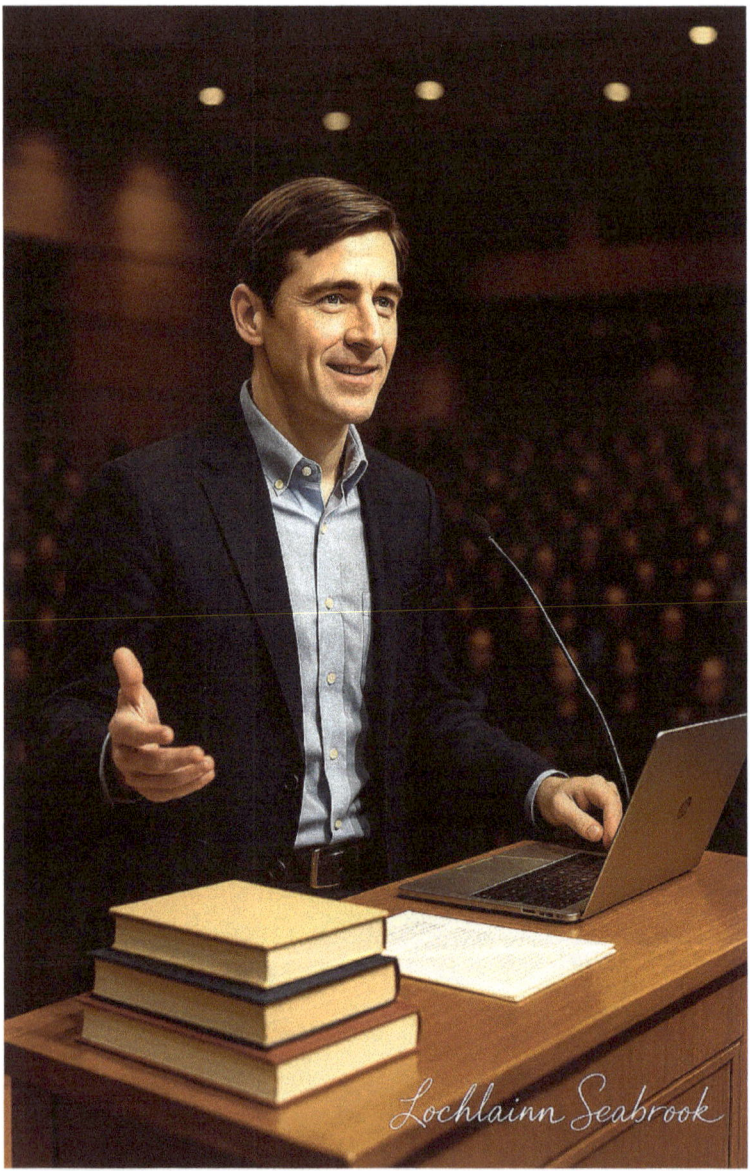

Emerson as he might look today as a successful author and lecturer. Copyright © Lochlainn Seabrook.

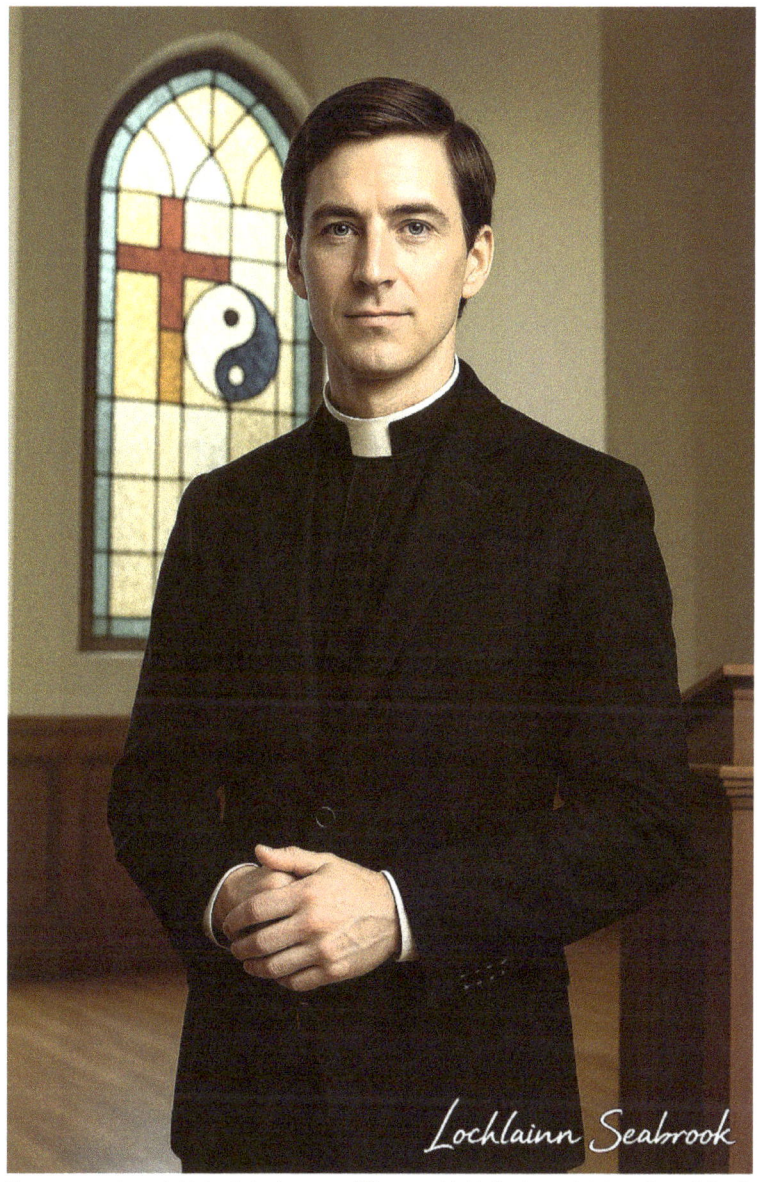

Emerson as he might look today as a 27 year old Unitarian minister. Copyright © Lochlainn Seabrook.

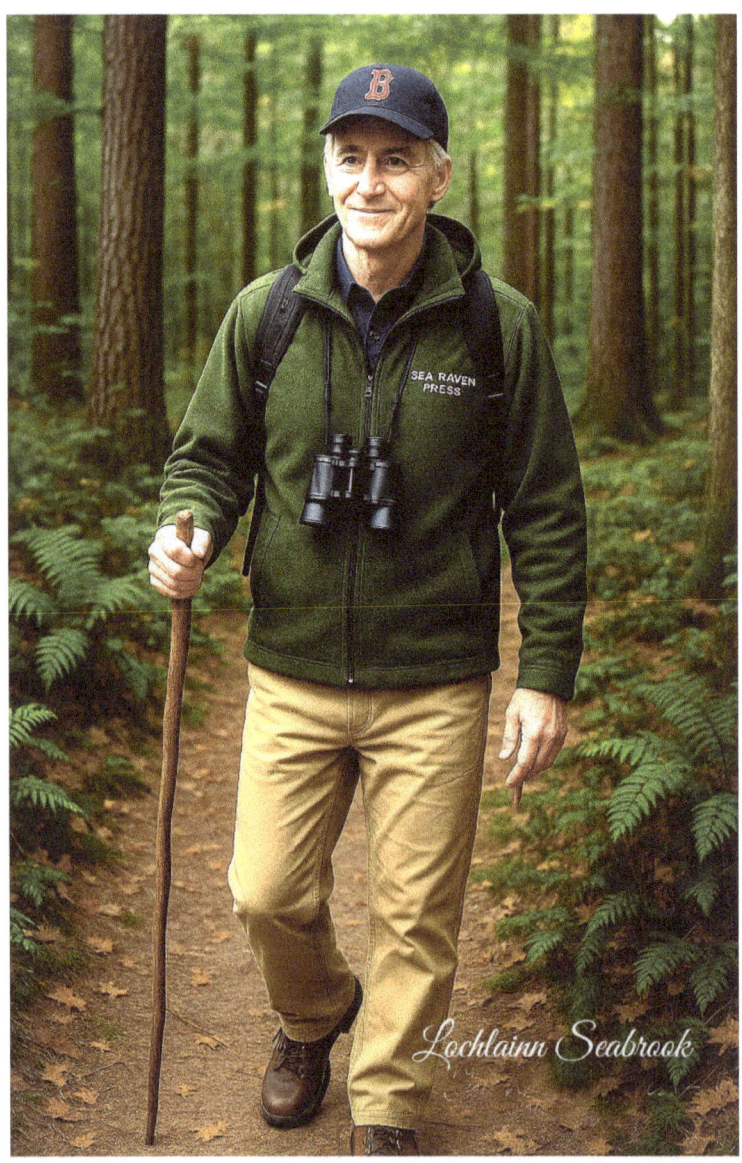

Ralph Waldo Emerson as he might look today enjoying one of his favorite pastimes: walking in the woods of Concord, Massachusetts. Copyright © Lochlainn Seabrook.

HENRY FORD

1863-1947, Michigan

Industrialist, entrepreneur, business magnate, automobile manufacturer, machinist, industrial engineer, electrical engineer, mechanical tinkerer, visionary inventor, agrarian proponent, founder of Ford Motor Company.

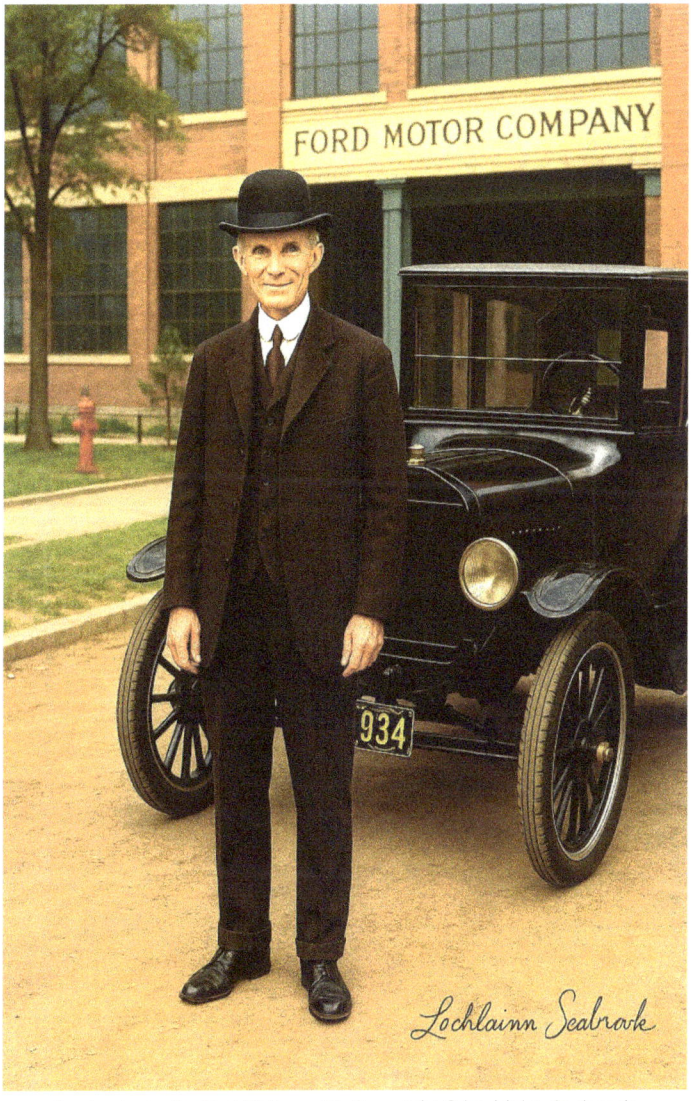

Ford as he looked in 1914, age 51. Copyright © Lochlainn Seabrook.

100 ∽ IF THEY WERE ALIVE TODAY

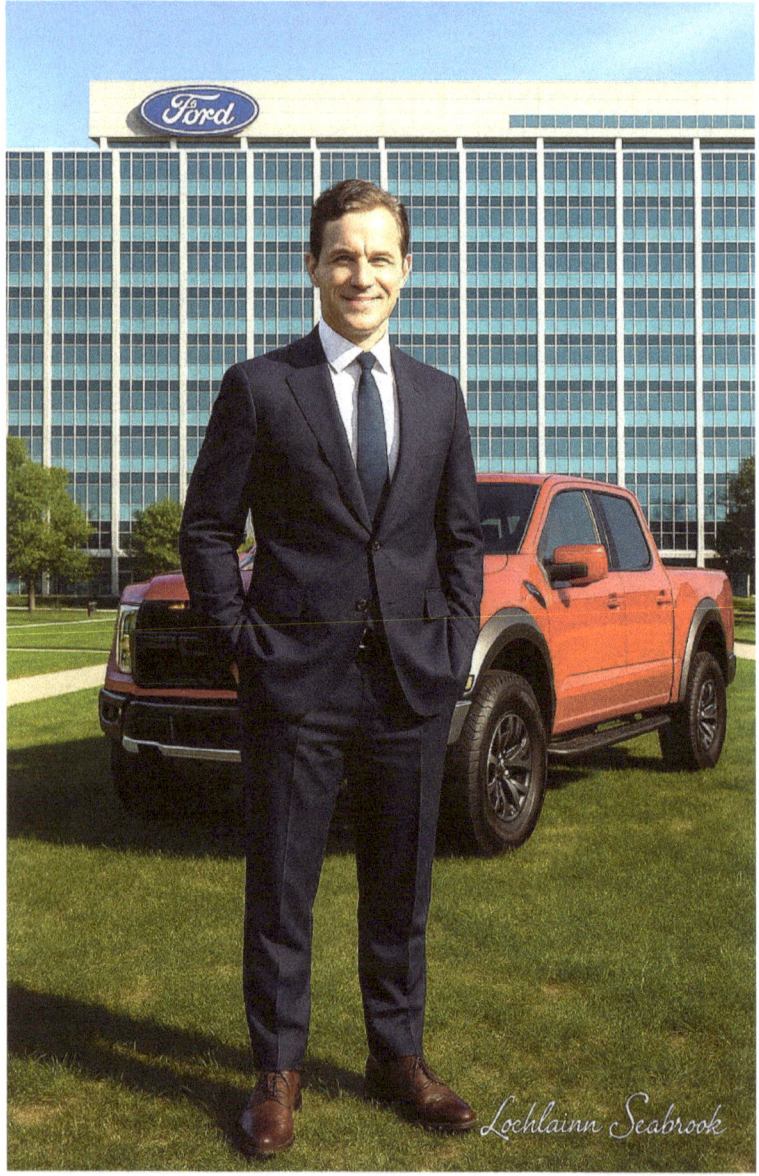

Ford as he might look today as the 39 year old president of Ford Motor Company, standing in front of the Ford World Headquarters, Dearborn, Michigan. Copyright © Lochlainn Seabrook.

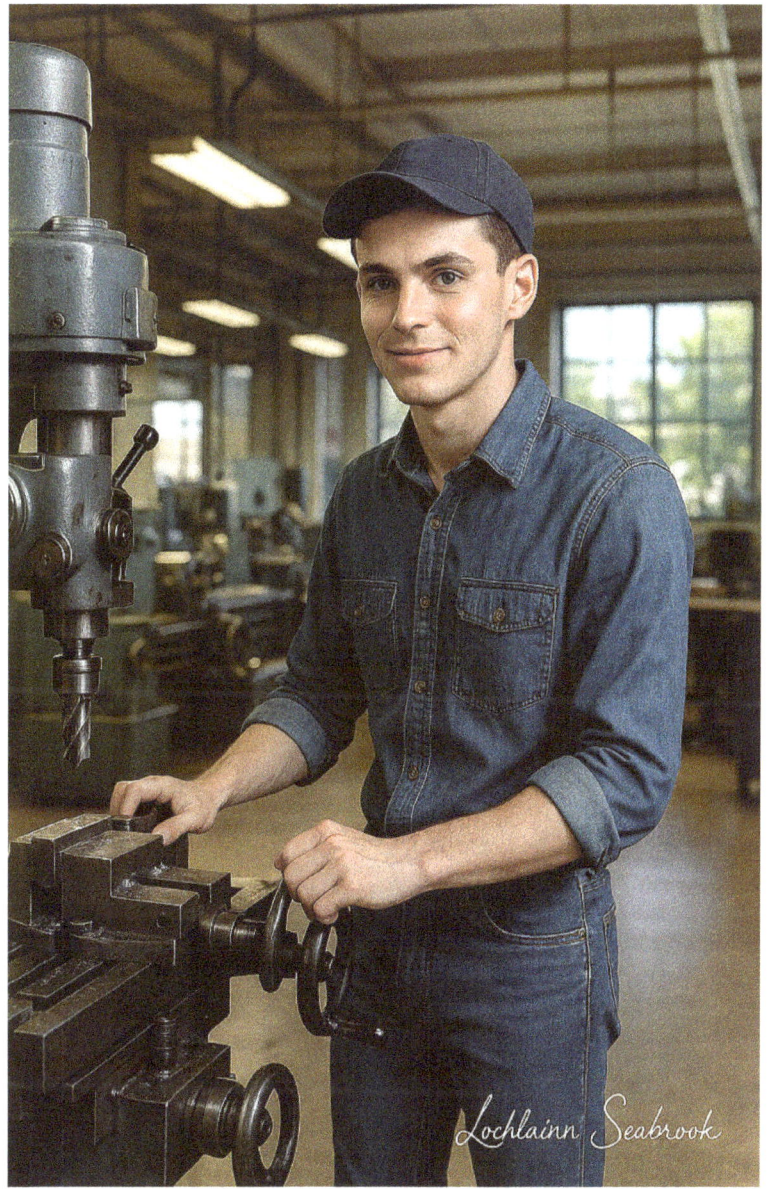

Ford as he might look today as an 18 year old machinist. Copyright © Lochlainn Seabrook.

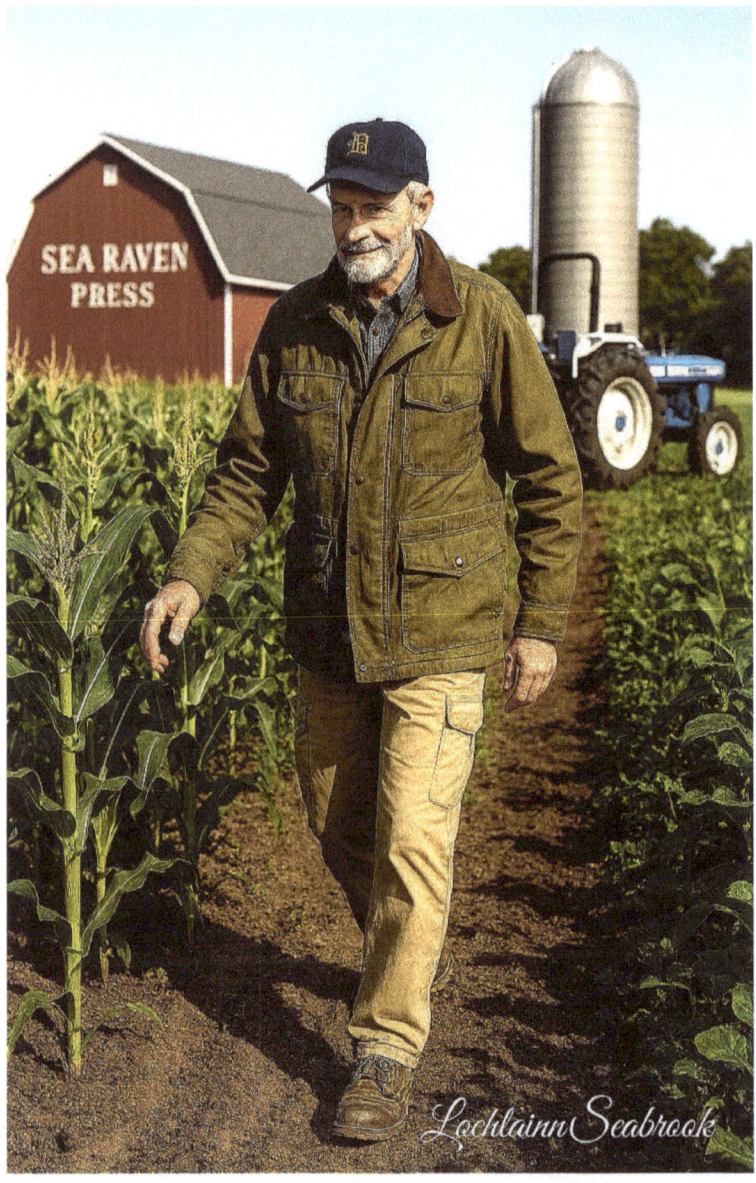

Henry Ford as he might look today as an 78 year old enjoying one of his favorite pastimes: overseeing one of his farms. Copyright © Lochlainn Seabrook.

NATHAN BEDFORD FORREST

1821-1877, Tennessee

Conservative businessman, entrepreneur, Confederate general, highly skilled equestrian, genius tactical commander, farmer, cotton planter, horse trader, cattle trader, real estate agent, land speculator, servant trader, railroad manager, public speaker, politician, equestrian, marksman, civil rights and racial unity advocate.

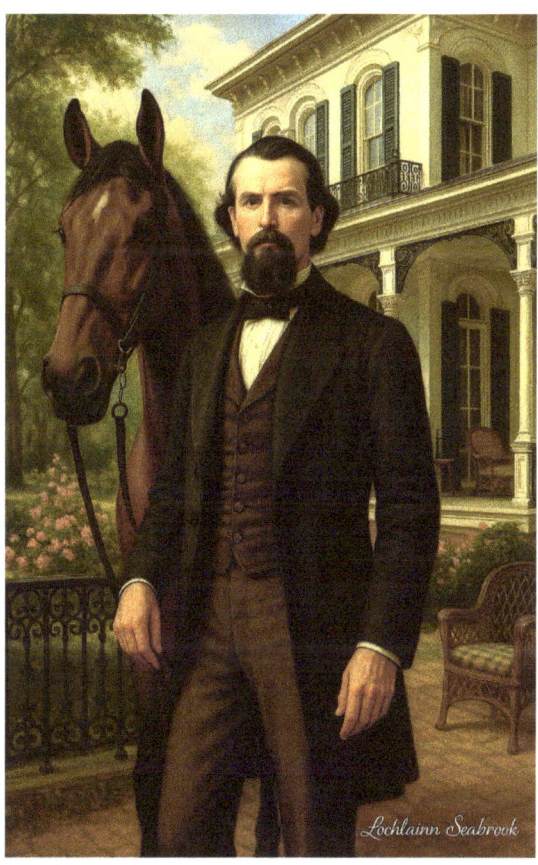

Forrest as he looked in 1855, age 33. Copyright © Lochlainn Seabrook.

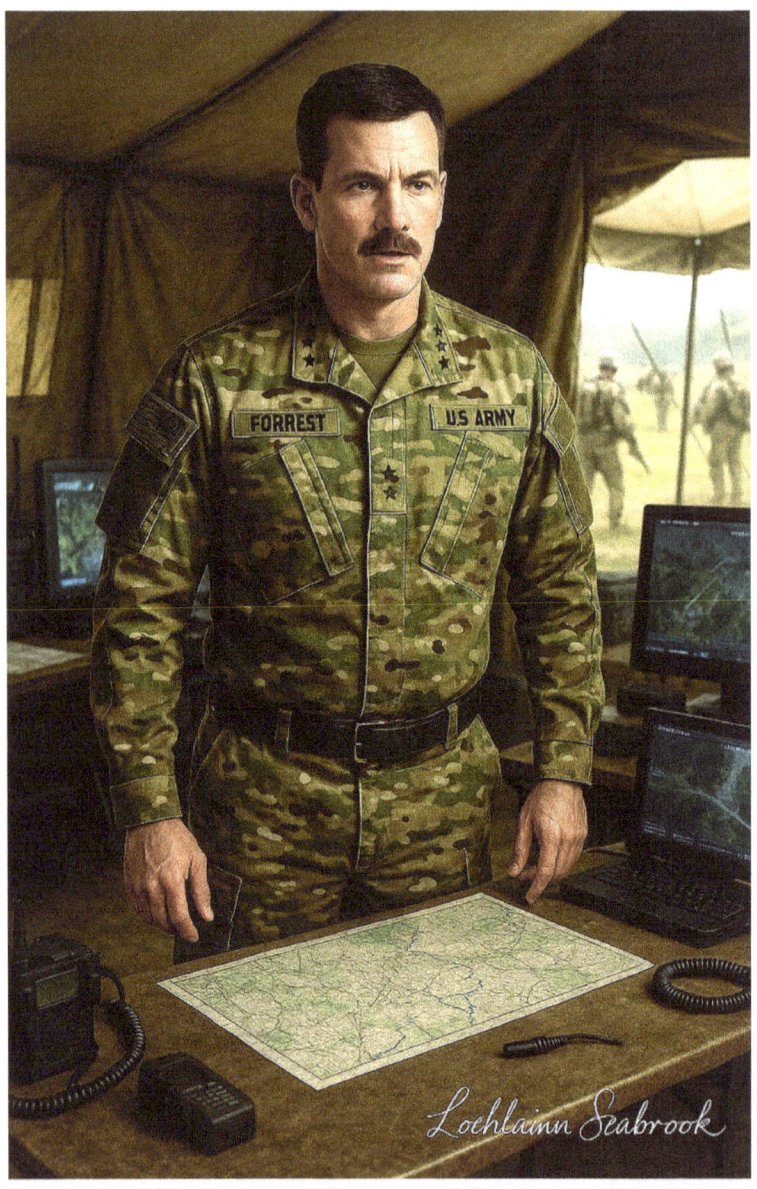

Forrest as he might look today as a U.S. army general. Copyright © Lochlainn Seabrook.

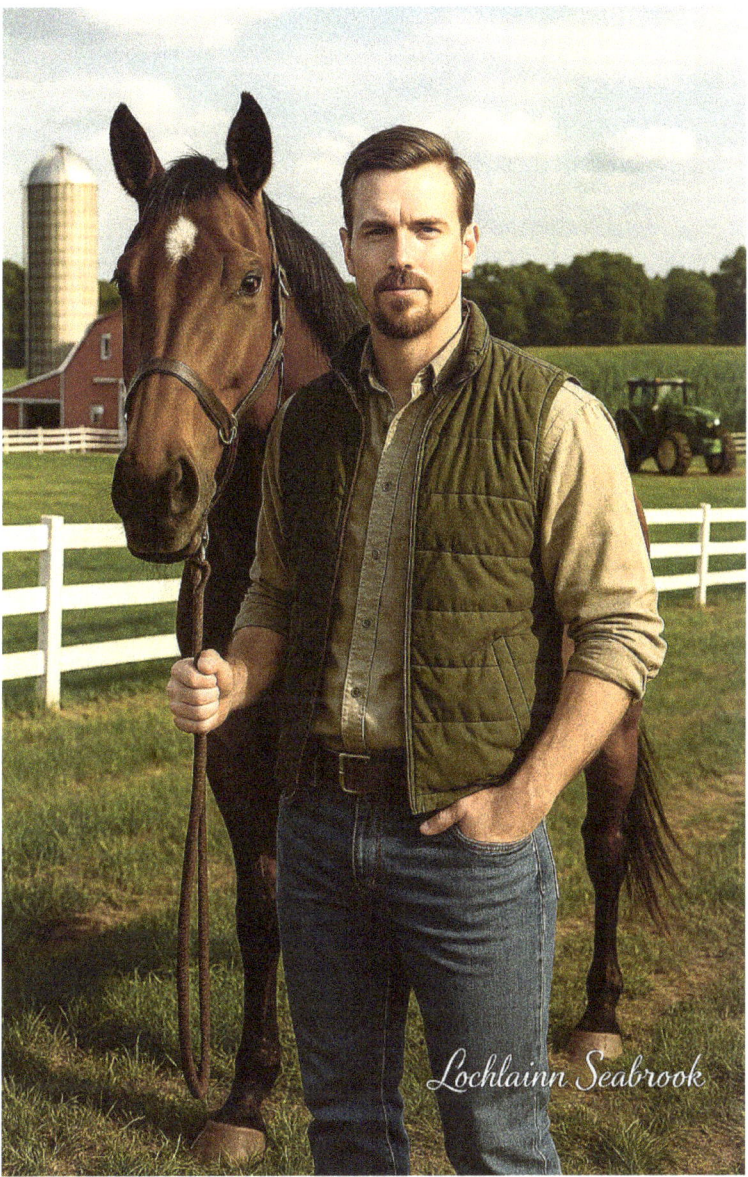

Forrest as he might look today as a wealthy young Mississippi farmer and horse rancher. Copyright © Lochlainn Seabrook.

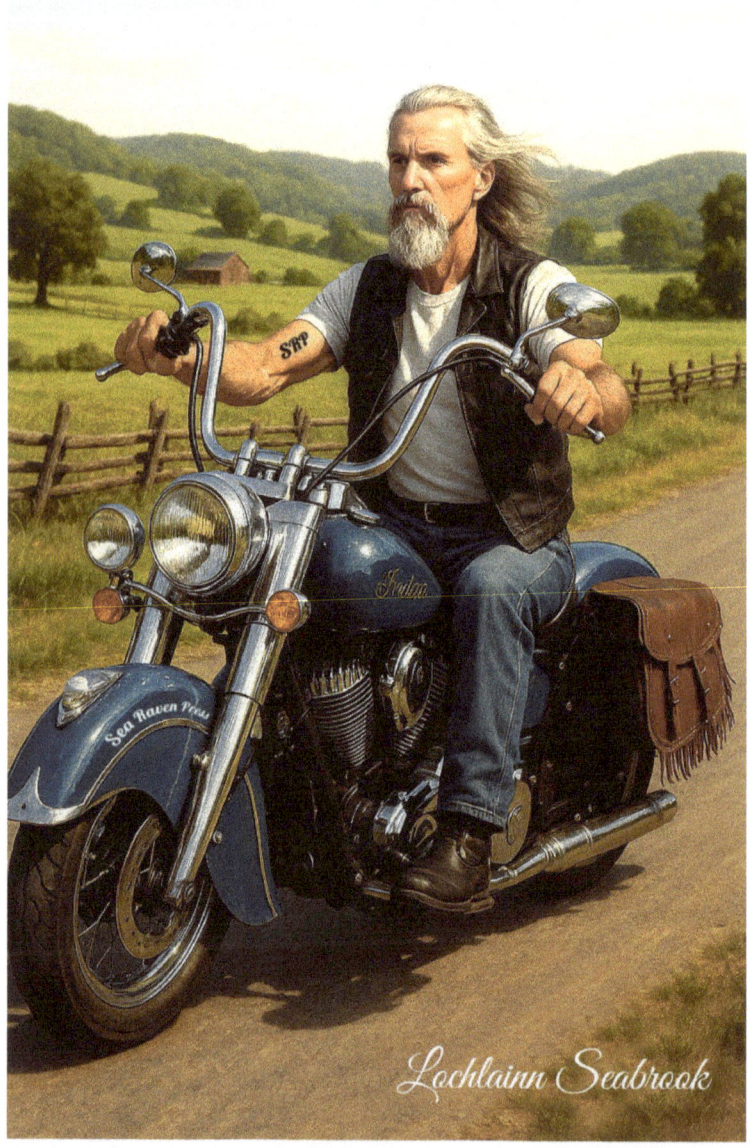

Ace equestrian and passionate equine lover Nathan Bedford Forrest as he might look today engaging in what would no doubt be one of his favorite pastimes: riding his "iron horse" in the Tennessee countryside Copyright © Lochlainn Seabrook.

BENJAMIN FRANKLIN

1706-1790, Massachusetts

American Founding Father, statesman, first U.S. postmaster general, Continental Congress delegate, diplomat, inventor, scientist, researcher, author, philosopher, public servant, printer, publisher, newspaper editor, legislator, ambassador to France, civic reformer, helped draft the Declaration of Independence.

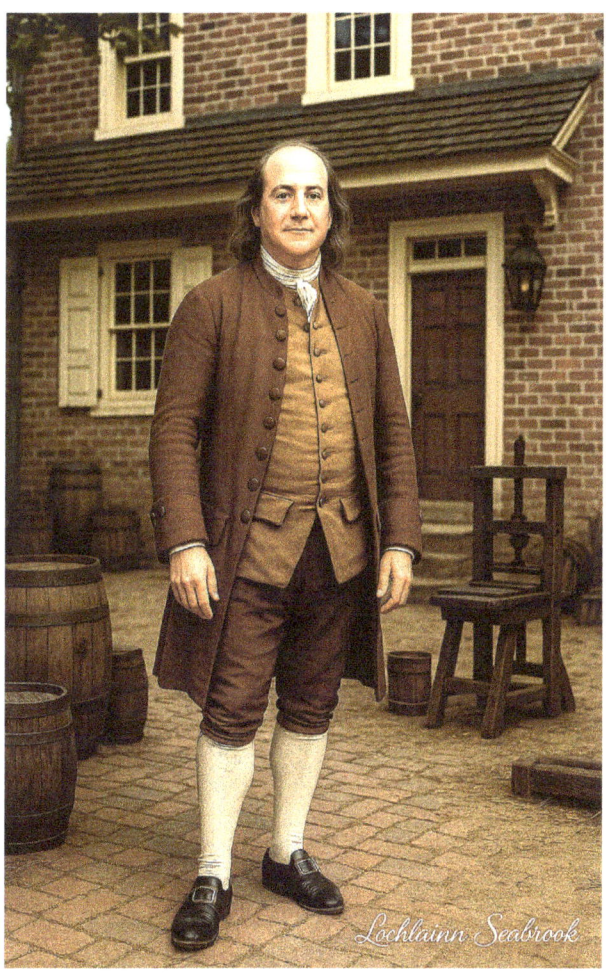

Franklin as he looked in 1750, age 44. Copyright © Lochlainn Seabrook.

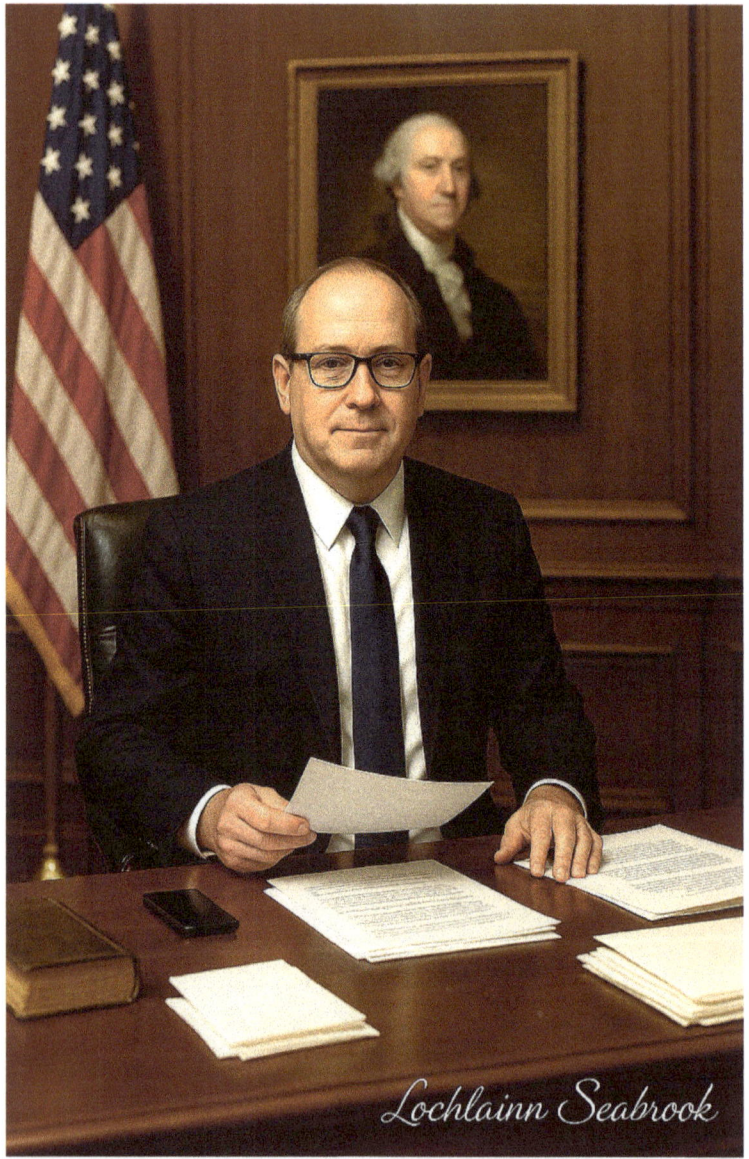

Franklin as he might appear today serving as an American statesman and international diplomat. Copyright © Lochlainn Seabrook.

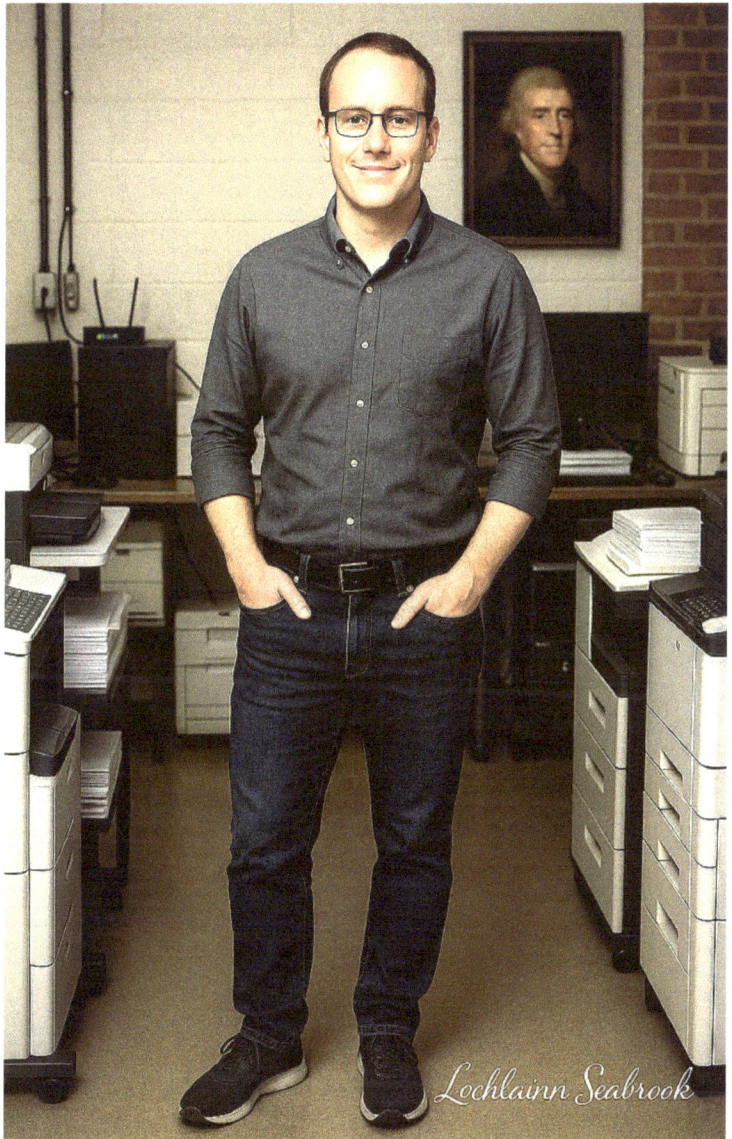

Franklin as he might look today as a 30 year old printing company owner. Copyright © Lochlainn Seabrook.

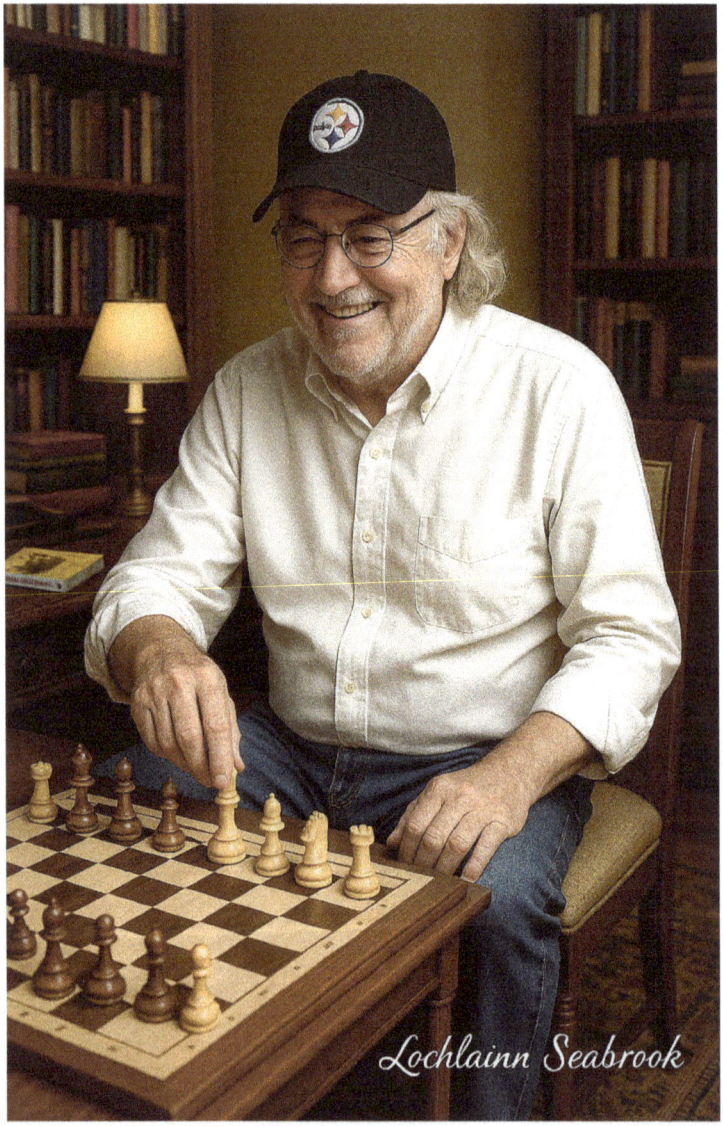

Benjamin Franklin as he might look today engaging in one of his favorite hobbies: chess. Copyright © Lochlainn Seabrook.

GERONIMO (GOYAHKLA)

1829-1909, New Mexico (now part of Arizona)

Chiricahua Apache leader, warrior, raider, tribal spokesman, resistance leader, marksman, equestrian, trader, hunter, farmer, public figure, performer, souvenir salesman.

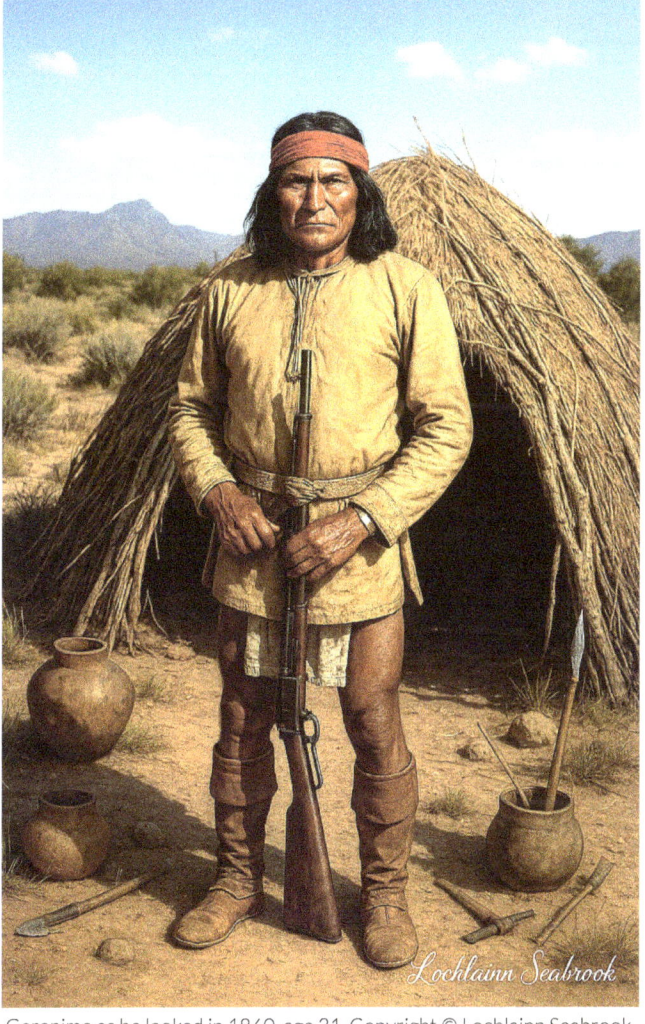

Geronimo as he looked in 1860, age 31. Copyright © Lochlainn Seabrook.

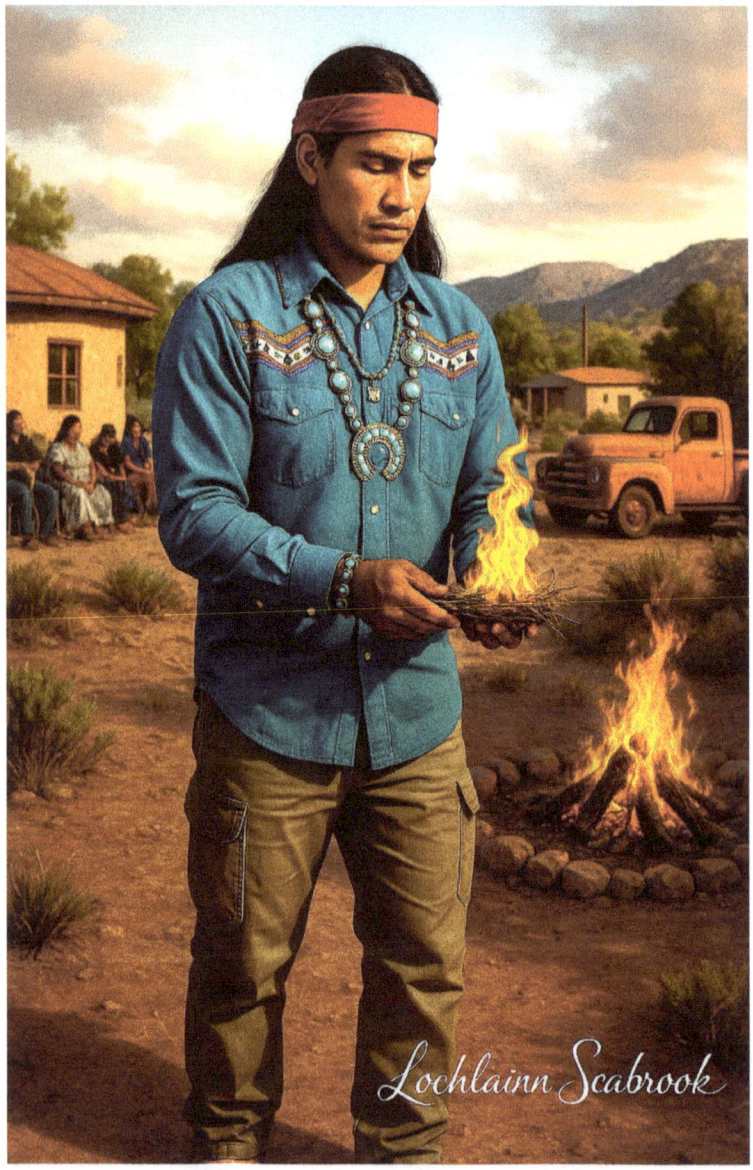

Geronimo as he might look today as a young Apache leader holding a traditional ceremony on an Arizona Apache reservation. Copyright © Lochlainn Seabrook.

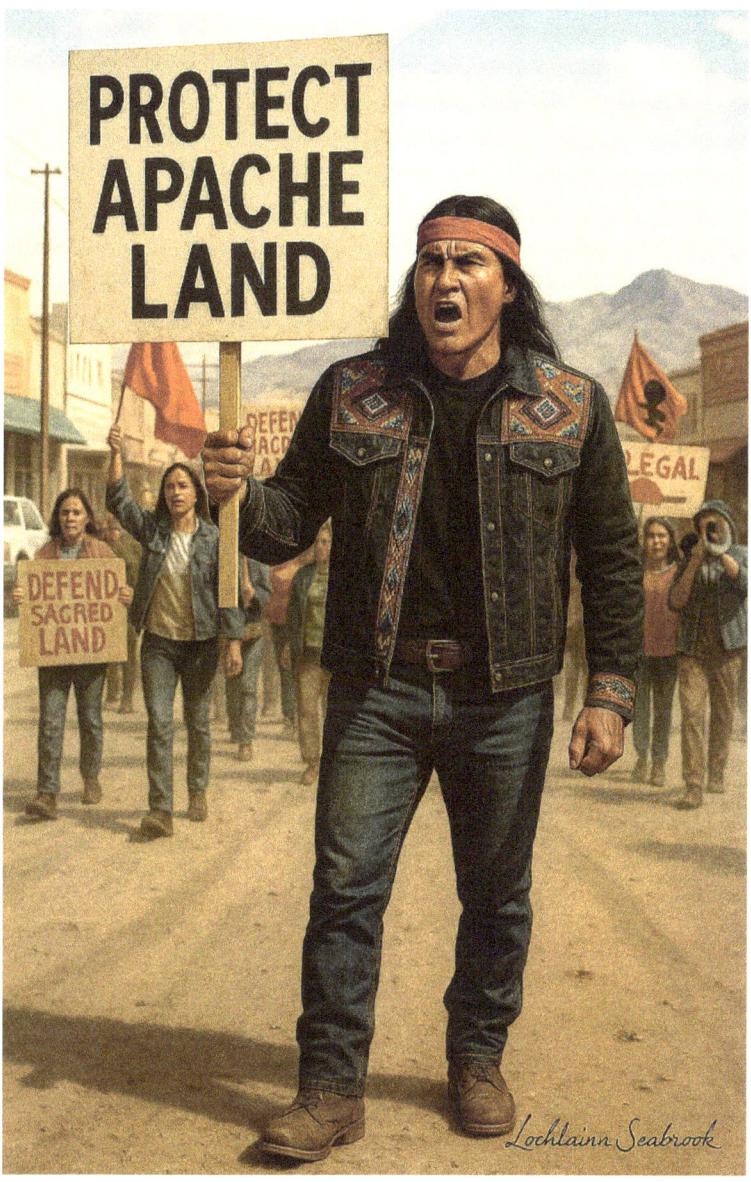

Geronimo as he might look today as an Apache civil rights activist leading a protest march in New Mexico. Copyright © Lochlainn Seabrook.

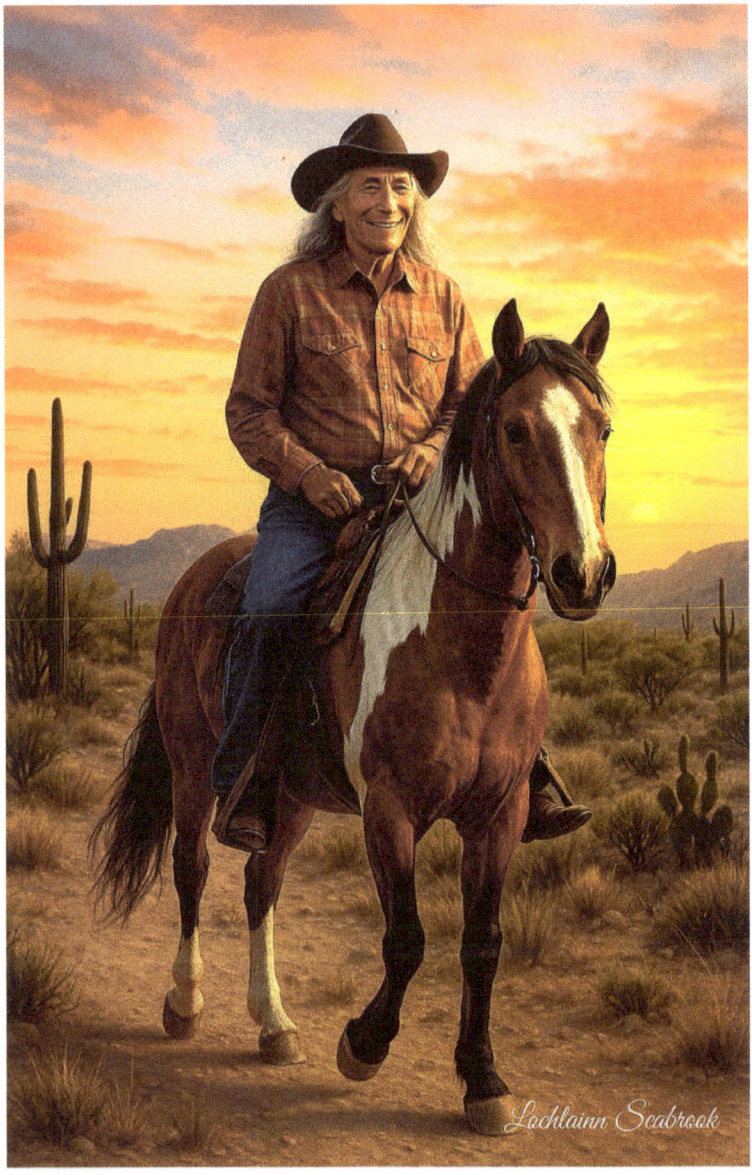

Geronimo (Goyahkla) as he might appear today as a 72 year old man engaging in one of his favorite hobbies: horseback riding. Copyright © Lochlainn Seabrook.

JOHN BROWN GORDON

1832-1904, Georgia

Governor of Georgia, U.S. senator from Georgia, political leader, public speaker, author, lawyer, businessman, entrepreneur, lecturer, coal mine operator, Confederate general, Confederate veterans benefactor and advocate, first commander-in-chief of United Confederate Veterans (UCV)—forerunner of today's Southern heritage organization: Sons of Confederate Veterans (SCV).

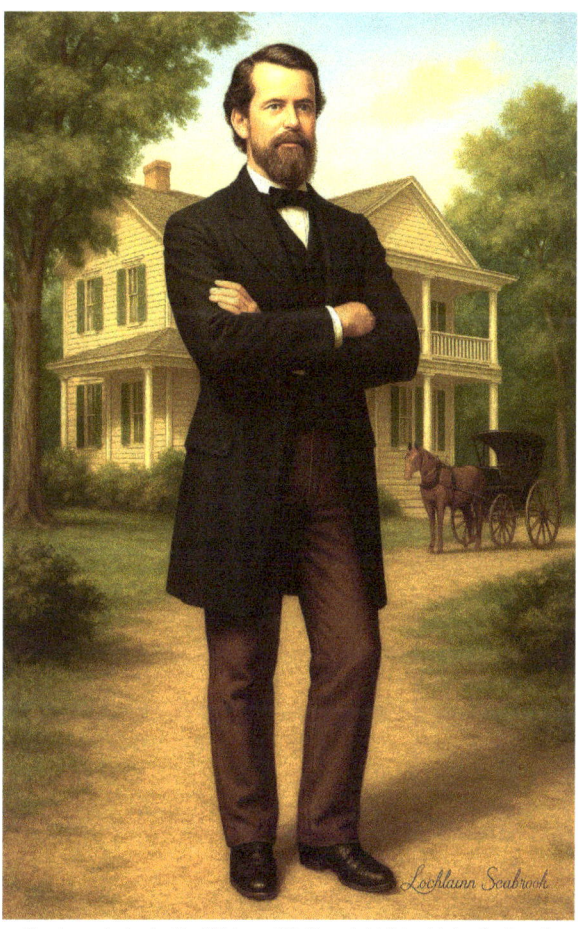

Gordon as he looked in 1864, age 32. Copyright © Lochlainn Seabrook.

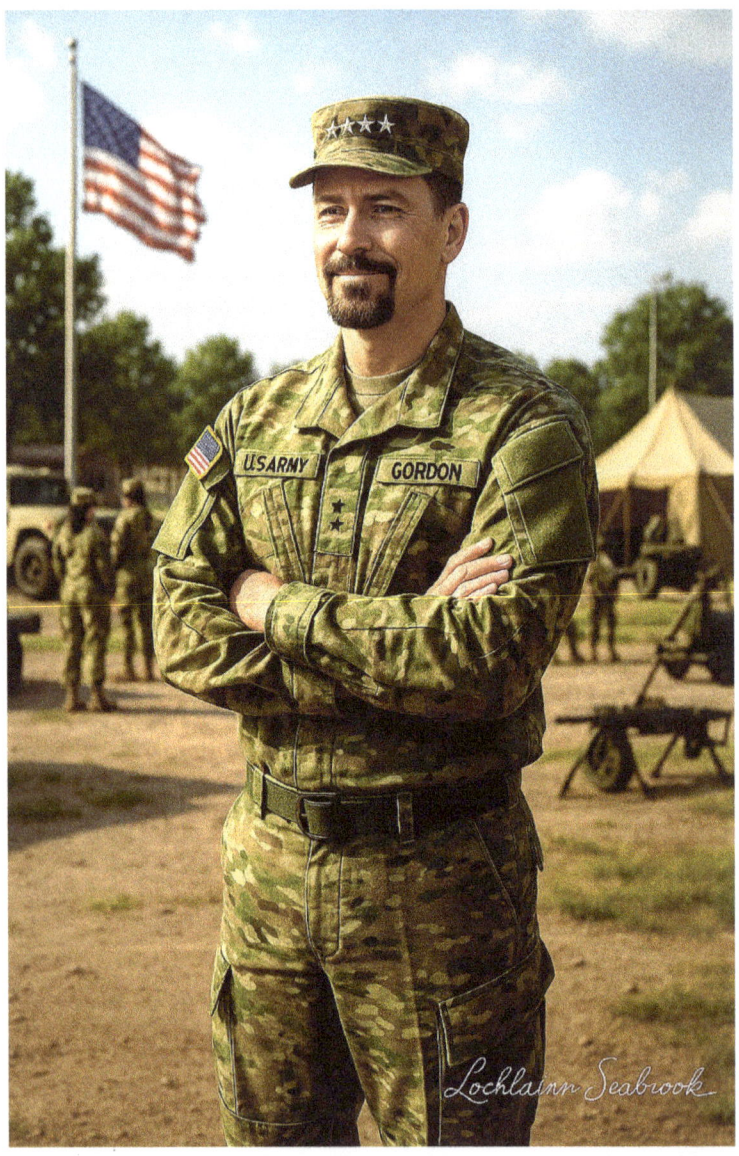

Gordon as he might look today as a 32 year old U.S. army general. Copyright © Lochlainn Seabrook.

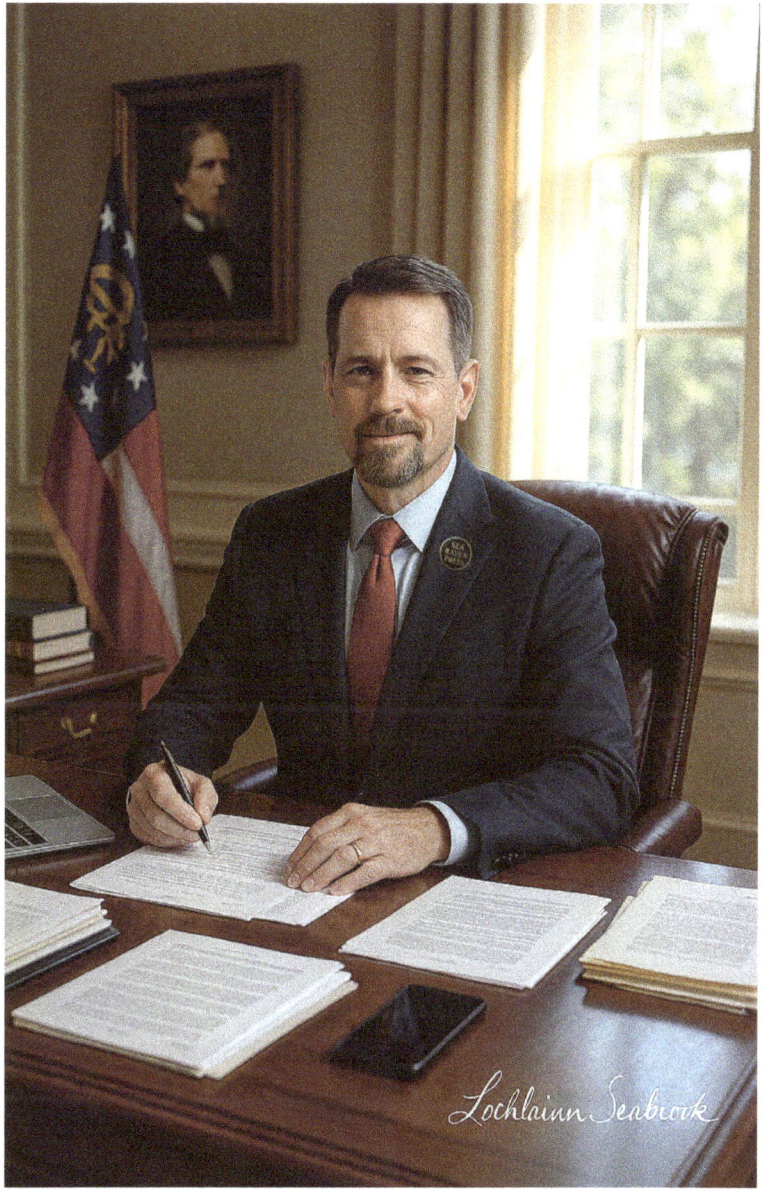

Gordon as he might appear today as a 56 year old Georgia governor. Copyright © Lochlainn Seabrook.

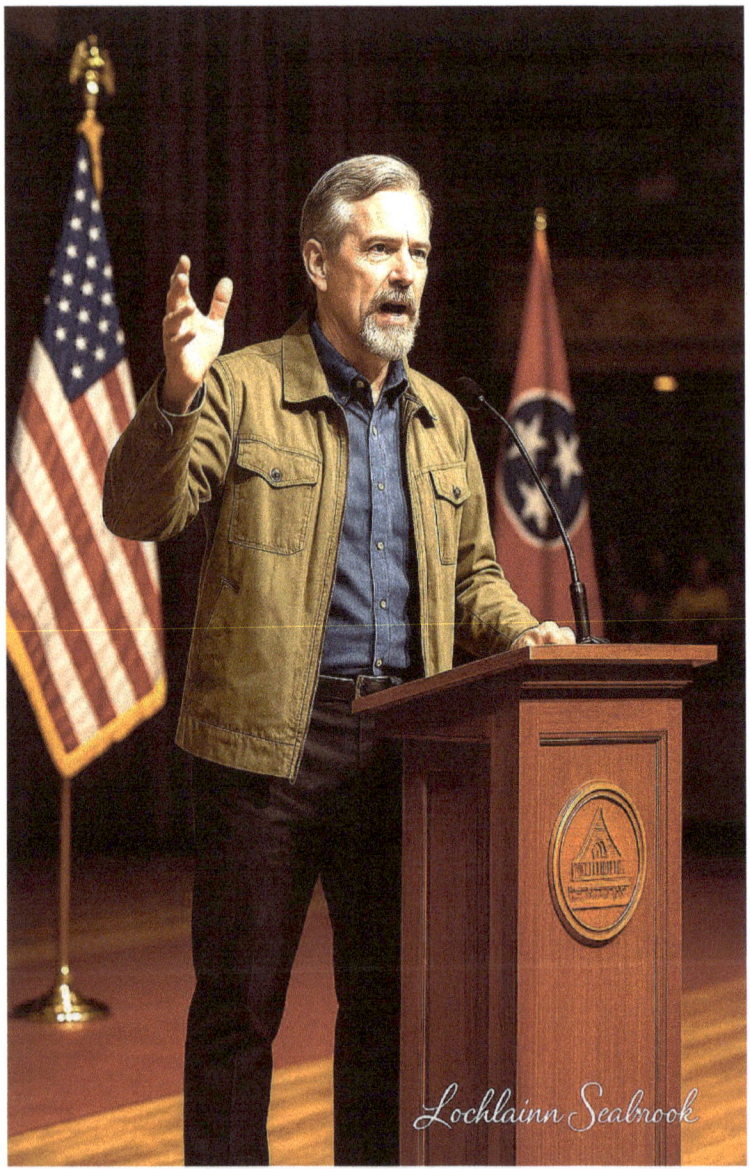

John Brown Gordon as he might look today as a 70 year old enjoying one of his favorite hobbies: public speaking on the importance of preserving authentic Confederate history. Copyright © Lochlainn Seabrook.

ROSE O'NEAL GREENHOW

1813-1864, Maryland

Influential Southern socialite, hostess, author, political confidante, American patriot, Confederate spy, informal Confederate foreign diplomat, traveler, tourist, political prisoner.

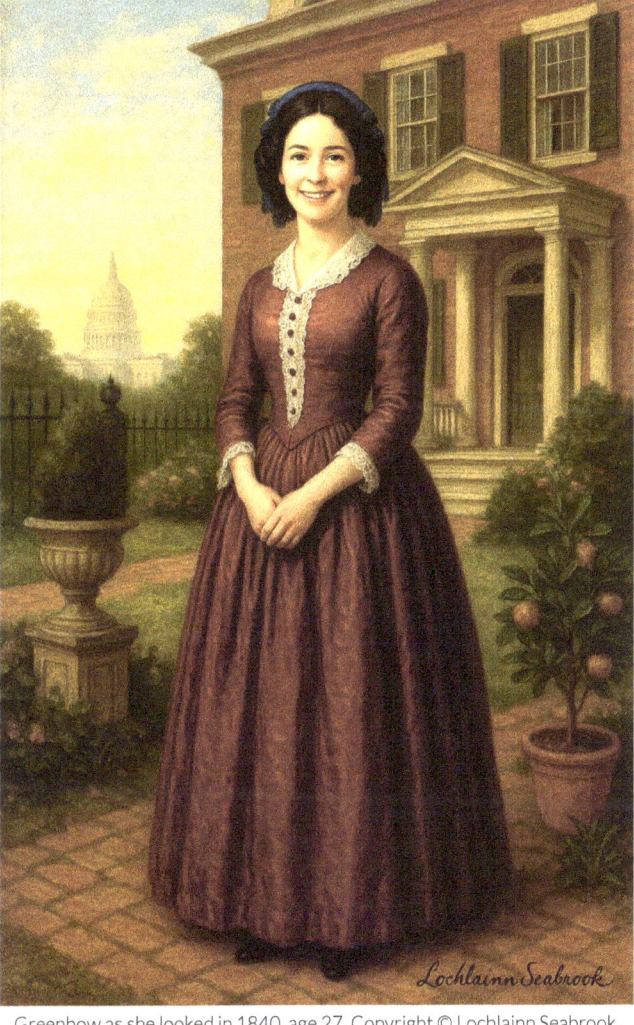

Greenhow as she looked in 1840, age 27. Copyright © Lochlainn Seabrook.

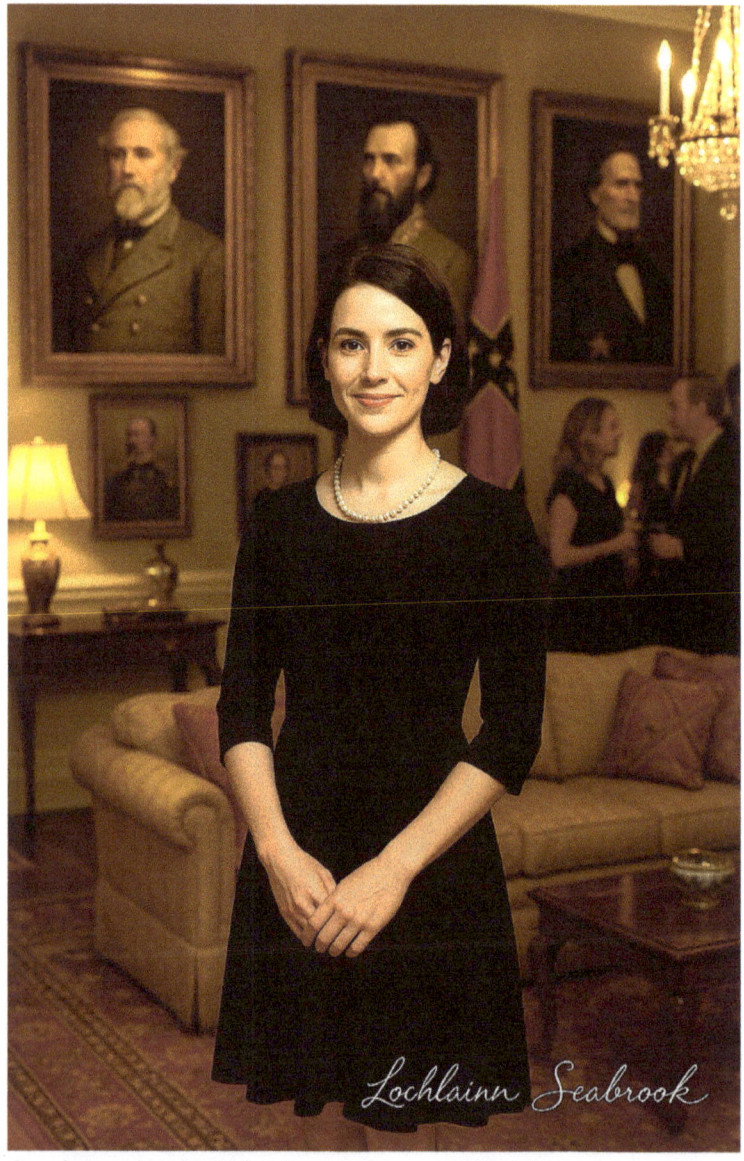

Greenhow as she might look today as a young married socialite living in Washington, D.C. Copyright © Lochlainn Seabrook.

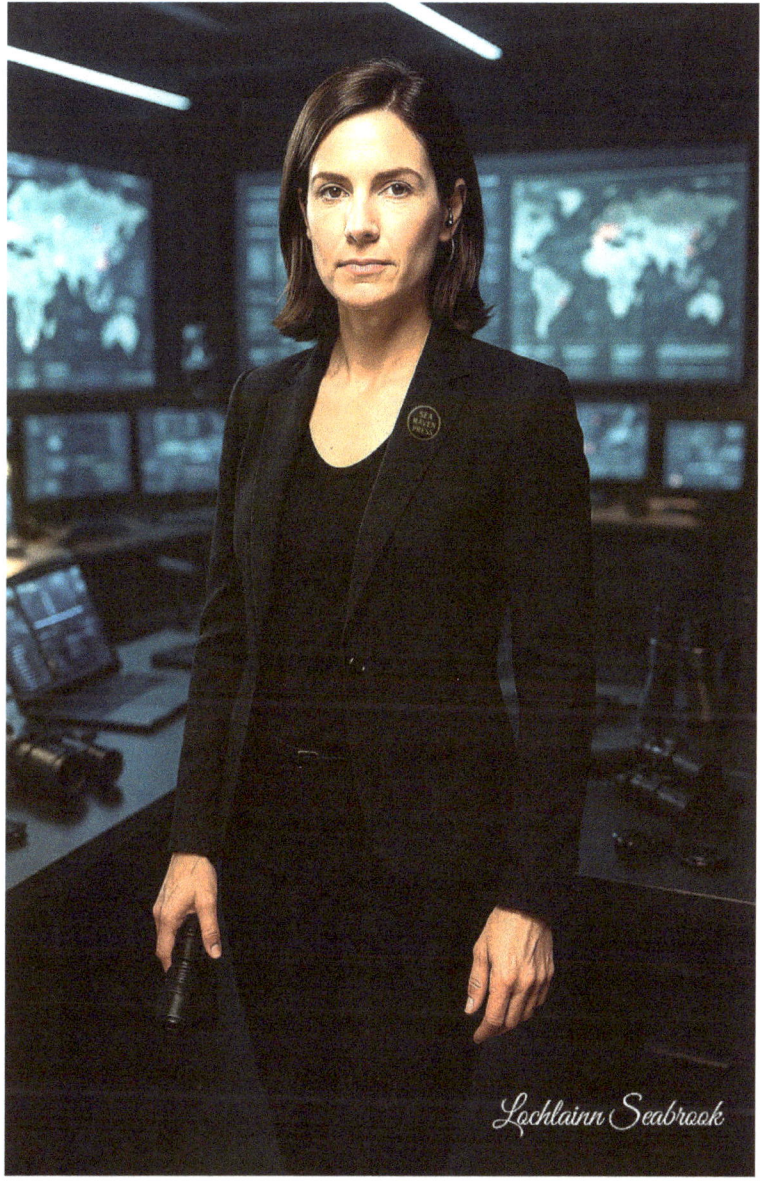

Greenhow as she might look today working as a spy for the U.S. government. Copyright © Lochlainn Seabrook.

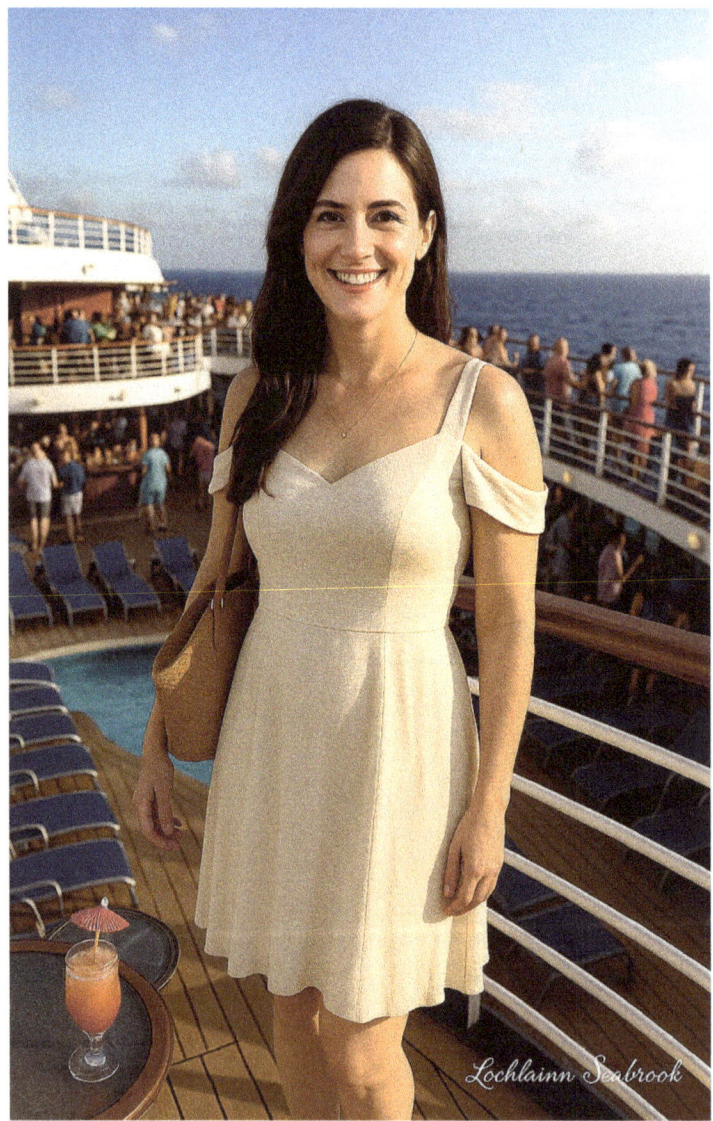

Maria Rosetta O'Neal (or O'Neale) Greenhow as she might look today engaging in one of her favorite pastimes: traveling. Copyright © Lochlainn Seabrook.

ALEXANDER HAMILTON

c. 1757-1804, Nevis, British West Indies

American Founding Father, U.S. Constitution signatory, Revolutionary War officer, first secretary of the Treasury, statesman, author, government official, lawyer, clerk, Federalist Party founder, founder of the First Bank of the U.S. as well as the U.S. mint.

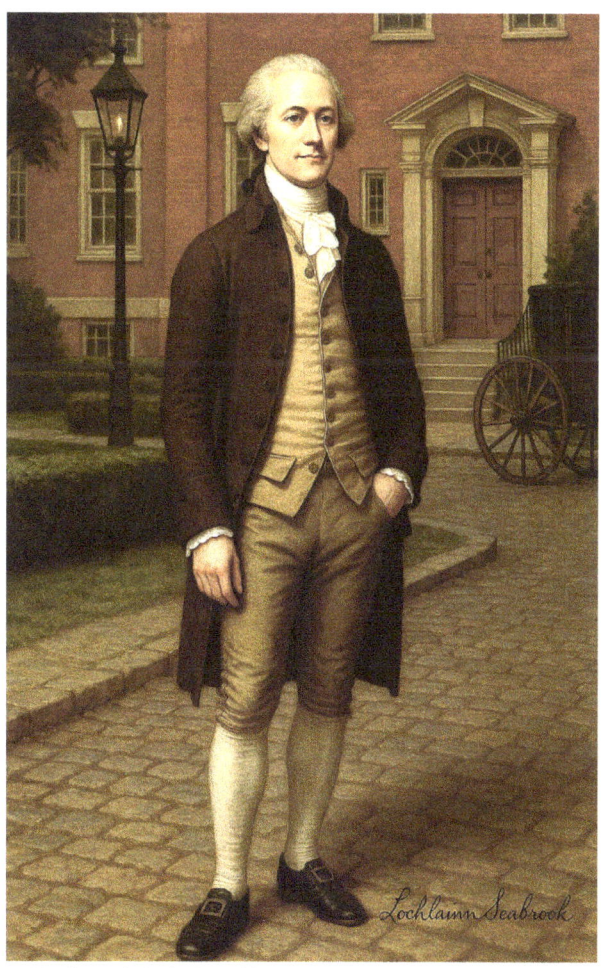

Hamilton as he looked in 1790, age 33. Copyright © Lochlainn Seabrook.

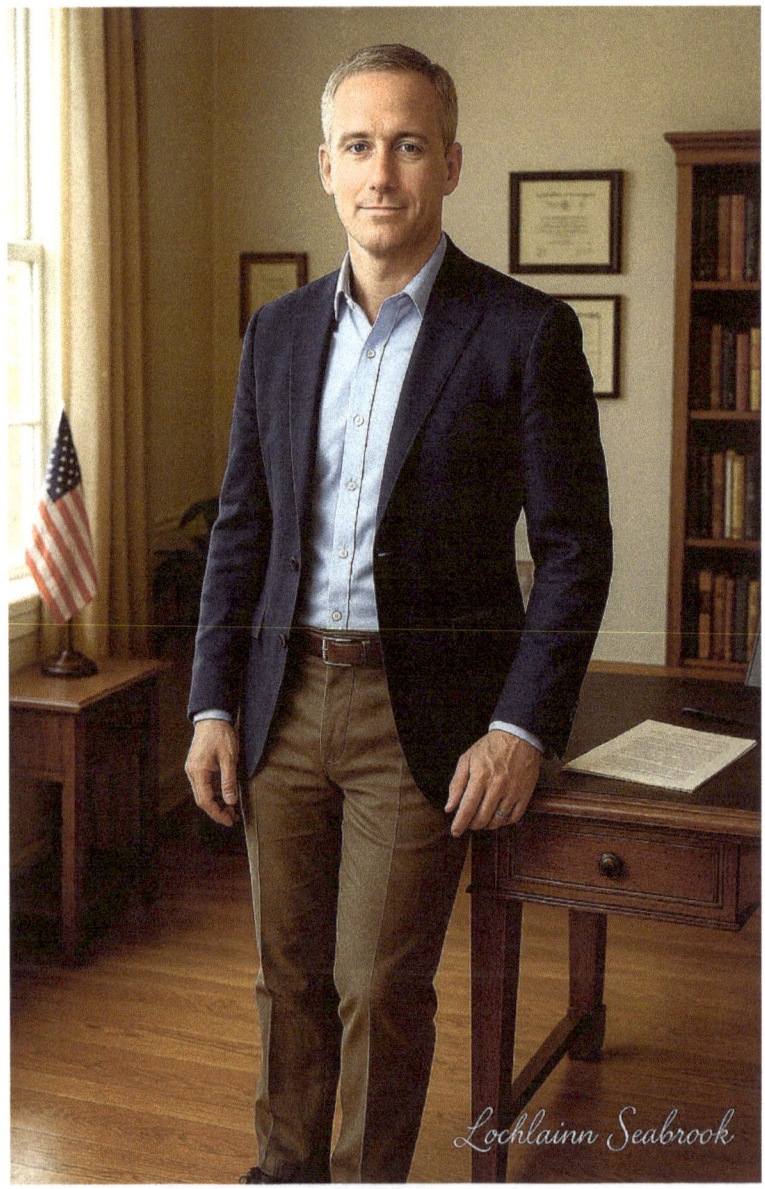

Hamilton as he might look today as a 45 year old U.S. statesman working out of his home office in New York. Copyright © Lochlainn Seabrook.

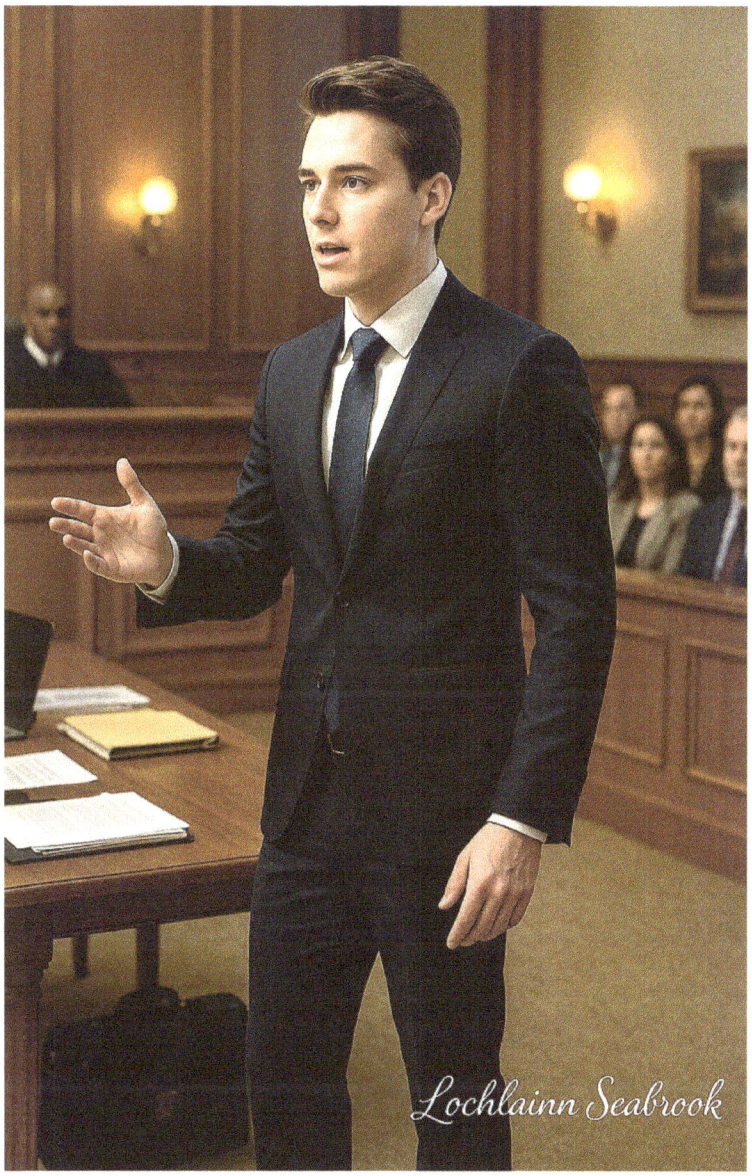

Hamilton as he might look today as a young attorney. Copyright © Lochlainn Seabrook.

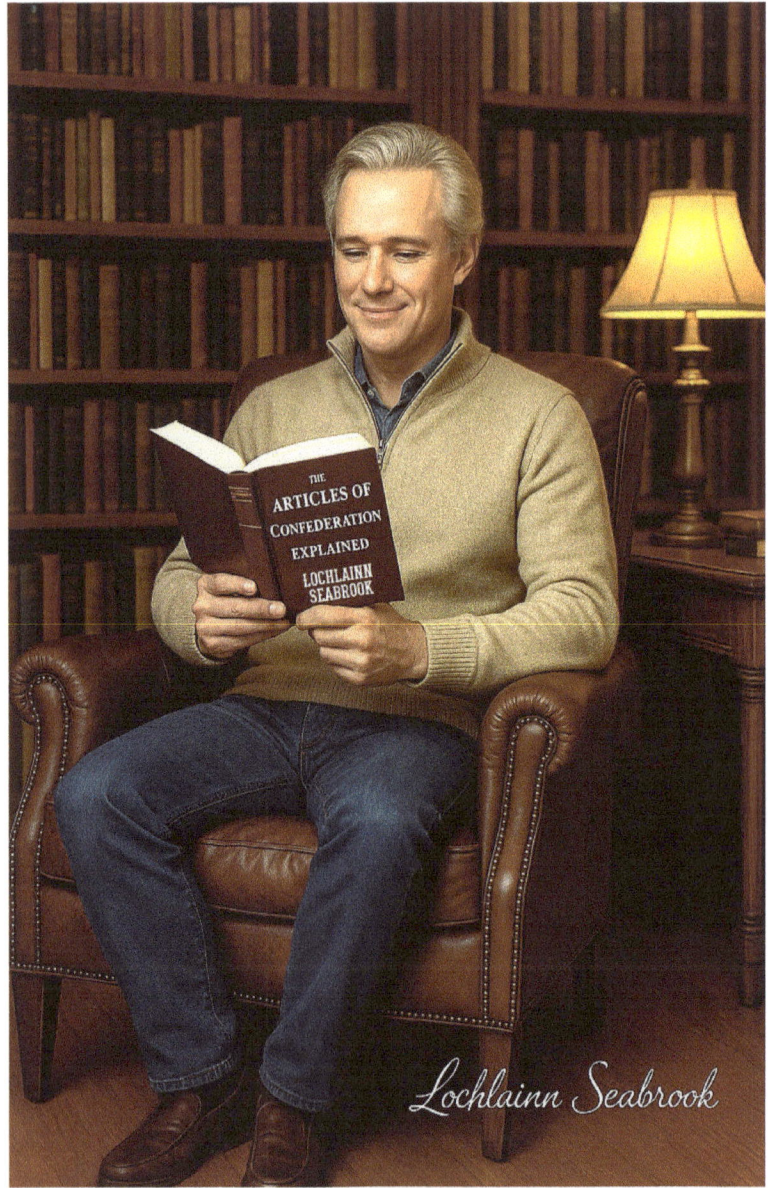

Alexander Hamilton, an ardent bibliophile, as he might look today engaging in one of his favorite hobbies: reading. Copyright © Lochlainn Seabrook.

NATHANIEL HAWTHORNE
1804-1864, Massachusetts

Conservative author, novelist, dark romanticist writer, editor, custom house clerk, surveyor, United States Consul at Liverpool, England, government patronage worker.

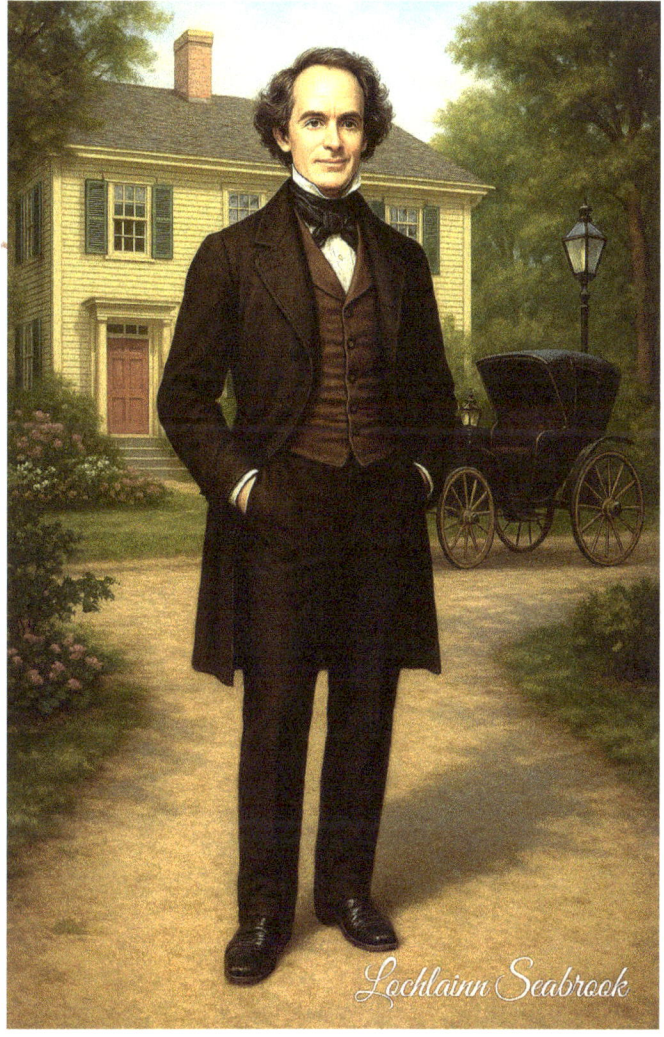

Hawthorne as he looked in 1846, age 42. Copyright © Lochlainn Seabrook.

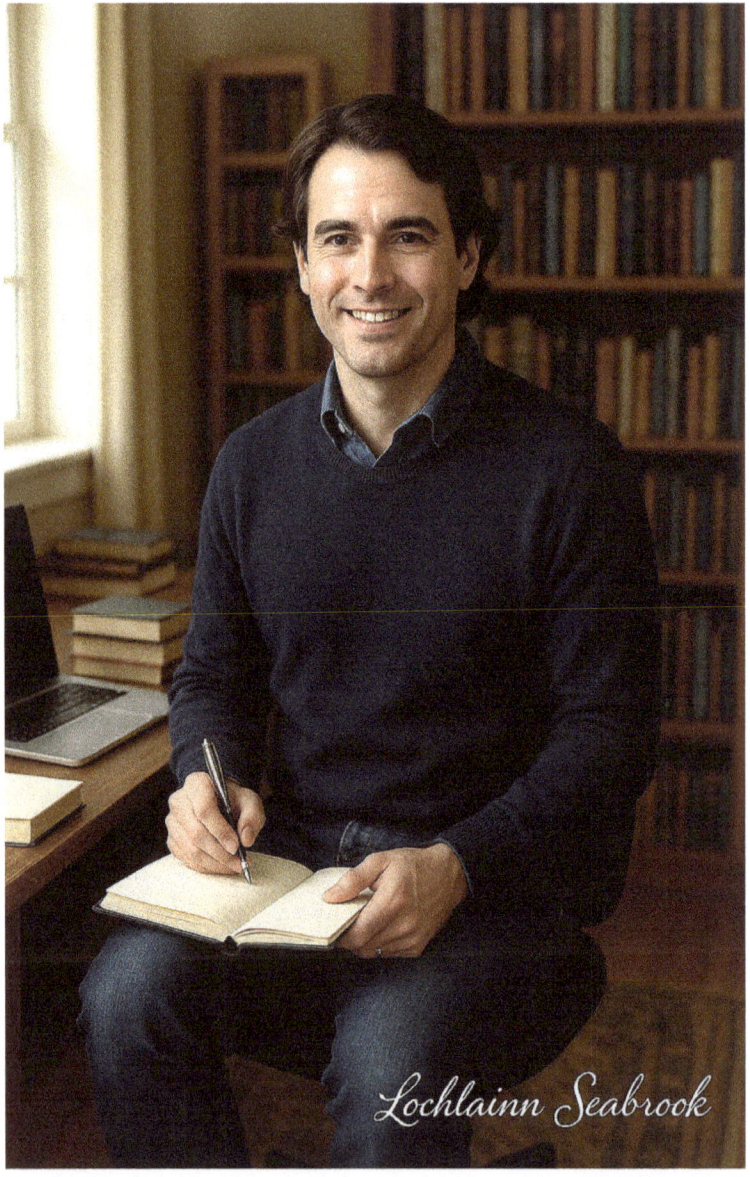

Hawthorne as he might look today as a successful 40 year old novelist. Copyright © Lochlainn Seabrook.

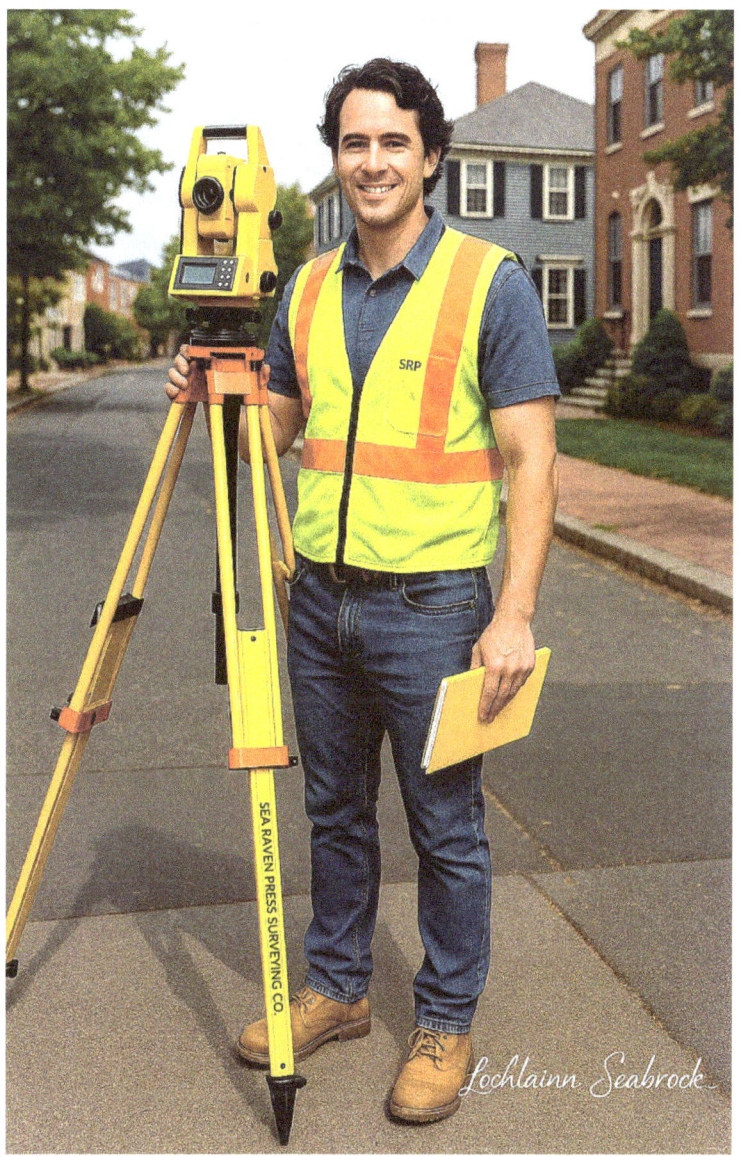

Hawthorne as he might look today working as a young surveyor in Salem, Massachusetts. Copyright © Lochlainn Seabrook.

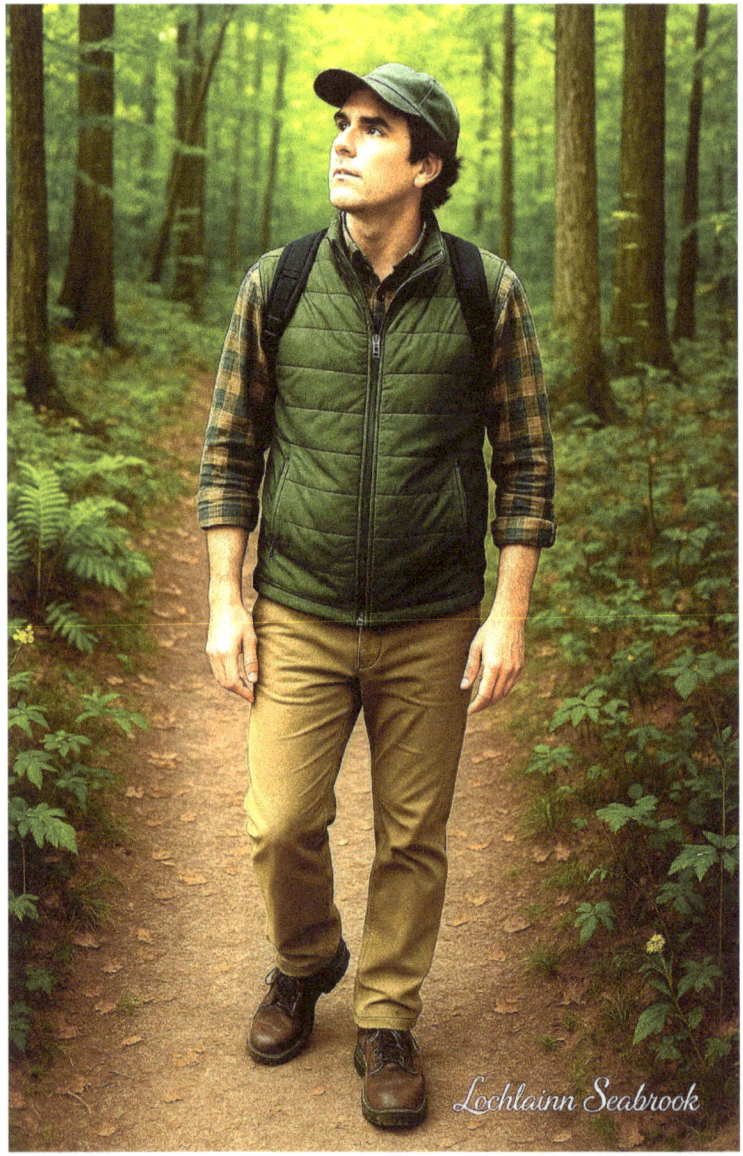

Nathaniel Hawthorne as he might look today engaging in one of his favorite pastimes: hiking the nature trails in and around Concord, Massachusetts. Copyright © Lochlainn Seabrook.

PATRICK HENRY

1736-1799, Virginia

American Founding Father, Conservative Revolutionary leader, governor of Virginia, member of the Continental Congress, statesman, lawyer, orator, member of the Virginia House of Burgesses, storekeeper, planter, anti-Federalist, fiery individual rights and limited government advocate.

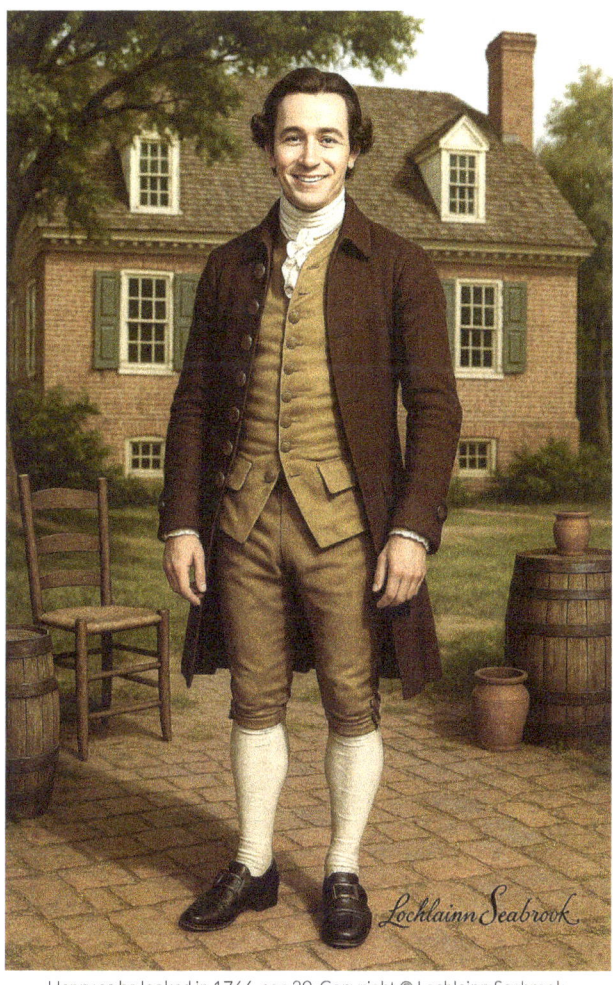

Henry as he looked in 1766, age 30. Copyright © Lochlainn Seabrook.

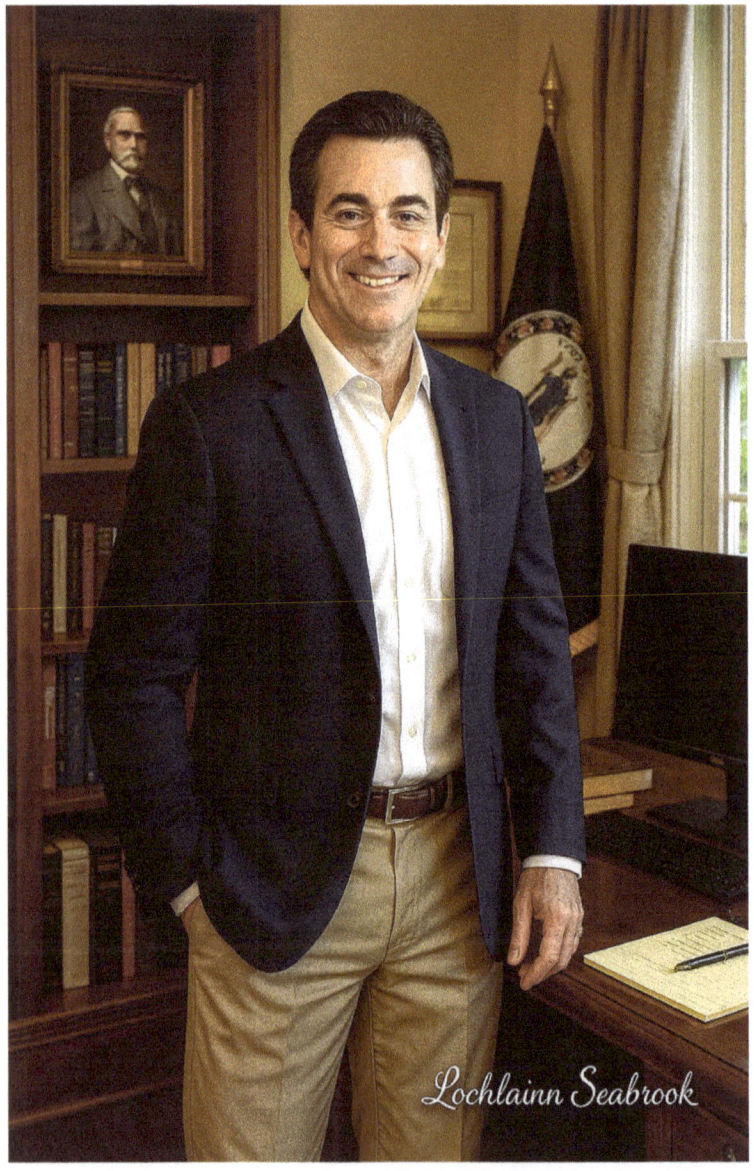

Henry as he might look today as governor of Virginia. Copyright © Lochlainn Seabrook.

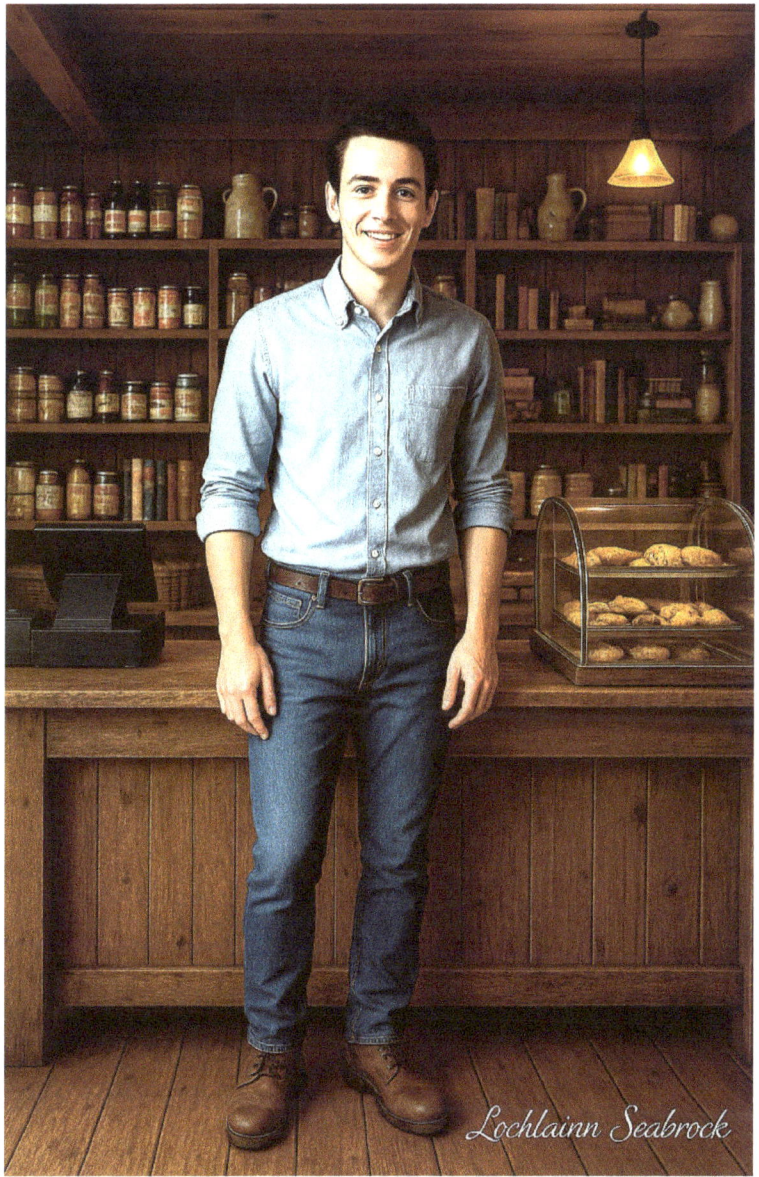

Henry as he might appear today as a 19 year old general store owner. Copyright © Lochlainn Seabrook.

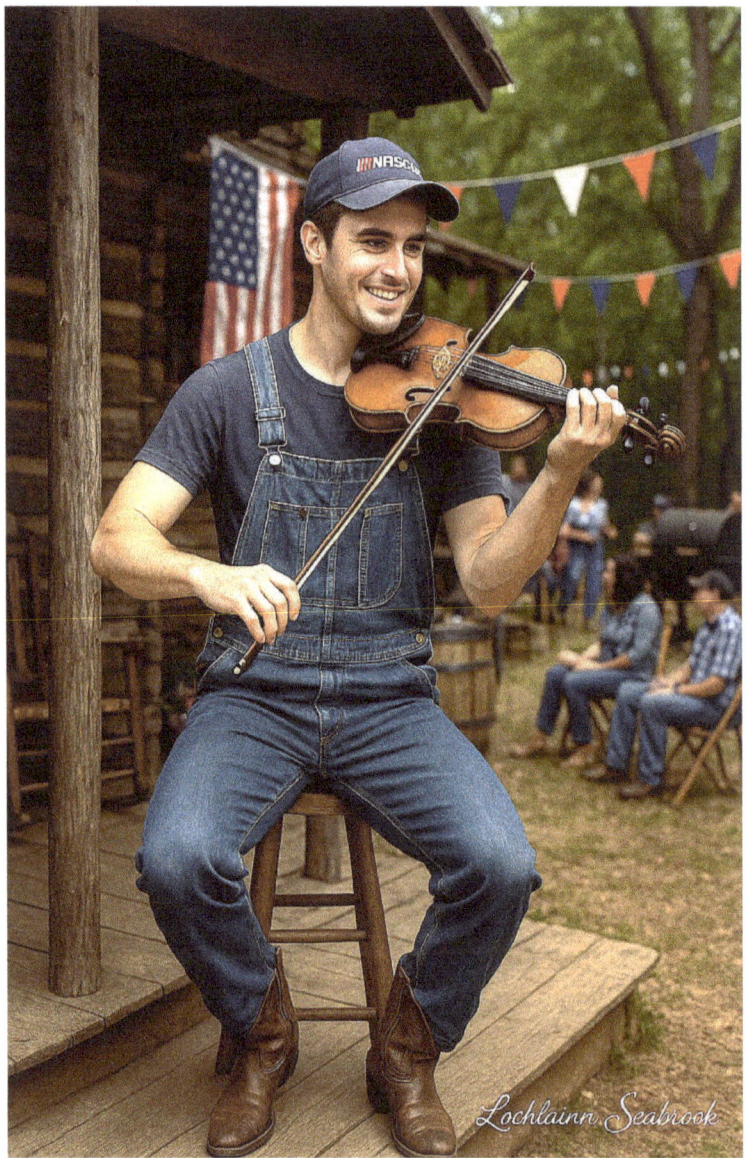

Patrick Henry as he might look today engaging in one of his favorite pastimes: playing fiddle at a country music event. Copyright © Lochlainn Seabrook.

SAM HOUSTON

1793-1863, Virginia

U.S. army officer, general and commander-in-chief of the Texian Army during the Texas Revolution, founding president of the Texas Republic, Tennessee and Texas governor, Tennessee congressman, Texas senator, War of 1812 veteran, schoolteacher, the "white Indian."

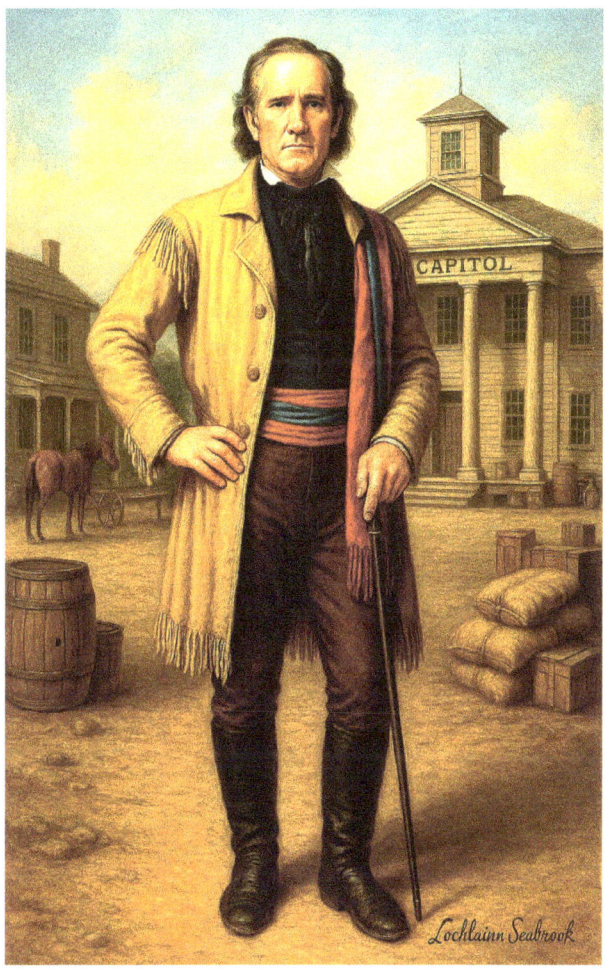

Houston as he looked in 1836, age 43. Copyright © Lochlainn Seabrook.

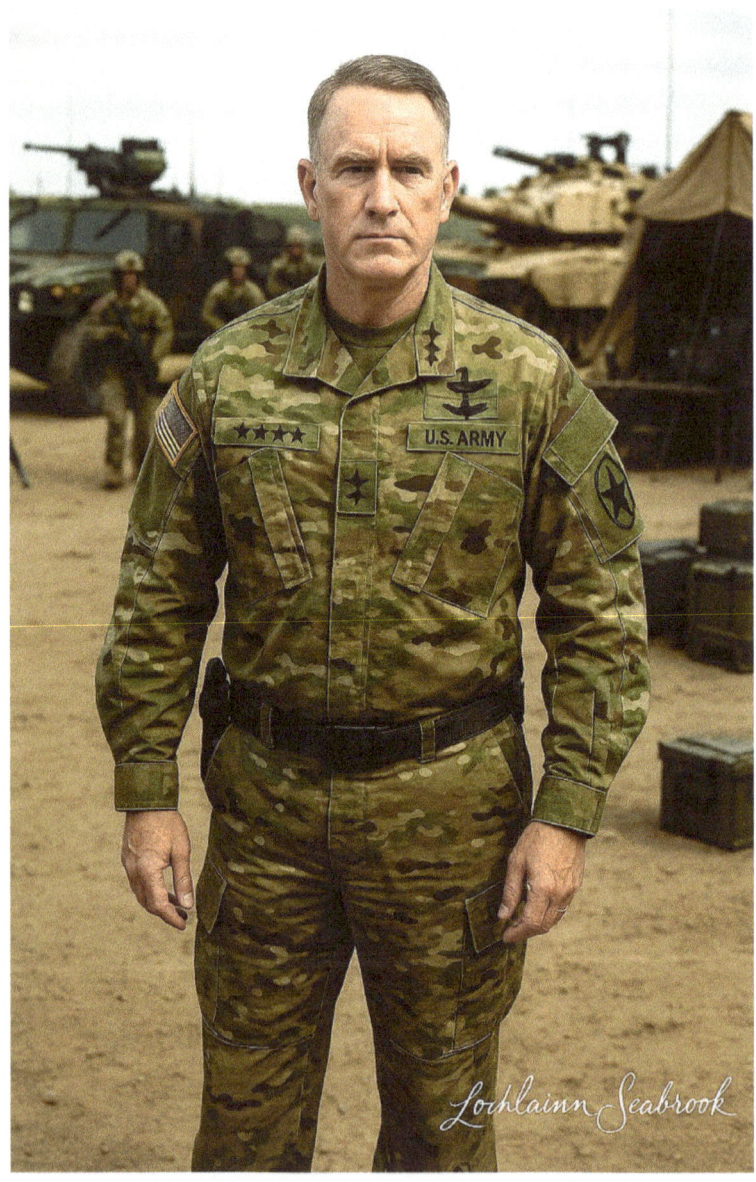

Houston as he might look today as a U.S. army general. Copyright © Lochlainn Seabrook.

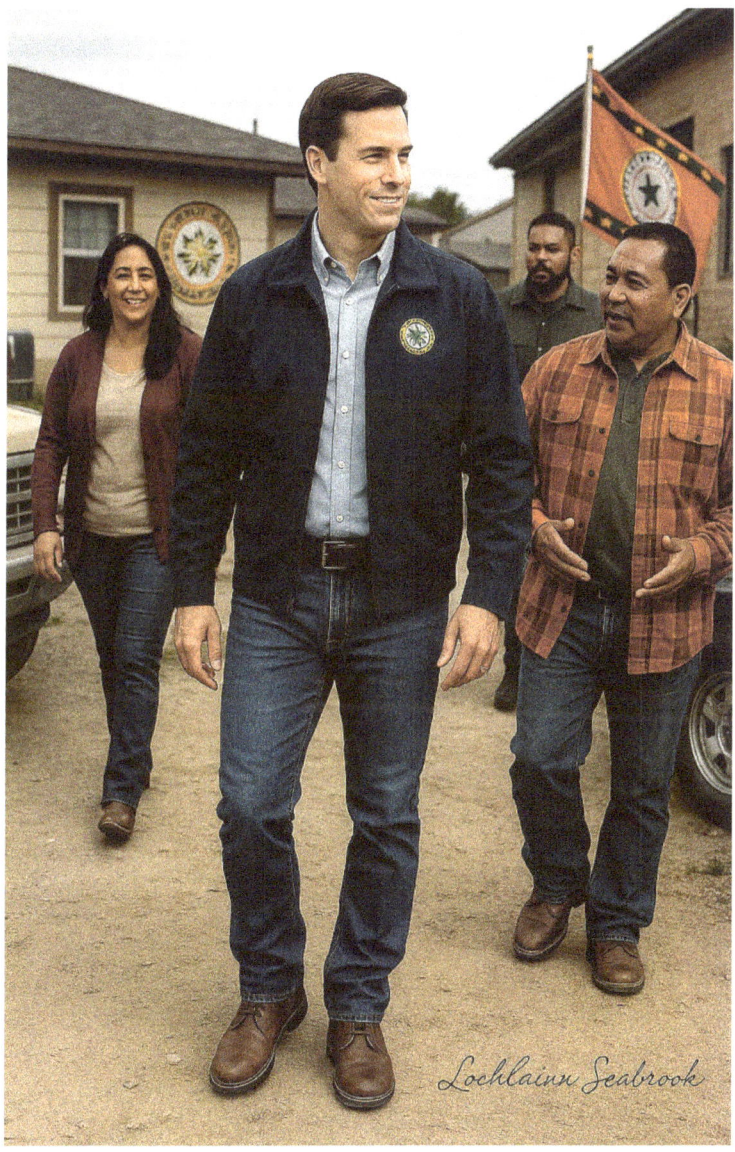

A lifelong champion of Native American rights, this is Houston as he might look today working as a young unofficial representative and advocate for the Cherokee people. Copyright © Lochlainn Seabrook.

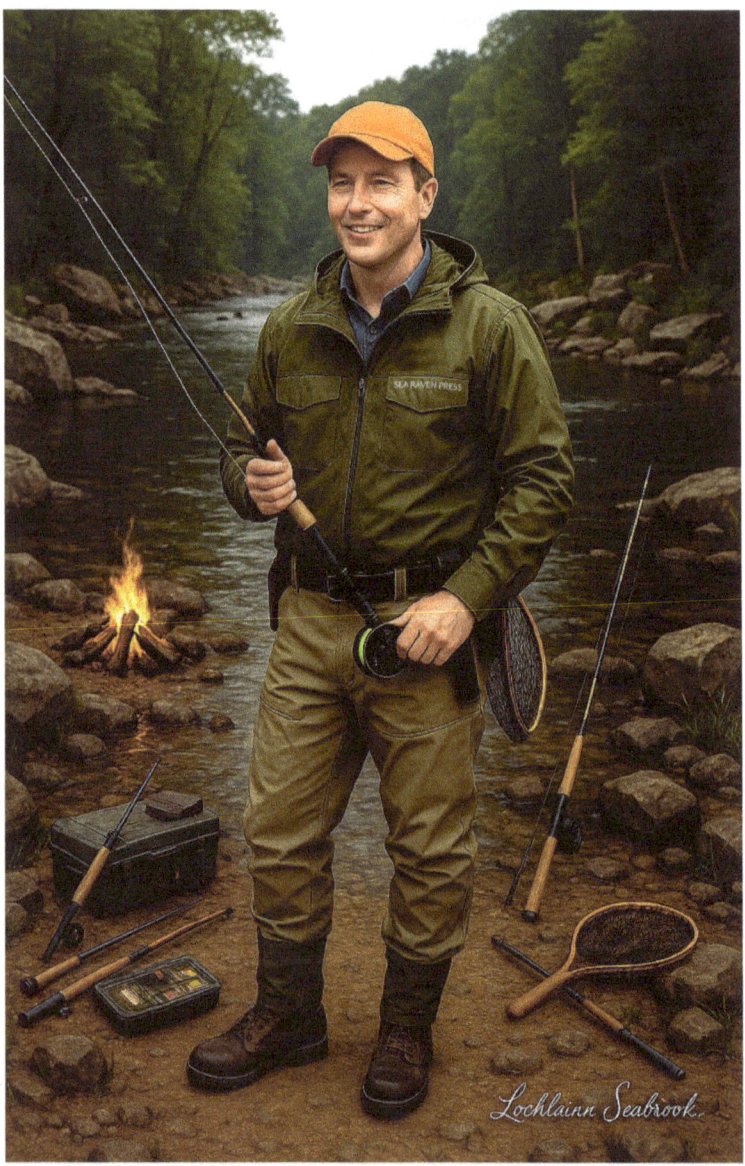

Samuel "Sam" Houston as he might look today engaging in a few of his favorite pastimes: fishing, hunting, and camping. Copyright © Lochlainn Seabrook.

ANDREW JACKSON

1767-1845, North Carolina

U.S. president, statesman, U.S. army general, lawyer, land speculator, real estate investor, judge, founded the modern Democratic Party (at the time conservative), "man of the people."

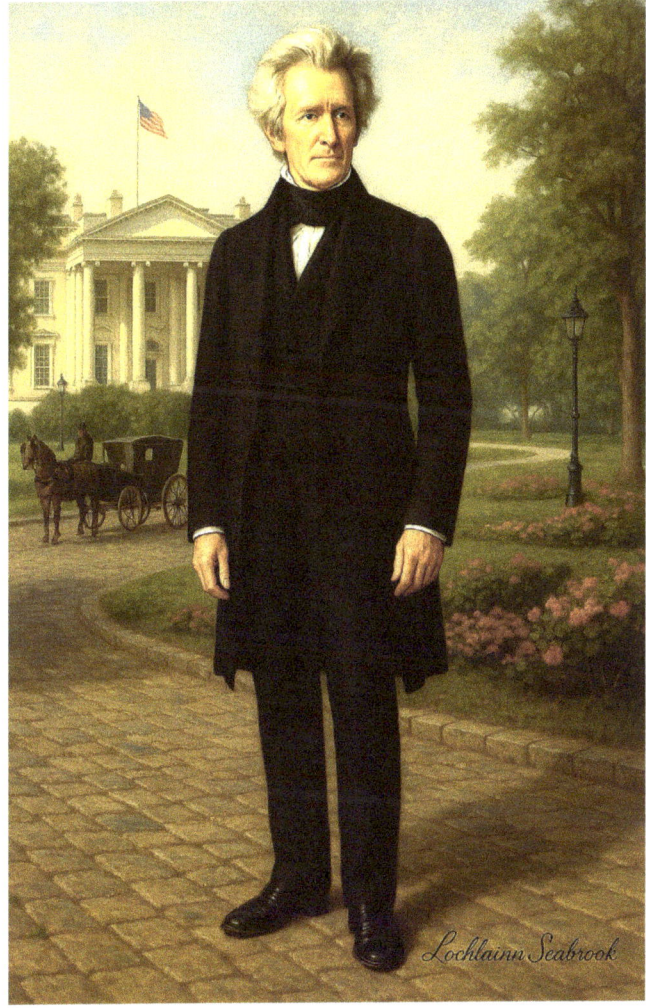

Jackson as he looked in 1832, age 65. Copyright © Lochlainn Seabrook.

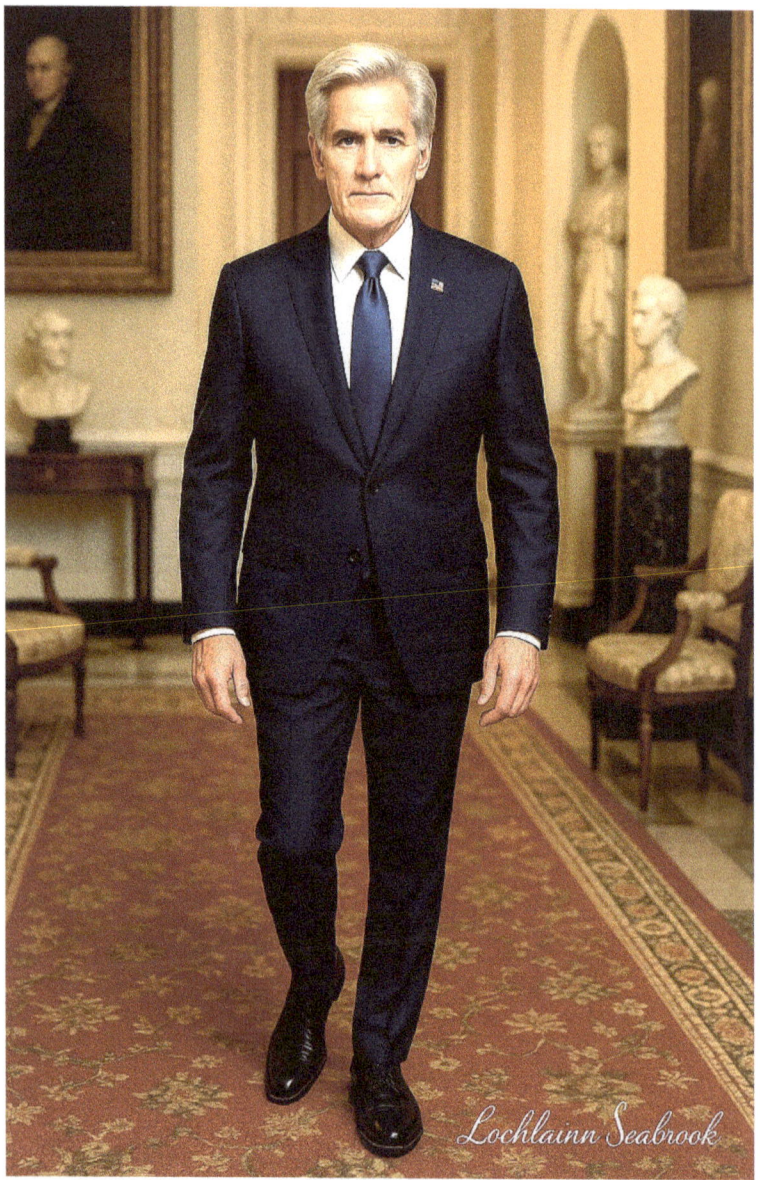

Jackson as he might look today as U.S. president. Copyright © Lochlainn Seabrook.

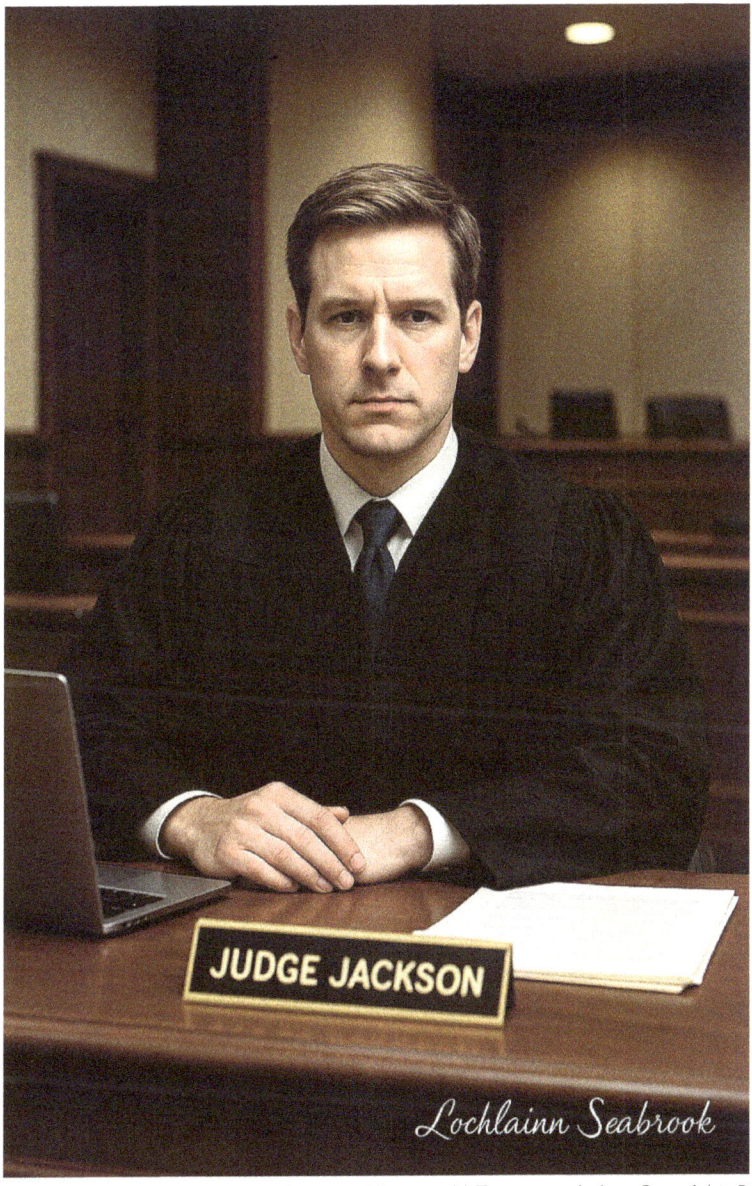

Jackson as he might appear today as a 31 year old Tennessee judge. Copyright © Lochlainn Seabrook.

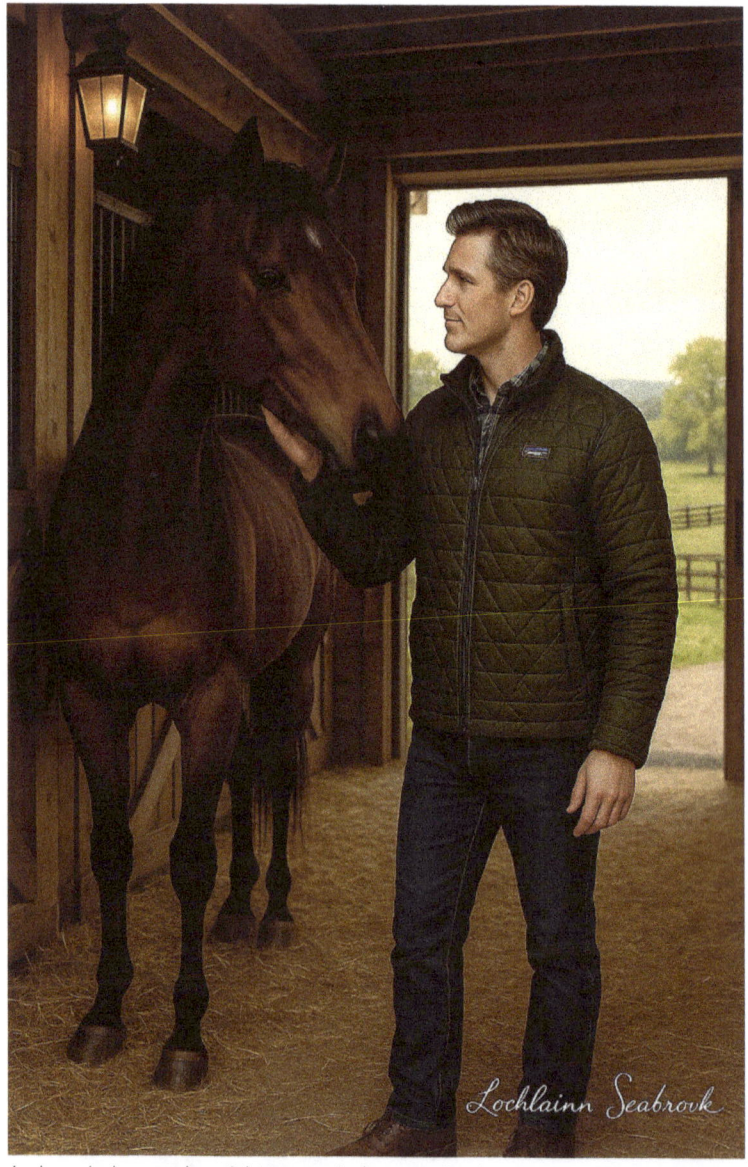

Andrew Jackson as he might appear today engaging in one of his favorite hobbies: breeding race horses. In this image he is overseeing the health of his prize champion thoroughbred, Truxton. Copyright © Lochlainn Seabrook.

THOMAS "STONEWALL" JACKSON

1824-1863, Virginia (now part of modern day West Virginia)

West Point graduate, Mexican-American War veteran, professor at Virginia Military Institute, weapons instructor, Confederate general, military genius, battlefield tactician, artillery expert, ardent Christian, health, nature, and outdoor enthusiast.

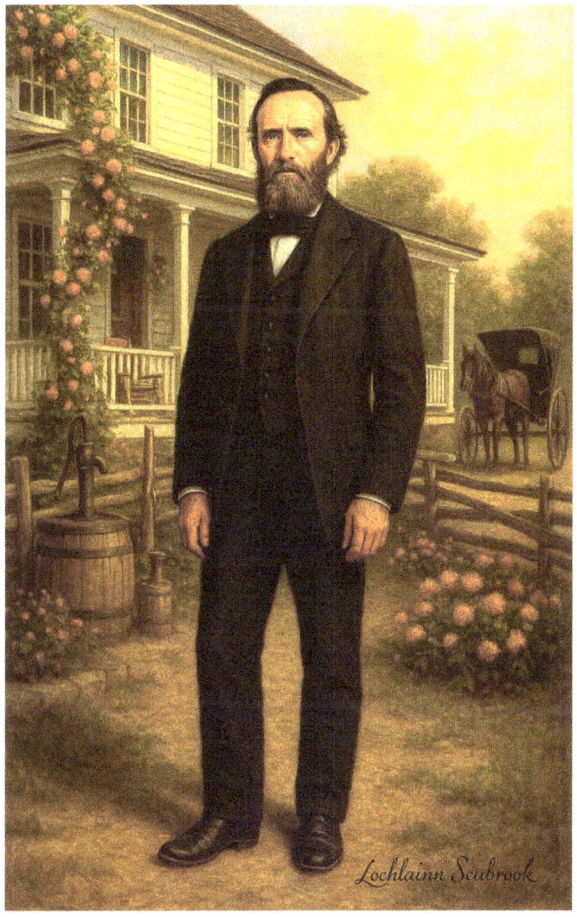

Jackson as he looked in 1862, age 38. Copyright © Lochlainn Seabrook.

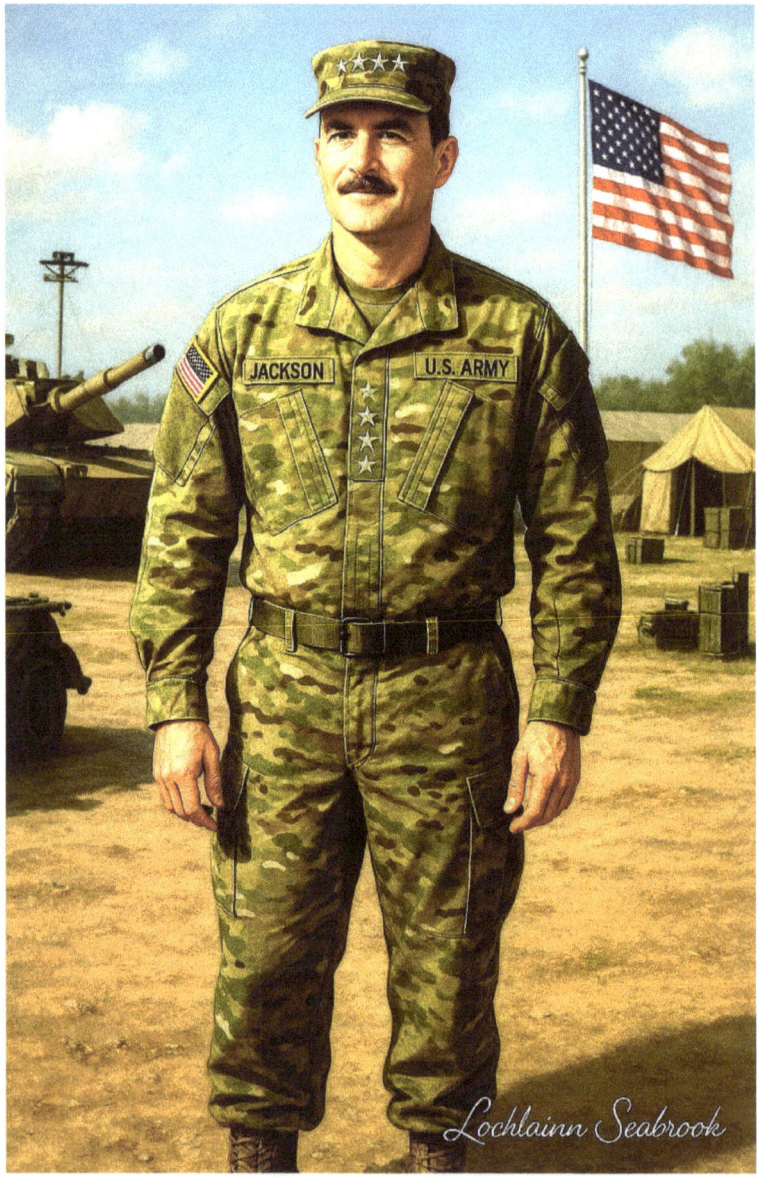

Jackson as he might look today as a 37 year old U.S. army general. Copyright © Lochlainn Seabrook.

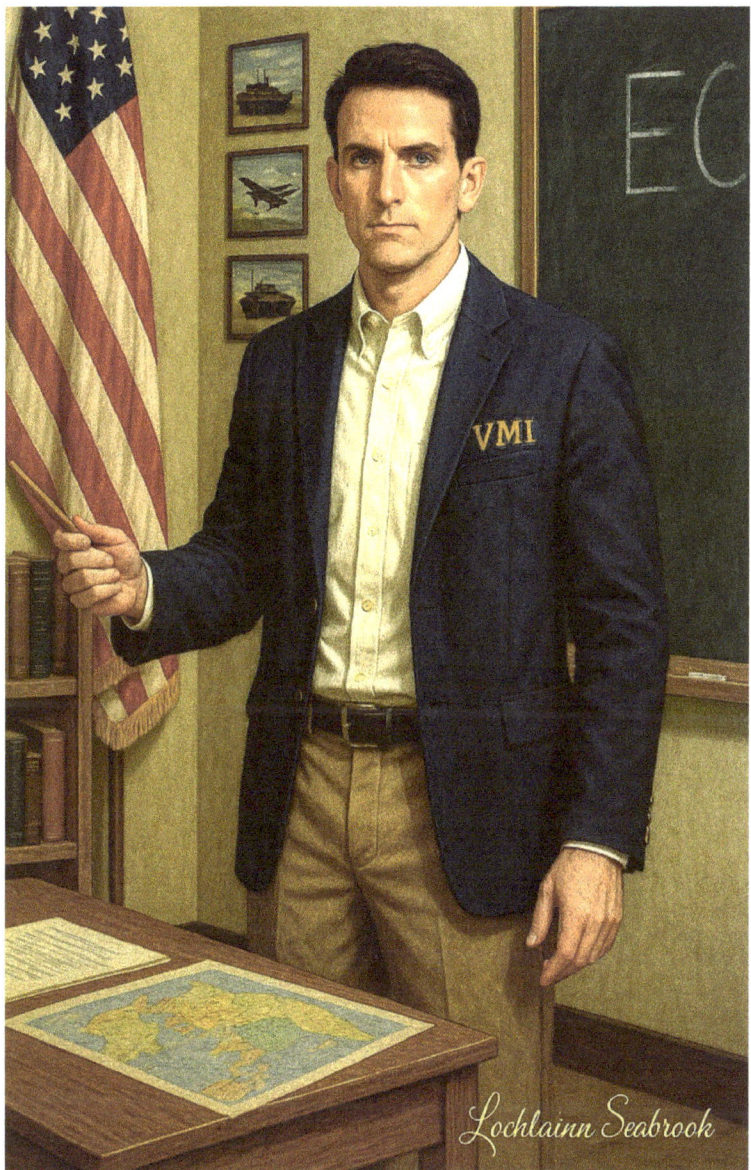

Jackson as he might appear today as a 27 year old professor of artillery tactics at Virginia Military Institute. Copyright © Lochlainn Seabrook.

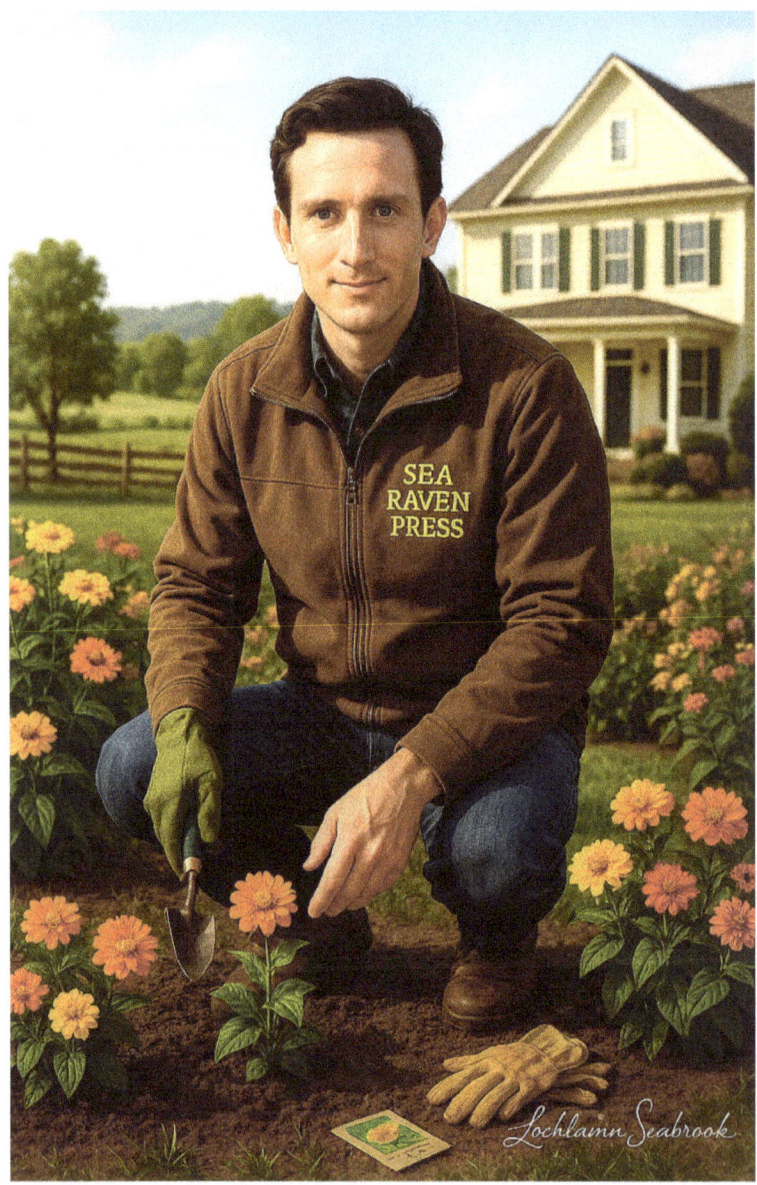

Thomas Jonathan "Stonewall" Jackson as he might look today as a 30 year old engaging in one of his favorite hobbies: gardening. Copyright © Lochlainn Seabrook.

THOMAS JEFFERSON

1743-1826, Virginia

Conservative U.S. president, U.S. vice president, U.S. secretary of state, U.S. minister to France, primary author of the Declaration of Independence, lawyer, planter, farmer, plantation owner, founder of the University of Virginia, passionate limited government and agrarian democracy advocate.

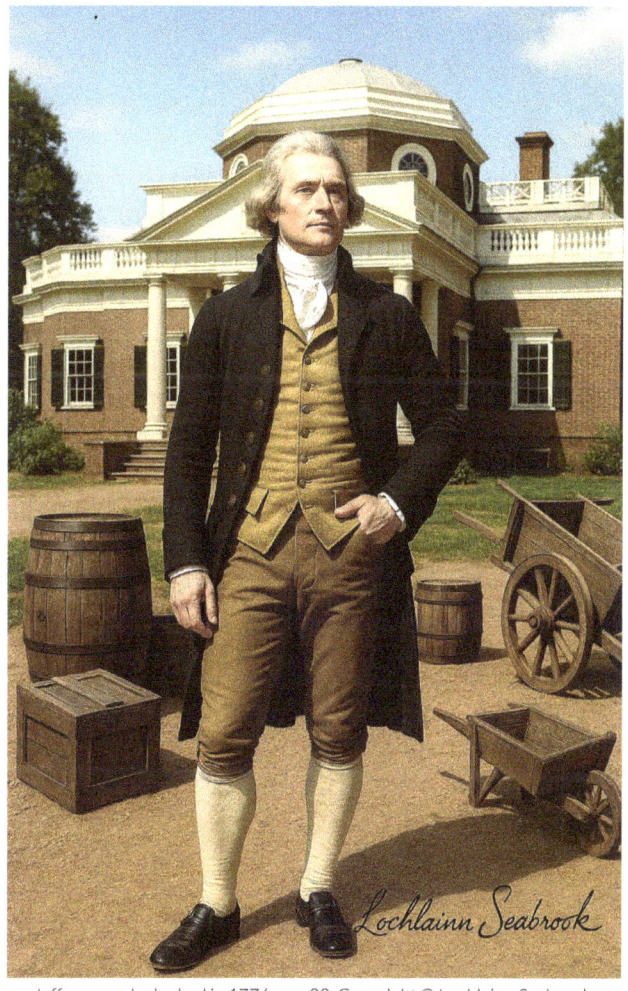

Jefferson as he looked in 1776, age 33. Copyright © Lochlainn Seabrook.

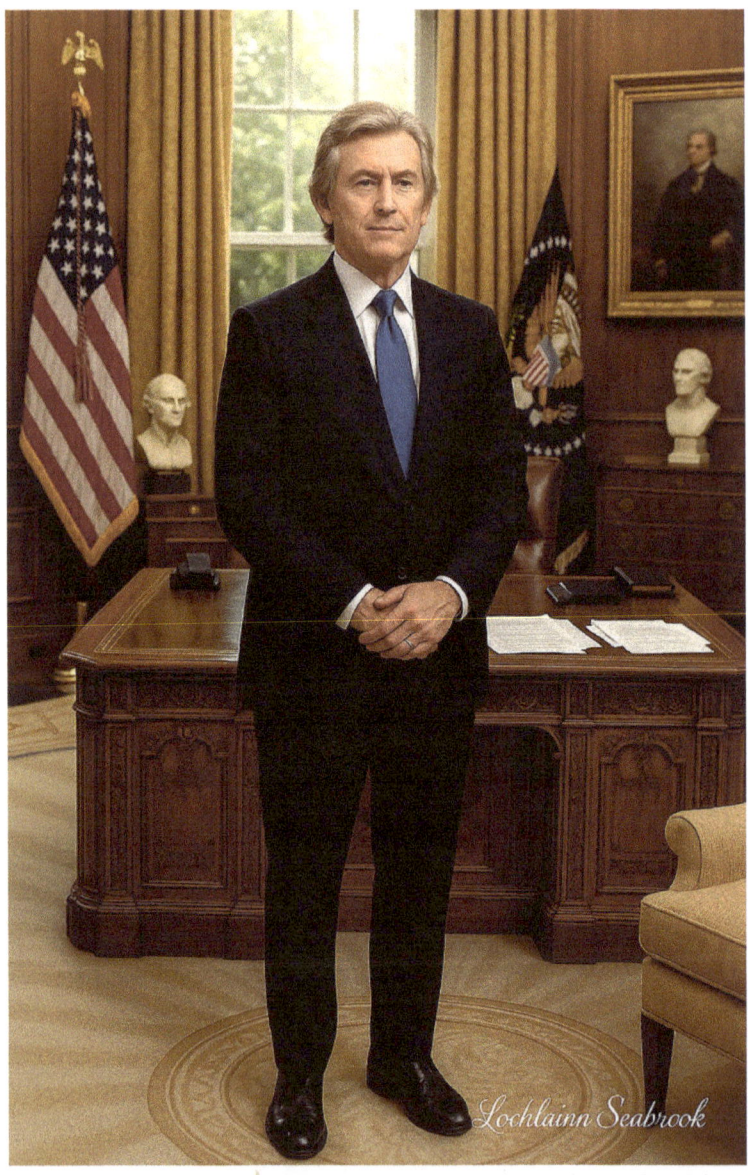

Jefferson as he might look today as president of the United States. Copyright © Lochlainn Seabrook.

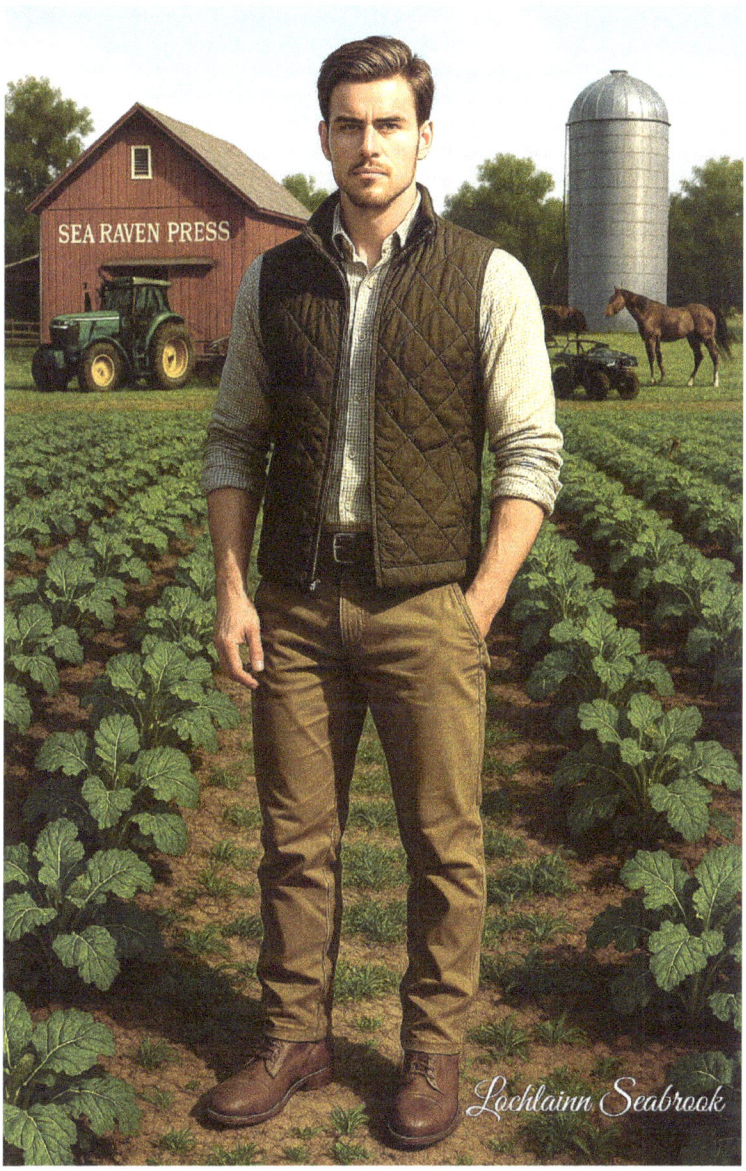

Jefferson as he might look today as a wealthy young large scale farm owner. Copyright © Lochlainn Seabrook.

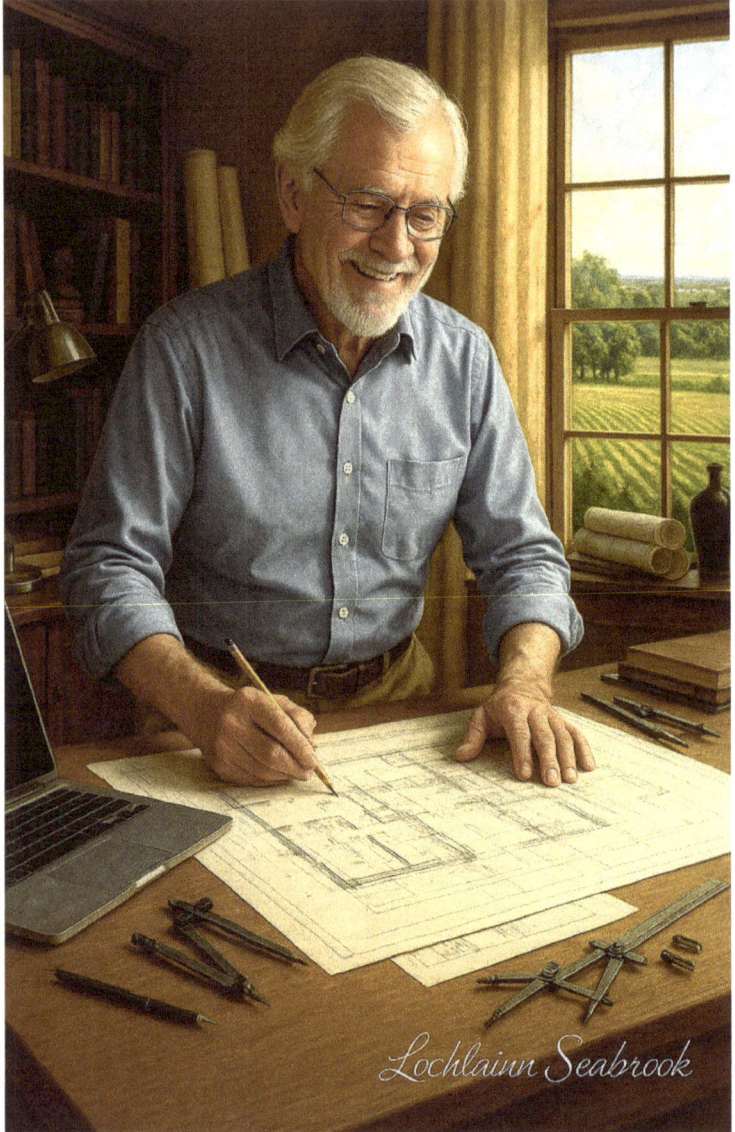

A 75 year old Thomas Jefferson as he might look today engaging in one of his favorite hobbies: architectural design. Copyright © Lochlainn Seabrook.

ROBERT E. LEE

1807-1870, Virginia

U.S. army career officer, commander of 2nd U.S. cavalry, Mexican-American War veteran, military engineer, West Point graduate, superintendent of West Point, Confederate general, commander-in-chief of Army of Northern Virginia, general-in-chief of all Confederate military forces, president of Washington College (now Washington and Lee University), educator-administrator, student mentor, virtuoso equestrian, one of American history's greatest military minds.

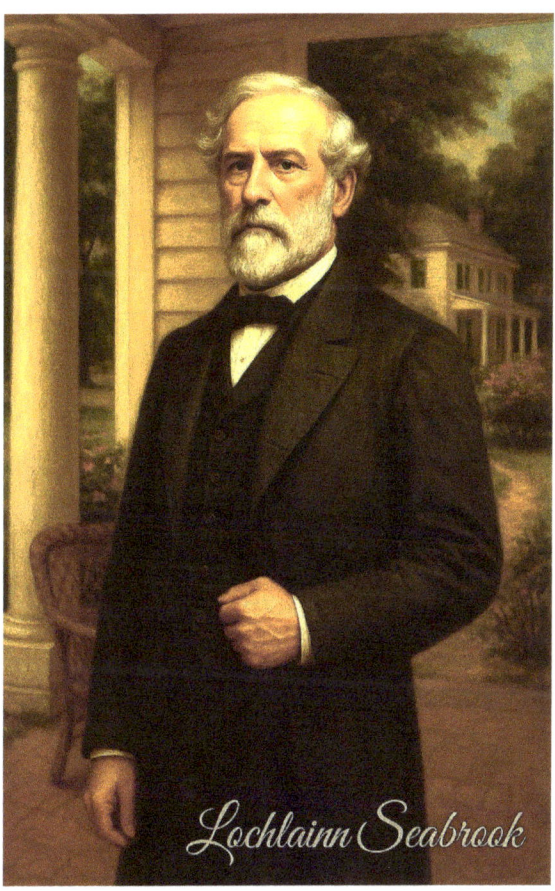

Lee as he looked in 1857, age 50. Copyright © Lochlainn Seabrook.

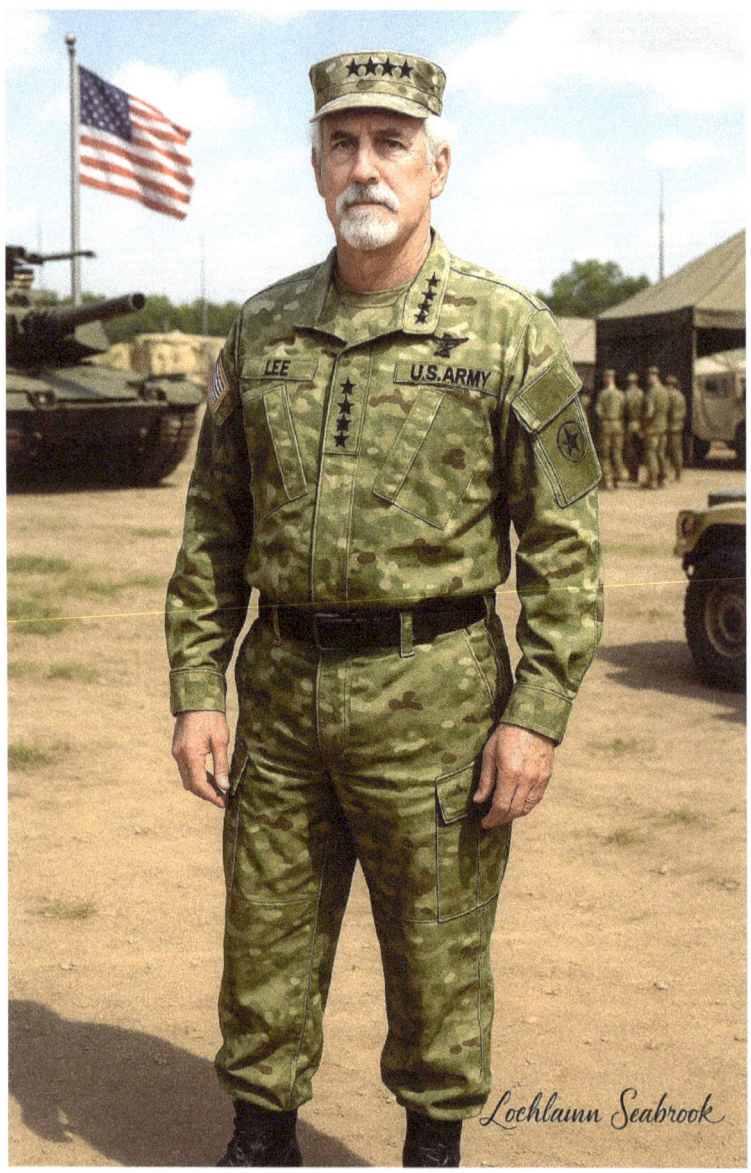

Lee as he might look today as a U.S. army general. Copyright © Lochlainn Seabrook.

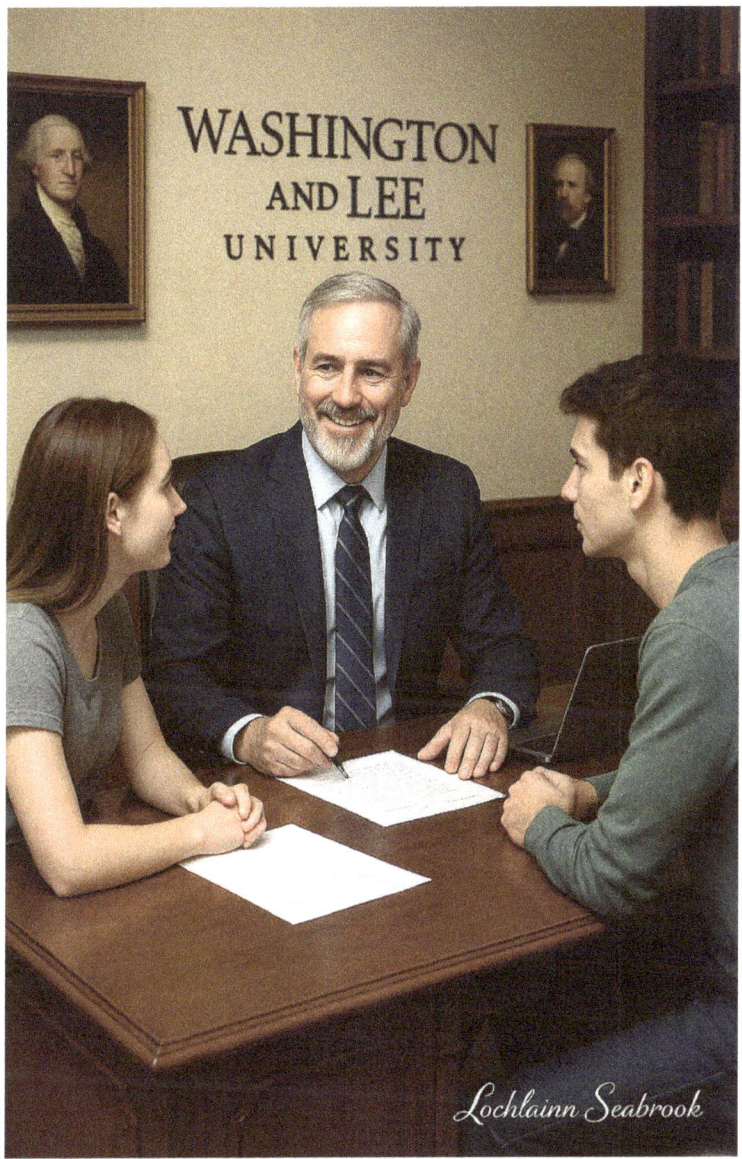

Lee as he might appear today serving as the president of Washington and Lee University. Copyright © Lochlainn Seabrook.

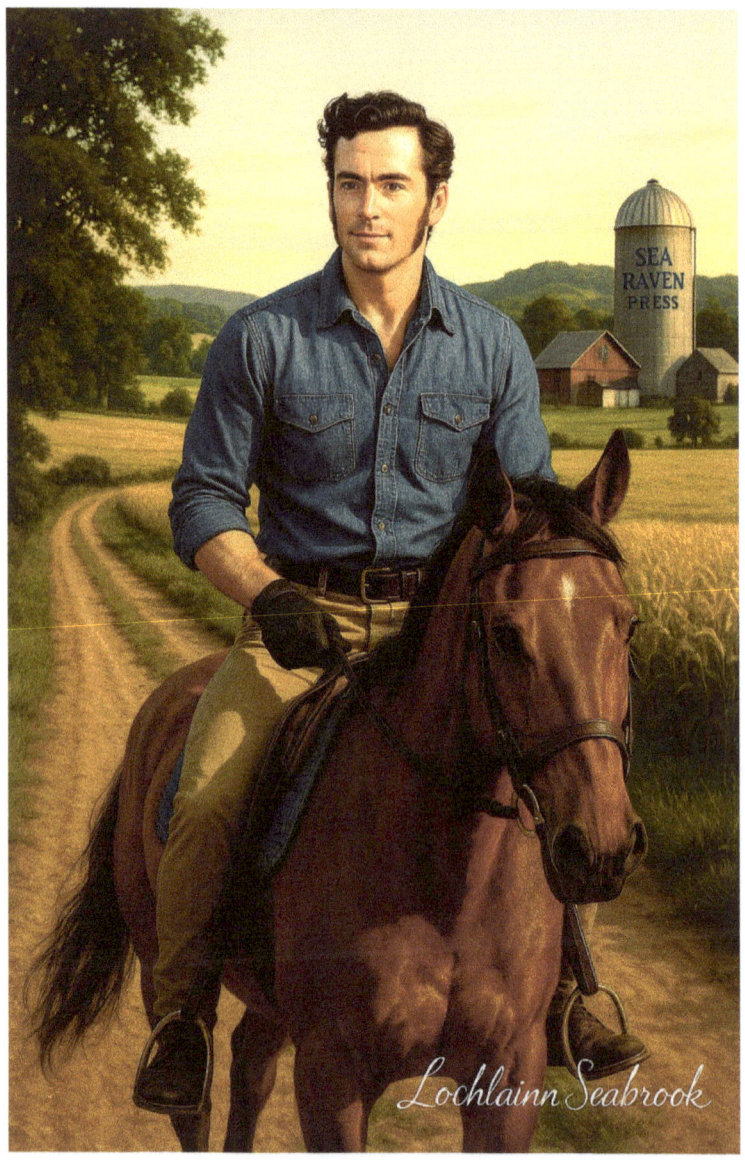

Robert Edward Lee as he might appear today as a 31 year old enjoying one of his favorite hobbies: horseback riding. Copyright © Lochlainn Seabrook.

MERIWETHER LEWIS

1774-1809, Virginia

Governor of the Louisiana Territory, U.S. army officer, pioneering American explorer, administrator, diplomat, personal secretary to U.S. President Thomas Jefferson, plantation manager, chief field scientist of the Lewis and Clark expedition.

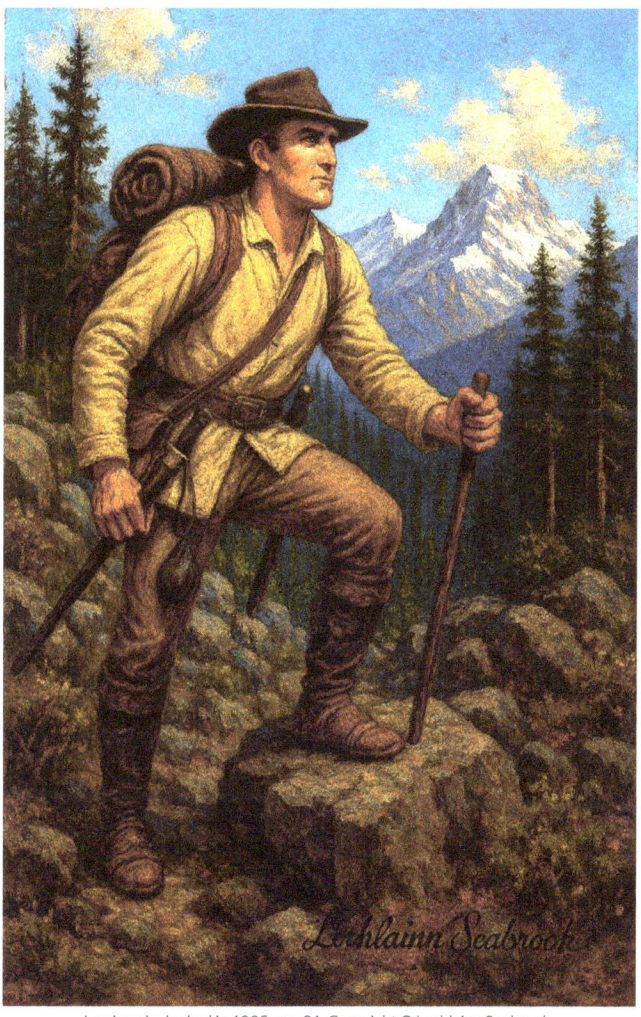

Lewis as he looked in 1805, age 31. Copyright © Lochlainn Seabrook.

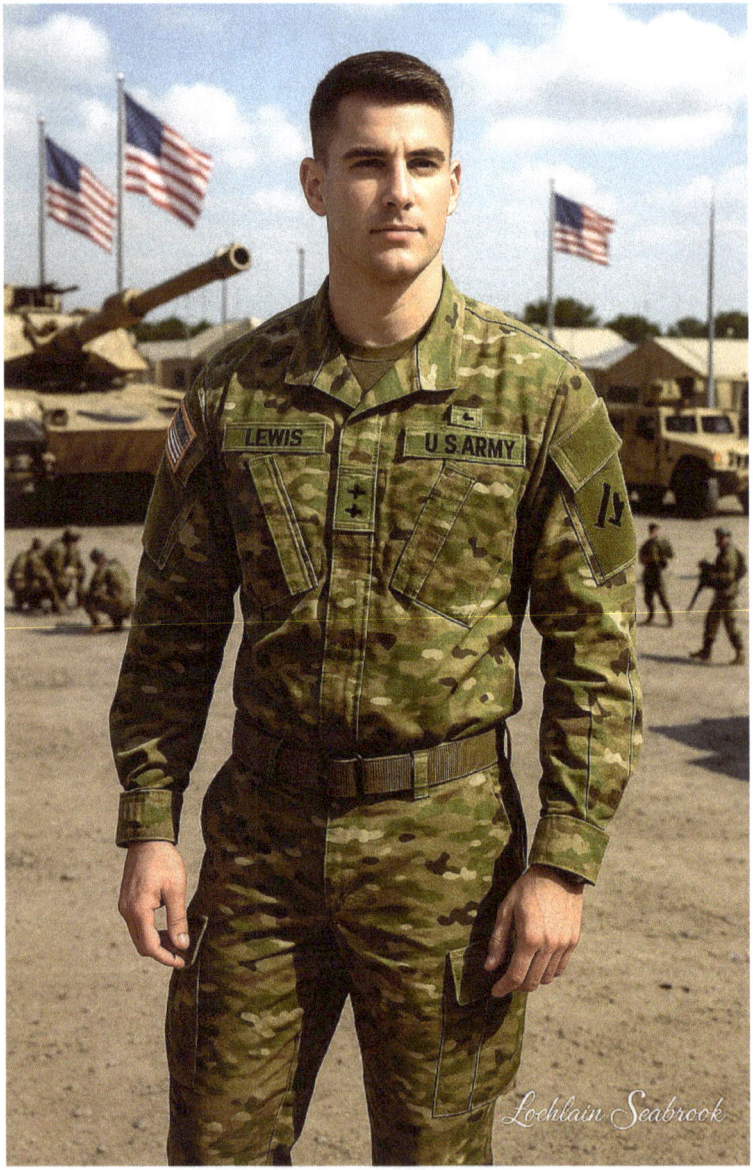

Lewis as he might look today as a young U.S. army captain. Copyright © Lochlainn Seabrook.

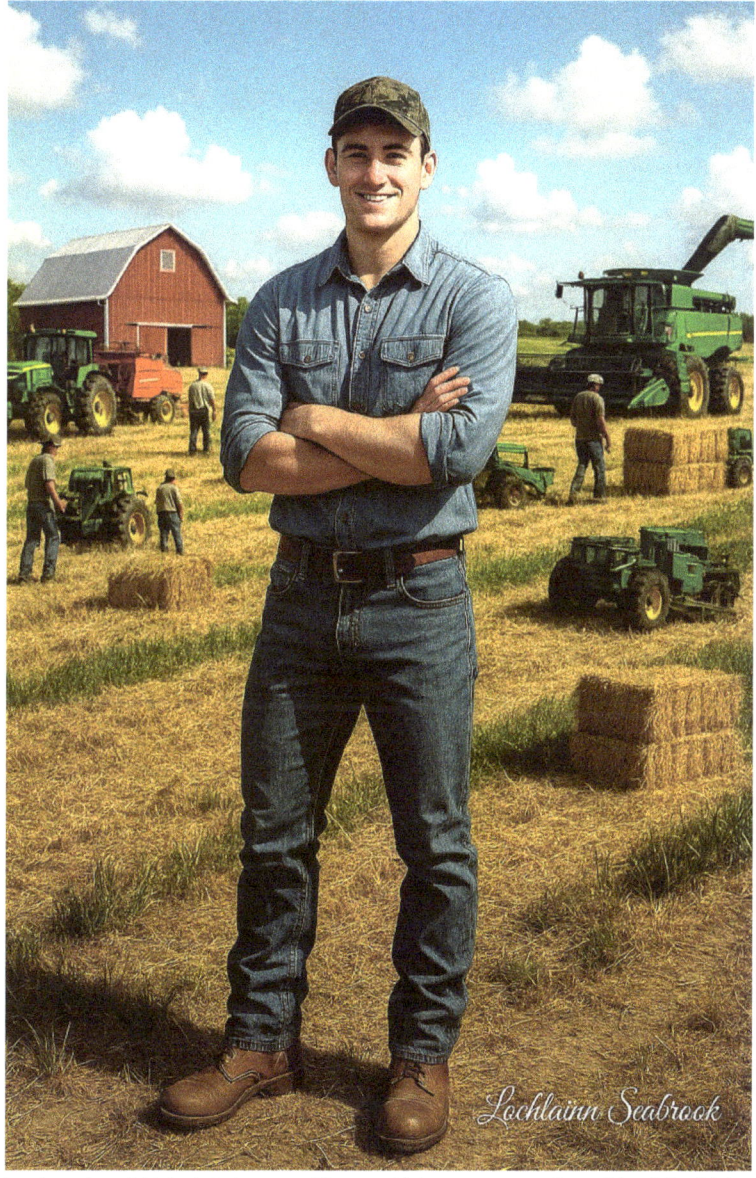

Lewis as he might look today as a 20 year old farm manager. Copyright © Lochlainn Seabrook.

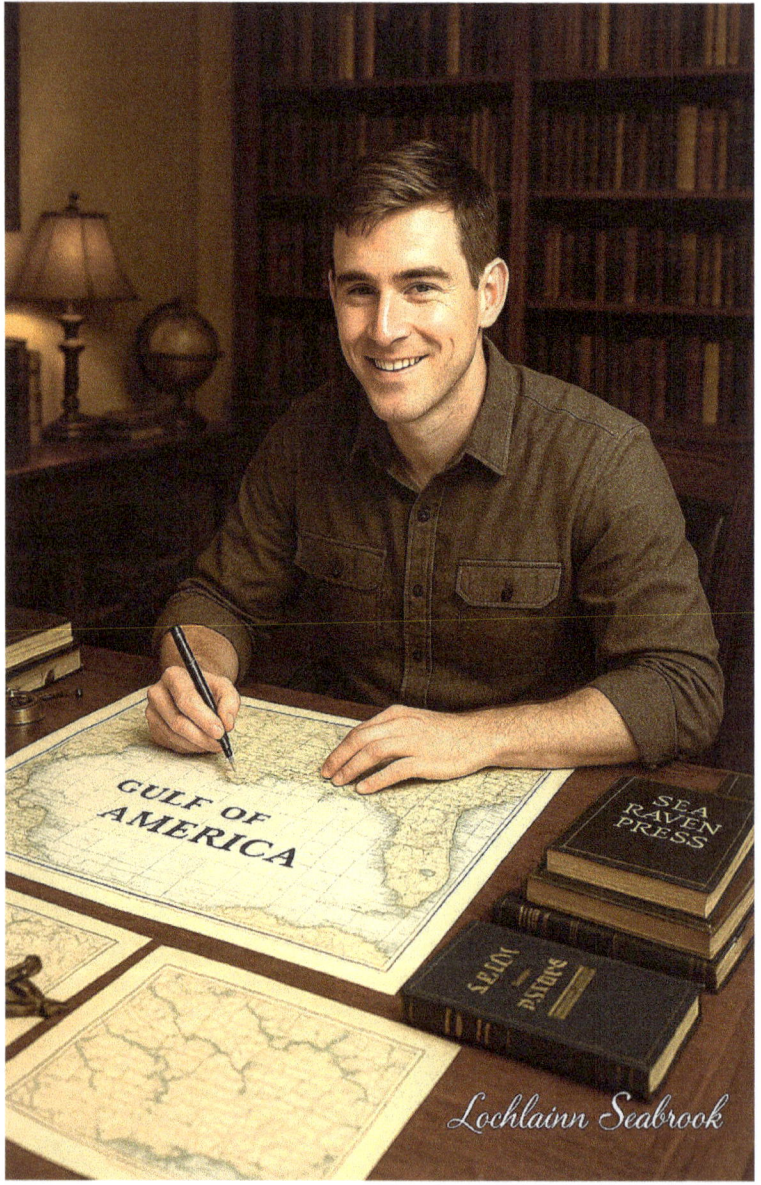

Meriwether Lewis as he might look today as a 25 year old engaging in one of his favorite hobbies: cartography. Copyright © Lochlainn Seabrook.

CHARLES LINDBERGH

1902-1974, Michigan

Pioneering aviator, transatlantic flight hero, record-setting pilot, visionary airman, aviation explorer, aviation consultant, U.S. airmail pilot, stunt pilot, parachutist, mechanic, Pulitzer Prize-winning author, scientific inventor, traditionalist, political Conservative and national isolationist, conservation advocate.

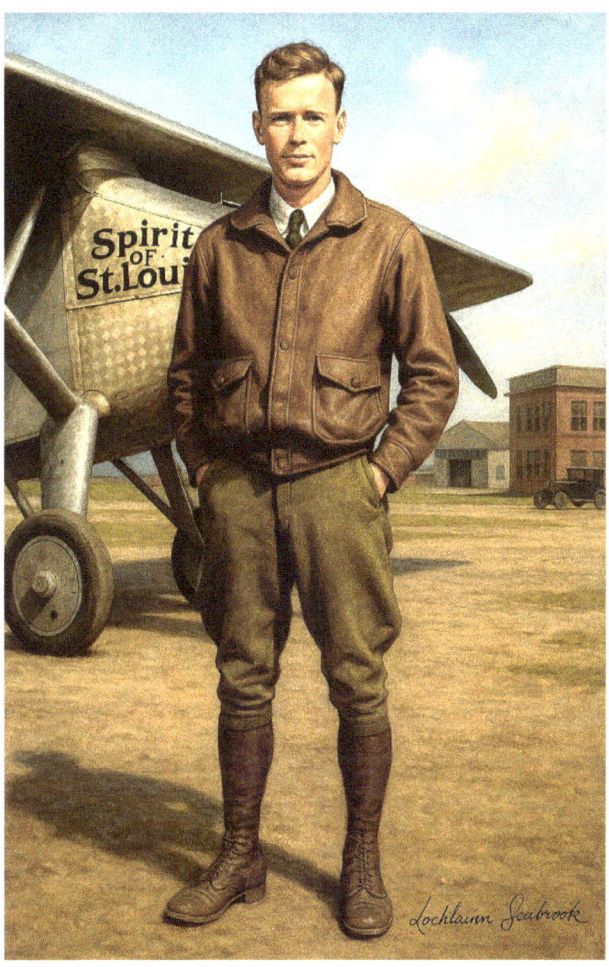

Lindbergh as he looked in 1927, age 25. Copyright © Lochlainn Seabrook.

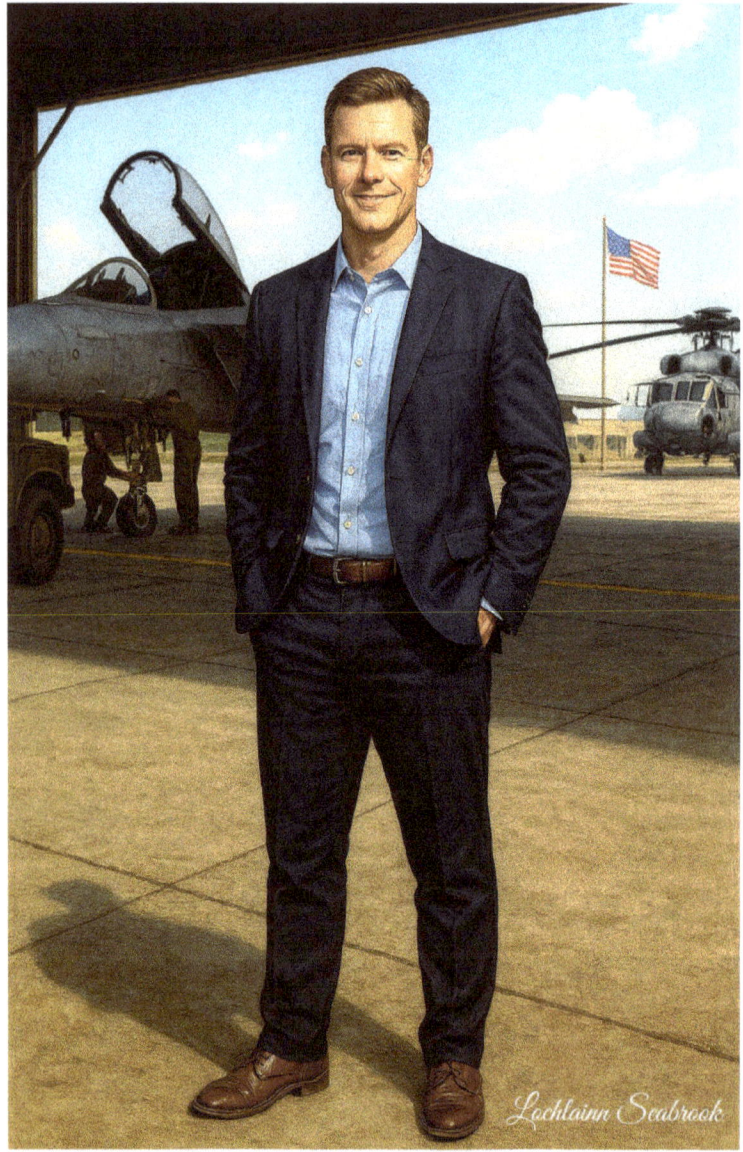

Lindbergh as he might look today working as a 21st-Century aviation consultant. Copyright © Lochlainn Seabrook.

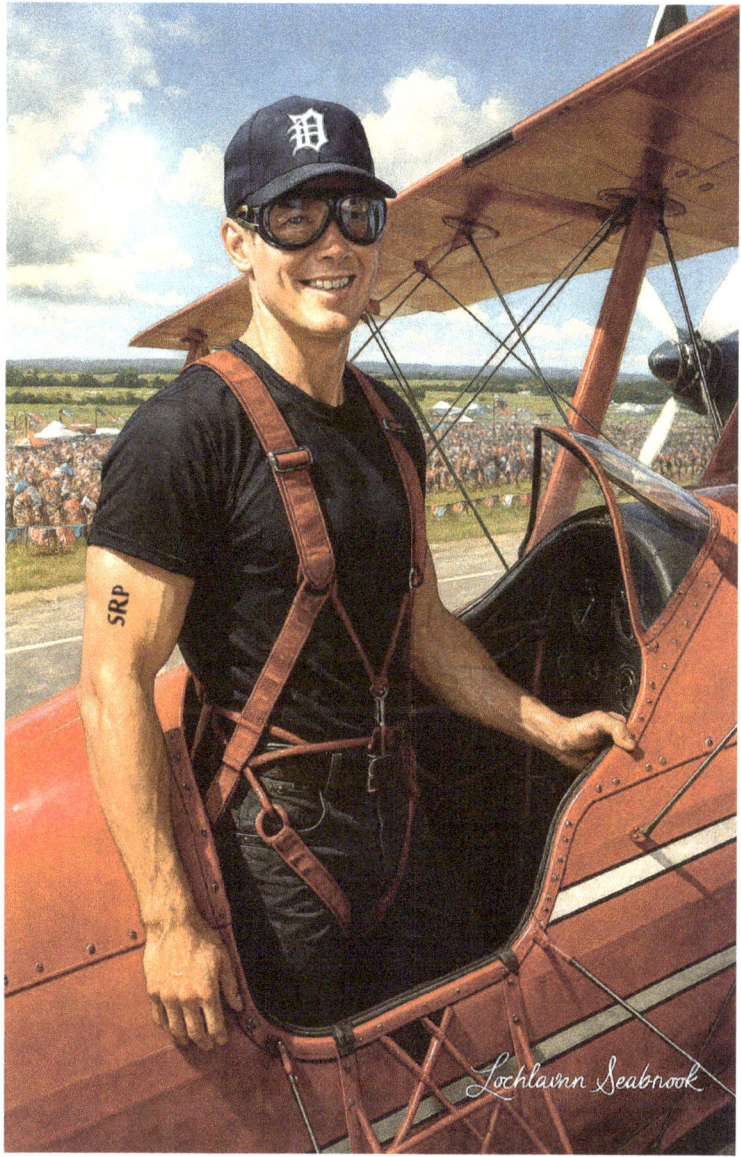

Lindbergh as he might look today as a popular young stunt flyer. Copyright © Lochlainn Seabrook.

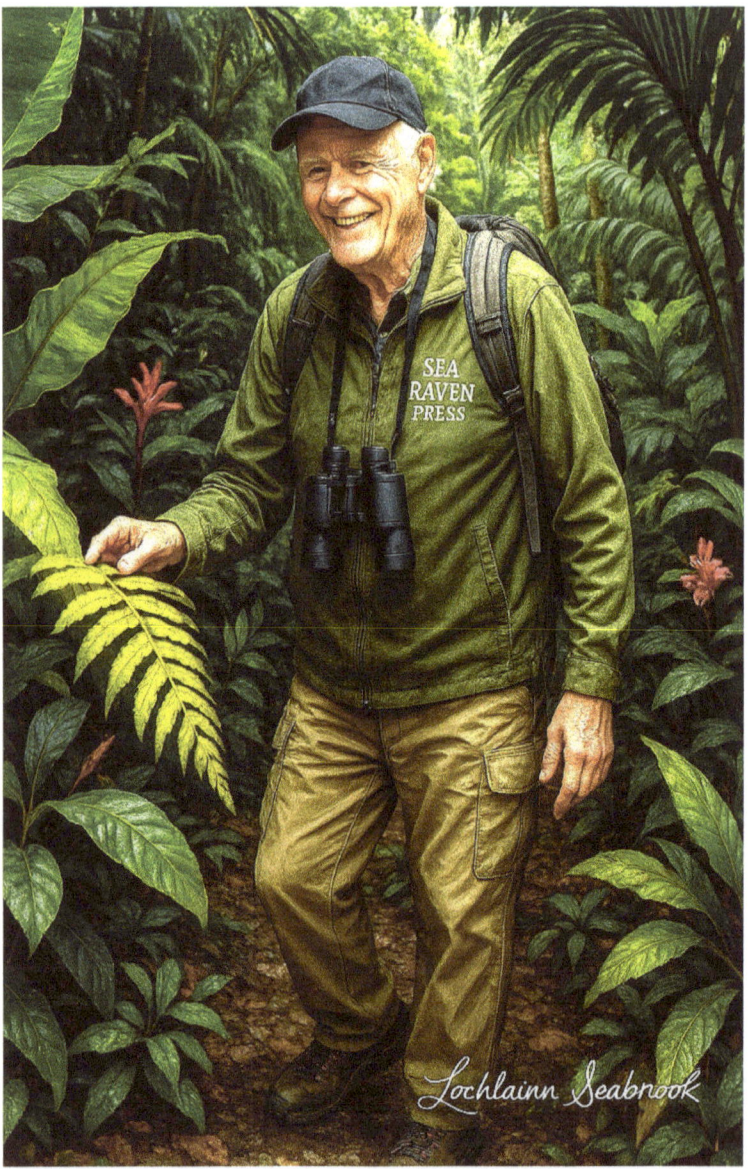

Charles Augustus Lindbergh as he might look today as a 70 year old nature lover, walking near his home in Kipahulu, Maui, Hawaii. Copyright © Lochlainn Seabrook.

HENRY WADSWORTH LONGFELLOW

1807-1882, Maine

Influential poet, author, novelist, literary scholar, literary celebrity, translator, college professor, foreign language teacher, international ambassador of American literature, textbook writer, traveler, left-leaning humanitarian and peace advocate.

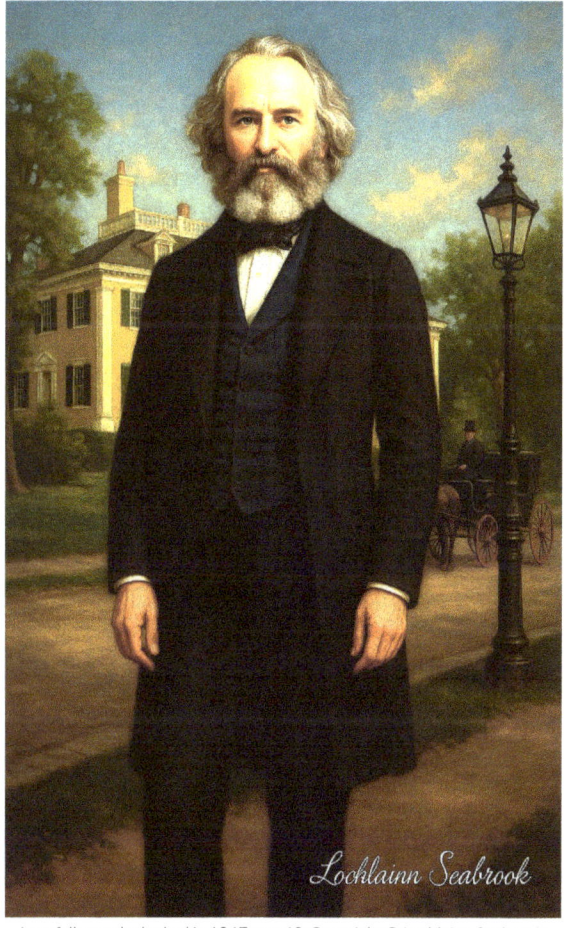

Longfellow as he looked in 1867, age 60. Copyright © Lochlainn Seabrook.

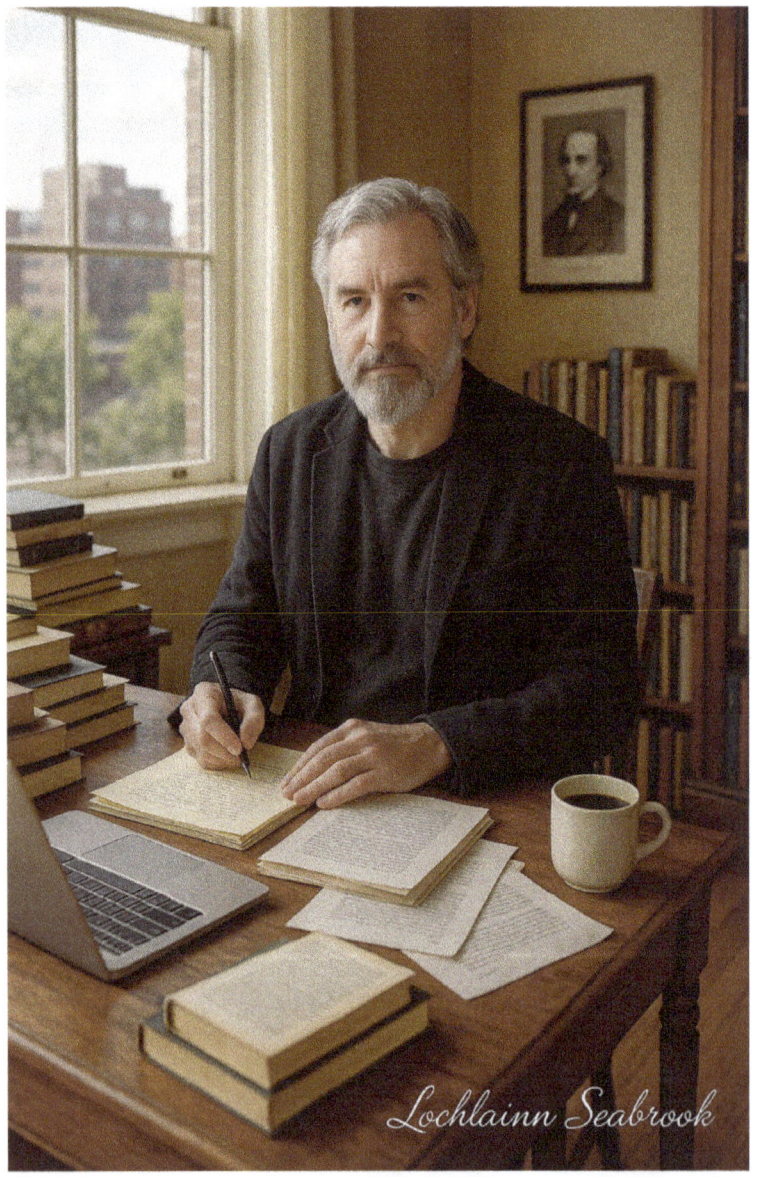

Longfellow as he might look today as a successful poet. Copyright © Lochlainn Seabrook.

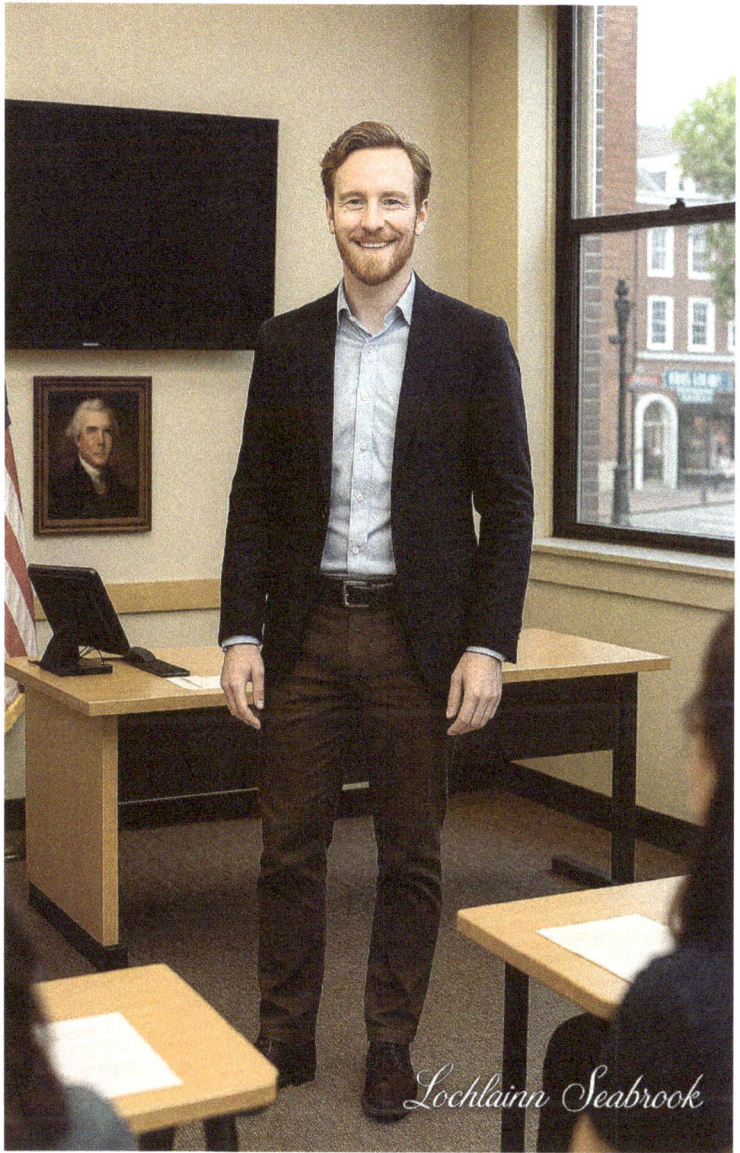

Longfellow as he might look today as a young Harvard professor of modern languages. Copyright © Lochlainn Seabrook.

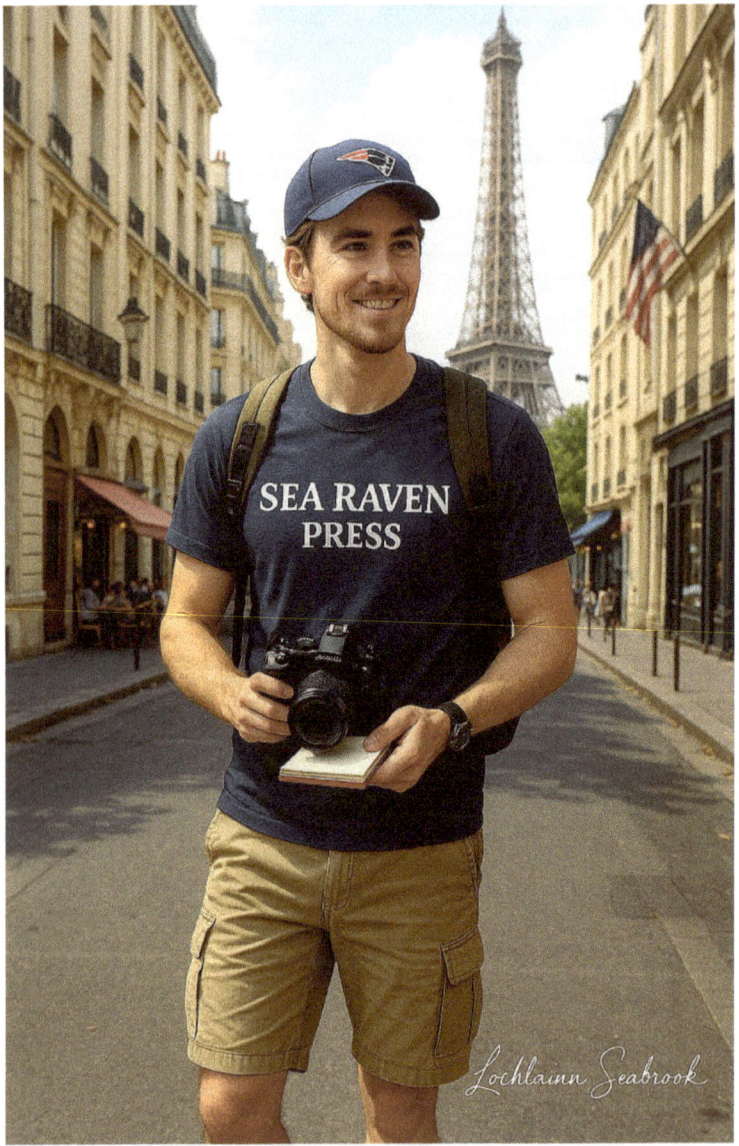

A youthful Henry Wadsworth Longfellow as he might look today engaging in one of his favorite pastimes: traveling in Europe. Copyright © Lochlainn Seabrook.

JAMES MADISON

1751-1836, Virginia

Conservative U.S. Founding Father, U.S. president, U.S. secretary of state, U.S. congressman, statesman, lawyer, farmer, political theorist, intellectual, key architect of the U.S. Constitution, author of the Bill of Rights, co-author of the *Federalist Papers*, limited government advocate.

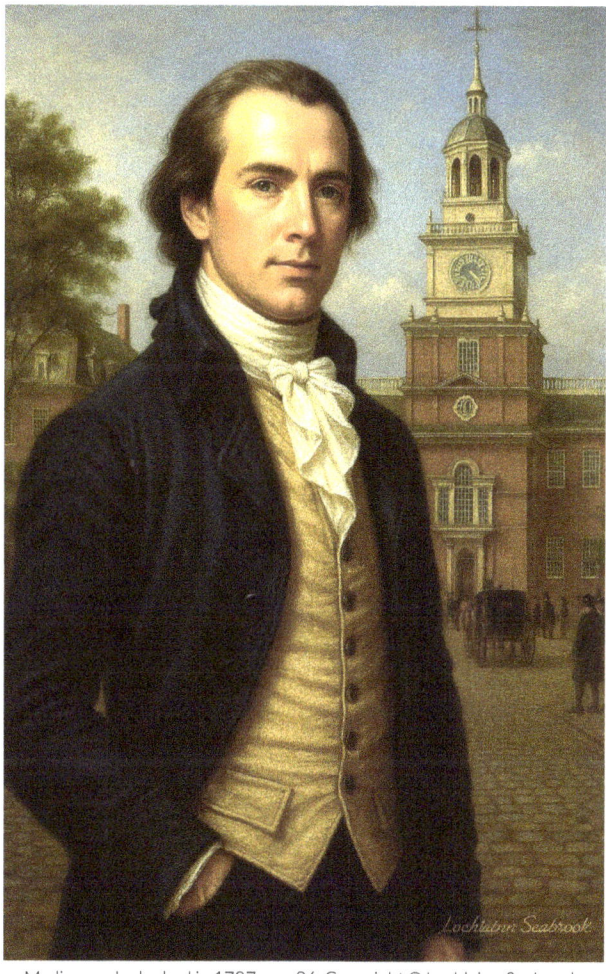

Madison as he looked in 1787, age 36. Copyright © Lochlainn Seabrook.

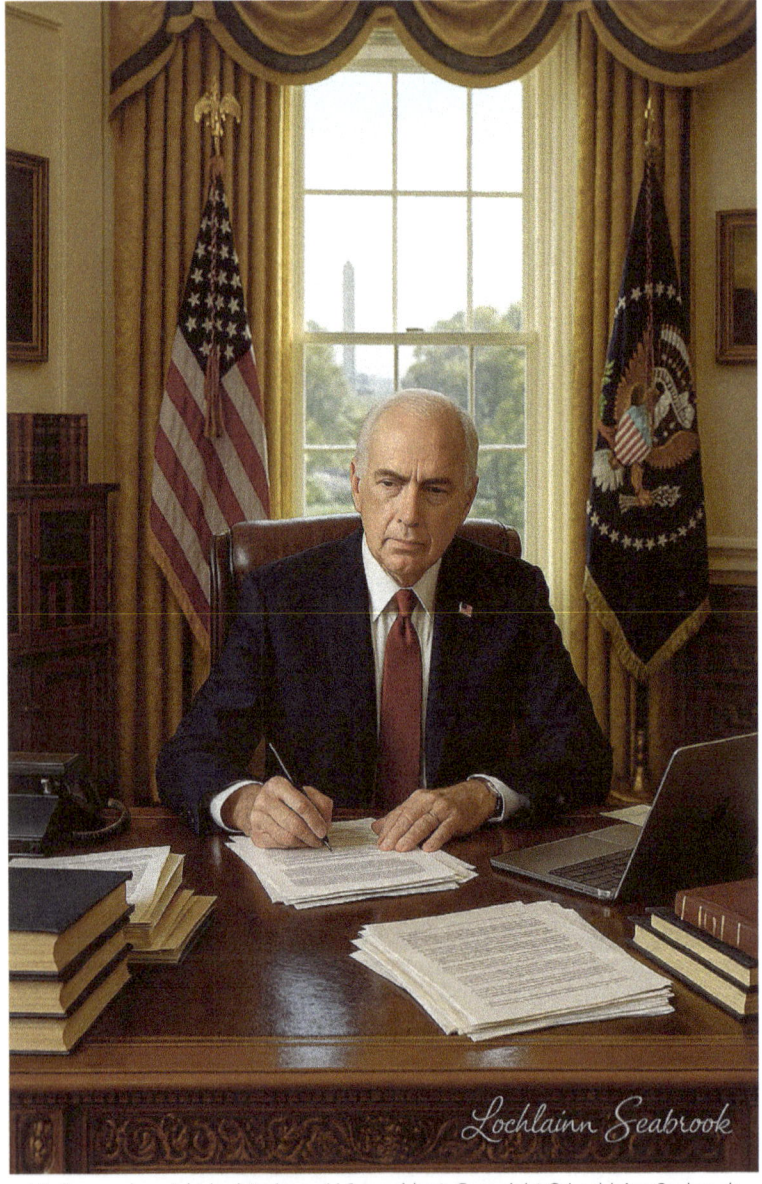

Madison as he might look today as U.S. president. Copyright © Lochlainn Seabrook.

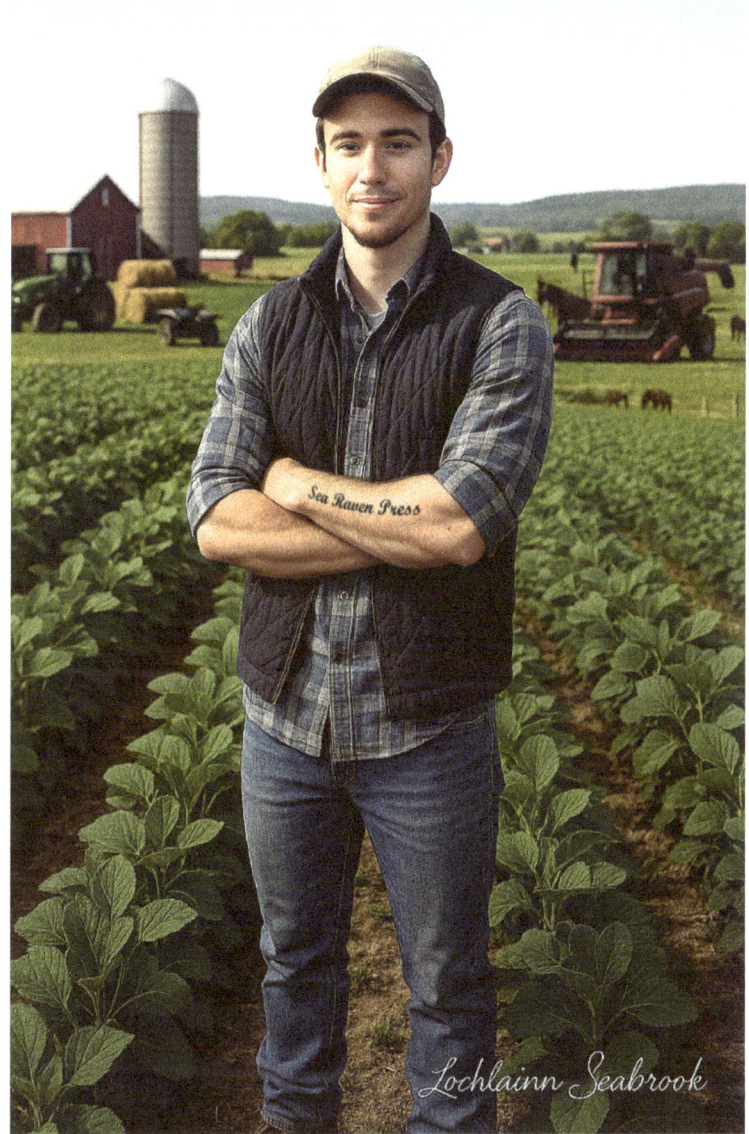

Madison as he might look in the 21st Century as a young farmer and estate manager. Copyright © Lochlainn Seabrook.

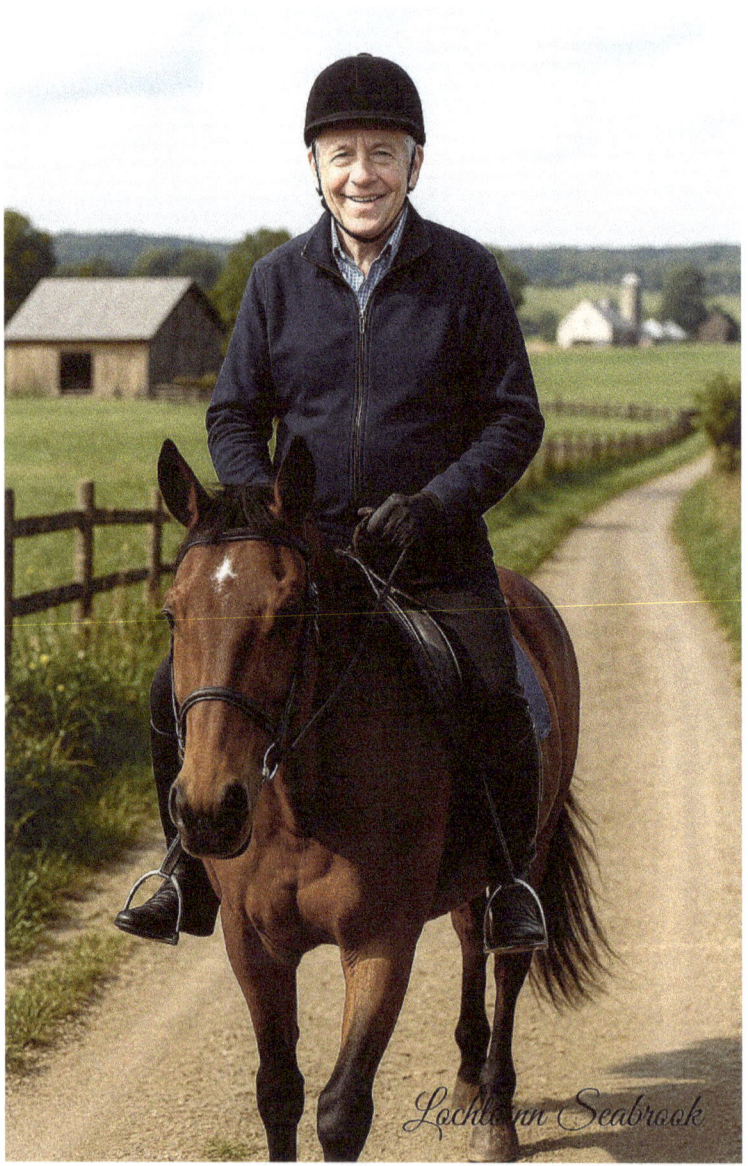

James Madison Jr. as he might look today enjoying one of his favorite hobbies: horseback riding. Copyright © Lochlainn Seabrook.

JOHN MUIR

1838-1914, Scotland

Naturalist, scientist, explorer, author, writer, lecturer, geologist, botanist, wilderness preservation advocate, machinist, inventor, wagon wheel factory worker, sheepherder, conservation movement leader, co-founder and first president of Sierra Club, "father of the national parks."

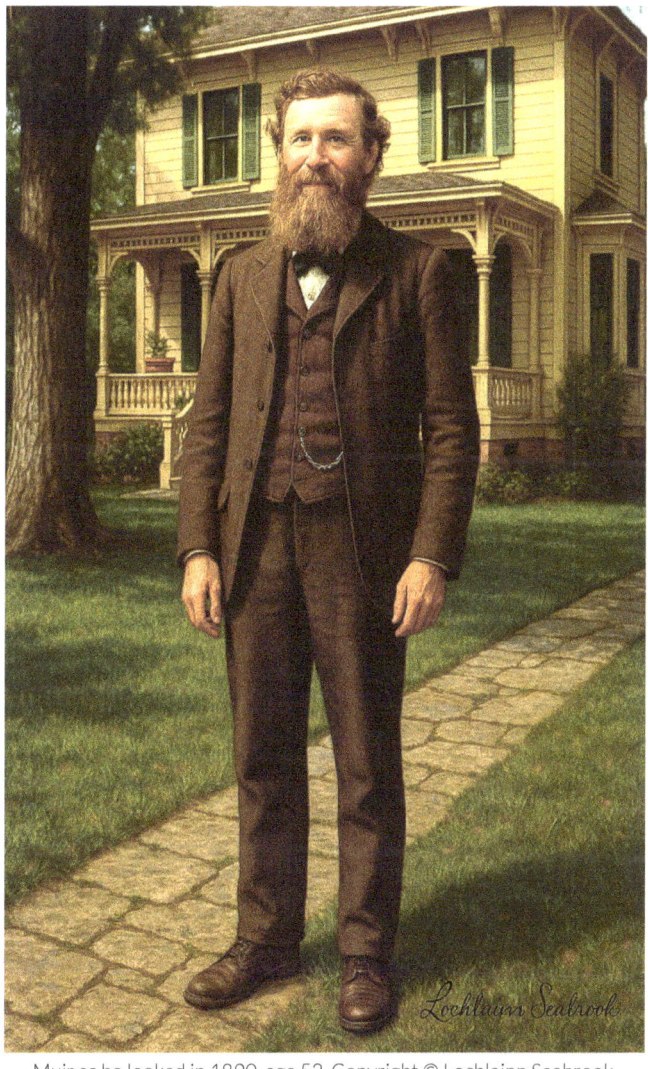

Muir as he looked in 1890, age 52. Copyright © Lochlainn Seabrook.

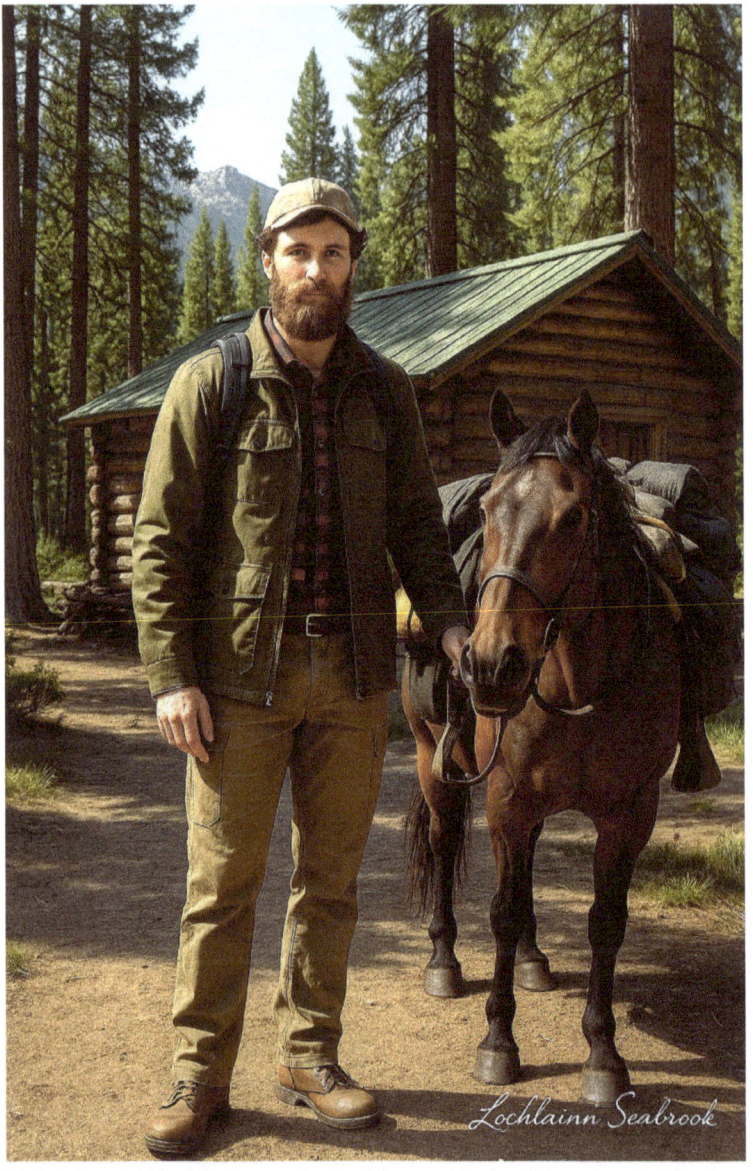

Muir as he might look today as a famous 31 year old naturalist, explorer, and author. Copyright © Lochlainn Seabrook.

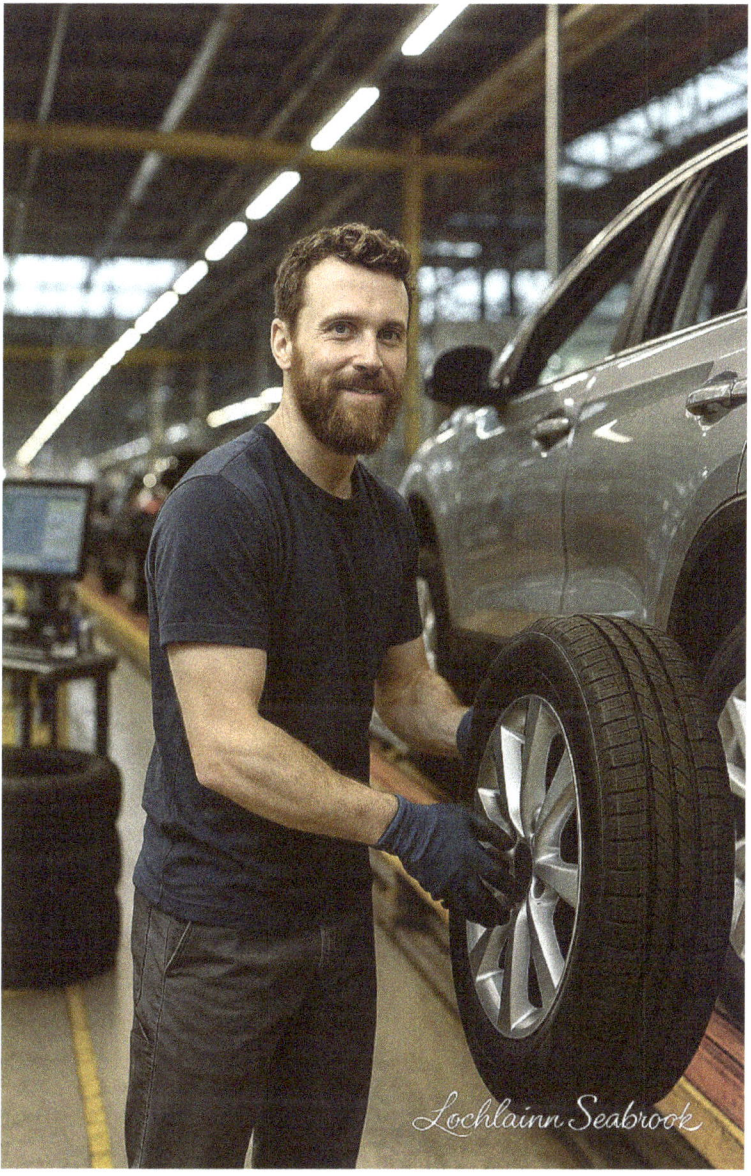

Muir as he might appear today as a 28 year old automobile factory worker. Copyright © Lochlainn Seabrook.

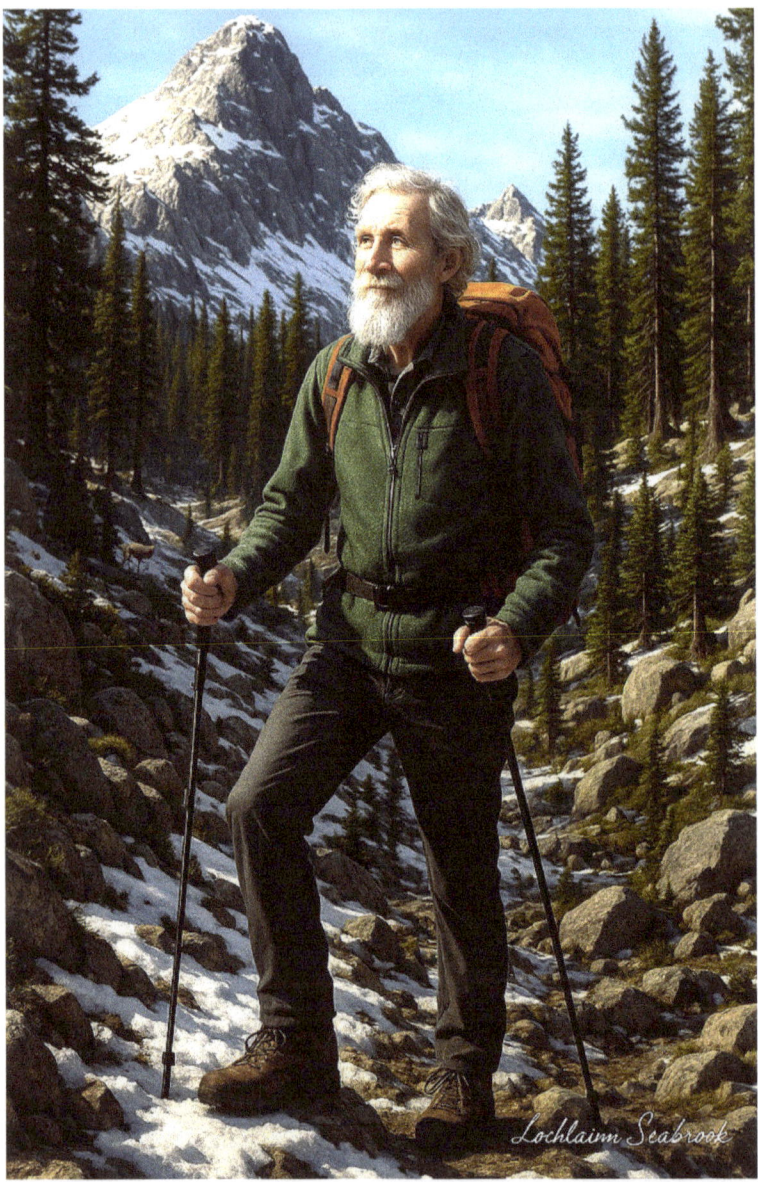

John Muir as he might look today as a 61 year old enjoying one of his favorite hobbies: mountaineering and collecting scientific data for his books. Copyright © Lochlainn Seabrook.

JOSÉ ANTONIO NAVARRO

1795-1871, Texas

Statesman, politician, landowner, Tejano leader in the Texas Revolution, Texas senator, Texas legislator, Texas congressional delegate, lawyer, merchant, trader, real estate investor, signer of the Texas Declaration of Independence, co-drafter of the Texas Constitution, Mexican-Texan civil rights advocate.

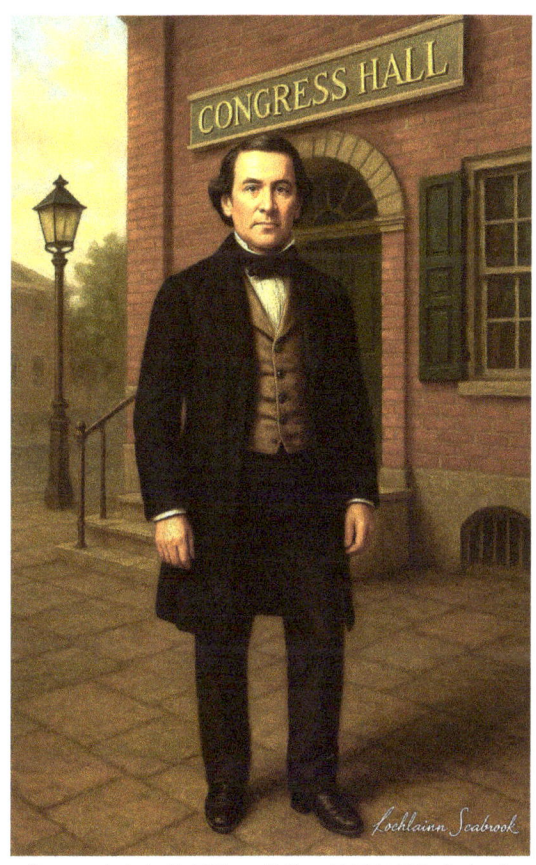

Navarro as he looked in 1836, age 41. Copyright © Lochlainn Seabrook.

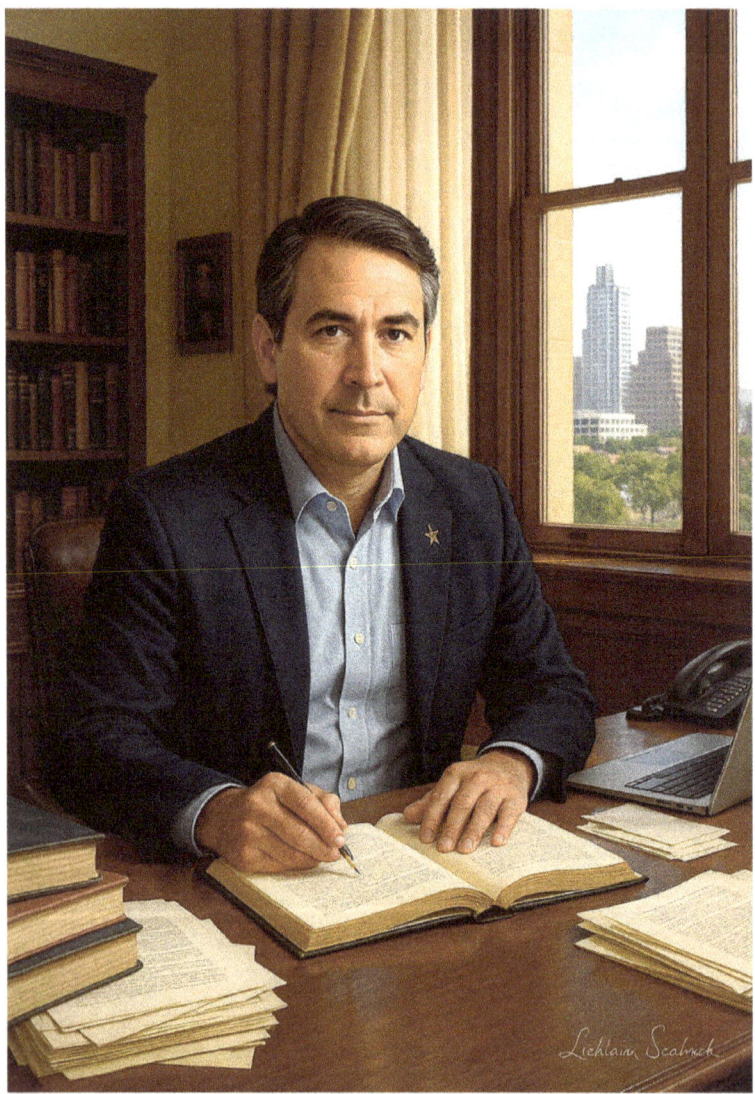

Navarro as he might look today as a Texas state senator. Copyright © Lochlainn Seabrook.

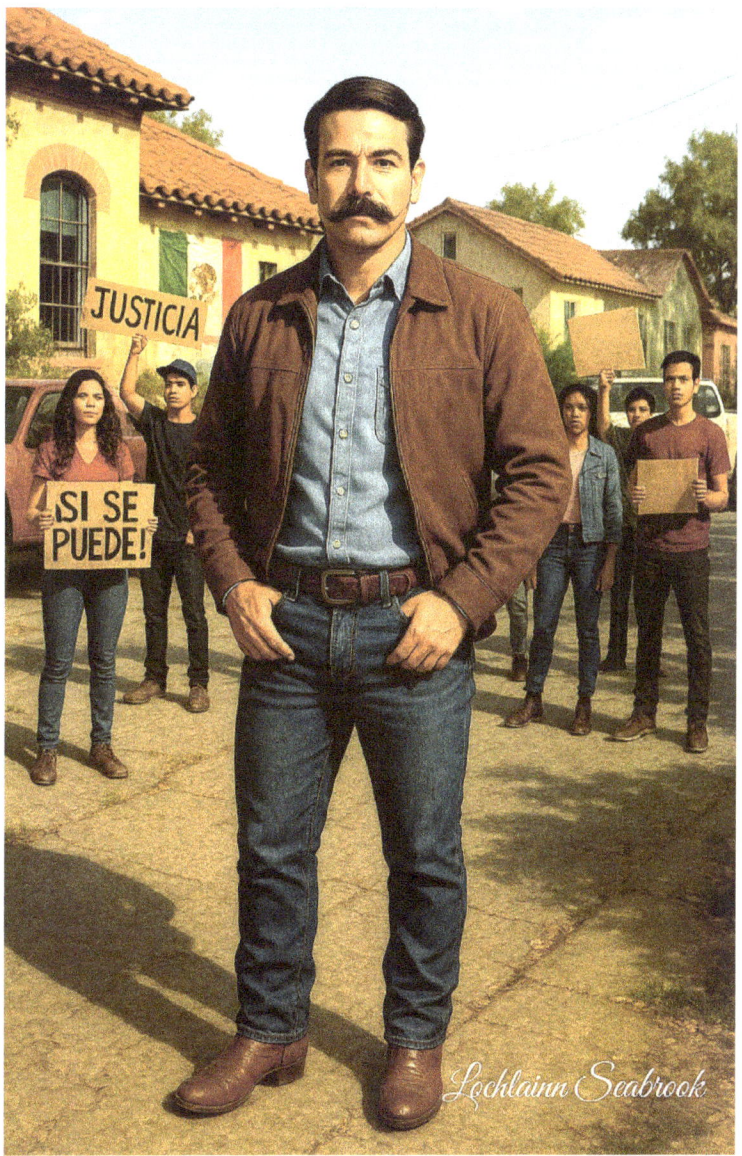

Navarro as he might look today as a Tejano civil rights activist. Copyright © Lochlainn Seabrook.

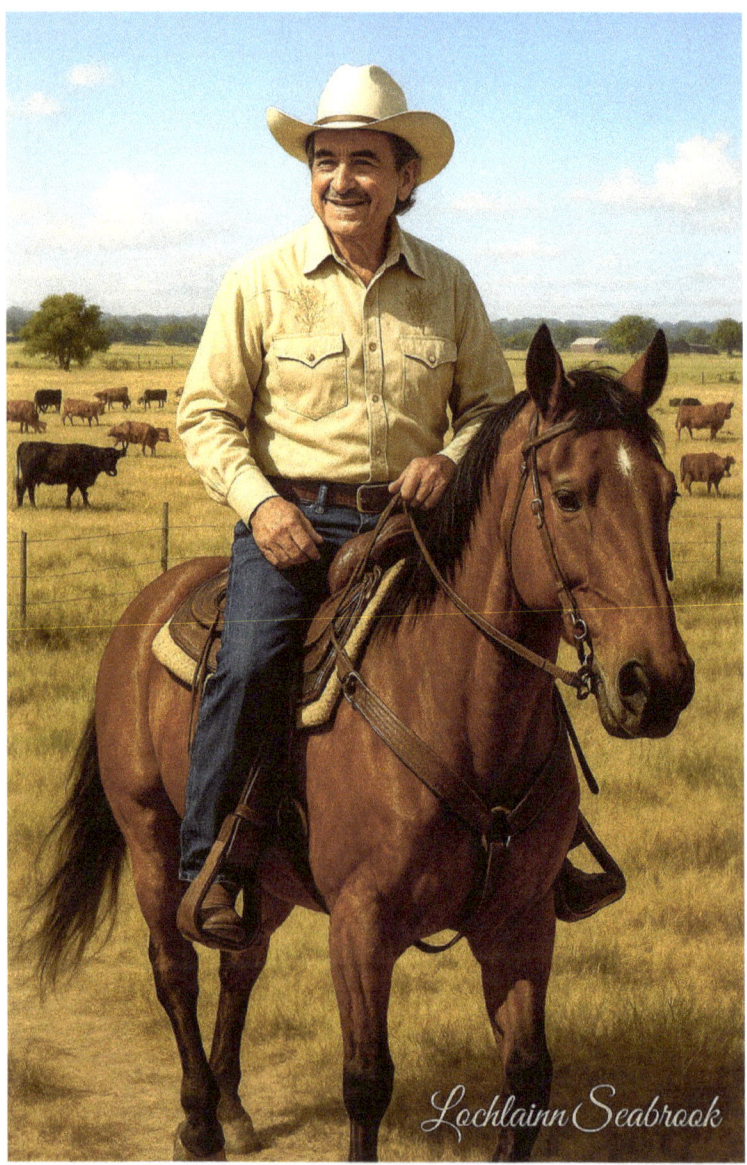

José Antonio Navarro as he might look today engaging in one of his favorite pastimes: ranching. Copyright © Lochlainn Seabrook.

FRANKLIN PIERCE

1804-1869, New Hampshire

Conservative U.S. president, U.S. senator, U.S. representative, state legislator, statesman, lawyer, Mexican-American War veteran, brigadier-general U.S. army, private citizen, strong states' rights advocate, passionate Confederate friend and supporter.

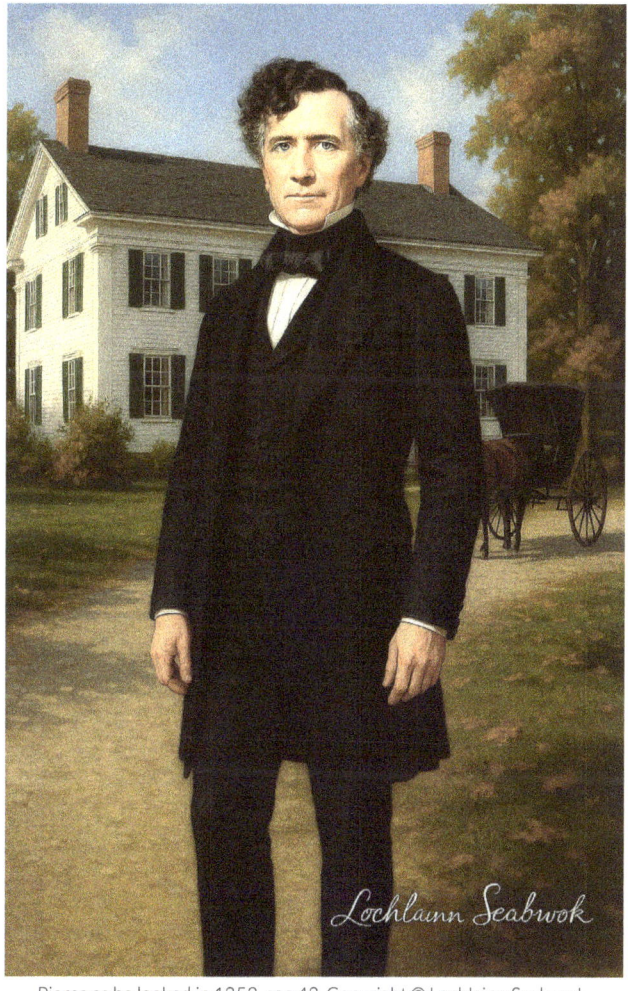

Pierce as he looked in 1853, age 48. Copyright © Lochlainn Seabrook.

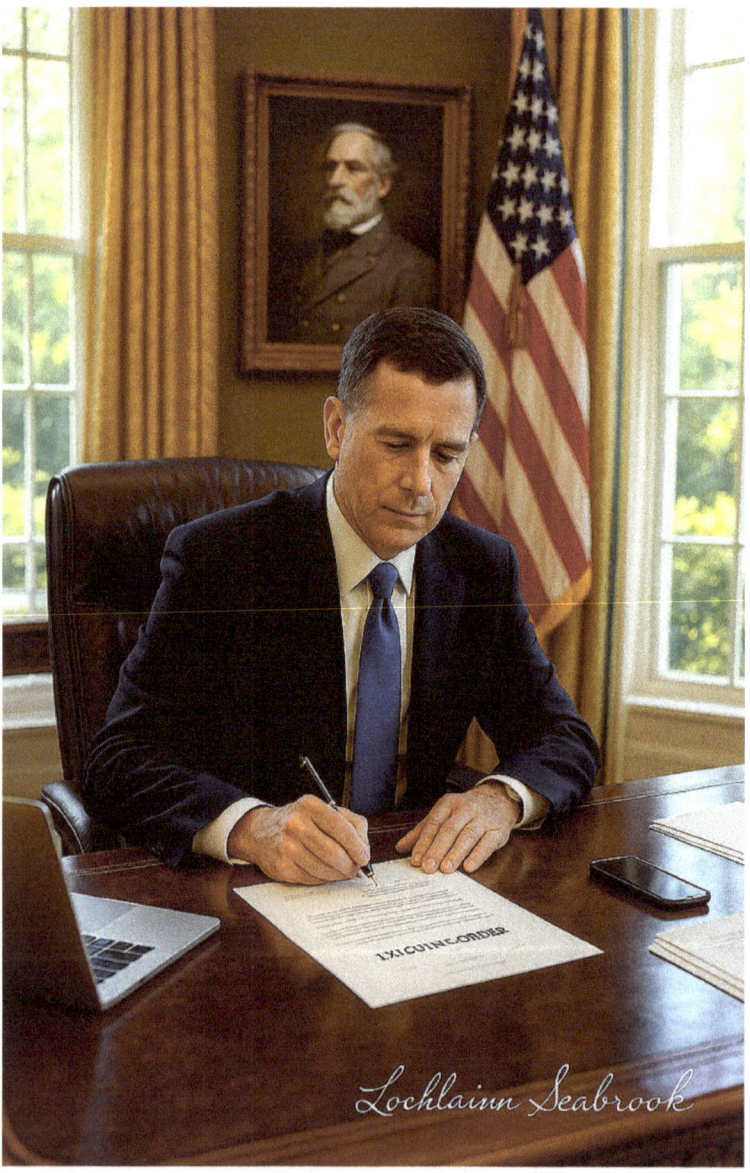

Pierce as he might look today as U.S. president, age 50. Copyright © Lochlainn Seabrook.

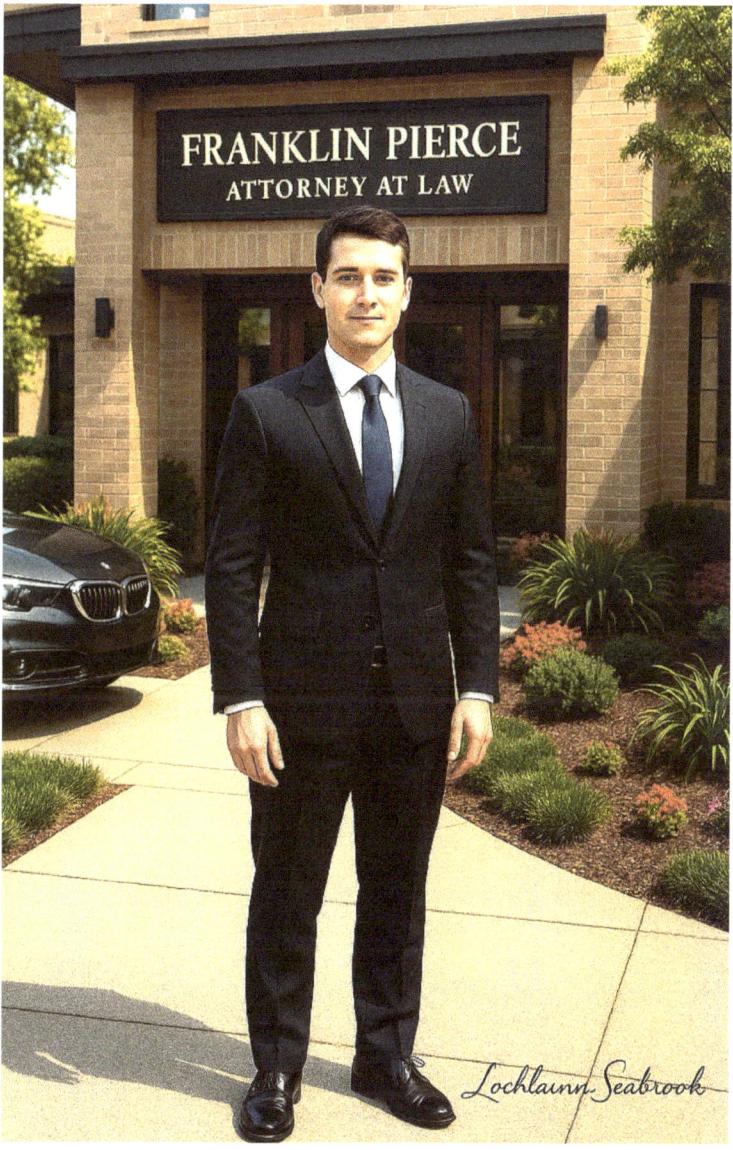

Pierce as he might appear today as a successful 23 year old New Hampshire lawyer. Copyright © Lochlainn Seabrook.

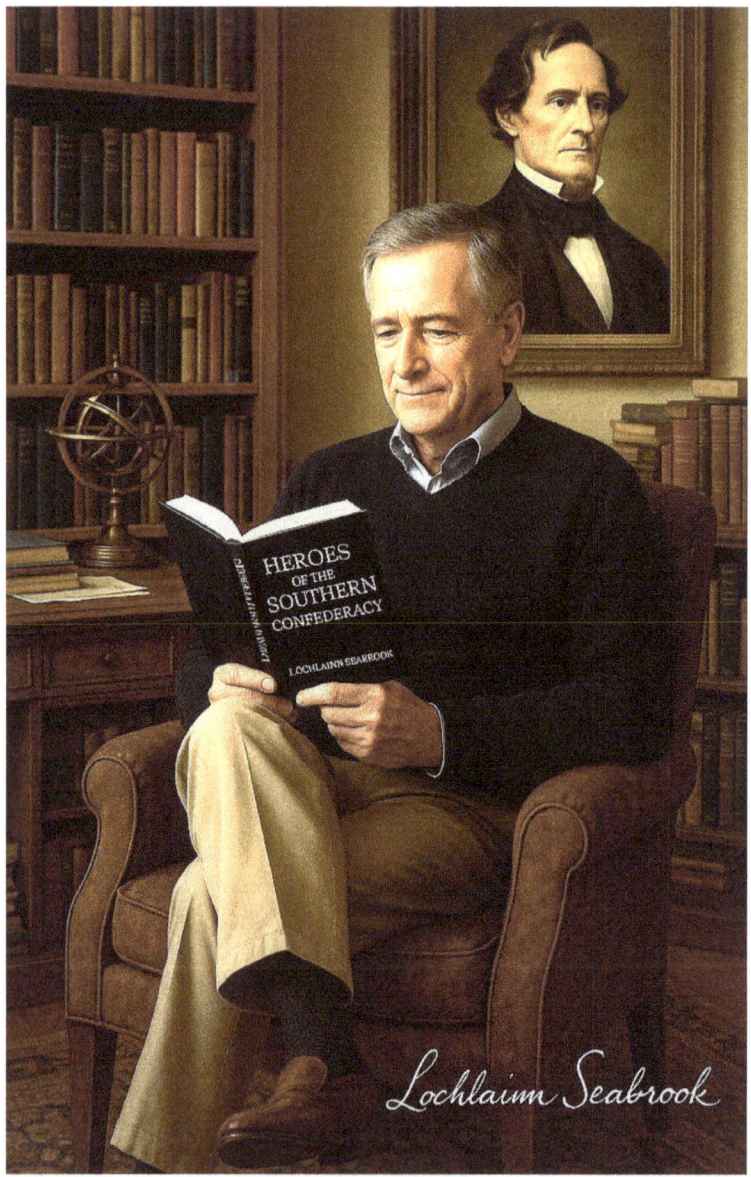

Franklin Pierce as he might look today as a 63 year old statesman enjoying one of his favorite hobbies: reading history books. Copyright © Lochlainn Seabrook.

EDGAR ALLAN POE

1809-1849, Massachusetts

Literary author, editor, poet, short story writer, literary critic, West Point cadet, U.S. army soldier, clerk, freelance journalist, book reviewer, helped develop American Gothic literature, the horror genre, and the modern detective genre.

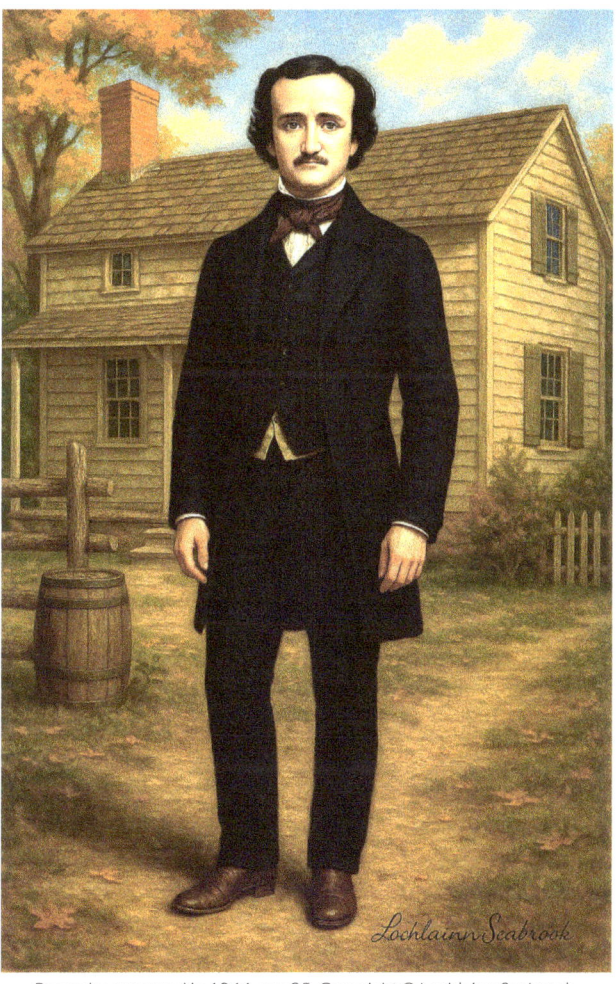

Poe as he appeared in 1844, age 35. Copyright © Lochlainn Seabrook.

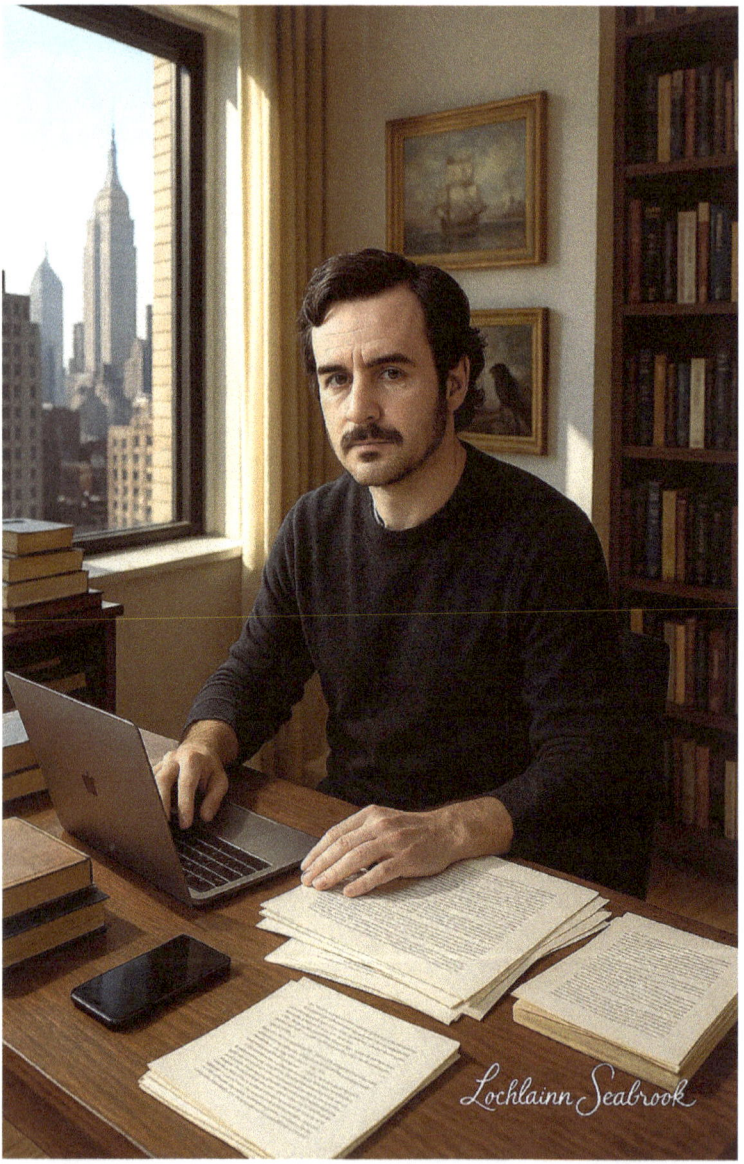

Poe as he might look today as a 40 year old literary author. Copyright © Lochlainn Seabrook.

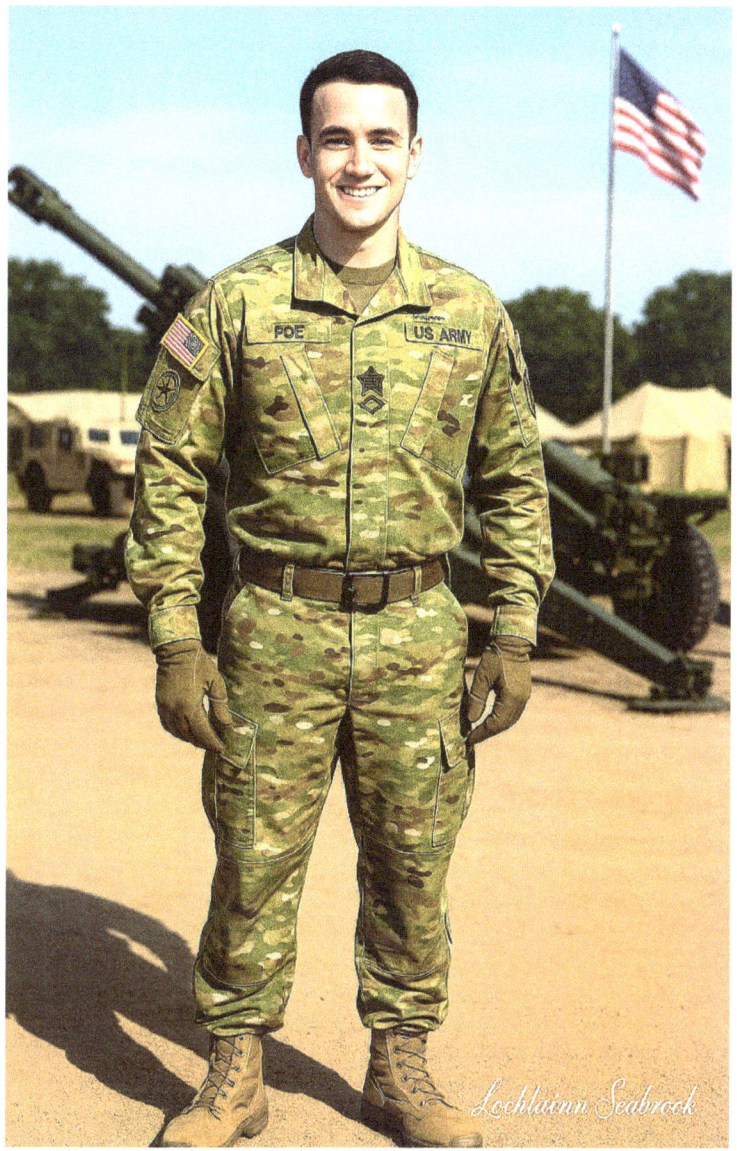

Poe as he might look today as a 19 year old U.S. army sergeant major of artillery. Copyright © Lochlainn Seabrook.

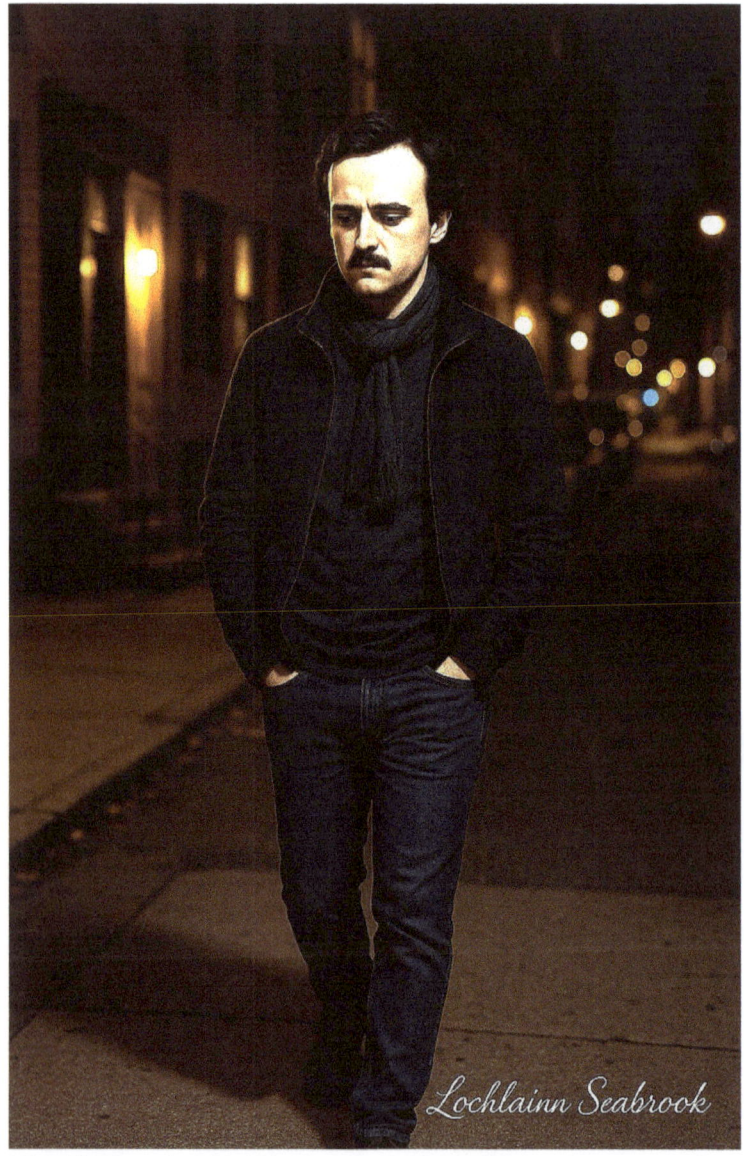

Edgar Allan Poe as he might look today engaging in one of his favorite pastimes: solitary night walking in the city. Copyright © Lochlainn Seabrook.

PAUL REVERE

1735-1818, Massachusetts

Political conservative, industrialist, businessman, entrepreneur, silversmith, engraver, founder of the Revere Copper Company, key player in the opening of the Revolutionary War, freedom lover, limited government proponent, copper production pioneer.

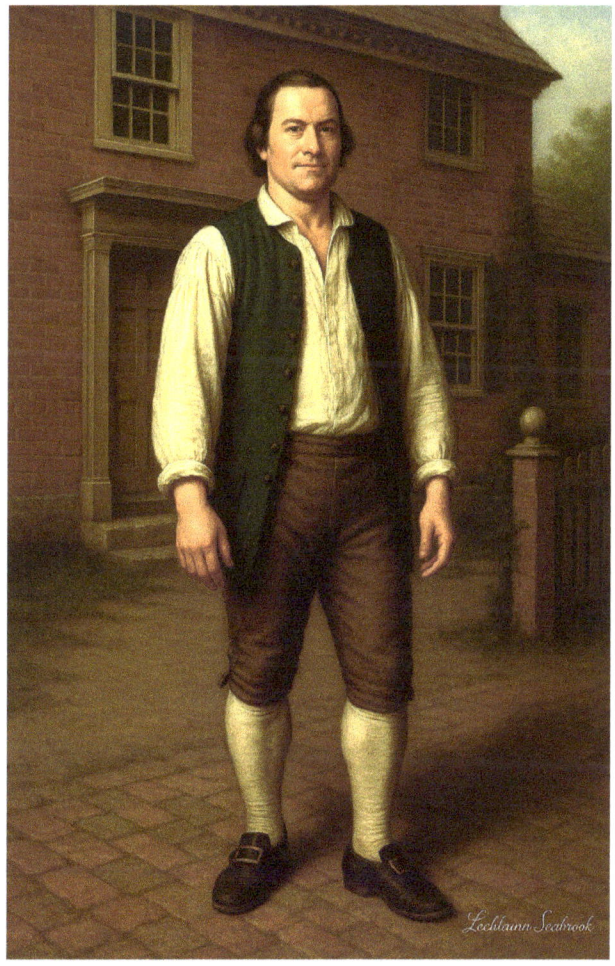

Revere as he looked in 1775, age 40. Copyright © Lochlainn Seabrook.

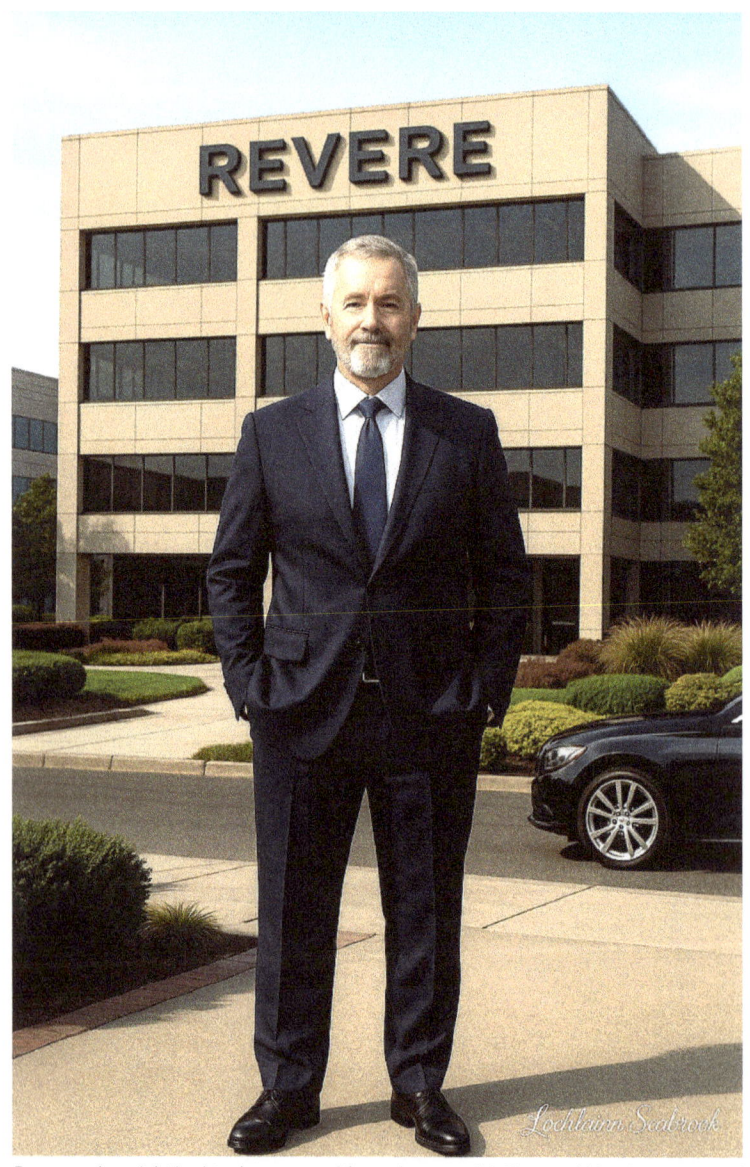

Revere as he might look today as a wealthy and successful 65 year old businessman and entrepreneur. Copyright © Lochlainn Seabrook.

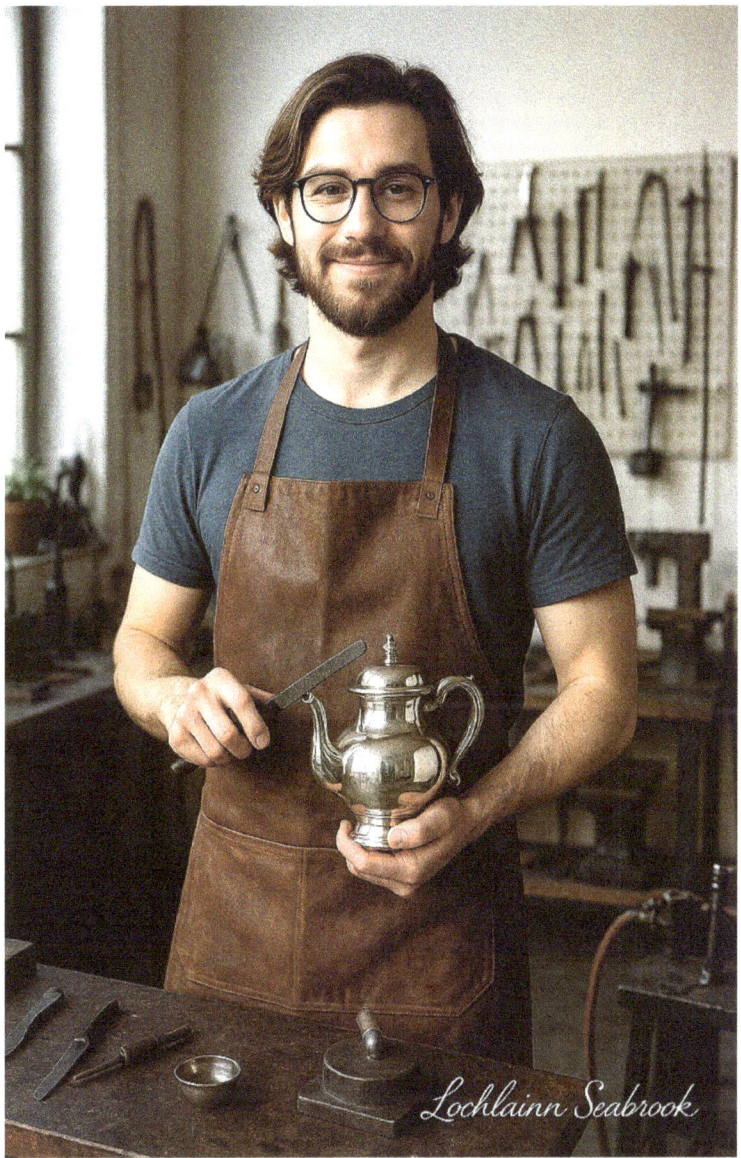

Revere as he might look today as a 25 year old artisan and silversmith. Copyright © Lochlainn Seabrook.

190 ∞ IF THEY WERE ALIVE TODAY

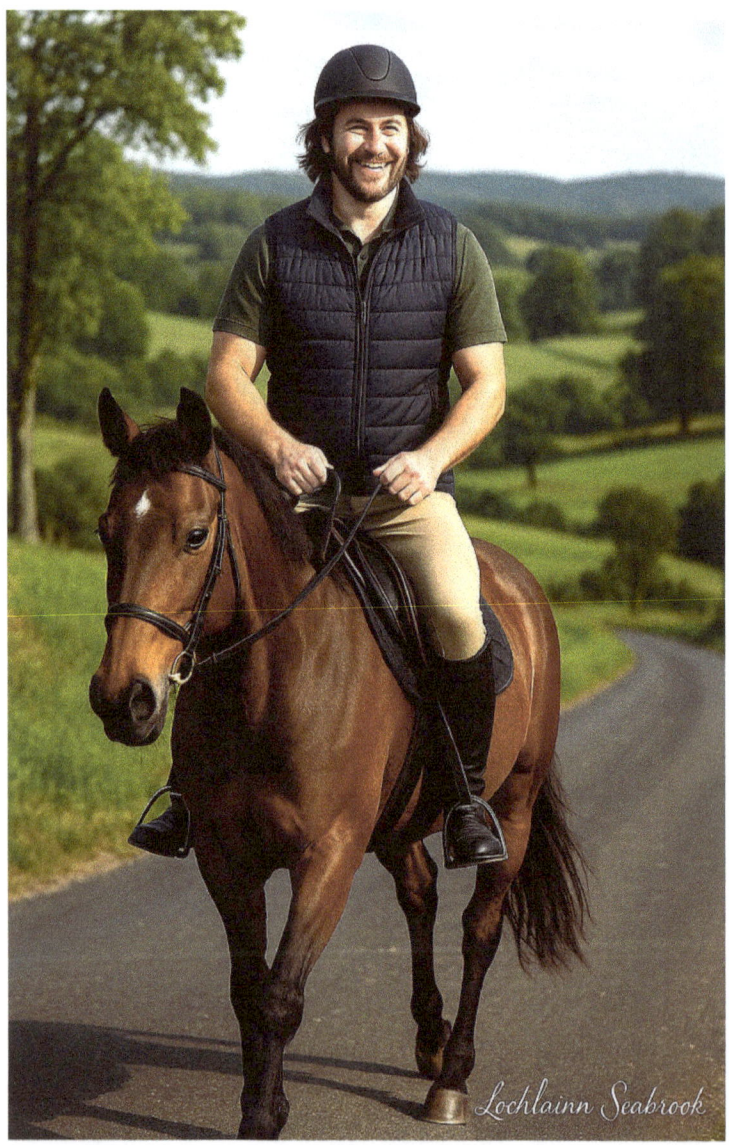

Paul Revere Jr. as he might look today engaging in one of his favorite activities: horseback riding in the New England countryside. Copyright © Lochlainn Seabrook.

THEODORE ROOSEVELT

1858-1919, New York

U.S. president, pro-Western nationalist, right-leaning progressive, statesman, reformer, international diplomat, New York state legislator, author, rancher, naturalist, NYC police commissioner, member of the U.S. Civil Service Commission, lecturer, founder of the Bull Moose Party, conservationist, established numerous national parks, Spanish-American War veteran, lieutenant colonel in the Rough Riders cavalry regiment, spear-headed the building of the Panama Canal, created the U.S. Forest Service, the "father of American conservation."

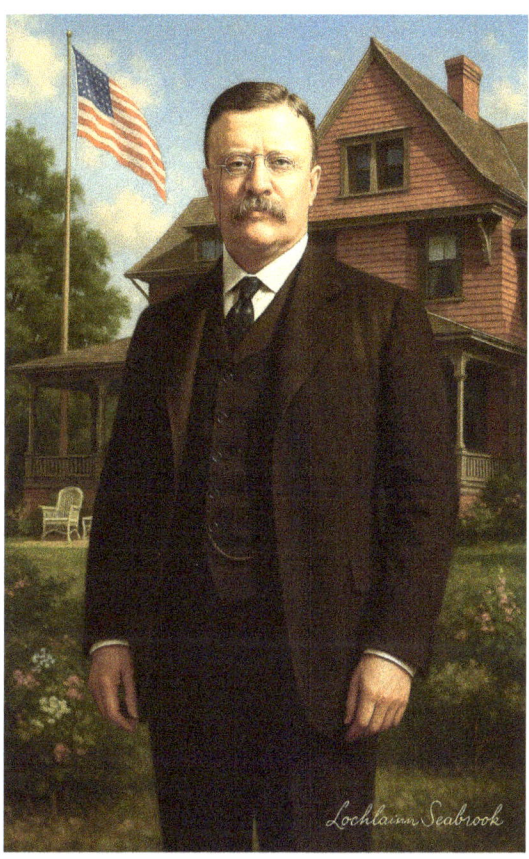

Roosevelt as he looked in 1906, age 48. Copyright © Lochlainn Seabrook.

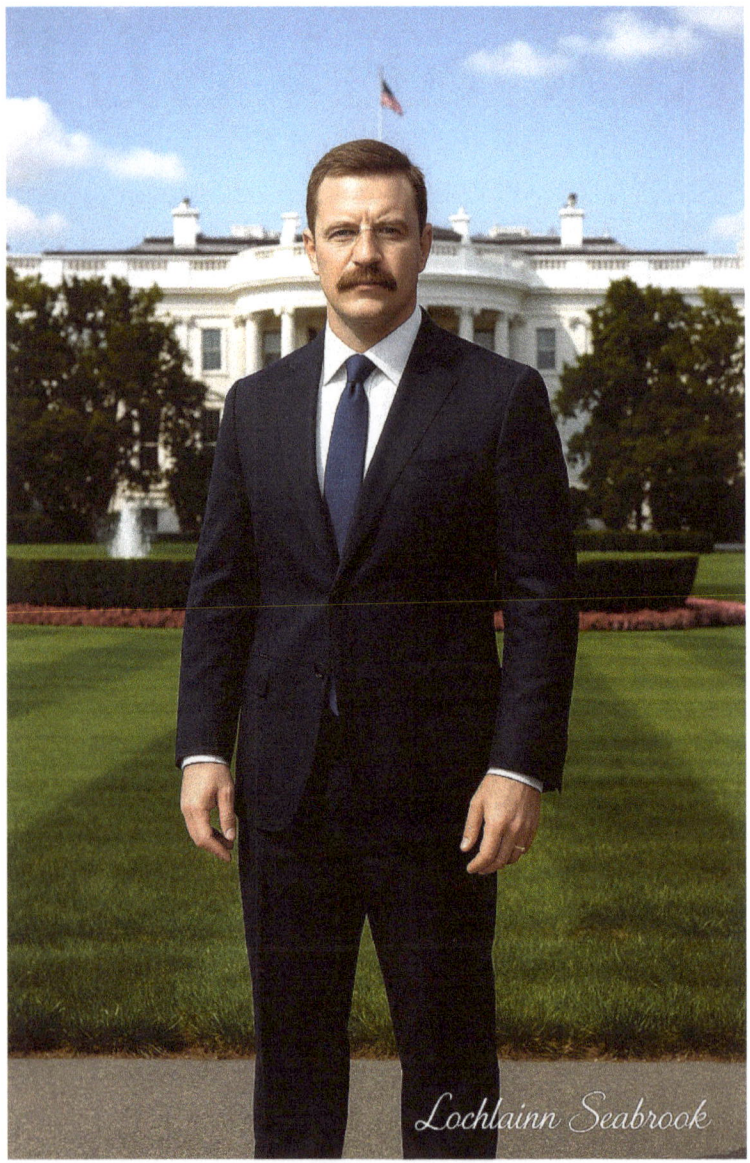

Roosevelt as he might look today as U.S. president. Copyright © Lochlainn Seabrook.

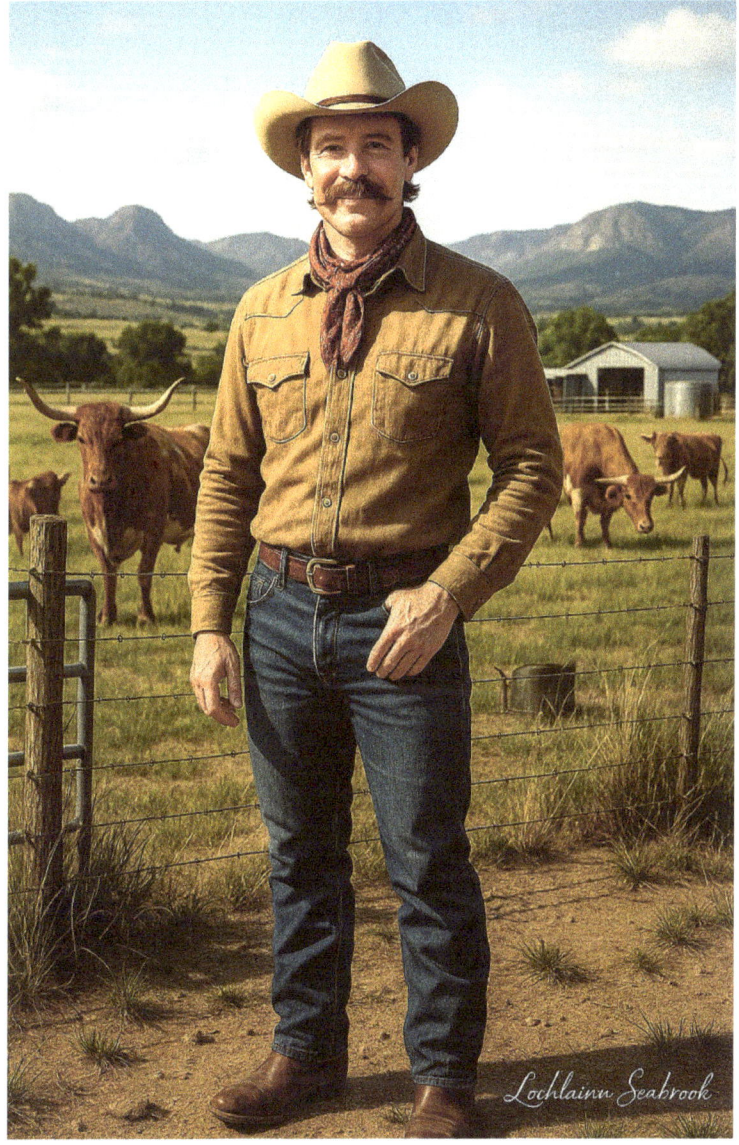

Roosevelt as he might appear today as a 30 year old North Dakota longhorn cattle rancher. Copyright © Lochlainn Seabrook.

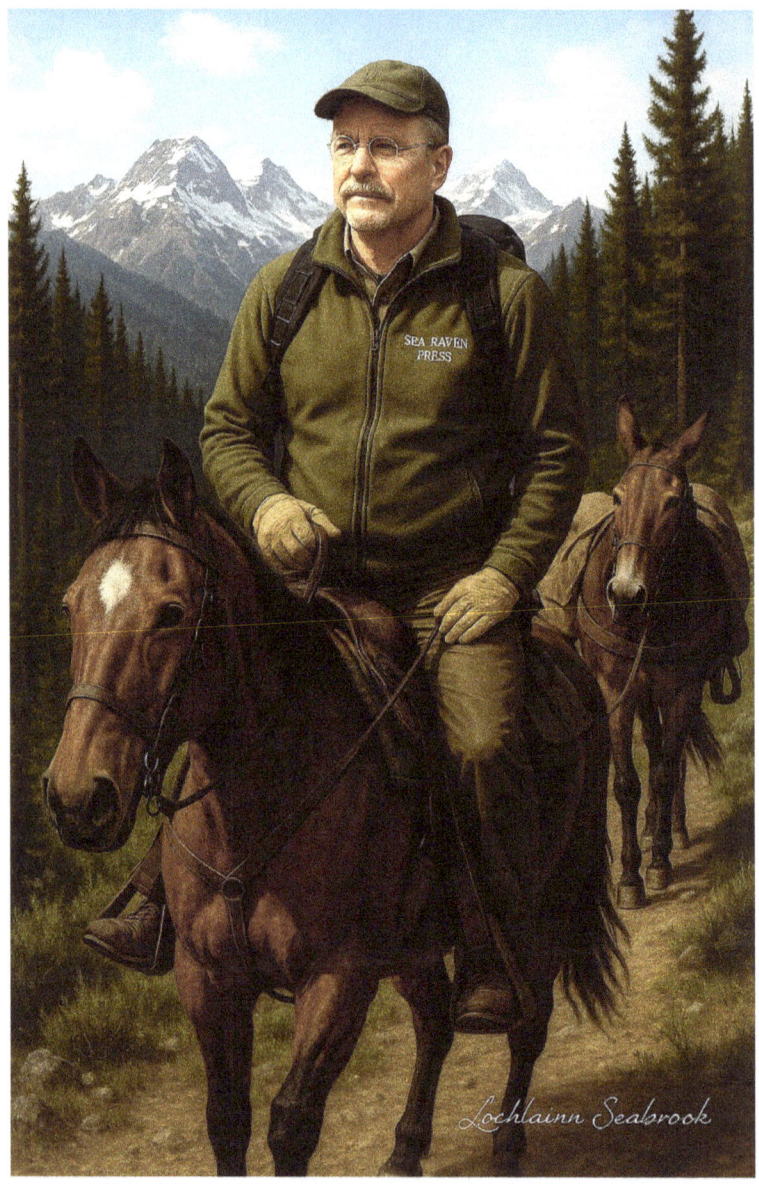

Theodore "Teddy" Roosevelt as he might look today as a 55 year old naturalist engaging in one of his favorite hobbies: wilderness exploration. Copyright © Lochlainn Seabrook.

MILDRED LEWIS RUTHERFORD

1851-1928, Georgia

Conservative Southern historian, American patriot, intellectual, author, orator, lecturer, Confederate advocate, Confederate memorialist, historian general of the United Daughters of the Confederacy (UDC), school principle, educator, school administrator, manager of the Lucy Cobb Institute (for Southern girls), publisher, UDC organizer, "Joan of Arc of the South."

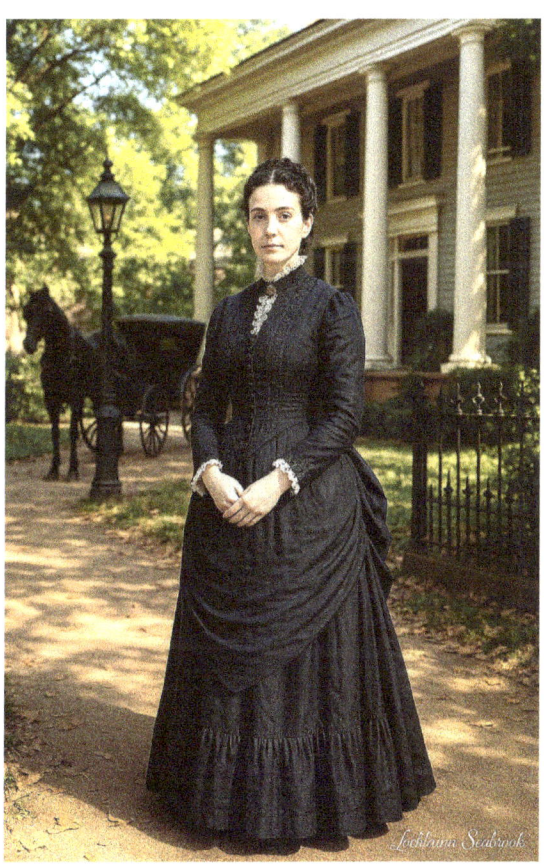

Rutherford as she looked in 1881, age 30. Copyright © Lochlainn Seabrook

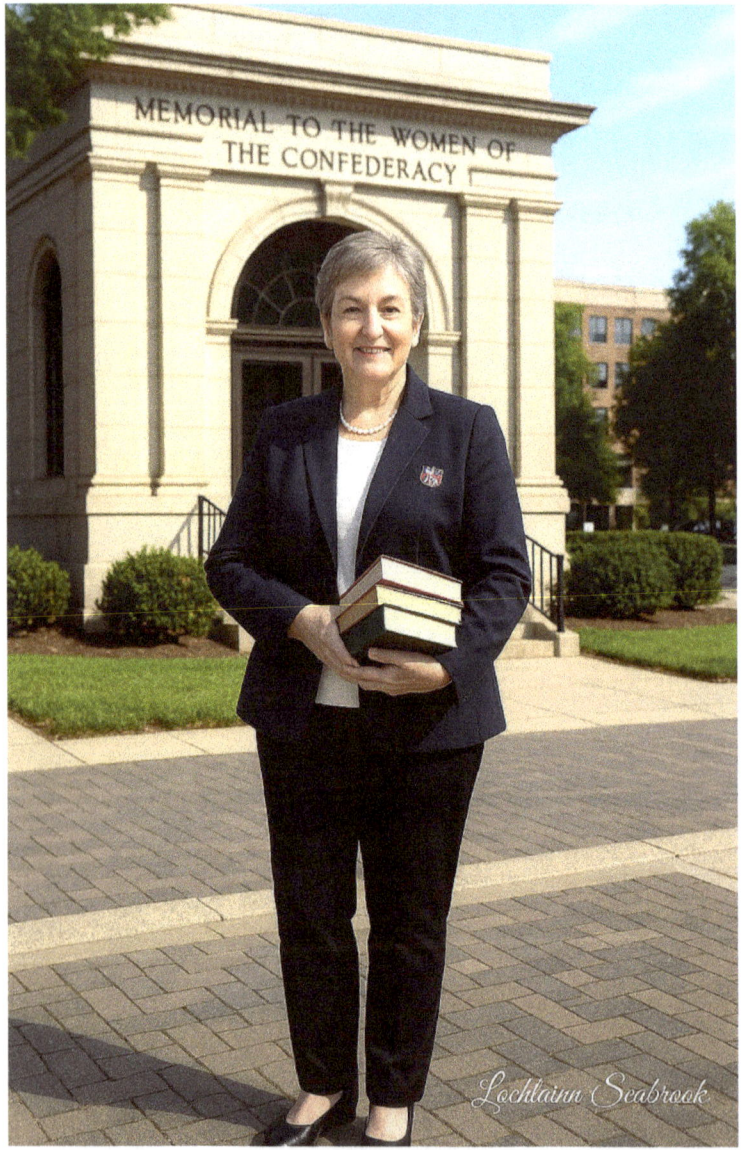

Rutherford as she might look today as Historian General of the United Daughters of the Confederacy, age 62. Copyright © Lochlainn Seabrook.

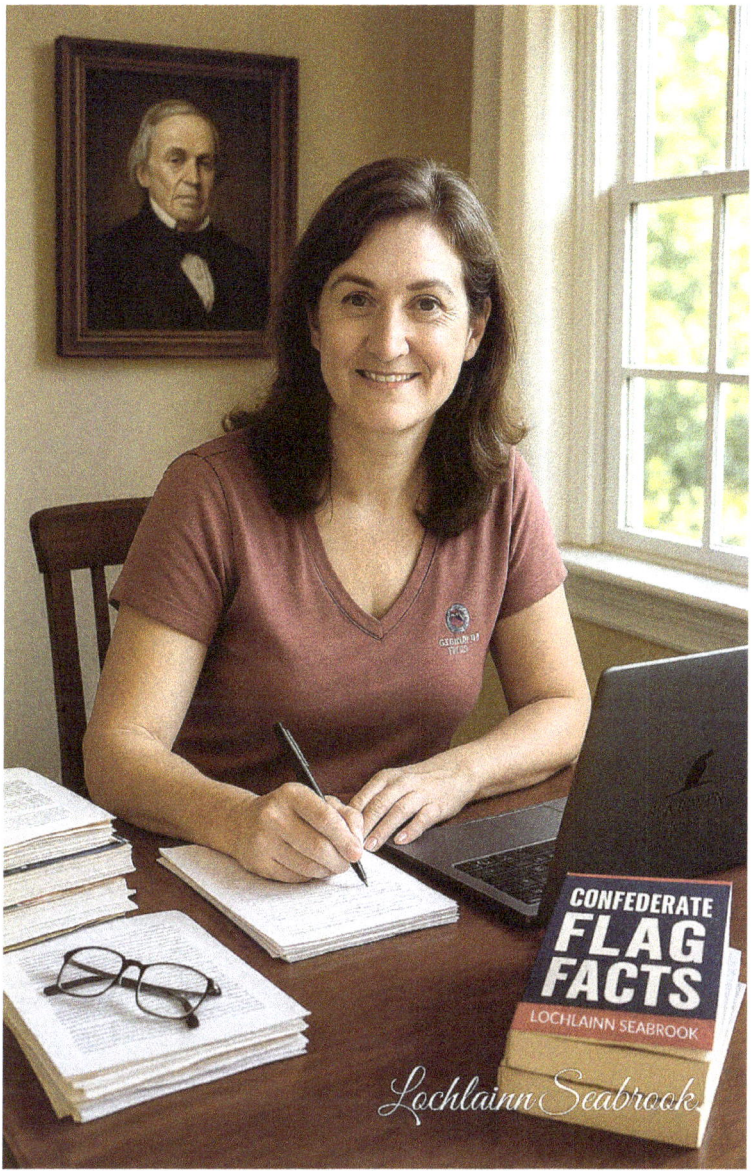

Rutherford as she might appear today as a 51 year old Southern writer and Confederate memorialist. Copyright © Lochlainn Seabrook.

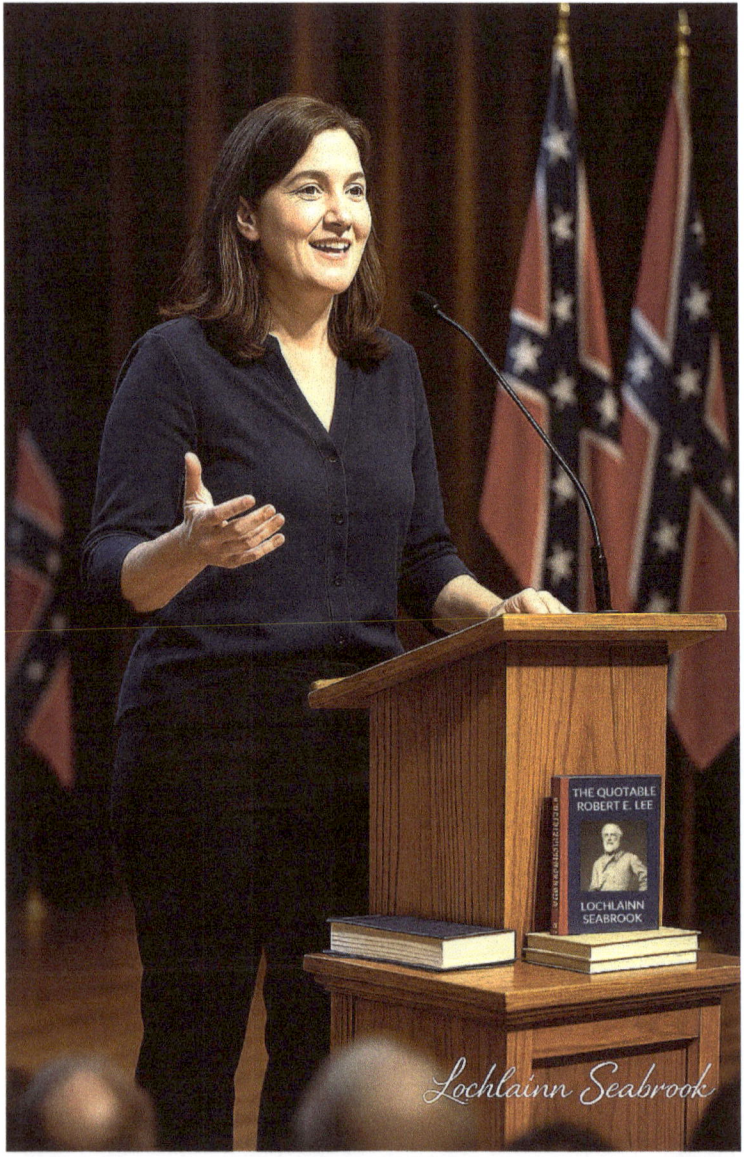

Mildred Lewis Rutherford as she might look today as a 42 year old pro-South public speaker, lecturer, and Confederate heritage preservation advocate. Copyright © Lochlainn Seabrook.

SITTING BULL

c. 1831-1890, South Dakota

Hunkpapa Lakota Sioux tribal leader, tribal spokesman, medicine man, military leader, spiritual leader, hunter, marksman, warrior, raider, equestrian, orator, storyteller, public performer in Buffalo Bill's Wild West Show, influenced the Battle of Little Bighorn.

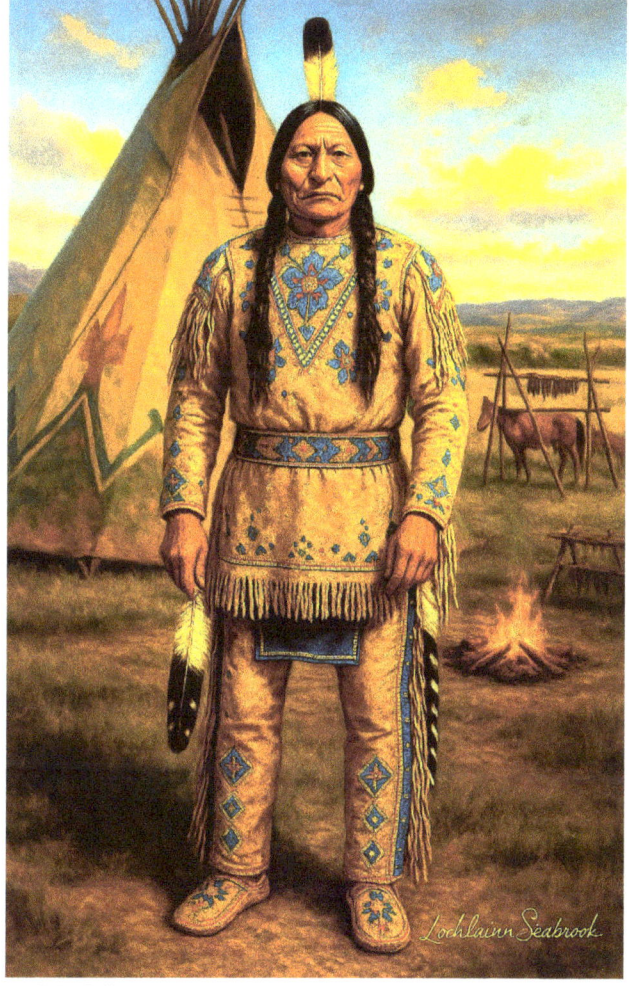

Sitting Bull as he appeared in 1876, age 45. Copyright © Lochlainn Seabrook.

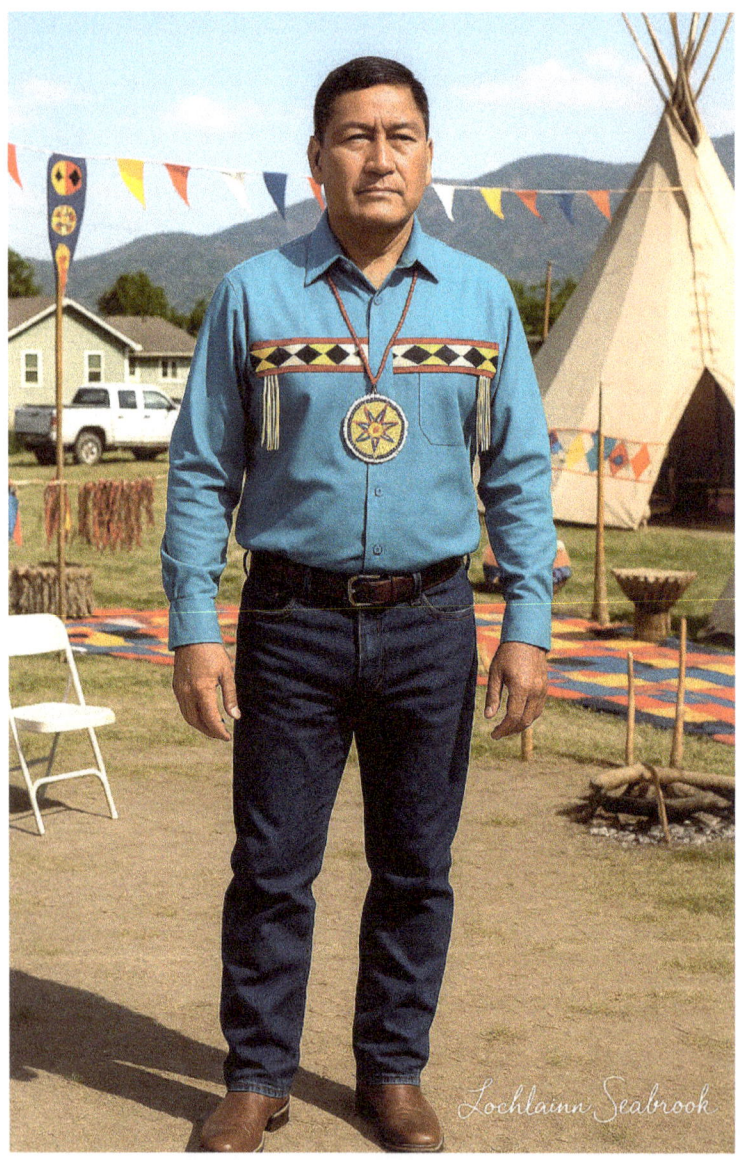

Sitting Bull as he might look today as a Hunkpapa Lakota Sioux tribal leader. Copyright © Lochlainn Seabrook.

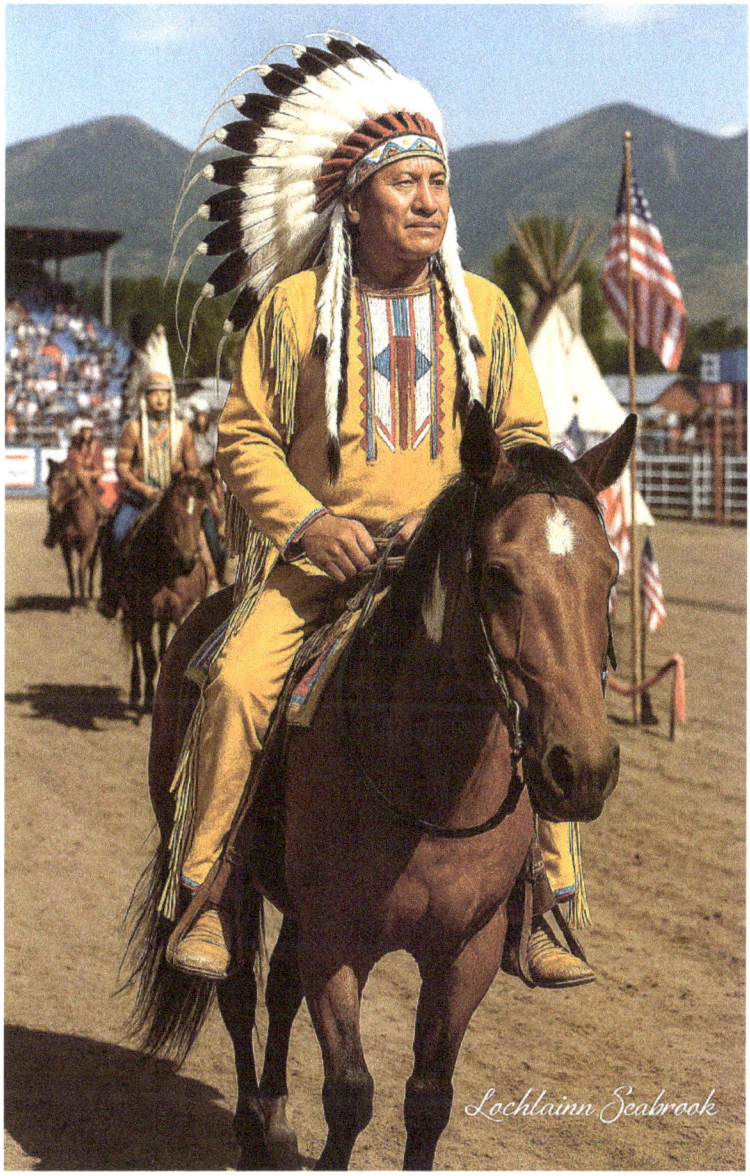

Sitting Bull as he might appear today as a public performer in a "Wild West Show." Copyright © Lochlainn Seabrook.

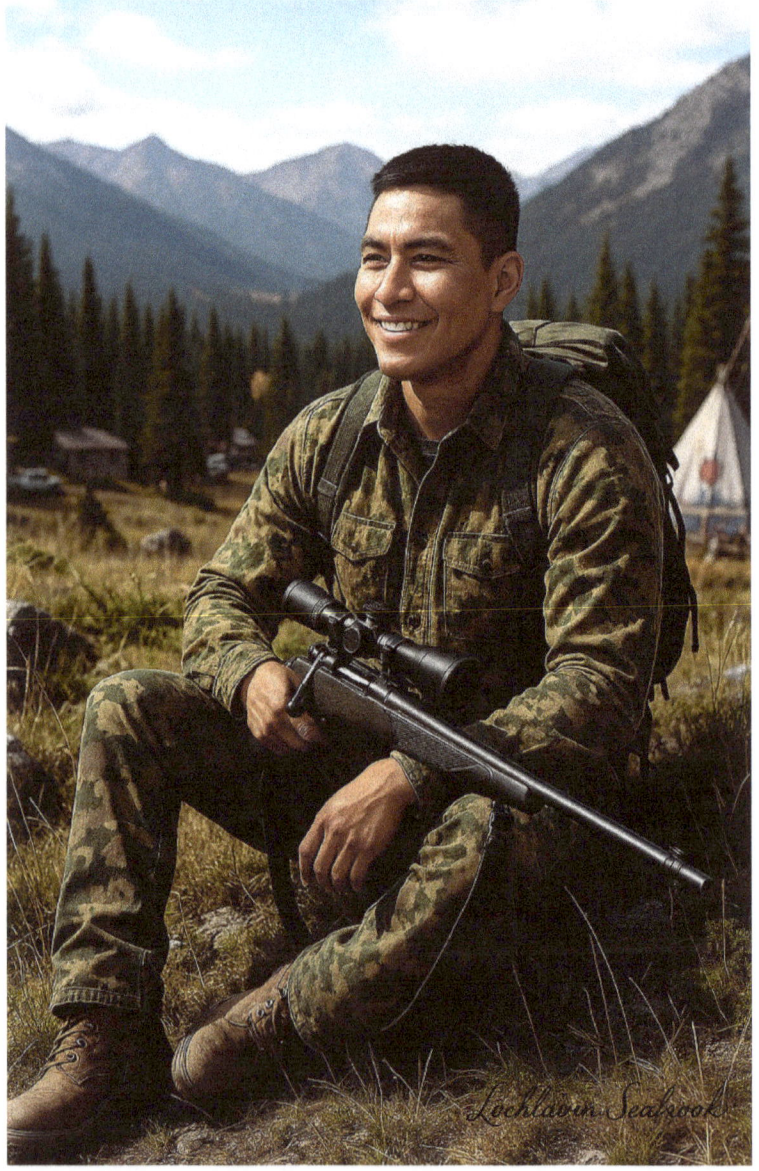

Sitting Bull (Tatanka Iyotake) as he might look today as a 35 year old engaging in one of his favorite pastimes: hunting. Copyright © Lochlainn Seabrook.

NIKOLA TESLA

1856-1943, (Serbian born in) Croatia

Ingenious experimental physicist and theoretical scientist, brilliant visionary, mechanical engineer, electrical engineer, inventor, businessman, entrepreneur, telegraph drafter, electrical designer, lecturer, Christian mystic, paranormalist, metaphysician, nature lover, futurist, invented the induction motor, pioneered wireless technology, founder of Tesla Electric Company.

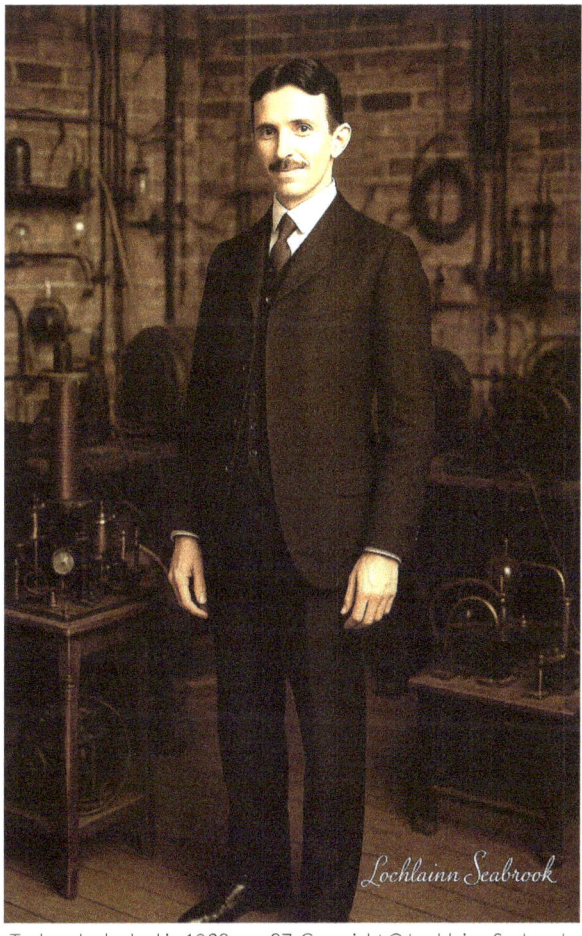

Tesla as he looked in 1893, age 37. Copyright © Lochlainn Seabrook.

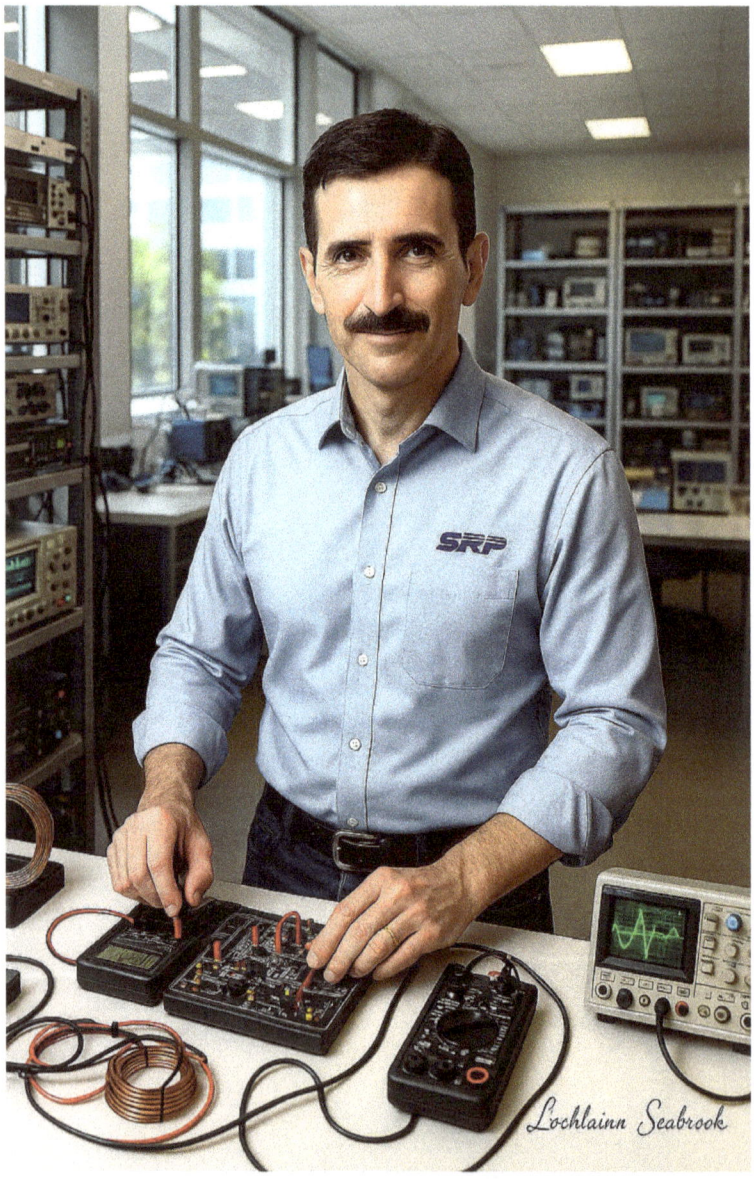

Tesla as he might look today as a successful 49 year old electrical engineer. Copyright © Lochlainn Seabrook.

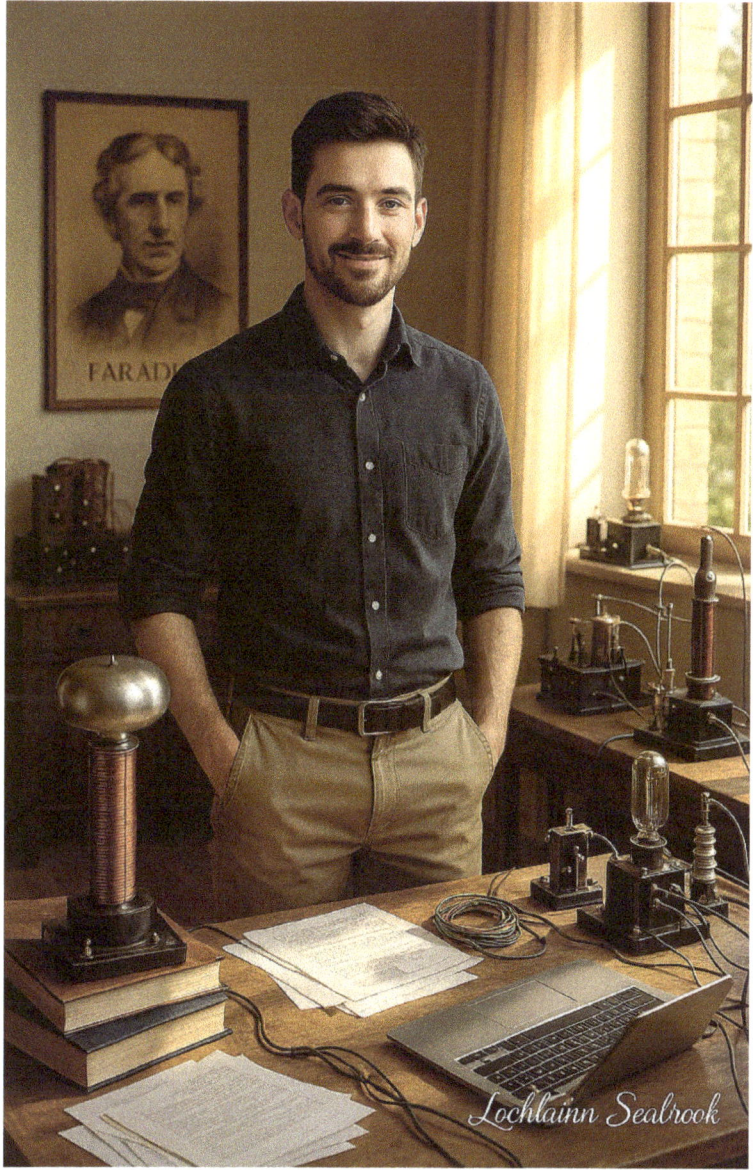

Tesla as he might appear today just starting his career as an 18 year old inventor. Copyright © Lochlainn Seabrook.

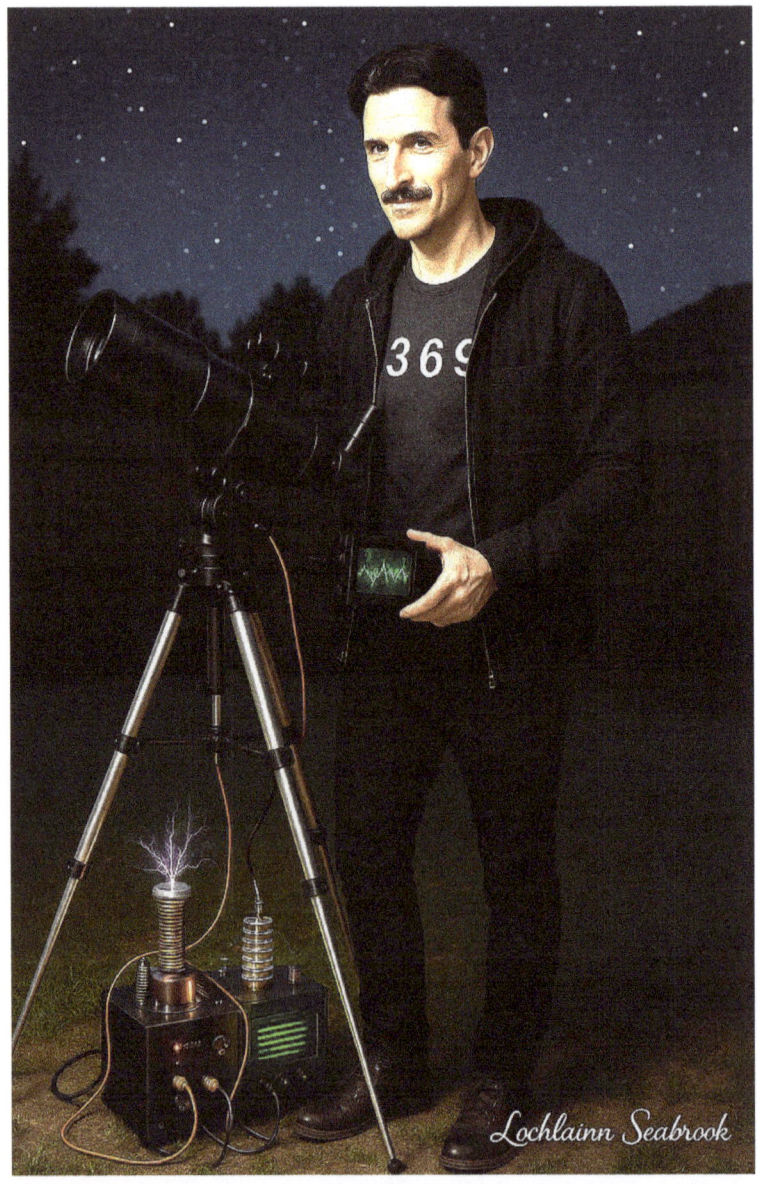

Nikola Tesla as he might appear today enjoying one of his favorite hobbies: searching for extraterrestrial signals using his high-voltage electronic devices.

HENRY DAVID THOREAU

1817-1862, Massachusetts

Naturalist, radical individualist, author, philosopher, lecturer, poet, schoolteacher, surveyor, pencil-maker, handyman, day laborer, Transcendentalist, environmentalist, libertarian social reformer, limited government advocate, anti-materialist, anti-capitalist, agrarian socialist, conservationist, Eastern-influenced Unitarian mystic, pantheist.

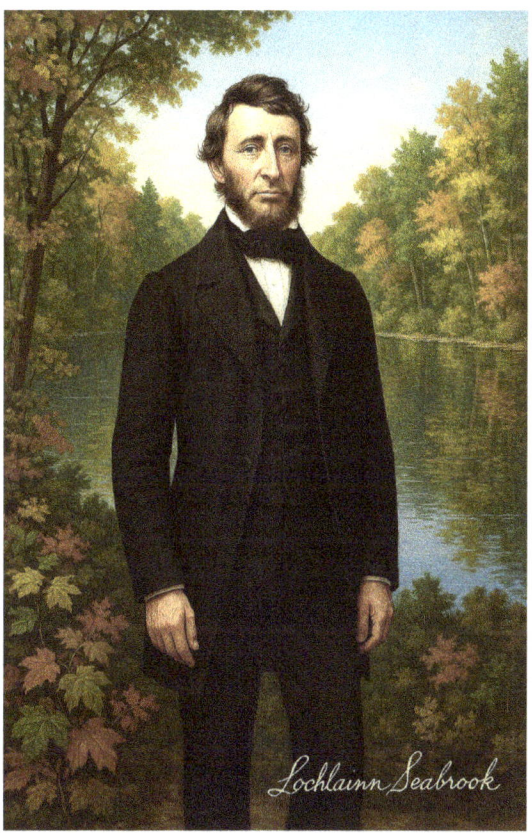

Thoreau as he looked in 1854, age 36. Copyright © Lochlainn Seabrook.

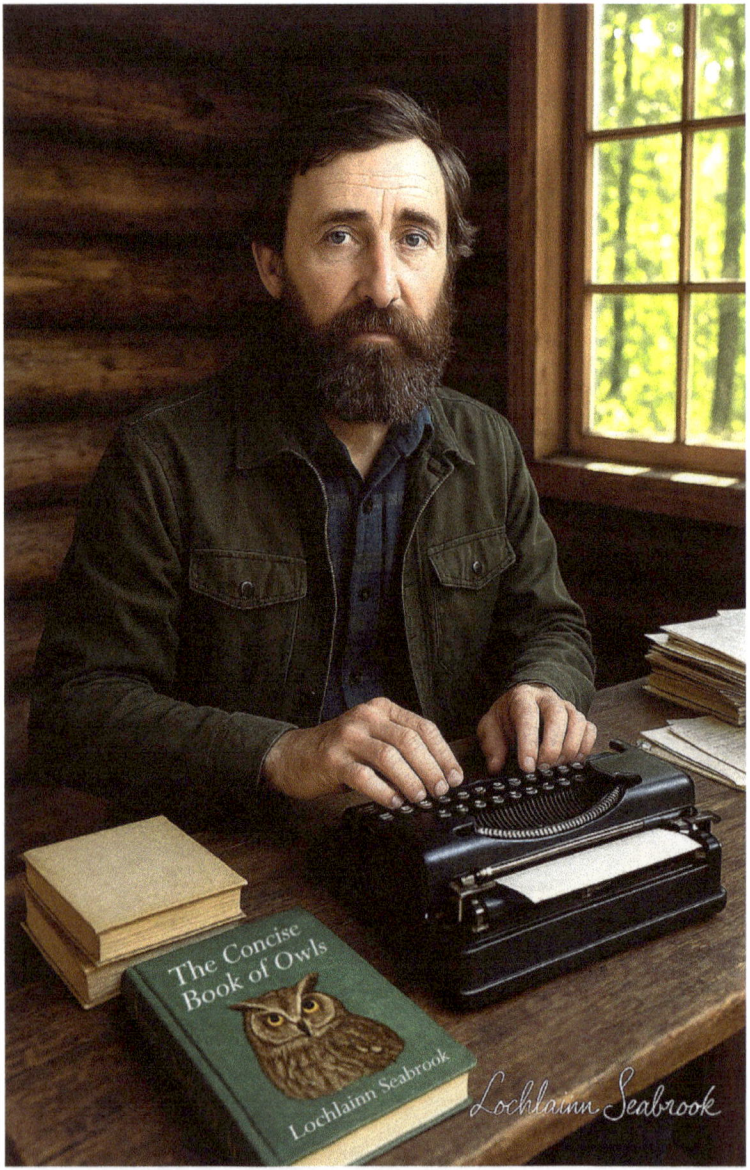

Thoreau as he might look today as a successful 40 year old nature writer. Copyright © Lochlainn Seabrook.

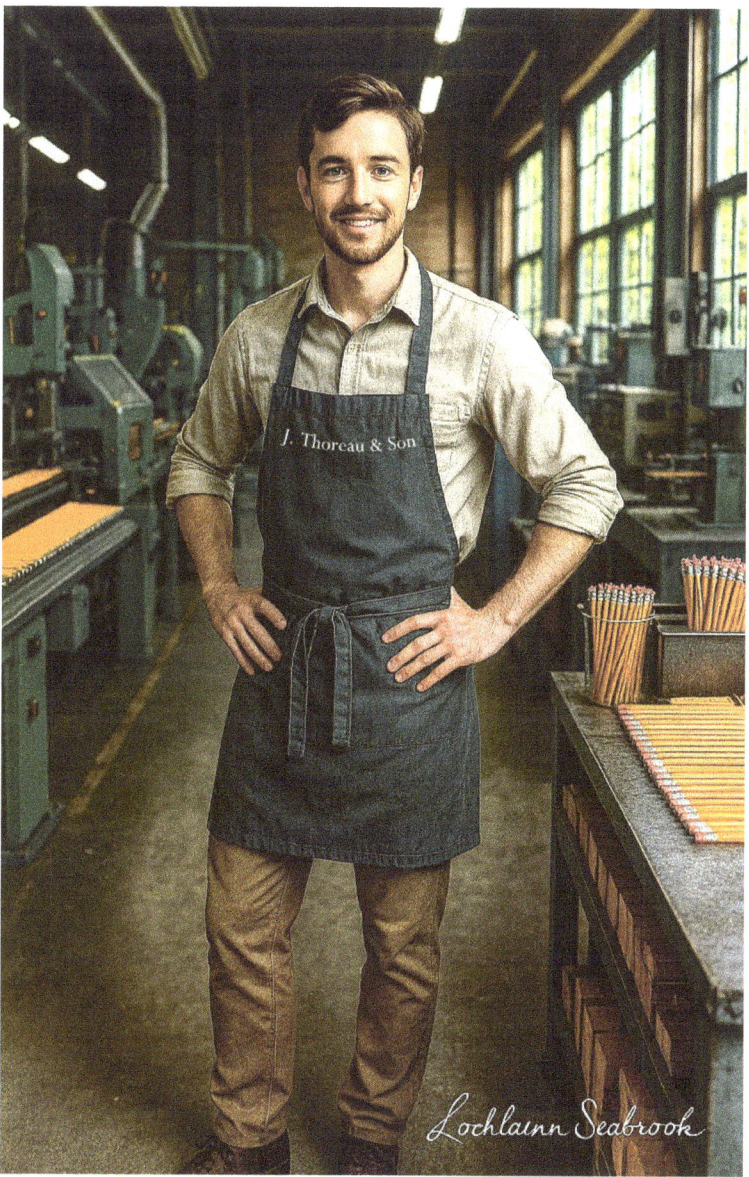

Thoreau as he might look today as a 20 year old partner in his family's pencil-making business in Concord, Massachusetts. Copyright © Lochlainn Seabrook.

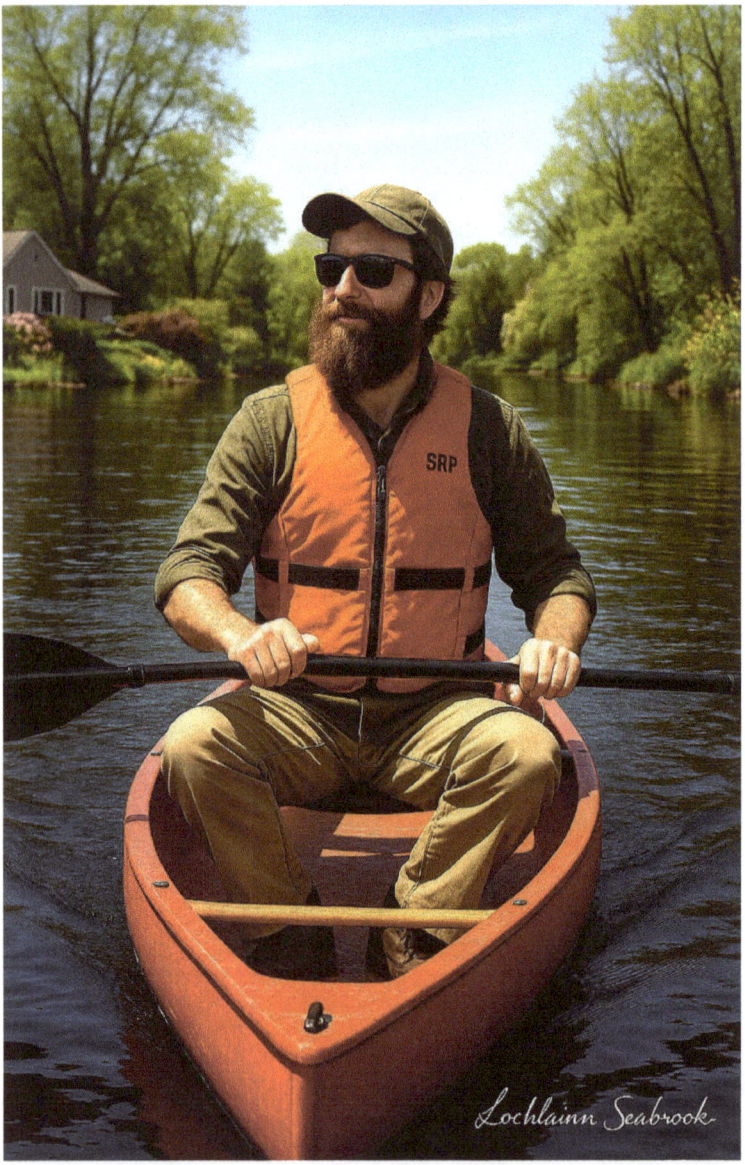

Henry David Thoreau as he might look today as a 41 year old engaging in one of his favorite pastimes: observing nature from his canoe. Copyright © Lochlainn Seabrook.

SALLY TOMPKINS

1833-1916, Virginia

Wealthy Southern aristocrat, charity worker, medical field worker, hospital administrator, nurse, Confederate captain (America's first female officer and the only commissioned female Confederate officer), humanitarian, Confederate veterans caregiver and benefactor, religious worker, welfare worker, "Angel of the Confederacy."

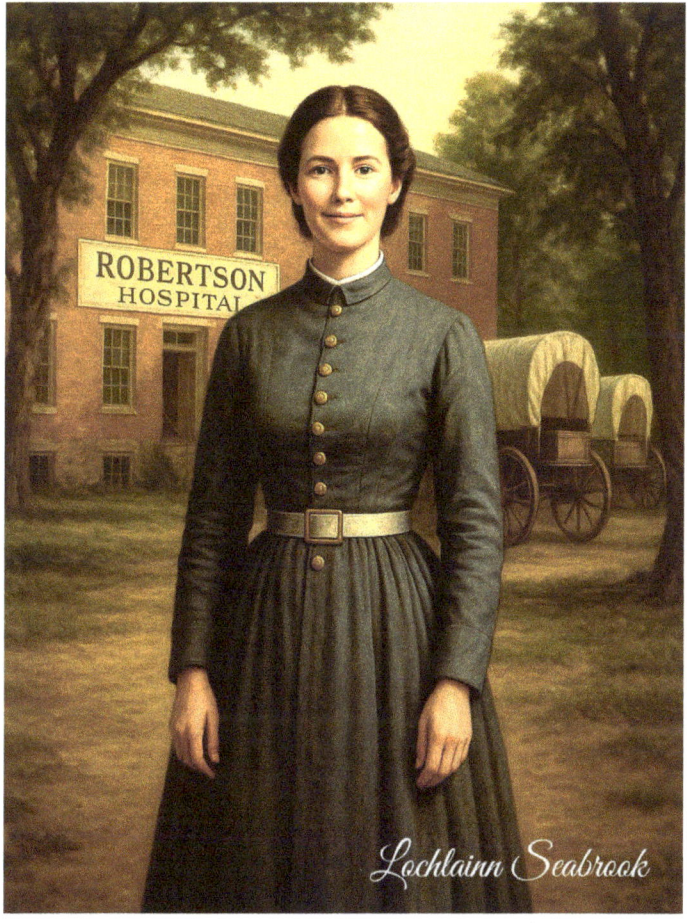

Tompkins as she looked in 1861, age 27. Copyright © Lochlainn Seabrook.

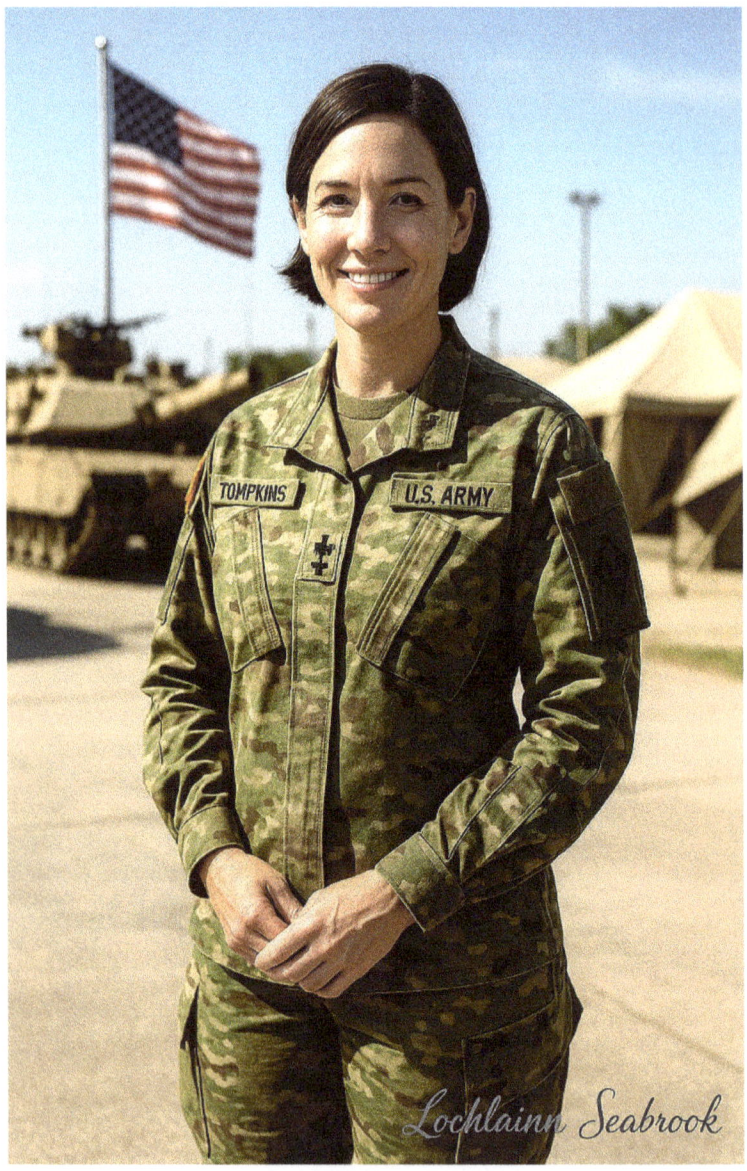

Tompkins as she might look today as a 31 year old U.S. army captain. Copyright © Lochlainn Seabrook.

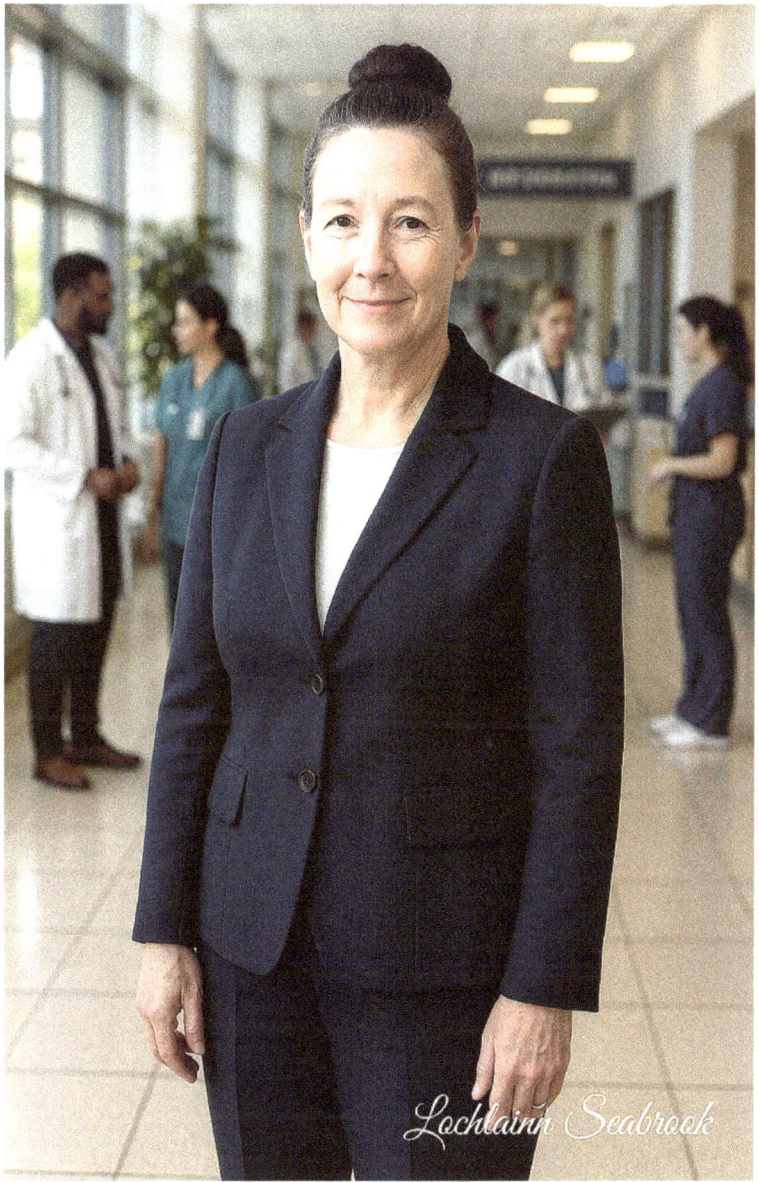

Tompkins as she might appear today as a middle aged hospital administrator. Copyright © Lochlainn Seabrook.

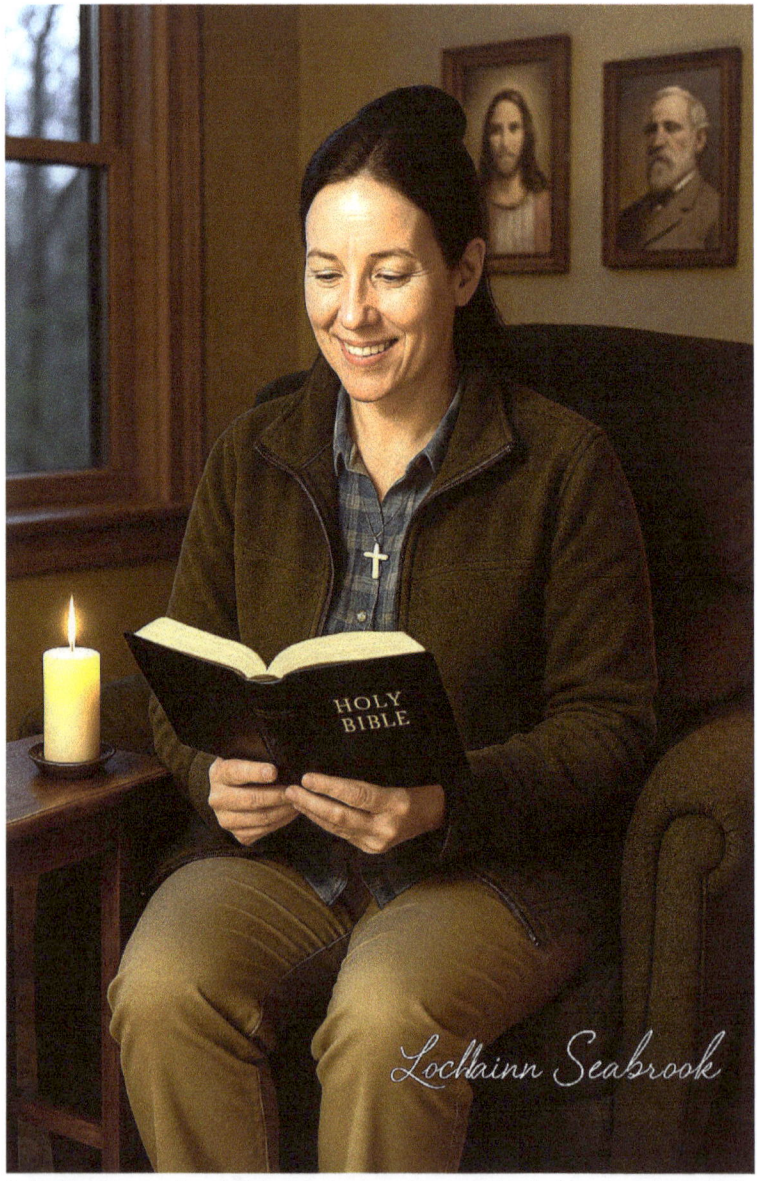

Sally Tompkins as she might look today as a 40 year old enjoying one of her favorite pastimes: religious studies. Copyright © Lochlainn Seabrook.

MARK TWAIN
1835-1910, Missouri

Left-leaning libertarian, internationally successful author, novelist, humorist, satirist, lecturer, public speaker, publisher, typesetter, printer, riverboat pilot, Confederate militia volunteer, journalist, businessman, entrepreneur, miner, silver and Gold Rush prospector, newspaper reporter, newspaper columnist, world traveler, cultural critic, social and political commentator.

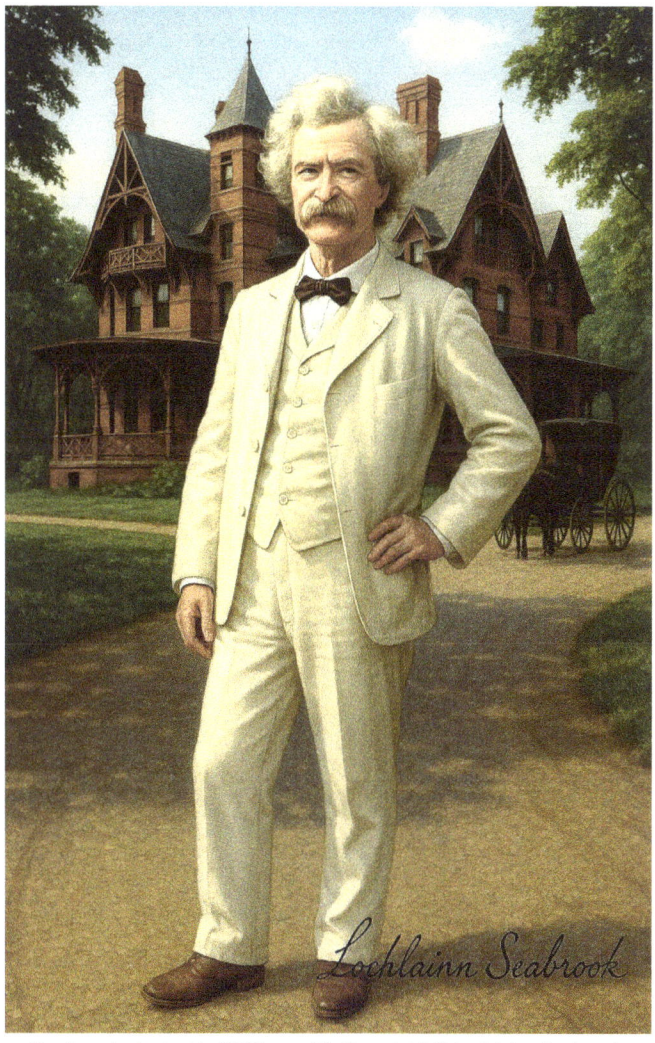

Twain as he looked in 1885, age 49. Copyright © Lochlainn Seabrook.

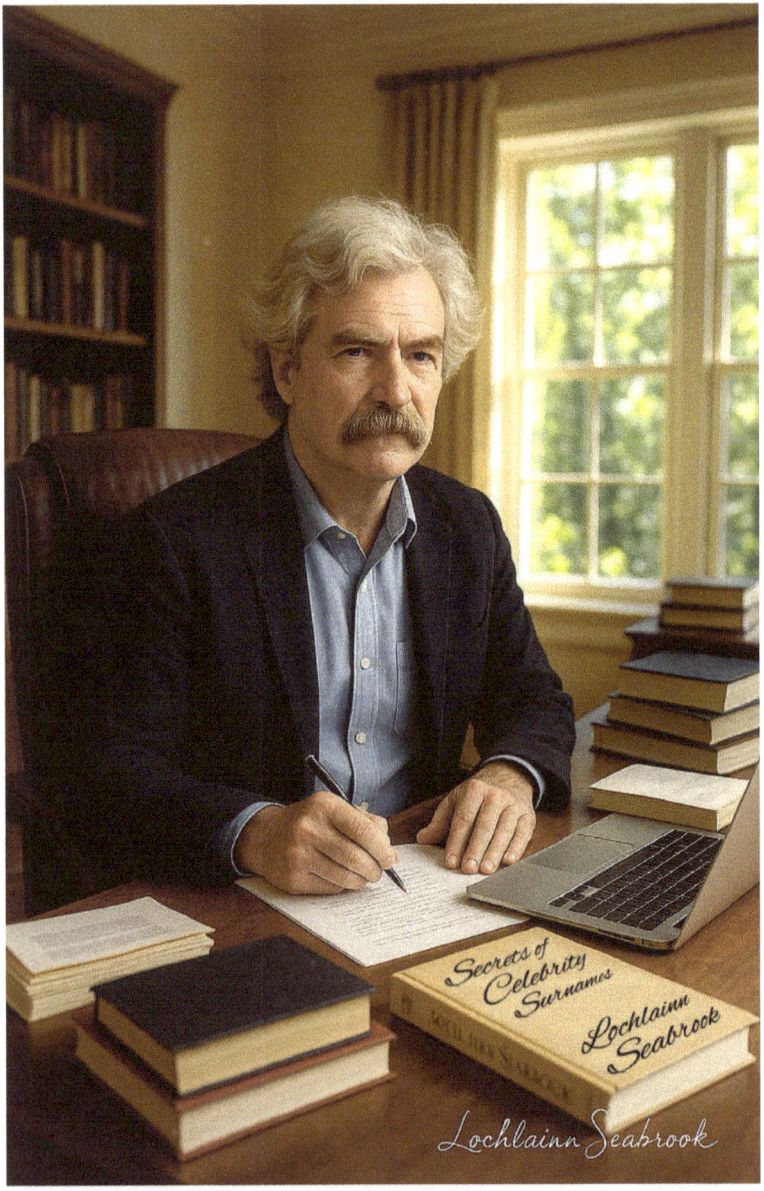

Twain as he might appear today as a successful and popular 65 year old author. Copyright © Lochlainn Seabrook.

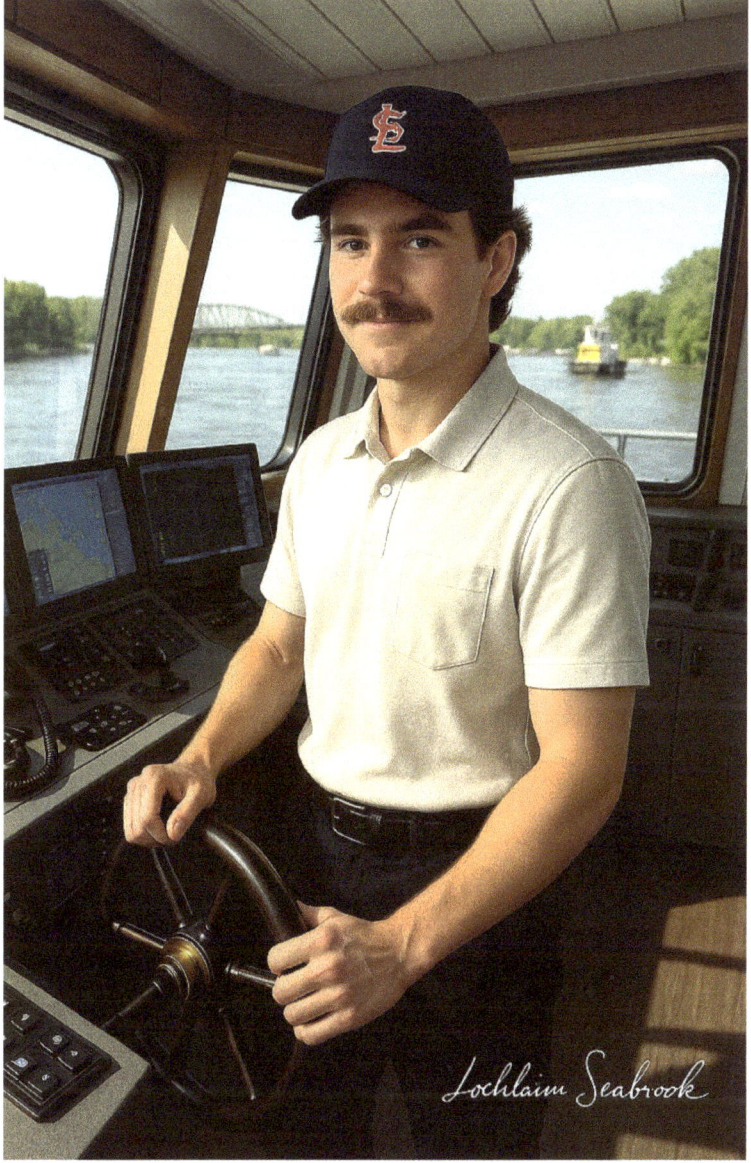

Twain as he might appear today as a 24 year old riverboat pilot in New Orleans, Louisiana. Copyright © Lochlainn Seabrook.

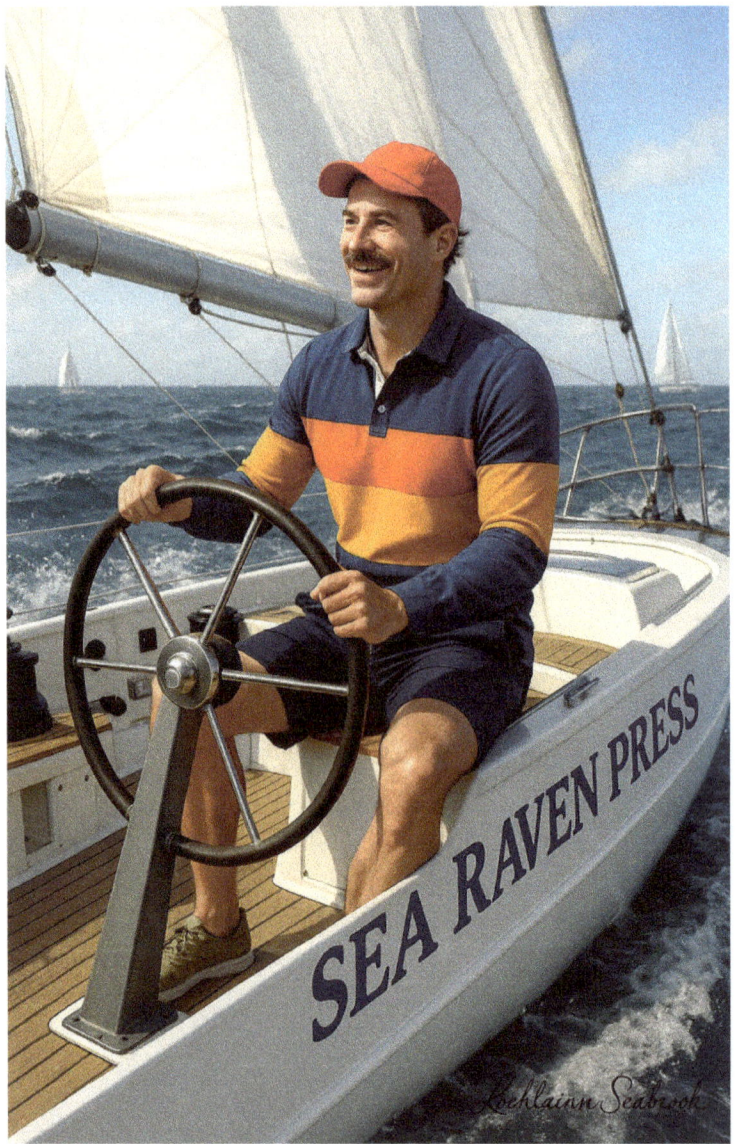

Samuel Langhorne Clemens ("Mark Twain") as he might look today as a 42 year old engaging in one of his favorite hobbies: yachting. Copyright © Lochlainn Seabrook.

BOOKER T. WASHINGTON

1856-1915, Virginia

Founder, first principle, and first president of Tuskegee University, author, writer, orator, public speaker, political adviser, national black leader, coal miner, salt packer, janitor, day school teacher, night school teacher, domestic house servant, houseboy, civil rights advocate, fundraiser, philanthropist, promoted black self-reliance.

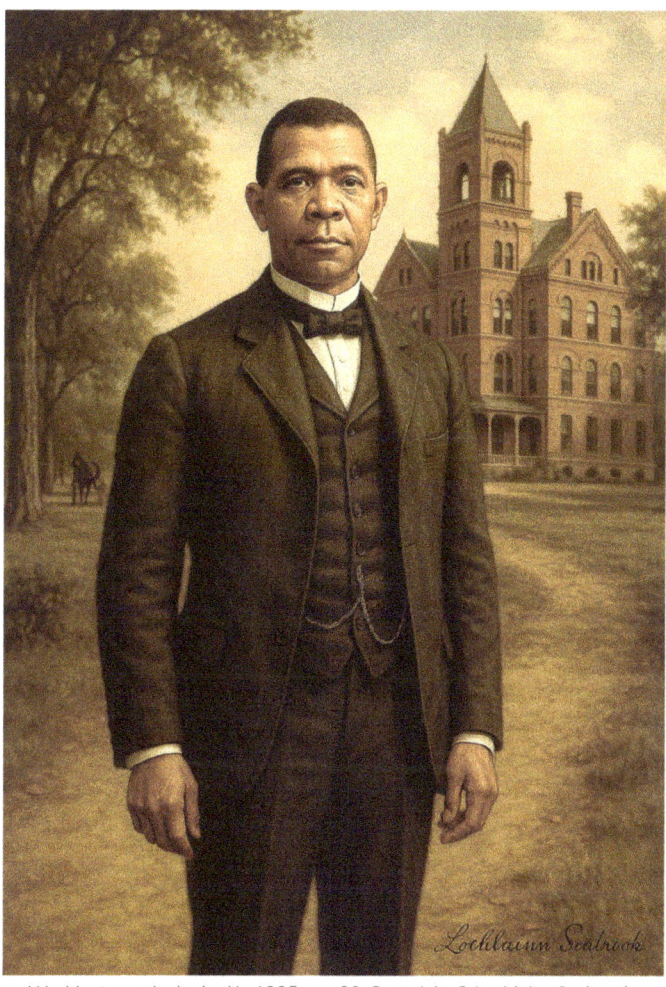

Washington as he looked in 1895, age 39. Copyright © Lochlainn Seabrook.

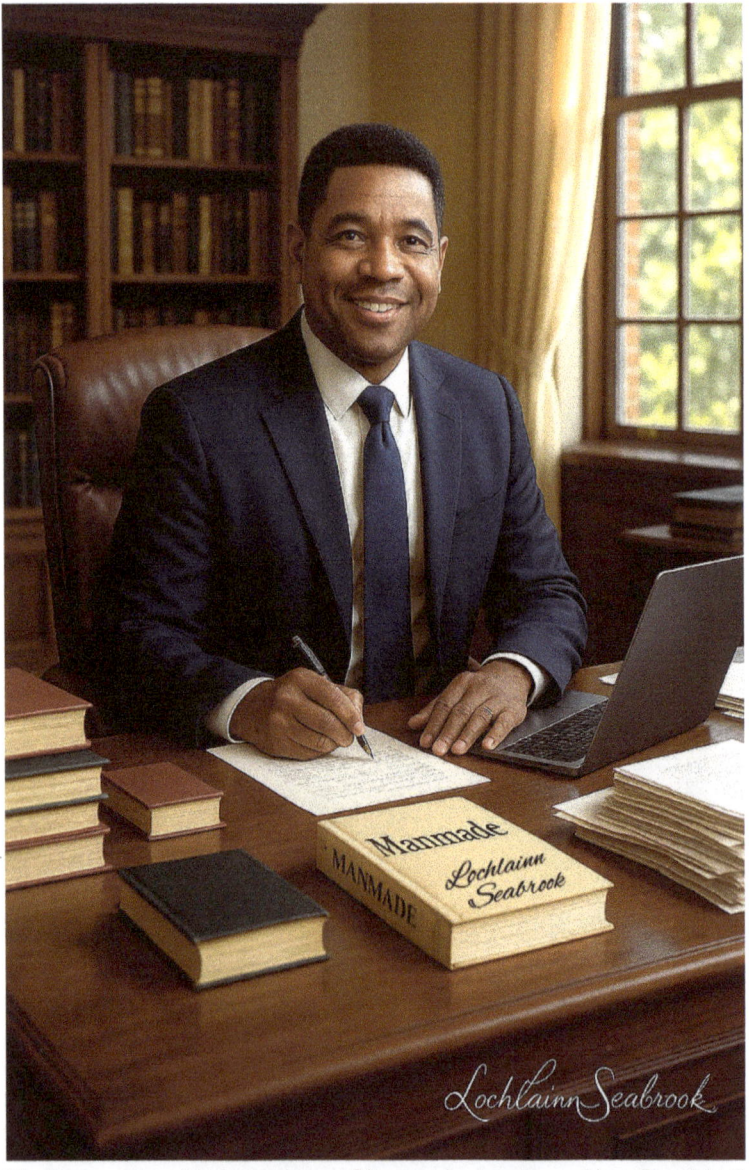

Washington as he might look today as a 50 year old university president. Copyright © Lochlainn Seabrook.

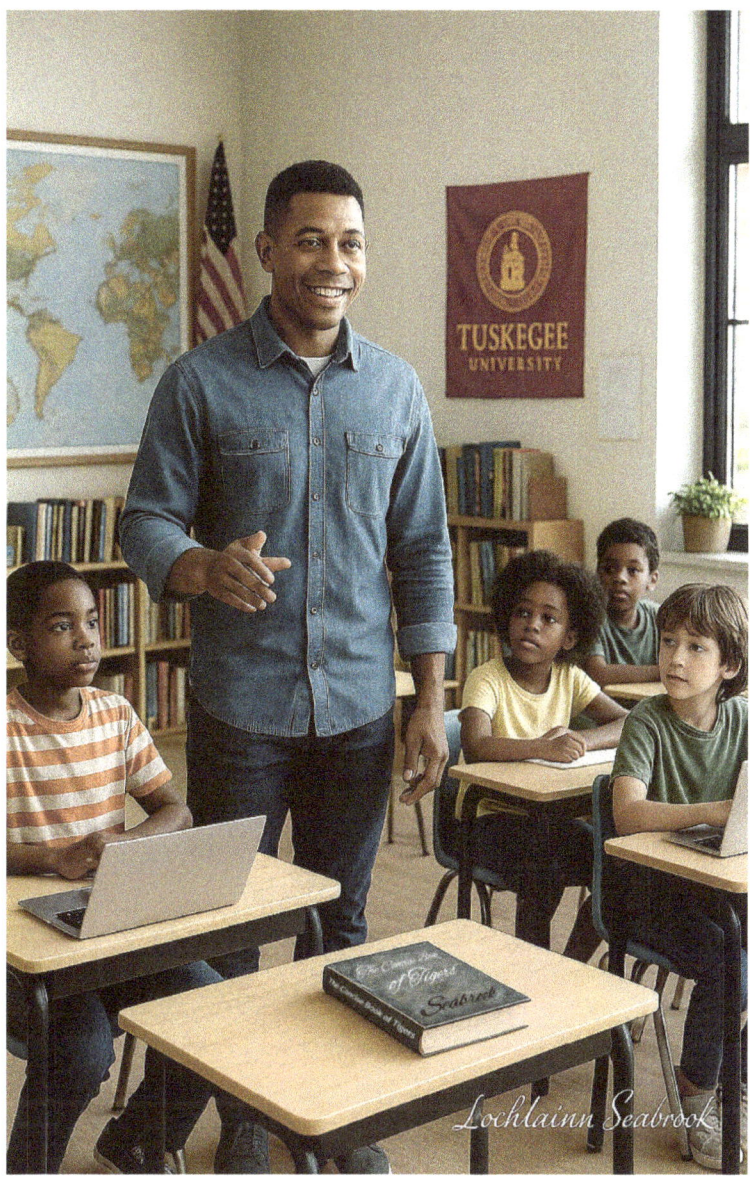

Washington as he might appear today as a 20 year old school teacher. Copyright © Lochlainn Seabrook.

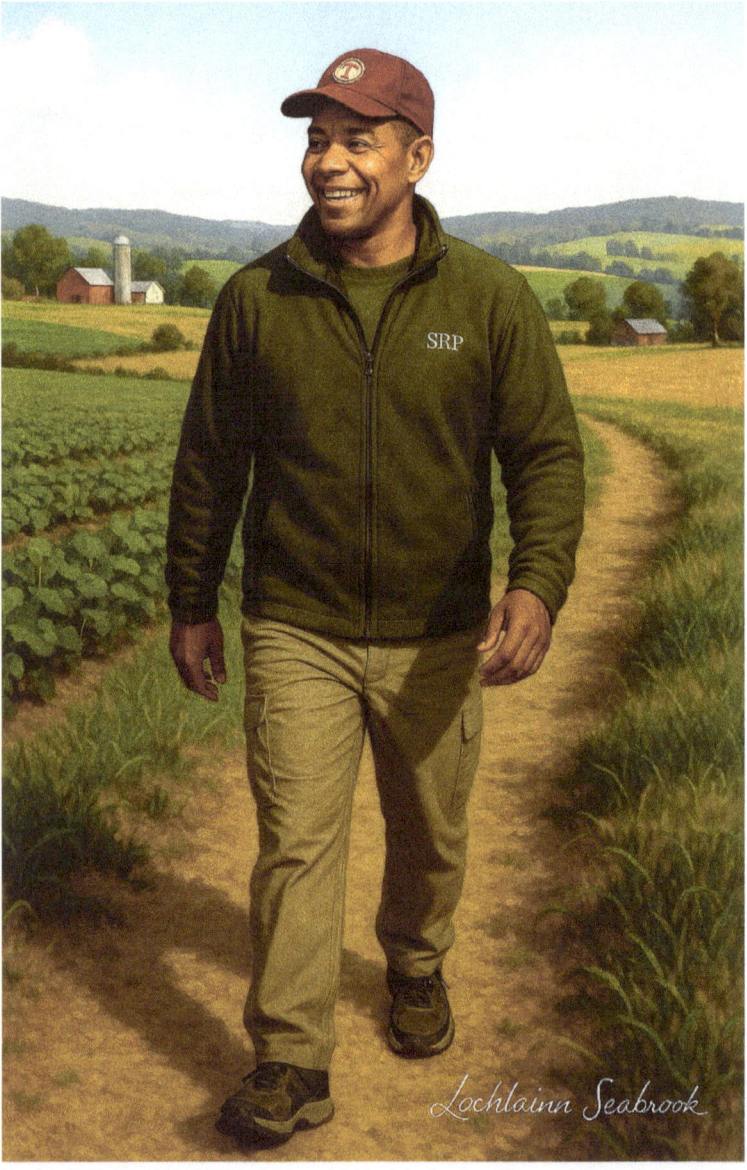

Booker Taliaferro Washington as he might look today as a 40 year old enjoying one of his favorite pastimes: nature walking in Virginia's farmland. Copyright © Lochlainn Seabrook.

GEORGE WASHINGTON

1732-1799, Virginia

First U.S. president, statesman, presiding officer (at 1787 Constitutional Convention), commander-in-chief of the Continental Army (during the American Revolutionary War), gentleman farmer and farm owner, land surveyor, military officer.

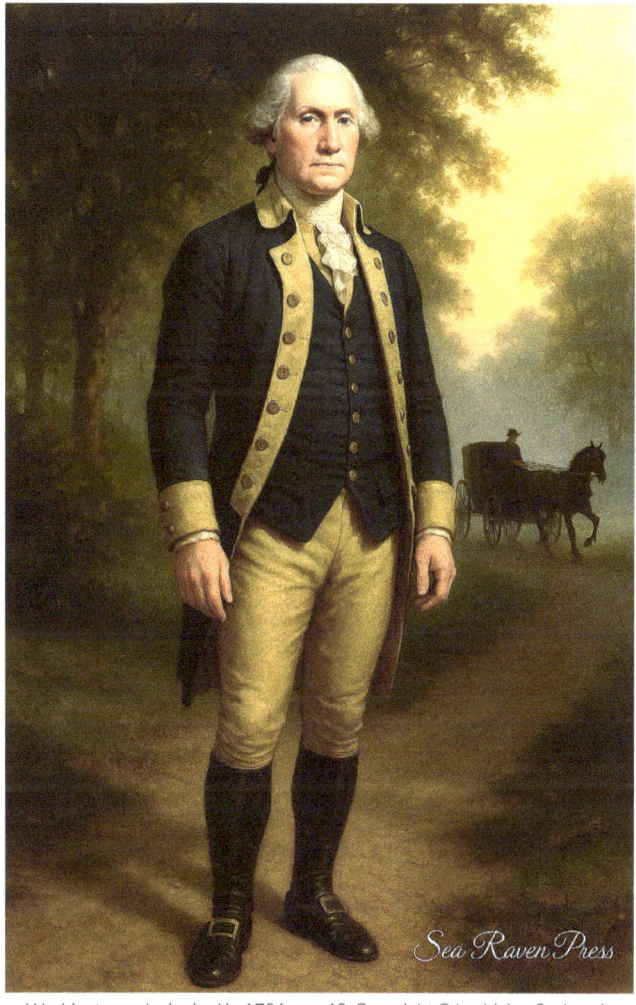

Washington as he looked in 1781, age 49. Copyright © Lochlainn Seabrook.

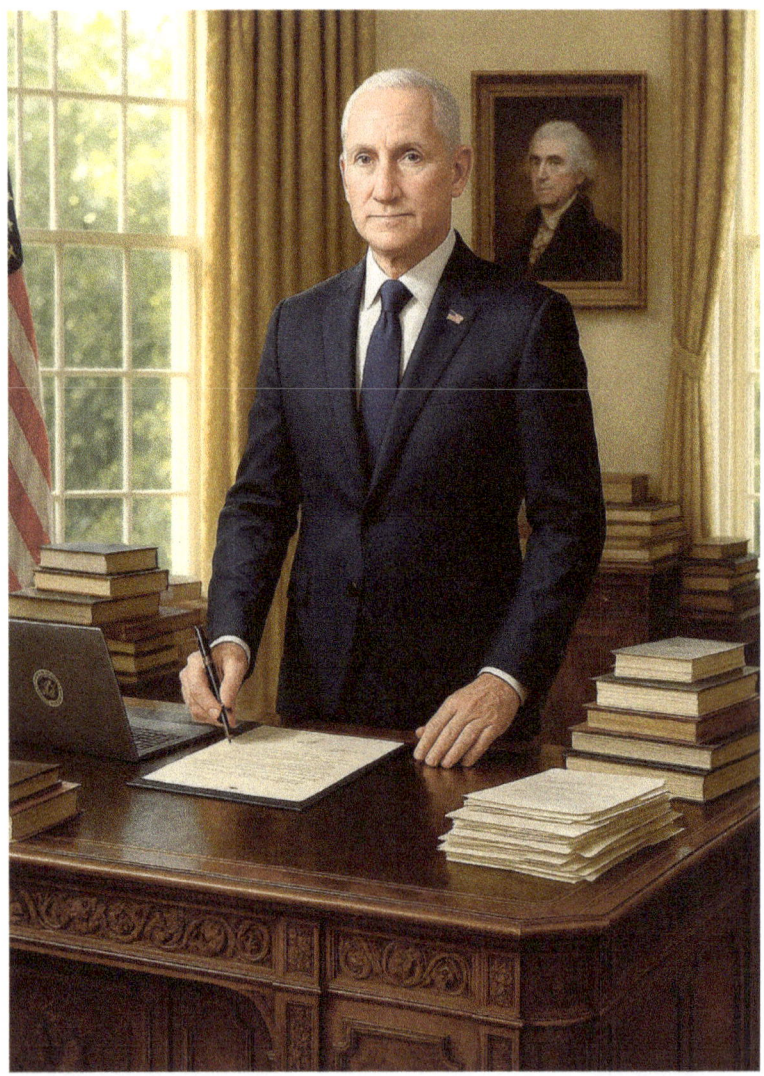

Washington as he might look today as a 60 year old U.S. president. Copyright © Lochlainn Seabrook.

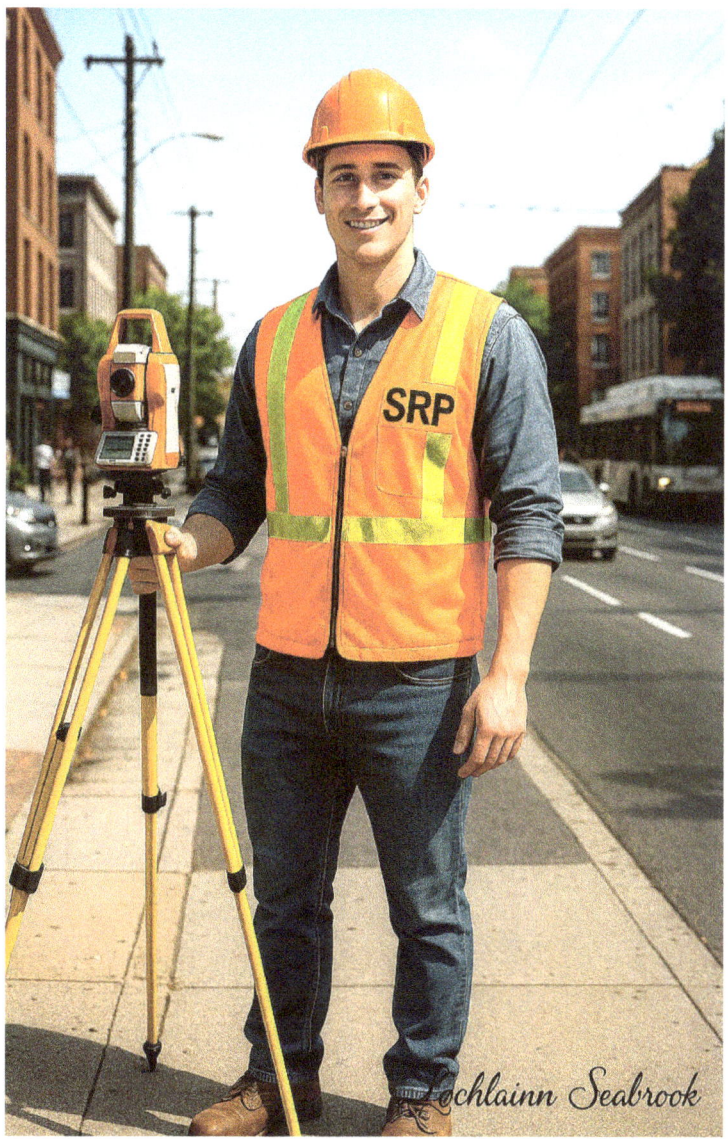

Washington as he might appear today as a 20 year old land surveyor. Copyright © Lochlainn Seabrook.

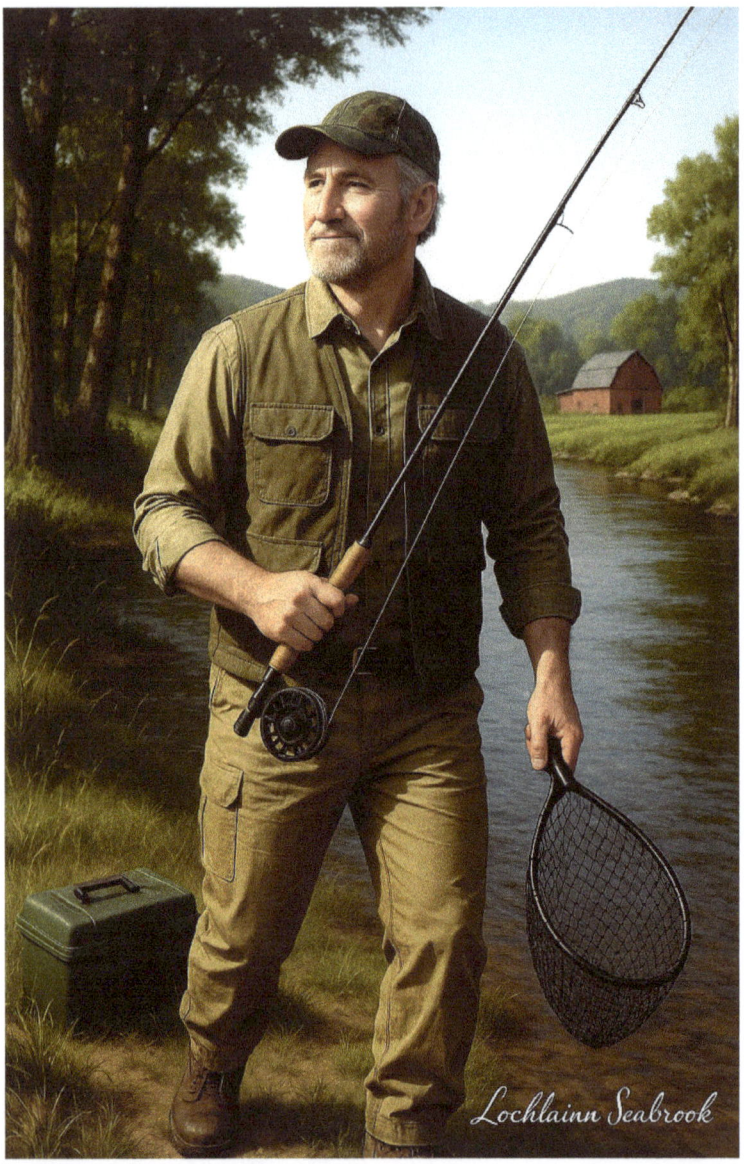

George Washington as he might look today as a 50 year old enjoying one of his favorite activities: fishing. Copyright © Lochlainn Seabrook.

STAND WATIE (DEGATAGA)

1806-1871, Georgia

Principal chief of the Cherokee Nation, tribal leader, Confederate general (led the 1st Cherokee Mounted Rifles), military strategist, guerrilla warfare tactician, farmer, lawyer, businessman, merchant, newspaper editor, publisher, entrepreneur, writer, plantation owner, salt works owner, trader, co-founder of the *Cherokee Phoenix* (the first Native American newspaper), last Confederate general to surrender.

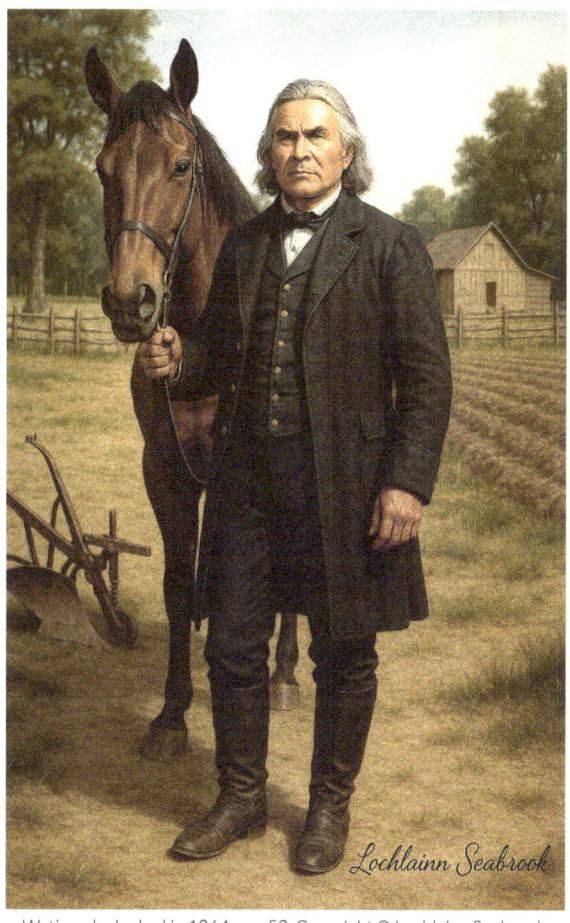

Watie as he looked in 1864, age 58. Copyright © Lochlainn Seabrook.

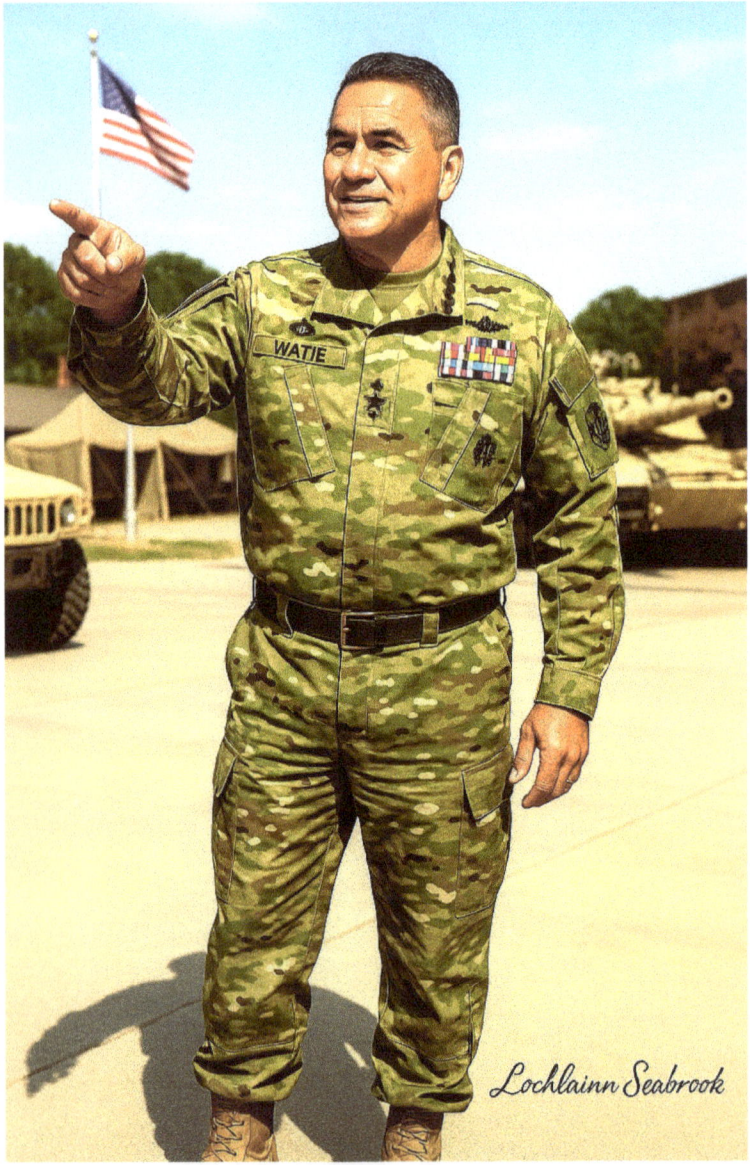

Watie as he might look today as a 60 year old U.S. army general. Copyright © Lochlainn Seabrook.

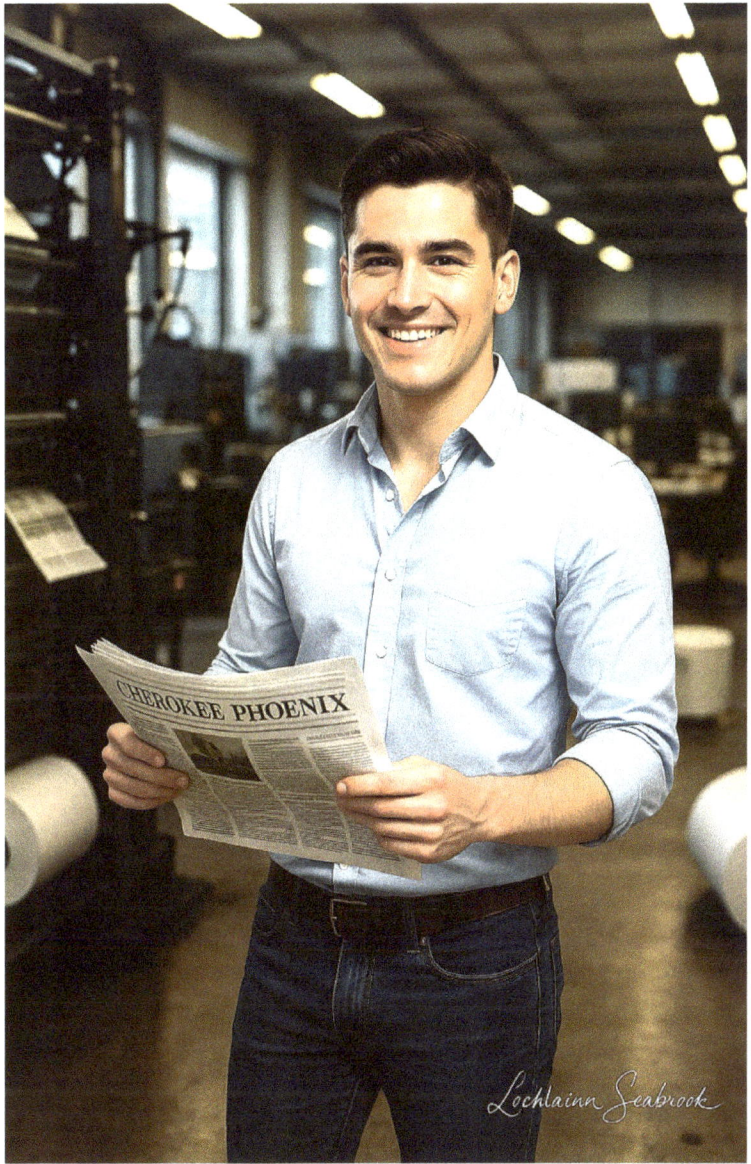

Watie as he might look today as a 22 year old newspaper editor and publisher. Copyright © Lochlainn Searbook.

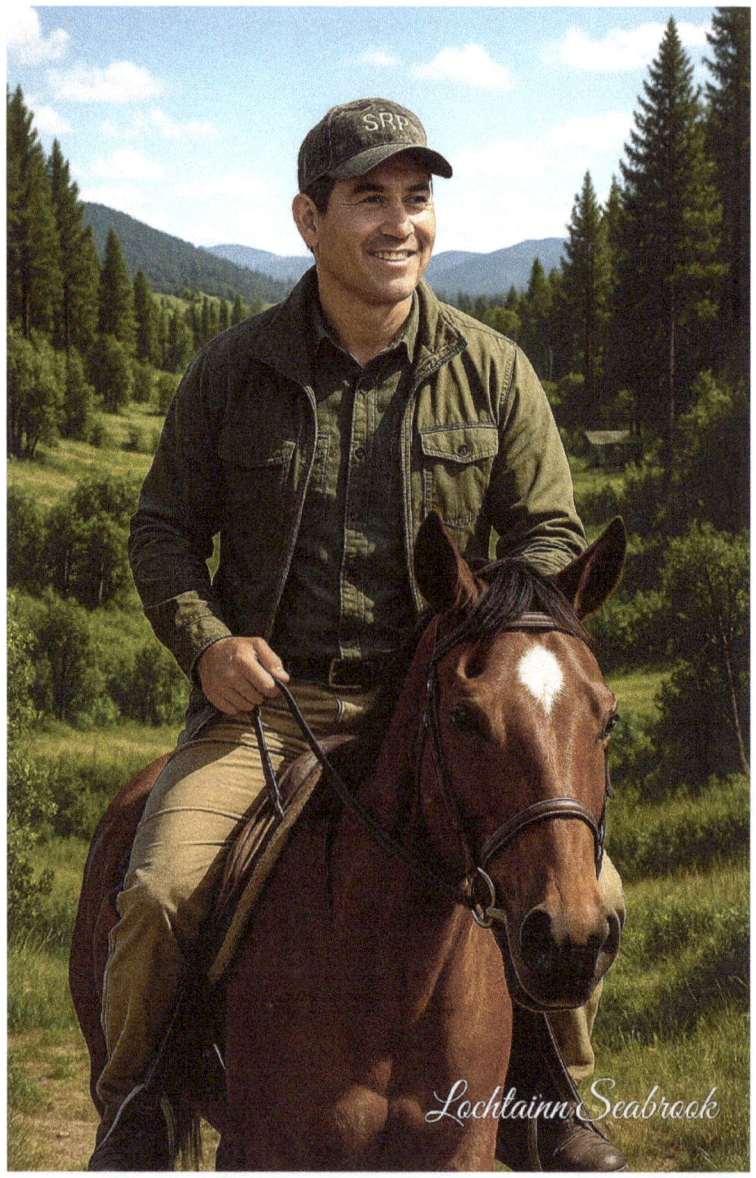

Stand Watie (Standhope Oowatie) as he might look today as a 40 year old enjoying one of his favorite pastimes: horseback riding in the Oklahoma wilderness. Copyright © Lochlainn Seabrook.

WALT WHITMAN
1819-1892, New York

Poet, essayist, lecturer, schoolteacher, journalist, newspaper editor, government clerk, freelance writer, short story writer, fiction writer, printer, printer's apprentice, typesetter, volunteer Union nurse (during the War Between the States).

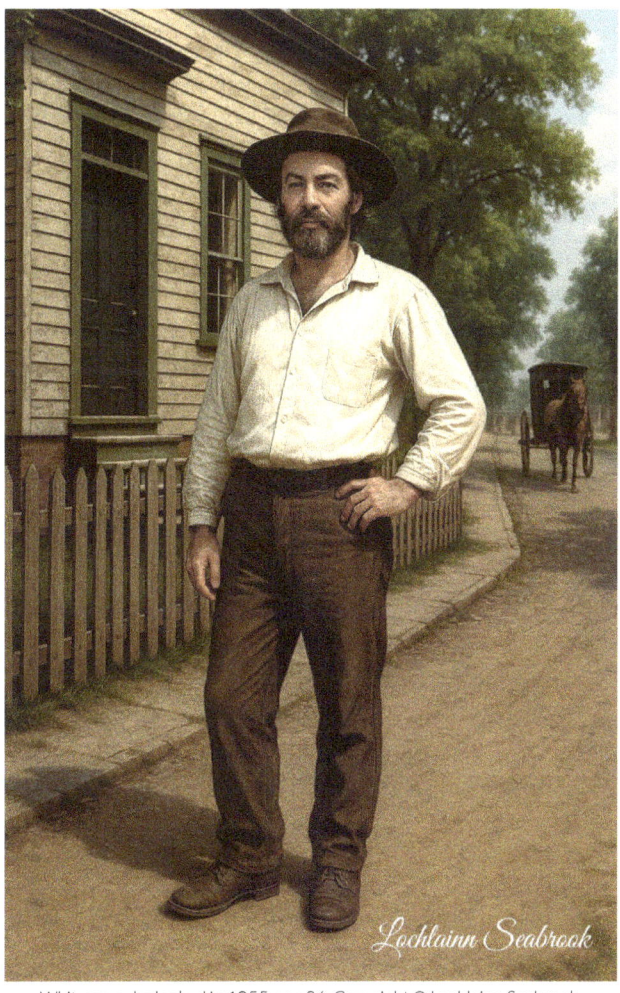

Whitman as he looked in 1855, age 36. Copyright © Lochlainn Seabrook.

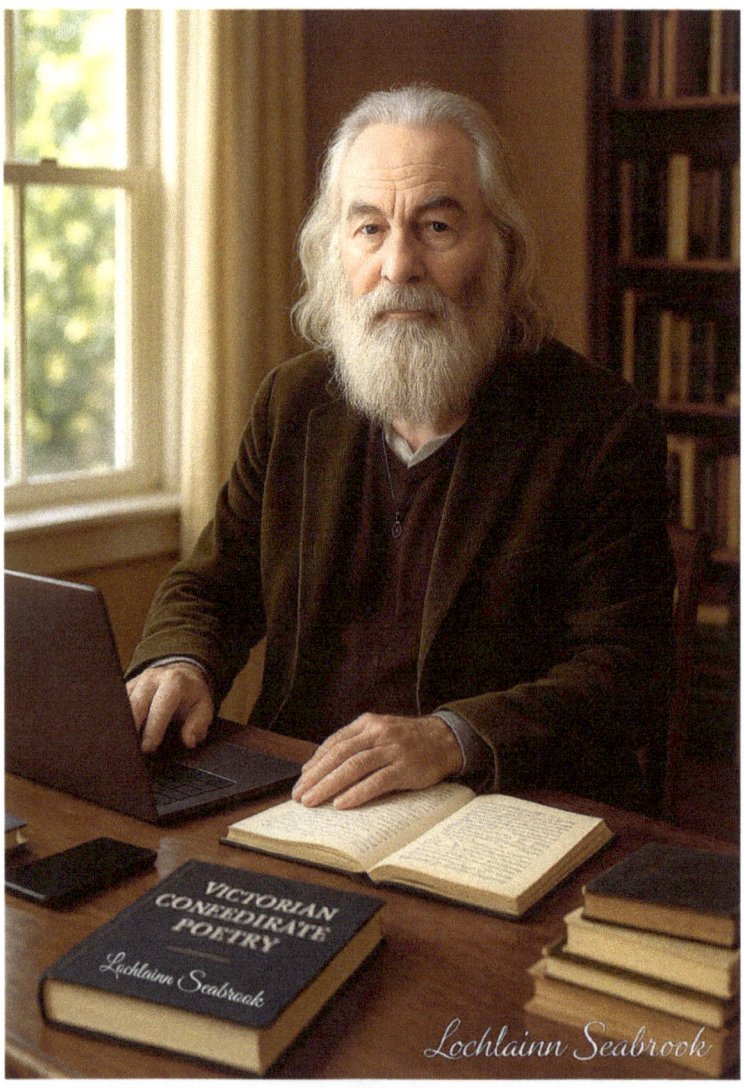

Whitman as he might look today as a successful 68 year old poet. Copyright © Lochlainn Seabrook.

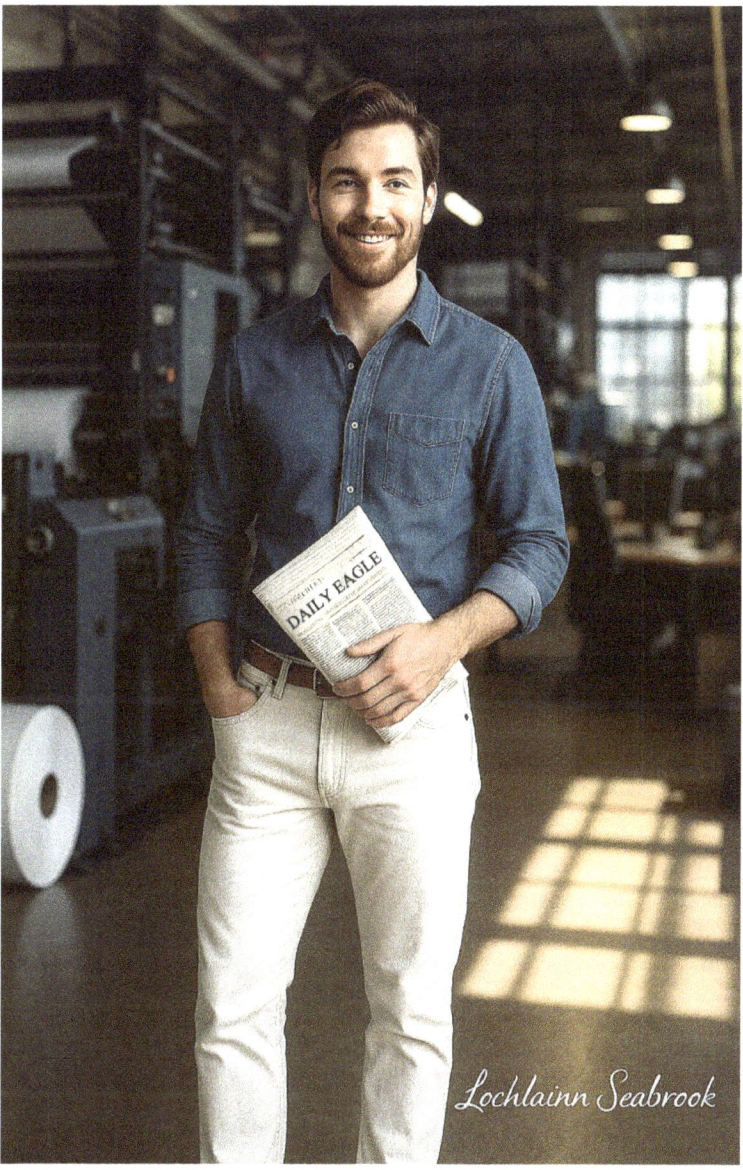

Whitman as he might appear today as a 27 year old newspaper editor. Copyright © Lochlainn Seabrook.

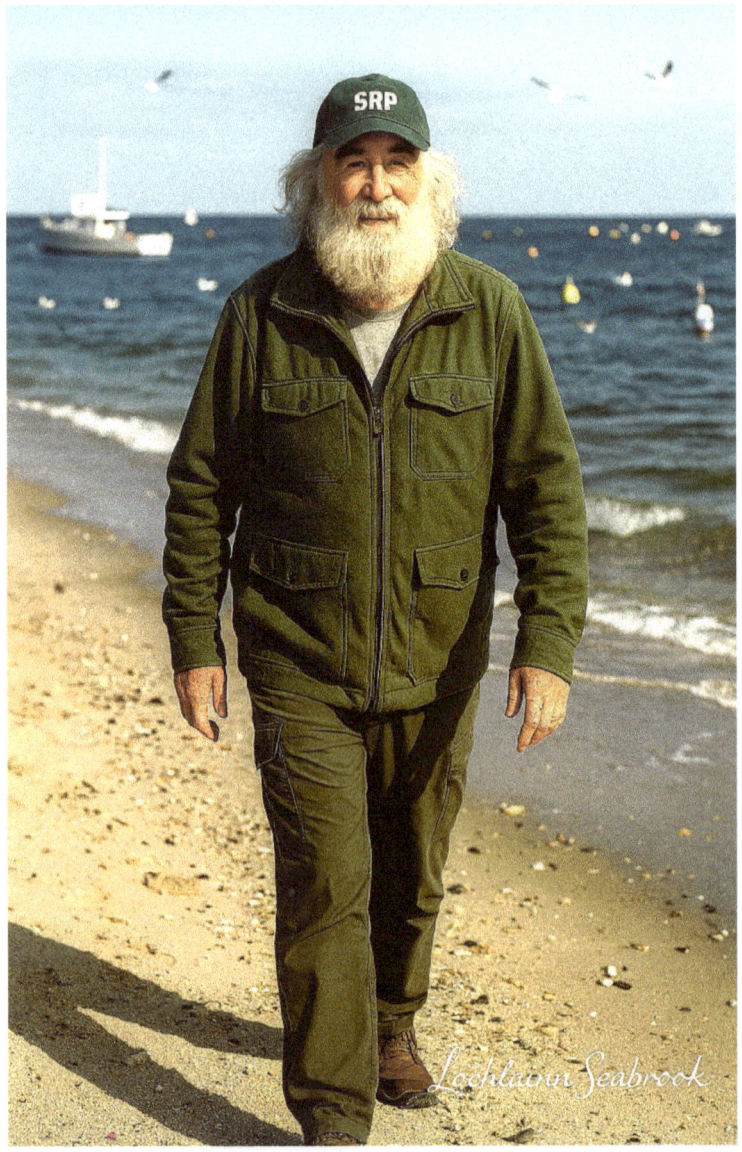

Walter "Walt" Whitman as might look today as a 72 year old enjoying one of his favorite hobbies: walking on the Long Island shoreline. Copyright © Lochlainn Seabrook..

ELI WHITNEY
1765-1825, Massachusetts

Mechanical engineer, industrial engineer, entrepreneur, businessman, industrialist, mechanic, inventor, schoolteacher, tutor, repairman (musical instruments and machinery), firearms manufacturer, farm laborer, engineering pioneer (interchangeable parts).

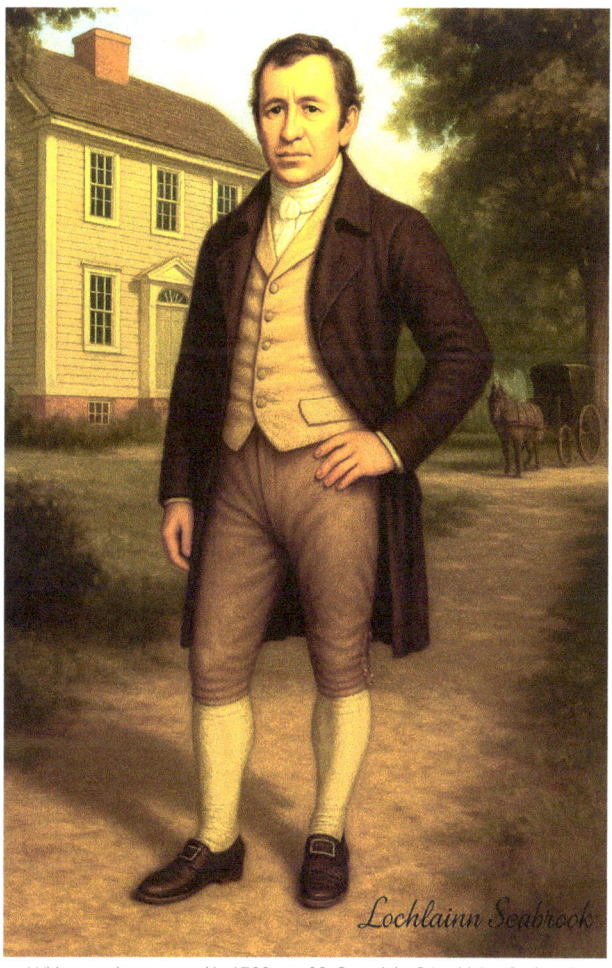

Whitney as he appeared in 1798, age 33. Copyright © Lochlainn Seabrook.

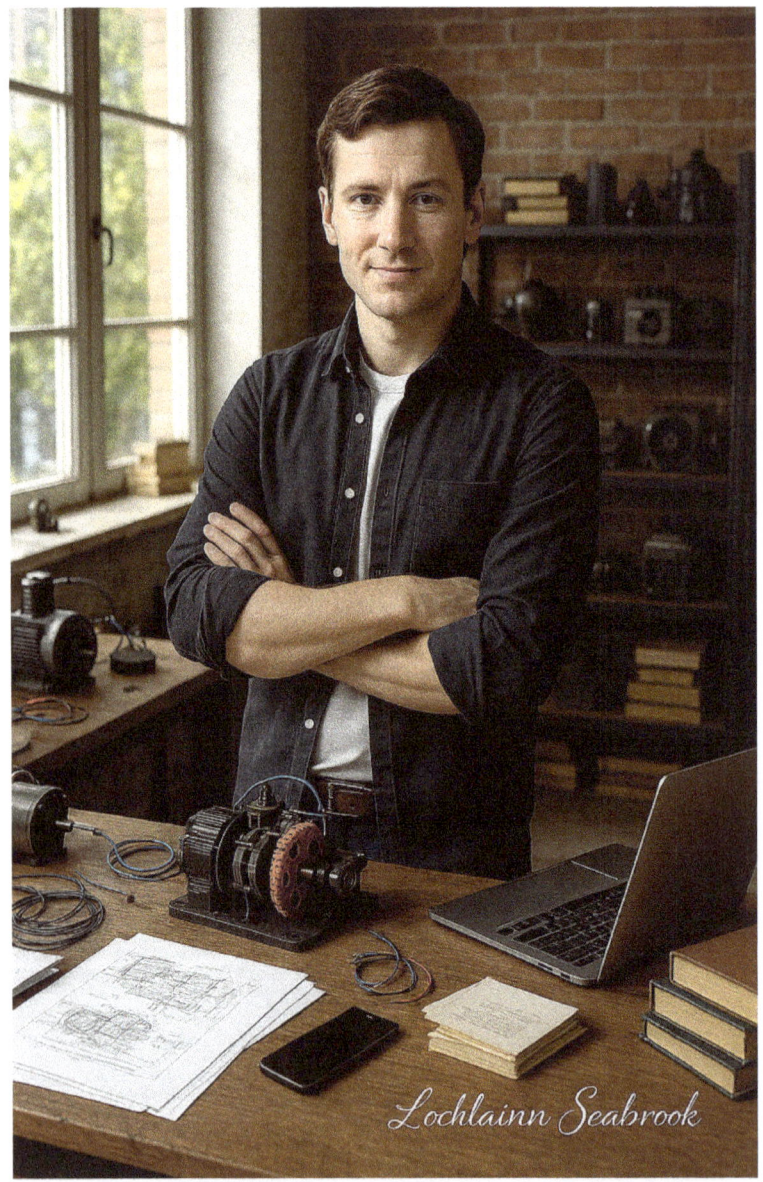

Whitney as he might look today as a successful 27 year old mechanical inventor. Copyright © Lochlainn Seabrook.

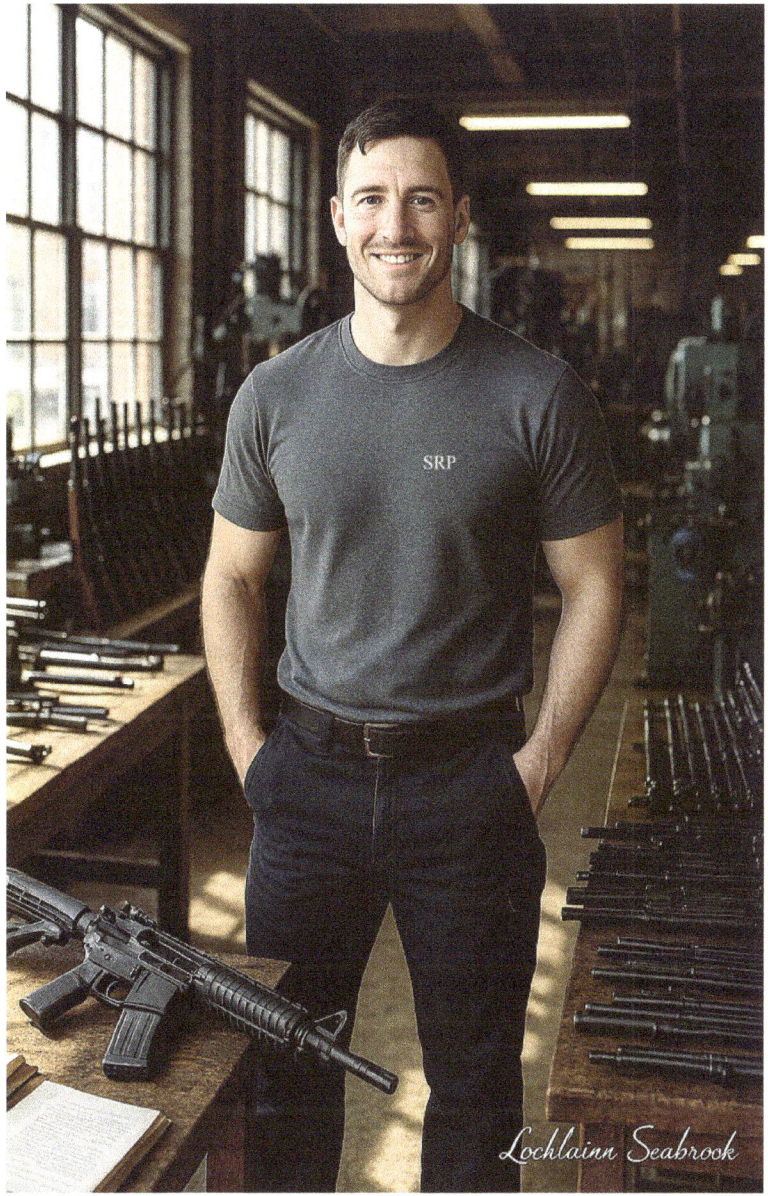

Whitney as he might look today as a 32 year old firearms manufacturer. Copyright © Lochlainn Seabrook.

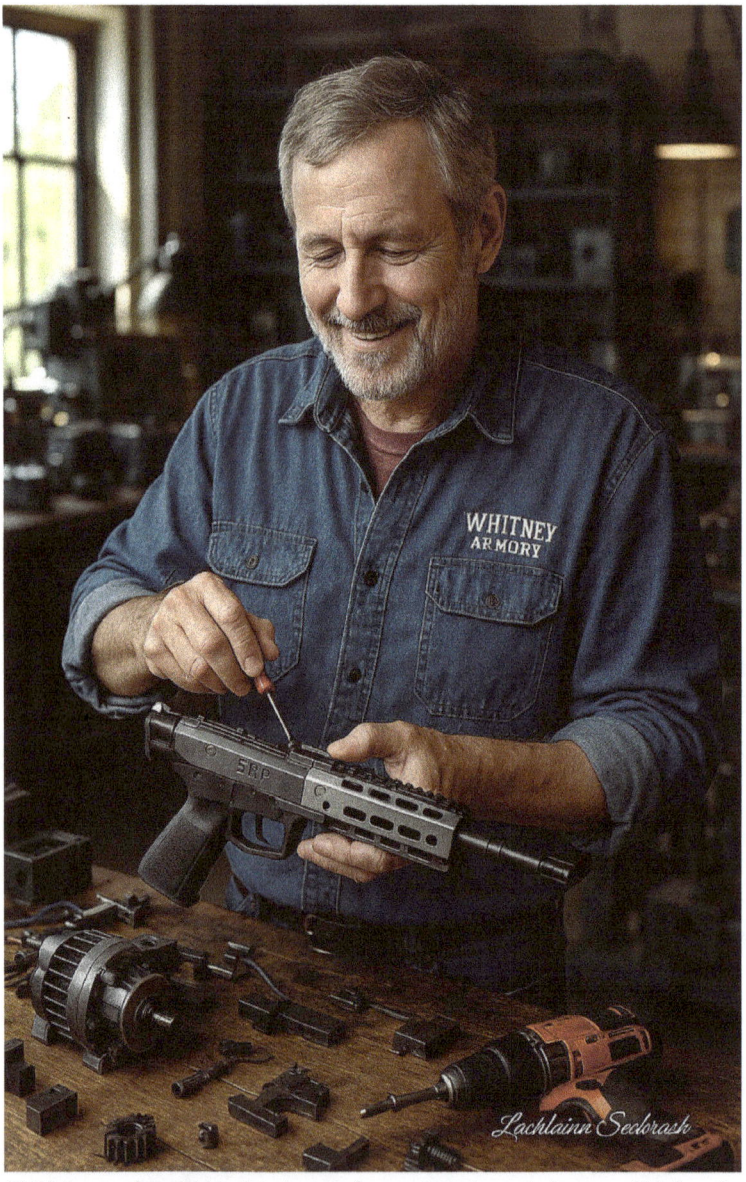

Eli Whitney as he might look today as a famous inventor enjoying one of his favorite pastimes: tinkering in his machine shop. Copyright © Lochlainn Seabrook.

BIBLIOGRAPHY

And Suggested Reading

Alderman, Edwin Anderson, and Joel Chandler Harris (eds.). *Library of Southern Literature: Biographical Dictionary of Authors*. Atlanta, GA: The Martin and Hoyt Co., 1907.
Alexander, Edward Porter. *Military Memoirs of a Confederate*. New York: Charles Scribner's Sons, 1907.
Allen, William. *An American Biographical and Historical Dictionary*. Boston, MA: William Hyde and Co., 1832.
Anderson, Mabel Washbourne. *Life of General Stand Watie: The Only Indian Brigadier General of the Confederate Army and the Last General to Surrender*. Pryor, OK: self-published, 1915.
A New Biographical Dictionary, of 3000 Contemporary Public Characters, British and Foreign, of All Ranks and Professions. London, UK: George B. Whittaker, 1825.
Appleyard, Rollo. *Pioneers of Electrical Communication*. Freeport, NY: Books for Libraries Press, 1930.
Armstrong, J. M. *The Biographical Encyclopedia of Kentucky of the Dead and Living Men of the Nineteenth Century*. Cincinnati, OH: J. M. Armstrong and Co., 1878.
Ashe, Samuel A'Court. *History of North Carolina*. 2 vols. Greensboro, NC: Charles L. Van Noppen, 1908.
Bachman, Frank P. *Great Inventors and Their Inventions*. New York: American Book Company, 1918.
Bellchambers, Edmund. *A General Biographical Dictionary: Containing Lives of the Most Eminent Persons of All Ages and Nations*. 4 vols. London, UK: Allan Bell and Co., 1835.
Blake, John L. *A Biographical Dictionary: Comprising a Summary Account of the Lives of the Most Distinguished Persons of All Ages, Nations, and Professions*. Philadelphia, PA: H. Cowperthwait, 1859.
Brown, John Howard (ed.). *Lamb's Biographical Dictionary of the United States*. Boston, MA: Federal Book Company of Boston, 1903
Bond, P. S. (ed.). *Military Science and Tactics: A Text and Reference for the Reserve Officers' Training Corps*. Washington, D.C.: P. S. Bond Publishing Co., 1938.
Borcke, Heros von. *Memoirs of the Confederate War for Independence*. 2 vols. Edinburgh, Scotland: William Blackwood and Sons, 1866.
Boyd, James P. *Parties, Problems, and Leaders of 1896: An Impartial Presentation of Living National Questions*. Chicago, IL: Publishers' Union, 1896.
Bradford, Gamaliel. *Confederate Portraits*. Boston, MA: Houghton Mifflin Co., 1913.
Brock, Robert Alonzo (ed.). *Southern Historical Society Papers*. 52 vols. Richmond, VA: Southern Historical Society, 1876-1943.
Browder, Earl. *Lincoln and the Communists*. New York, NY: Workers Library Publishers, Inc., 1936.
Bryan, William Jennings. *The First Battle: A Story of the Campaign of 1896*. Chicago, IL: W. B. Conkey Co., 1896.
Buhle, Mari Jo. *Women and American Socialism, 1870-1920*. Chicago, IL: University of Illinois Press, 1981.
Burke, Bernard. *A Genealogical and Heraldic History of the Peerage and Baronetage*. London, UK: Harrison and Sons, 1885.
Burns, James MacGregor. *The Vineyard of Liberty*. New York, NY: Alfred A. Knopf, 1982.
Carpenter, Stephen D. *Logic of History - Five Hundred Political Texts: Being Concentrated Extracts of Abolitionism; Also Results of Slavery Agitation and Emancipation; Together With

Sundry Chapters on Despotism, Usurpations and Frauds. Madison, WI: self-published, 1864.
Casson, Herbert N. *The History of the Telephone*. Chicago, IL: A. C. McClurg, 1910.
Chalmers, Alexander. *The General Biographical Dictionary: Containing an Historical and Critical Account of the Lives and Writings of the Most Eminent Persons in Every Nation; Particularly the British and the Irish, From the Earliest Accounts to the Present Time*. London, UK: self-published, 1812.
Chambers, Robert. *Lives of Illustrious and Distinguished Scotsman, Forming a Complete Scottish Biographical Dictionary*. 4 vols. Glasgow, Scotland: Blackie and Son, 1834.
Christian, George Llewellyn. *Abraham Lincoln: An Address Delivered Before R. E. Lee Camp, No. 1 Confederate Veterans at Richmond, VA, October 29, 1909*. Richmond, VA: L. H. Jenkins, 1909.
———. *A Capitol Disaster: A Chapter of Reconstruction in Virginia*. Richmond, VA: self-published, 1915.
———. *Confederate Memories and Experiences*. Richmond, VA: self-published, 1915.
Cochrane, Robert. *Heroes of Invention and Discovery: Lives of Eminent Inventors and Pioneers*. Edinburgh, Scotland: W. P. Nimmo, Hay, and Mitchell, 1897.
Commons, John R., David J. Saposs, Helen L. Sumner, E. B. Mittelman, H. E. Hoagland, John B. Andrews, Selig Perlman. *History of Labour in the United States*. New York: Macmillan Co., 1918.
Confederate Veteran (Sumner Archibald Cunningham, ed., 1893-1913; Edith Drake Pope, ed., 1914-1932). 40 vols (original forty year run). Nashville, TN: Confederate Veteran, 1893-1932.
Cooke, John Esten. *Mohun; or, The Last Days of Lee and His Paladins: Final Memoirs of a Staff Officer Serving in Virginia*. New York: F. J. Huntington and Co., 1869.
Cooper, Thompson. *A Biographical Dictionary: Containing Concise Notices of Eminent Persons of All Ages and Countries*. London, UK: George Bell and Sons, 1890.
Cooper, William Ricketts. *An Archaic Dictionary: Biographical, Historical, and Mythological; From the Egyptian, Assyrian, and Etruscan Monuments and Papyri*. London, UK: Samuel Bagster and Sons, 1876.
Curry, Jabez Lamar Monroe. *The Southern States of the American Union Considered in Their Relations to the Constitution of the United States and to the Resulting Union*. New York: G. P. Putnam's Sons, 1894.
Dean, Henry Clay. *Crimes of the Civil War, and Curse of the Funding System*. Baltimore, MD: self-published, 1869.
Deitch, JoAnne Weisman (ed.). *A Nation of Inventors: Researching American History*. Carlisle, MA: Discovery Enterprises, Ltd., 2001.
Derby, George. *The National Cyclopaedia of American Biography: Being an Analytical Study of American History and Biography*. New York: James T. White and Co., 1906.
Dickson, William Kennedy Laurie, and Antonia Dickson. *The Life and Inventions of Thomas Alva Edison*. London, UK: Chatto and Windus, 1894.
Dircks, Henry. *Inventors and Inventions*. London, UK: E. and F. N. Spon, 1867.
Doubleday, Russell. *Stories of Inventors: The Adventures of Inventors and Engineers—True Incidents and Personal Experiences*. New York: Doubleday Page and Company, 1904.
Dodd, Bella. *School of Darkness*. New York, NY: P. J. Kennedy and Sons, 1954.
Early, Jubal Anderson. *A Memoir of the Last Year of the War for Independence, in the Confederate States of America*. Lynchburg, VA: Charles W. Button, 1867.
Edmonds, George. *Facts and Falsehoods Concerning the War on the South, 1861-1865*. Memphis, TN: self-published, 1904.
Evans, Clement Anselm (ed.). *Confederate Military History*. 12 vols. Atlanta, GA: Confederate Publishing Co., 1899.
Ewing, E. W. R. *Northern Rebellion, Southern Secession*. Philadelphia, PA: The John C. Winston Co., 1904.
Fitzhugh, George. *Cannibals All! Or, Slaves Without Masters*. Richmond, VA: A. Morris, 1857.
Franklin, John Hope. *Reconstruction After the Civil War*. Chicago, IL: University of

Chicago Press, 1961.
Garbit, Frederick J. *The Phonograph and Its Inventor, Thomas Alvah Edison: Being a Description of the Invention and a Memoir of Its Inventor*. Boston, MA: Gunn, Bliss and Company, 1878.
Gardiner, C. *Acts of the Republican Party as Seen by History*. Washington, D.C.: self-published, 1906.
Gould, John. *Biographical Dictionary of Eminent Artists: Comprising Painters, Sculptors, Engravers, and Architects*. 2 vols. London, UK: Effingham Wilson, 1835.
Green, B. M. (ed.). *Who's Who and Why: 1919-1920*. Vancouver, CAN: International Press Limited, 1912.
——. (ed.). *Who's Who in Canada: An Illustrated Biographical Record of Men and Women of the Time: 1925-1926*. Vancouver, CAN: International Press Limited, 1925.
Gruber, Helmut, and Pamela Graves (eds). *Women and Socialism, Socialism and Women: Europe Between the Two World Wars*. Oxford, UK: Berghahn Books, 1998.
Hale, Edward E. *Stories of Invention Told by Inventors and Their Friends*. Boston, MA: Roberts Brothers, 1889.
Hardie, James. *The New Universal Biographical Dictionary, and American Remembrancer of Departed Merit*. New York: Johnson and Stryker, 1801.
Hart, Charles. *Agriculture v. The Cotton Trade*. London, UK: self-published, 1852.
Hasselberg, P. D. (ed.). *Parliamentary Debates: First Session, Fortieth Parliament, 1982, House of Representatives* (Vol. 445). Wellington, New Zealand: Government Printer, 1982.
Hays, Will H. *Motion Pictures: An Outline of the History and Achievements of the Screen From its Earliest Beginnings to the Present Day*. Garden City, NY: Doubleday, Doran and Co., 1929.
Herbermann, Charles G. (ed.). *The Catholic Encyclopedia*. New York: The Encyclopedia Press, 1914.
Henderson, George Francis Robert. *Stonewall Jackson and the American Civil War*. 2 vols. London, UK: Longmans, Green, and Co., 1898.
Hole, Charles. *A Brief Biographical Dictionary*. New York: Hurd and Houghton, 1866.
Johnson, Robert Underwood, and Clarence Clough Buel (eds.). *Battles and Leaders of the Civil War*. 4 vols. New York, NY: The Century Co., 1884-1888.
Johnson, Rossiter (ed.). *The Twentieth Century Biographical Dictionary of Notable Americans*. Boston, MA: The Biographical Society, 1904.
Johnstone, Huger William. *Truth of War Conspiracy, 1861*. Idylwild, GA: H. W. Johnstone, 1921.
Jones, Francis Arthur. *Thomas Alva Edison: Sixty Years of an Inventor's Life*. New York: Thomas Y. Crowell and Co., 1907.
Jones, John William. *Christ in the Camp: or Religion in Lee's Army*. Richmond, VA: B. F. Johnson and Co., 1887.
——. *The Davis Memorial Volume; Or Our Dead President, Jefferson Davis and the World's Tribute to His Memory*. Richmond, VA: B. F. Johnson, 1889.
Jones, Stephen (ed.). *A New Biographical Dictionary; Or, Pocket Compendium: Containing a Brief Account of the Lives and Writings of the Most Eminent Persons in Every Age and Nation*. London, UK: G. G. Robinson, 1794.
Kamman, William F. *Socialism in German American Literature*. Philadelphia, PA: Americana Germanica Press, 1917.
La Bree, Ben. *The Confederate Soldier in the Civil War, 1861-1865*. Louisville, KY: The Prentice Press, 1897.
Landman, Isaac (ed.). *The Universal Jewish Encyclopedia: An Authoritative and Popular Presentation of Jews and Judaism Since the Earliest Times*. New York: The Universal Jewish Encyclopedia, 1943.
Lenin, Vladimir. *"Left Wing" Communism: An Infantile Disorder*. Detroit, MI: The Marxian Educational Society, 1921.
Leonard, John William. (ed.). *Who's Who in Pennsylvania: A Biographical Dictionary of Contemporaries*. New York: L. R. Hamersly and Co., 1908.

———. *Who's Who in Finance, Banking and Insurance: A Biographical Dictionary of Contemporary Bankers, Capitalists and Others Engaged in Financial Activities in the United States and Canada.* New York: Joseph and Sefton, 1911.

———. *Woman's Who's Who of America: 1914-1915.* New York: The American Commonwealth Co., 1914.

Livermore, Thomas L. *Numbers and Losses in the Civil War in America, 1861-65.* 1900. Carlisle, PA: John Kallmann, 1996 ed.

Macleod, Henry Dunning. *A Dictionary of Political Economy: Biographical, Bibliographical, Historical, and Practical.* London, UK: Longman, Green, Longman, Roberts, and Green, 1863.

Magliocca, Gerard N. *The Tragedy of William Jennings Bryan: Constitutional Law and the Politics of Backlash.* New Haven, CT: Yale University Press, 2011.

Marquis, Albert Nelson. *The Book of Chicagoans: A Biographical Dictionary of Leading Living Men of the City of Chicago.* Chicago, IL: A. N. Marquis and Co., 1911.

———. (ed.) *Who's Who in New England: A Biographical Dictionary of Leading Living Men and Women.* Chicago, IL: A. N. Marquis and Co., 1916 ed.

Martin, Gloria. *Socialist Feminism: The First Decade, 1966-76.* Seattle, WA: Freedom Socialist Publications, 1978.

Martin, Thomas Commerford. *The Inventions, Researches and Writings of Nikola Tesla: With Special Reference to His Work in Polyphase Currents and High Potential Lighting.* New York: The Electrical Engineer, 1894.

Marx, Karl, and Frederick Engels. *Manifesto of the Communist Party.* Chicago, IL: Charles H. Kerr and Co., 1906.

Mather, Frank Lincoln (ed.). *Who's Who of the Colored Race: A General Biographical Dictionary of Men and Women of African Descent.* Chicago, IL: self-published, 1915.

Maunder, Samuel. *The Biographical Treasury: A Dictionary of Universal Biography.* London, UK: Longman, Brown, Green, Longmans, and Roberts, 1856.

McCabe, Joseph (ed.). *A Biographical Dictionary of Modern Rationalists.* London, UK: Watts and Co., 1920.

McCarty, Burke (ed.). *Little Sermons in Socialism by Abraham Lincoln.* Chicago, IL: The Chicago Daily Socialist, 1910.

McClellan, Henry Brainerd. *The Life and Campaigns of Major-General J.E.B. Stuart, Commander of the Cavalry of the Army of Northern Virginia.* Boston, MA: Houghton, Mifflin and Co., 1885.

McClure, James Baird (ed.). *Edison and His Inventions: Including the Many Incidents, Anecdotes, and Interesting Particulars Connected With the Life of the Great Inventor.* Chicago, IL: Rhodes and McClure, 1879.

Meriwether, Elizabeth Avery (pseudonym, "George Edmonds"). *Facts and Falsehoods Concerning the War on the South, 1861-1865.* Memphis, TN: A. R. Taylor and Co., 1904.

Messer-Kruse, Timothy. *The Yankee International: Marxism and the American Reform Tradition, 1848-1876.* Chapel Hill, NC: University of North Carolina Press, 1998.

Miller, Francis Trevelyan, and Robert S. Lanier (eds.). *The Photographic History of the Civil War.* 10 vols. New York, NY: The Review of Reviews Co., 1911.

Minutes of the Eighth Annual Meeting and Reunion of the United Confederate Veterans, Atlanta, GA, July 20-23, 1898. New Orleans, LA: United Confederate Veterans, 1907.

Minutes of the Ninth Annual Meeting and Reunion of the United Confederate Veterans, Charleston, SC, May 10-13, 1899. New Orleans, LA: United Confederate Veterans, 1907.

Minutes of the Twelfth Annual Meeting and Reunion of the United Confederate Veterans, Dallas, TX, April 22-25, 1902. New Orleans, LA: United Confederate Veterans, 1907.

Mottlelay, Paul Fleury. *Bibliographical History of Electricity and Magnetism: Chronologically Arranged.* London, UK: Charles Griffin and Co., 1922.

Mowry, William A., and Arthur May Mowry. *American Inventions and Their Inventors.* New York: Silver, Burdett and Company, 1900.

Muir, John. *The Story of My Boyhood and Youth.* Boston, MA: Houghton Mifflin Co.,

1913.
Muzzey, David Saville. *The United States of America: Vol. 1, To the Civil War*. Boston, MA: Ginn and Co., 1922.
——. *The American Adventure: Vol. 2, From the Civil War*. 1924. New York, NY: Harper and Brothers, 1927 ed.
Neilson, William (ed.). *Webster's Biographical Dictionary: A Dictionary of Names of Noteworthy Persons With Pronunciations and Concise Biographies* (1st edition). Springfield, MA: G. and C. Merriam Company, 1943.
Nichols, John. *The "S" Word: A Short History of an American Tradition . . . Socialism*. London, UK: Verso, 2011.
Nicolay, John G., and John Hay (eds.). *Abraham Lincoln: A History*. 10 vols. New York, NY: The Century Co., 1890.
——. *Complete Works of Abraham Lincoln*. 12 vols. 1894. New York, NY: Francis D. Tandy Co., 1905 ed.
——. *Abraham Lincoln: Complete Works*. 12 vols. 1894. New York, NY: The Century Co., 1907 ed.
Nolan, Melanie (ed.). *Australian Dictionary of Biography*. Acton, Australia: The Australian National University Press, 2021.
ORA (full title: *The War of the Rebellion: A Compilation of the Official Records of the Union and Confederate Armies*). 128 vols. Washington, DC: Government Printing Office, 1880.
ORN (full title: *Official Records of the Union and Confederate Navies in the War of the Rebellion*). 30 vols. Washington, DC: Government Printing Office, 1894.
Palmer, Samuel. *A General History of Printing*. London, UK: A. Bettesworth, 1733.
Perry, Frances M. *Four American Inventors: Robert Fulton, Eli Whitney, Samuel F. B. Morse, Thomas A. Edison*. New York: American Book Company, 1901.
Pollard, Edward Alfred. *The Lost Cause*. New York, NY: E. B. Treat and Co., 1867.
Powers, William Dudley. *Uncle Isaac; Or, Old Days in the South. A Remembrance of the South*. Richmond, VA: B. F. Johnson Co., 1899.
Ramsaye, Terry. *A Million and One Nights: A History of the Motion Picture*. New York: Simon and Schuster, 1926.
Randall, James Garfield. *Constitutional Problems Under Lincoln*. New York: D. Appleton and Co., 1926.
Rawle, William. *A View of the Constitution of the United States of America*. Philadelphia, PA: self-published, 1825.
Richardson, John Anderson. *Richardson's Defense of the South*. Atlanta, GA: A. B. Caldwell, 1914.
Robinson, Henry. *Inventors and Inventions*. New York: self-published, 1911.
Rogers, Thomas J. (ed.). *A New American Biographical Dictionary*. Easton, PA: self-published, 1824.
Rogers, William P. *The Three Secession Movements in the United States: Samuel J. Tilden, the Democratic Candidate for Presidency; the Advisor, Aider and Abettor of the Great Secession Movement of 1860; and One of the Authors of the Infamous Resolution of 1864; His Claims as a Statesman and Reformer Considered*. Boston, MA: John Wilson and Son, 1876.
Rose, Hugh James. *New General Biographical Dictionary*. 12 vols. London, UK: B. Fellowes, 1848.
Ross, Earle Dudley. *The Liberal Republican Movement*. New York: Henry Holt and Co., 1919.
Rove, Karl. *The Triumph of William McKinley: Why the Election of 1896 Still Matters*. New York, NY: Simon and Schuster, 2015.
Rutherford, Mildred Lewis. *Truths of History: A Fair, Unbiased, Impartial, Unprejudiced and Conscientious Study of History*. Athens, GA: n.p., 1920.
Sanderson, John. *Biography of the Signers to the Declaration of Independence*. Philadelphia, PA: R. W. Pomeroy, 1823.
Scharf, John Thomas. *History of the Confederate States Navy From its Organization to the Surrender of its Last Vessel*. New York: Rogers and Sherwood, 1887.

Schlüter, Herman. *Lincoln, Labor and Slavery: A Chapter From the Social History of America.* New York: Socialist Literature Co., 1913.

Shore, Thomas T. (ed.). *Cassell's Biographical Dictionary.* London, UK: Caseel, Petter, and Galpin, 1867.

Seabrook, Lochlainn. *Carnton Plantation Ghost Stories: True Tales of the Unexplained from Tennessee's Most Haunted Civil War House!* 2005. Franklin, TN, 2016 ed.

———. *Nathan Bedford Forrest: Southern Hero, American Patriot.* 2007. Franklin, TN, 2010 ed.

———. *Abraham Lincoln: The Southern View.* 2007. Franklin, TN: Sea Raven Press, 2013 ed.

———. *The McGavocks of Carnton Plantation: A Southern History - Celebrating One of Dixie's Most Noble Confederate Families and Their Tennessee Home.* 2008. Franklin, TN, 2011 ed.

———. *A Rebel Born: A Defense of Nathan Bedford Forrest.* 2010. Franklin, TN: Sea Raven Press, 2011 ed.

———. *Everything You Were Taught About the Civil War is Wrong, Ask a Southerner!* 2010. Franklin, TN: Sea Raven Press, 2024 ed.

———. *The Quotable Jefferson Davis: Selections From the Writings and Speeches of the Confederacy's First President.* Franklin, TN: Sea Raven Press, 2011.

———. *The Quotable Robert E. Lee: Selections From the Writings and Speeches of the South's Most Beloved Civil War General.* Franklin, TN: Sea Raven Press, 2011 Sesquicentennial Civil War Edition.

———. *Lincolnology: The Real Abraham Lincoln Revealed In His Own Words.* Franklin, TN: Sea Raven Press, 2011.

———. *The Unquotable Abraham Lincoln: The President's Quotes They Don't Want You To Know!* Franklin, TN: Sea Raven Press, 2011.

———. *Honest Jeff and Dishonest Abe: A Southern Children's Guide to the Civil War.* Franklin, TN: Sea Raven Press, 2012.

———. *Encyclopedia of the Battle of Franklin - A Comprehensive Guide to the Conflict that Changed the Civil War.* Franklin, TN: Sea Raven Press, 2012.

———. *The Quotable Nathan Bedford Forrest: Selections From the Writings and Speeches of the Confederacy's Most Brilliant Cavalryman.* Spring Hill, TN: Sea Raven Press, 2012.

———. *Forrest! 99 Reasons to Love Nathan Bedford Forrest.* Spring Hill, TN: Sea Raven Press, 2012.

———. *Give 'Em Hell Boys! The Complete Military Correspondence of Nathan Bedford Forrest.* Spring Hill, TN: Sea Raven Press, 2012.

———. *The Constitution of the Confederate States of America Explained: A Clause-by-Clause Study of the South's Magna Carta.* Spring Hill, TN: Sea Raven Press, 2012 Sesquicentennial Civil War Edition.

———. *The Great Impersonator: 99 Reasons to Dislike Abraham Lincoln.* Spring Hill, TN: Sea Raven Press, 2012.

———. *The Old Rebel: Robert E. Lee As He Was Seen By His Contemporaries.* Spring Hill, TN: Sea Raven Press, 2012 Sesquicentennial Civil War Edition.

———. *The Quotable Stonewall Jackson: Selections From the Writings and Speeches of the South's Most Famous General.* Spring Hill, TN: Sea Raven Press, 2012 Sesquicentennial Civil War Edition.

———. *Saddle, Sword, and Gun: A Biography of Nathan Bedford Forrest for Teens.* Spring Hill, TN: Sea Raven Press, 2013.

———. *The Alexander H. Stephens Reader: Excerpts From the Works of a Confederate Founding Father.* Spring Hill, TN: Sea Raven Press, 2013.

———. *The Quotable Alexander H. Stephens: Selections From the Writings and Speeches of the Confederacy's First Vice President.* Spring Hill, TN: Sea Raven Press, 2013 Sesquicentennial Civil War Edition.

———. *Give This Book to a Yankee! A Southern Guide to the Civil War for Northerners.* Spring Hill, TN: Sea Raven Press, 2014.

———. *The Articles of Confederation Explained: A Clause-by-Clause Study of America's First Constitution.* Spring Hill, TN: Sea Raven Press, 2014.

———. *Confederate Blood and Treasure: An Interview With Lochlainn Seabrook*. Spring Hill, TN: Sea Raven Press, 2015.

———. *Nathan Bedford Forrest and the Battle of Fort Pillow: Yankee Myth, Confederate Fact*. Spring Hill, TN: Sea Raven Press, 2015.

———. *Everything You Were Taught About American Slavery War is Wrong, Ask a Southerner!* Spring Hill, TN: Sea Raven Press, 2015.

———. *Confederacy 101: Amazing Facts You Never Knew About America's Oldest Political Tradition*. Spring Hill, TN: Sea Raven Press, 2015.

———. *The Great Yankee Coverup: What the North Doesn't Want You to Know About Lincoln's War!* Spring Hill, TN: Sea Raven Press, 2015.

———. *Slavery 101: Amazing Facts You Never Knew About America's "Peculiar Institution."* Spring Hill, TN: Sea Raven Press, 2015.

———. *Confederate Flag Facts: What Every American Should Know About Dixie's Southern Cross*. Spring Hill, TN: Sea Raven Press, 2016.

———. *Nathan Bedford Forrest and the Ku Klux Klan: Yankee Myth, Confederate Fact*. Spring Hill, TN: Sea Raven Press, 2016.

———. *Everything You Were Taught About African-Americans and the Civil War is Wrong, Ask a Southerner!* Spring Hill, TN: Sea Raven Press, 2016.

———. *Nathan Bedford Forrest and African-Americans: Yankee Myth, Confederate Fact*. Spring Hill, TN: Sea Raven Press, 2016.

———. *Women in Gray: A Tribute to the Ladies Who Supported the Southern Confederacy*. Spring Hill, TN: Sea Raven Press, 2016.

———. *Lincoln's War: The Real Cause, the Real Winner, the Real Loser*. Spring Hill, TN: Sea Raven Press, 2016.

———. *The Unholy Crusade: Lincoln's Legacy of Destruction in the American South*. Spring Hill, TN: Sea Raven Press, 2017.

———. *Abraham Lincoln Was a Liberal, Jefferson Davis Was a Conservative: The Missing Key to Understanding the American Civil War*. Spring Hill, TN: Sea Raven Press, 2017.

———. *All We Ask is to be Let Alone: The Southern Secession Fact Book*. Spring Hill, TN: Sea Raven Press, 2017.

———. *The Ultimate Civil War Quiz Book: How Much Do You Really Know About America's Most Misunderstood Conflict?* Spring Hill, TN: Sea Raven Press, 2017.

———. *Rise Up and Call Them Blessed: Victorian Tributes to the Confederate Soldier, 1861-1901*. Spring Hill, TN: Sea Raven Press, 2017.

———. *Victorian Confederate Poetry: The Southern Cause in Verse, 1861-1901*. Spring Hill, TN: Sea Raven Press, 2018.

———. *Confederate Monuments: Why Every American Should Honor Confederate Soldiers and Their Memorials*. Spring Hill, TN: Sea Raven Press, 2018.

———. *The God of War: Nathan Bedford Forrest as He Was Seen by His Contemporaries*. Spring Hill, TN: Sea Raven Press, 2018.

———. *The Battle of Spring Hill: Recollections of Confederate and Union Soldiers*. Spring Hill, TN: Sea Raven Press, 2018.

———. *I Rode With Forrest! Confederate Soldiers Who Served With the World's Greatest Cavalry Leader*. Spring Hill, TN: Sea Raven Press, 2018.

———. *The Battle of Nashville: Recollections of Confederate and Union Soldiers*. Spring Hill, TN: Sea Raven Press, 2018.

———. *The Battle of Franklin: Recollections of Confederate and Union Soldiers*. Spring Hill, TN: Sea Raven Press, 2018.

———. *A Rebel Born: The Screenplay* (for the film). Written 2011. Franklin, TN: Sea Raven Press, 2020.

———. (ed.) *A Short History of the Confederate States of America* (Jefferson Davis, Belford Company, NY, 1890). A Sea Raven Press Reprint. Spring Hill, TN: Sea Raven Press, 2020.

———. (ed.) *Prison Life of Jefferson Davis: Embracing Details and Incidents in his Captivity, With Conversations on Topics of Public Interest* (John J. Craven, Sampson, Low, Son, and Marston, London, UK, 1866). A Sea Raven Press Reprint. Spring Hill, TN: Sea

Raven Press, 2020.
———. *What the Confederate Flag Means to Me: Americans Speak Out in Defense of Southern Honor, Heritage, and History*. Spring Hill, TN: Sea Raven Press, 2021.
———. *Heroes of the Southern Confederacy: The Illustrated Book of Confederate Officials, Soldiers, and Civilians*. Spring Hill, TN: Sea Raven Press, 2021.
———. *Support Your Local Confederate: Wit and Humor in the Southern Confederacy*. Spring Hill, TN: Sea Raven Press, 2021.
———. *America's Three Constitutions: Complete Texts of the Articles of Confederation, Constitution of the United States of America, and Constitution of the Confederate States of America*. Spring Hill, TN: Sea Raven Press, 2021.
———. *Vintage Southern Cookbook: 2,000 Delicious Dishes From Dixie*. Spring Hill, TN: Sea Raven Press, 2021.
———. *The Bittersweet Bond: Race Relations in the Old South as Described by White and Black Southerners*. Spring Hill, TN: Sea Raven Press, 2022.
———. (ed.) *The Rise and Fall of the Confederate Government* (Jefferson Davis, D. Appleton, New York, 1881). 2 vols. A Sea Raven Press Facsimile Reprint. Spring Hill, TN: Sea Raven Press, 2022.
———. *Secrets of Celebrity Surnames: An Onomastic Dictionary of Famous People*. Cody, WY: Sea Raven Press, 2023.
———. *I, Confederate: Why Dixie Seceded and Fought in the Words of Southern Soldiers*. Spring Hill, TN: Sea Raven Press, 2023.
———. *Twelve Years in Hell: Victorian Southerners Expose the Myth of Reconstruction, 1865-1877*. Cody, WY: Sea Raven Press, 2023.
———. *Seabrook's Complete Battle Book: The War Between the States, 1861-1865*. Cody, WY: Sea Raven Press, 2023.
———. *The Hampton Roads Conference: The Southern View*. Cody, WY: Sea Raven Press, 2024.
———. *We Called Him Jeb: James Ewell Brown Stuart as He Was Seen by His Contemporaries*. Cody, WY: Sea Raven Press, 2024.
———. *Authentic Victorian Ghost Stories: Genuine Early Reports of Apparitions, Wraiths, Poltergeists, and Haunted Houses*. Cody, WY: Sea Raven Press, 2024.
———. *Manmade: Male Inventors Who Created the Modern World*. Cody, WY: Sea Raven Press, 2025.
———. *The Hunter-Gatherer Principle: Evolutionary Biology and the Case for Sex-Based Female Sports*. Cody, WY: Sea Raven Press, 2025.
Smith, William, and Henry Wace (eds.). *A Dictionary of Christian Biography, Literature, Sects and Doctrines*. Boston, MA: Little, Brown, and Company, 1877.
Stark, John. *Biographia Scotica: Or Scottish Biographical Dictionary; Containing a Short Account of the Lives and Writings of the Most Eminent Persons and Remarkable Characters, Natives of Scotland, From the Earliest Ages to the Present Time*. Edinburgh, Scotland: 1805.
Steel, Samuel Augustus. *The South Was Right*. Columbia, SC: R. L. Bryan Co., 1914.
Steele, Matthew Forney. *American Campaigns*. 2 vols. Washington, D.C.: Byron S. Adams, 1909.
Stephen, Leslie. *Dictionary of National Biography*. New York: Macmillan and Co., 1886.
Stephens, Alexander Hamilton. *Speech of Mr. Stephens, of Georgia, on the War and Taxation*. Washington, D.C.: J & G. Gideon, 1848.
———. *A Constitutional View of the Late War Between the States: Its Causes, Character, Conduct and Results*. 2 vols. Philadelphia, PA: National Publishing, Co., 1870.
———. *Recollections of Alexander H. Stephens: His Diary Kept When a Prisoner at Fort Warren, Boston Harbour, 1865*. New York, NY: Doubleday, Page, and Co., 1910.
Sturgis, Russell. *A Dictionary of Architecture and Building: Biographical, Historical, and Descriptive*. New York: Macmillan and Co., 1905.
The Biographical Dictionary of the Society for the Diffusion of Useful Knowledge. London, UK: Longman, Brown, Green, and Longmans, 1843.
The Encyclopedia Britannica: A Dictionary of Arts, Sciences, Literature and General Information.

11th ed. New York: The Encyclopedia Britannica Company, 1911.

The United States Biographical Dictionary and Portrait Gallery of Eminent and Self-Made Men. Chicago, IL: American Biographical Publishing Co., 1877.

Thompson, Holland. *The New South: A Chronicle of Social and Industrial Evolution.* New Haven, CT: Yale University Press, 1920.

Toner, Joseph M. *George Washington as an Inventor and Promoter of the Useful Arts.* An Address Delivered at Mount Vernon, April 10, 1891. Washington, D.C.: U.S. Government Printing Office, 1891.

Traub, Hamilton P. *The American Literary Yearbook: A Biographical and Bibliographical Dictionary of Living North American Authors.* Henning, MN: self-published, 1919.

Warner, Ezra J. *Generals in Gray: Lives of the Confederate Commanders.* 1959. Baton Rouge, LA: Louisiana State University Press, 1989 ed.

——. *Generals in Blue: Lives of the Union Commanders.* 1964. Baton Rouge, LA: Louisiana State University Press, 2006 ed.

Watkins, John. *Universal Biographical Dictionary.* London, UK: Longman, Rees, Orme, Brown, and Green, 1830.

Wheeler, Joseph M. *A Biographical Dictionary of Freethinkers of All Ages and Nations.* London, UK: Progressive Publishing Co., 1889.

Wile, Frederic William. *A Century of Industrial Progress.* Garden City, NY: Doubleday, Doran and Co., 1928.

Wilkes, John. *A Christian Biographical Dictionary.* London, UK: Longman, Hurst, Rees, Orme, and Brown, 1821.

Woodcroft, Bennet. *Brief Biographies of Inventors of Machines for the Manufacture of Textile Fabrics.* London, UK: Longman, Green, Longman, Roberts, and Green, 1863.

——. *Alphabetical Index of Patentees and Applicants for Patents of Invention, for the Year 1870.* London, UK: Office of the Commissioners of Patents for Inventions, 1871.

Woods, Thomas E., Jr. *The Politically Incorrect Guide to American History.* Washington, D.C.: Regnery, 2004.

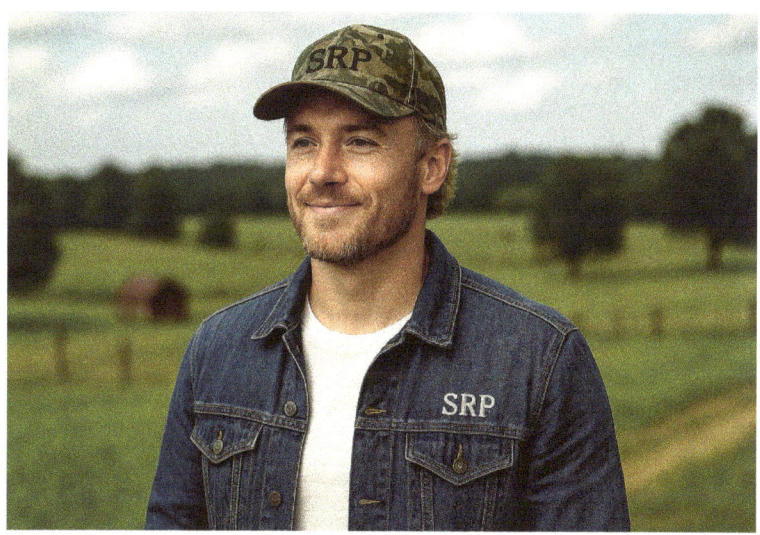

A 30 year old Thomas Jefferson as I imagine him today on his Virginia farm. Copyright © Lochlainn Seabrook.

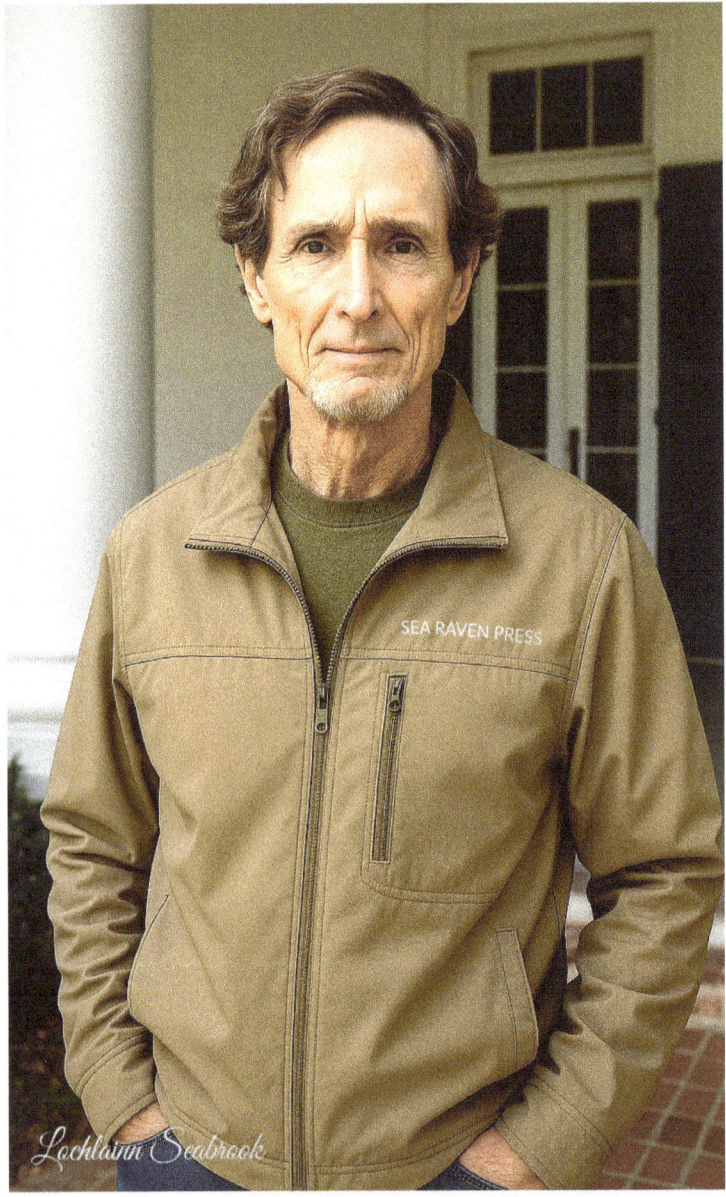

Jefferson Davis as I imagine he might look today standing on the porch of his Mississippi home, Beauvoir. Copyright © Lochlainn Seabrook.

MEET THE AUTHOR

"Bestselling author, award-winning historian, and esteemed nature writer Lochlainn Seabrook straddles multiple genres with ease, seamlessly weaving together history, science, politics, philosophy, and spirituality with the authority of a scholar and the flair of a storyteller."
— SEA RAVEN PRESS

AMERICAN POLYMATH LOCHLAINN SEABROOK is a bestselling author, award-winning historian, and world acclaimed artist. A descendant of the families of Alexander Hamilton Stephens, John Singleton Mosby, Edmund Winchester Rucker, and William Giles Harding, the neo-Victorian scholar is a 7th generation Kentuckian, and one of the most prolific and widely read traditional writers in the world today. Known by literary critics as the "new Shelby Foote," the "American Robert Graves," the "Southern Joseph Campbell," and the "Rocky Mountain Richard Jefferies," and by his fans as the "the best author ever," he is a recipient of the United Daughters of the Confederacy's prestigious Jefferson Davis Historical Gold Medal, and is considered the foremost Southern interpreter of American Civil War history—or what he refers to as the War for the Constitution (1861-1865).

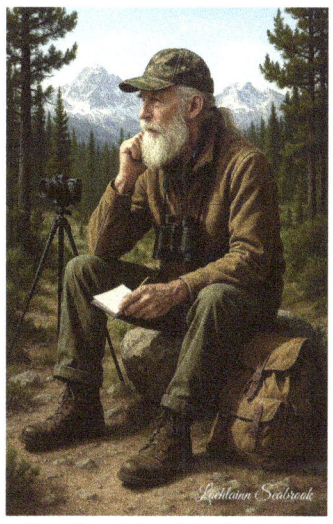

Copyright © Lochlainn Seabrook.

A lifelong litterateur, the Sons of Confederate Veterans member has authored and edited books ranging in topics from ancient and modern history, politics, science, comparative religion, diet and nutrition, spirituality, astronomy, entertainment, military, biography, mysticism, anthropology, cryptozoology, photography, and Bible studies, to natural history, technology, paleography, music, humor, gastronomy, etymology, paleontology, onomastics, mysteries, alternative health and fitness, wildlife, alternate history, comparative mythology, genealogy, Christian history, and the paranormal; books that his readers describe as "game changers," "transformative," and "life altering."

One of America's most popular living historians, nature writers, and Transcendentalists, he is a 17th generation Southerner of Appalachian heritage who descends from dozens of patriotic Revolutionary War soldiers and Confederate soldiers from Kentucky, Tennessee, North Carolina, and Virginia. Also a history, wildlife, and nature preservationist, the well-respected scrivener began life as a child prodigy, later maturing into an archetypal Renaissance Man.

Besides being cofounder and co-CEO of Sea Raven Press, an accomplished writer, author, historian, biographer, lexicographer, encyclopedist, neologist, publisher, editor, poet, creative, onomastician, etymologist, and Bible authority, the influential prosateur is also a Kentucky Colonel, eagle scout, entrepreneur, businessman, composer, screenwriter, nature, wildlife, and landscape photographer, videographer, and filmmaker, artist, artisan, painter, watercolorist, sculptor, ceramic artist, visual artist, sketch artist, pen and ink artist, graphic artist, graphic designer, book designer, book formatter, editorial designer, book cover designer, publishing designer, Web designer, poster artist, cartoonist, content creator, inventor, aquarist, genealogist, jewelry designer, jewelry maker, former history museum docent, and a former Red Cross certified lifeguard, ranch hand, zookeeper, and wrangler. A contemporary songwriter (of some 3,000 songs in a dozen genres), he is also a pianist, organist, drummer, bass player, rhythm guitarist, rhythm mandolinist, percussionist, electronic musician, synthesist, clavichordist, harpsichordist, classical composer, jingle composer, film composer (currently his musical work has been featured in 11 movies), lyricist, band leader, multi-instrument musician, lead vocalist, backup vocalist, session player, music producer, and recording studio mixing engineer, who has worked and performed with some of Nashville's top musicians and singers.

Currently Seabrook is the multi-genre author and editor of over 100 adult and children's books (totaling some 30,000 pages and 15,000,000 words) that have earned him accolades from around the globe. His works, which have sold on every continent except Antarctica, have introduced hundreds of thousands to vital facts that have been left out of our mainstream books. He has been endorsed internationally by leading experts, museum curators, award-winning historians, chart-topping authors, celebrities, filmmakers, noted scientists, well regarded educators, TV show hosts and producers, renowned military artists, venerable heritage organizations, and distinguished academicians of all races, creeds, and colors.

He currently holds two interesting world records: He is the author of the most books on American military officer Nathan Bedford Forrest (12 in total), and he was the first to publicize and describe the 19th-Century platform reversal of America's two main political parties, namely that Civil War era Democrats (primarily in the South—the Confederacy) were Conservatives, while Civil War era Republicans (primarily in the North—the Union) were Liberals.

Of northern, western, and central European ancestry, he is the 6th great-grandson of the Earl of Oxford and a descendant of European royalty through his Kentucky father and West Virginia mother. A proud descendant of Appalachian coal miners, trainmen, mountain folk, and wilderness pioneers, his modern day cousins include: Johnny Cash, Elvis Presley, Lisa Marie Presley, Billy Ray and Miley Cyrus, Patty Loveless, Tim McGraw, Lee Ann Womack, Dolly Parton, Pat Boone, Naomi, Wynonna, and Ashley Judd, Ricky Skaggs, the Sunshine Sisters, Martha Carson, Chet Atkins, Patrick J. Buchanan, Cindy Crawford, Bertram Thomas Combs (Kentucky's 50th governor), Edith Bolling (second wife of President Woodrow Wilson), Andy Griffith, Riley Keough, George C. Scott, Robert Duvall, Reese Witherspoon, Lee Marvin, Rebecca Gayheart, and Tom Cruise.

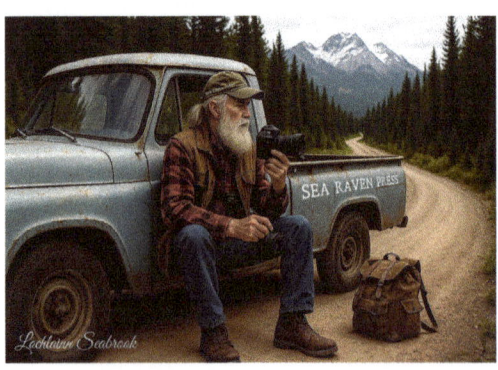

Copyright © Lochlainn Seabrook.

A constitutionalist, avid outdoorsman, wilderness conservationist, and gun rights advocate, Seabrook is the author of the international blockbuster, *Everything You Were Taught About the Civil War is Wrong, Ask a Southerner!* He lives with his wife and family in the magnificent Rocky Mountains, heart of the American West, where you will find him writing, hiking, and filming.

For more information on Mr. Seabrook visit
LochlainnSeabrook.com

Praise for Author-Historian-Artist
Lochlainn Seabrook

Comments from our readers around the world

✭ "Lochlainn Seabrook is a genius writer!" — STEVEN WARD

✭ "Best author ever." — EMILY (last name withheld)

✭ "We get asked a lot what books we use and read. We don't do many modern historians, but we make an exception for some, and Lochlainn Seabrook is one of them. His works are completely well researched from original documents, and heavily footnoted and documented." — SOUTHERN HISTORICAL SOCIETY

✭ "Looking forward to more Lochlainn Seabrook books, my favourite historian!" — ALBERTO IGLESIAS

✭ "Lochlainn Seabrook is one of the finest authors on true history in this century. His books should be on every student's desk." — RONDA SAMMONS RENO

✭ "All of Col. Seabrook's books are great. I have bought most of them and want to end up buying them all." — DAVID VAUGHN

✭ "Lochlainn pulls together such arcane facts with relative ease, compiling these into ordinary prose that strike to the heart with substance, no fluff-speak. I am awestruck! Really. He is an inspiration to me. . . . He is truly a revolutionist. He dares to speak what others whisper; he writes with a boldness and an authoritative knowledge that is second to none." — JAY KRUIZENGA

✭ "Mr. Lochlainn Seabrook is . . . the most well researched and heavily documented author I've ever read. His books are must haves. Everything he writes should be required reading! I assure you, you won't be disappointed. One simply cannot go wrong with his books. Mr. Seabrook is awesome! . . . I have never read any other author as well researched and footnoted as him. I've been in love with Mr. Seabrook for almost 5 years now. His quick wit and logic is enough reason to purchase his books. But the mere fact that he's so extensively researched is icing on the cake. Mr. Seabrook is my favorite, hands down." — LANI BURNETTE RINKEL

✭ "My favorite book is the Bible. Lochlainn Seabrook wrote my second favorite book." — RICHARD FINGER

✭ "I have a new favorite author and his name is Lochlainn Seabrook." — J. EWING

✭ "Lochlainn Seabrook is an incredible writer and I love all of his books on the South. . . . His writing is brilliant. . . . I look forward to reading more of his masterpieces. Thank you." — JOEY (last name withheld)

✭ "It's hard to choose just one of Lochlainn's books!" — ROSANNE STEELE

✭ "Mr. Seabrook, thank you ever so much for blessing us with your most enlightening works." — LAURENCE DRURY

✭ "I recommend anything written by Lochlainn Seabrook." — HOTRODMOB

✭ "Awesome books . . . by a great writer of truth, Lochlainn. Thank you so much. Keep up the great work you do." — WILDBUNCH19INF

★ "I love Lochlainn Seabrook's style and approach. It's not the 'norm.' What a miracle his books are. . . . He is a literal life changing author! Amazing books!" — KEITH PARISH

★ "I adore Mr. Seabrook's style and I love his books. I love an author that does proper research, and still finds a way to engage the reader. Mr. Seabrook does an admirable job of both." — DONALD CAUL

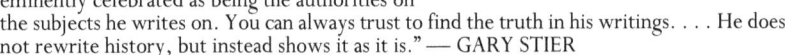

★ "Lochlainn Seabrook's books are much more well researched and authoritative than those eminently celebrated as being the authorities on the subjects he writes on. You can always trust to find the truth in his writings. . . . He does not rewrite history, but instead shows it as it is." — GARY STIER

★ "I love all of Colonel Seabrook's books. They are informative and enlightening, and his warm Southern hospitality writing style makes you feel right at home." — KEITH CRAVEN

★ "Lochlainn Seabrook's work is an absolute treasure of scholarship and historic scope." — MARK WAYNE CUNNINGHAM

★ "Mr. Seabrook's command of . . . history is breathtaking. . . . He deserves great renown—check out his books!" — MARGARET SIMMONS

★ "I love Seabrook's writings. LOVE!!! . . . So grateful to know the truth! Keep writing Lochlainn!!!" — REBECCA DALRYMPLE

★ "Lochlainn Seabrook . . . [has] probably [written] the best book on mental science in existence by a living author. Along with Thomas Troward, Emmet Fox, and Jack Addington, Mr. Seabrook is one of the top four mental science authors of all time, since biblical times." - IAN BARTON STEWART

★ "Glad I discovered Mr. Seabrook! . . . He writes eye opening books! Unbelievable the facts he unearths - and he backs it all up with truth, notes, footnotes, and bibliography! . . . He always amazes me! His books always see the whole picture. His timelines and bibliographies are incredible. He always provides carefully reasoned arguments! He's the best. To me I think he's better than the late great Shelby Foote! America needs more like Lochlainn Seabrook. I can't wait to own all of his books on the war someday. Everyone who wants the Truth, who seeks the Truth and wants the full story, should read his books." — JOHN BULL BADER

★ "I love all of Colonel Seabrook's books!" — DEBBIE SIDLE

★ "Lochlainn Seabrook is well educated and versed in what he writes and I'm impressed with the delivery." — THOMAS L. WHITE

★ "Lochlainn Seabrook is the author of great works of scholarship." — JOHN B. (last name withheld)

★ "Thank you Lochlainn Seabrook for your wonderful books! You are the real deal! You are an amazing author and I love your books!!" — SOPHIA MEOW CELLIST

★ "I really enjoy Mr. Seabrook's books! His knowledge is beyond belief!" — SANDRA FISH

★ "Love Lochlainn Seabrook. Awesome!!" — ROBIN HENDERSON ARISTIDES

★ "Kudos to Lochlainn Seabrook who is a very good and informative professional truthful historian. We need more like him!" — AMY VACHON

LOCHLAINN SEABROOK ~ 253

Nurture Your Mind, Body, and Spirit!

READ THE BOOKS OF

SEA RAVEN PRESS

Visit our Webstore for a wide selection of wholesome, family-friendly, evidence-based, educational books for all ages. You'll be glad you did!

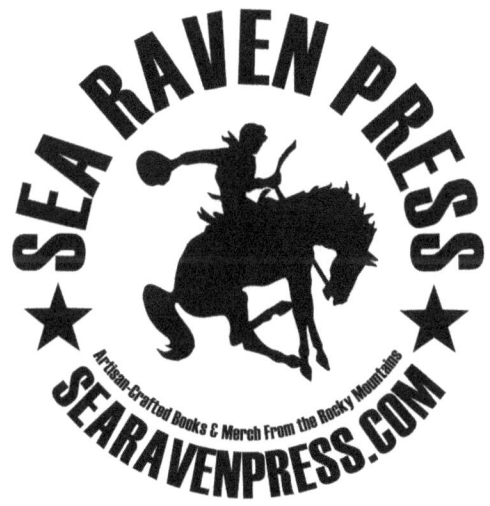

Artisan-Crafted Books & Merch From the Rocky Mountains

SeaRavenPress.com

LochlainnSeabrook.com
TheBestCivilWarBookEver.com
YouTube.com/user/SeaRavenPress
YouTube.com/@SeabrookFilms
Rumble.com/user/SeaRavenPress
AmbianceGoneWild.com
Pond5.com/artist/LochlainnSeabrook

OUR CONNECTION TO THE CONFEDERACY

WHY WE SUPPORT, WRITE ABOUT, & PUBLISH BOOKS ON THE SOUTHERN CONFEDERACY

MANY PEOPLE HAVE ASKED US why we are involved with Southern, and more specifically, Confederate history. The answer is that we are 17th generation Southerners, with deep ancestral roots dating back to Jamestown, Virginia, with associated family tree branches in Kentucky, North Carolina, West Virginia, and Tennessee, as well as blood and historical ties to all of the other Southern states. Like most folks around the world, we are proud of our heritage as well as our ancestors—many who fought for the Confederacy and made the ultimate sacrifice during the South's struggle to preserve the U.S. Constitution (1861-1865).

Of course, being traditionalists and constitutionalists there is far more to our affection for the American South than just ancestral pride. For those who are not aware, the two major parties were reversed in the 1860s: At that time the Democratic Party was the Conservative Party and was made up primarily of right-wing Confederates in the South, while the Republican Party was then the Liberal Party, comprised mainly of left-wing Unionists in the North. (For more on this topic see my book, *Abraham Lincoln Was a Liberal, Jefferson Davis Was a Conservative: The Missing Key to Understanding the American Civil War*).

Thus the South as a whole, including the Southern people and the Confederate States of America, was a *Conservative* body, one that represented:

Americanism, Western traditions, European culture, rugged individualism, self-government, states' rights, agrarianism, a strong Christian worldview, Christian moral values, a Christian educational system, love of family, personal honor, deep ties to the land, nature, and animals, chivalry, military valor, warm hospitality, and resistance to centralized government and industrial modernism; that is, an instinctual inclination toward decentralization of federal power and an unyielding opposition to leftist politics—including modern liberalism, progressivism, nazism, socialism, communism, and Marxism.

This is unaltered *real history*, something the Left does not tolerate or accept. Preferring its own brand of history—that is, revisionist *fake history*—to this end it defamed the proud and noble Southern people, demonized their symbols, slandered their beliefs, and entirely rewrote their history, all to accord with their unpopular progressive ideology, to wit: Western society, along with all of its cultural accoutrements, is evil and must be destroyed—a concept right out of Karl Marx's playbook (*The Communist Manifesto*). Little wonder that conservative Civil War era Southerners correctly referred to the liberal North's attack on the South in 1861 as a "Yankee communist revolution," for thanks to the then Left-wing Republicans, that is exactly what it was.

In short, what you were taught about the South in history class was a sham, manufactured by America-loathing radicals whose only unifying principles are a hatred of those who do not agree with them and a desire to sow discord and destruction. According to they themselves, their "ends can be attained only by the forcible overthrow of all existing social conditions." Bear in mind that it is the so-called "historians" from this extremist "by any means necessary" group who wrote our mainstream history; that is, the accepted canonical history of both the so-called "Civil War" and the United States of America. Should the writings of such individuals be trusted? The answer is obvious.

We take history very seriously here at Sea Raven Press, particularly our family history, our regional history, and our country's history. If you do too, you will find our books a refreshing and uplifting change from the heavily redacted, and thus thoroughly nonsensical, mainstream Civil War propaganda fabricated by those whose only interest is promoting their nihilistic ideologies rather than objective facts. Read our books and discover the Truth for yourself.

If you enjoyed this book you may be interested in some of Colonel Seabrook's other popular titles:

☞ SECRETS OF CELEBRITY SURNAMES: AN ONOMASTIC DICTIONARY OF FAMOUS PEOPLE
☞ EVERYTHING YOU WERE TAUGHT ABOUT THE CIVIL WAR IS WRONG, ASK A SOUTHERNER!
☞ THE GREATEST JESUS MYSTERY OF ALL TIME: WHERE WAS CHRIST BETWEEN THE AGES OF 12 AND 30?
☞ THE CONCISE BOOK OF OWLS: A GUIDE TO NATURE'S MOST MYSTERIOUS BIRDS
☞ WHEN MONSTERS RULED: THE 25 SCARIEST ANIMALS OF THE PREHISTORIC WORLD
☞ UFOs AND ALIENS: THE COMPLETE GUIDEBOOK

Available from Sea Raven Press and wherever fine books are sold

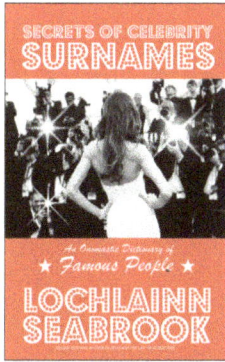
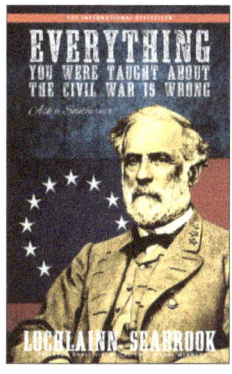
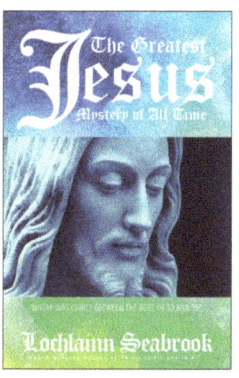
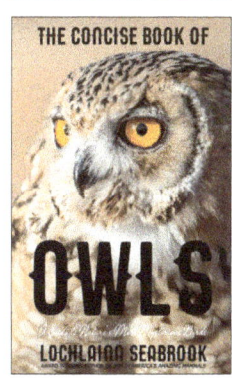
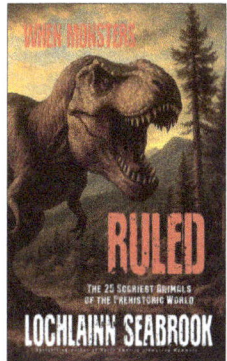
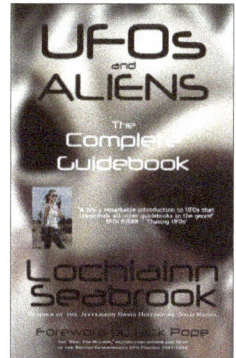

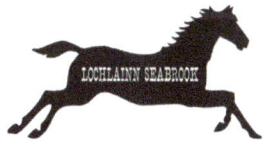

SeaRavenPress.com

www.ingramcontent.com/pod-product-compliance
Lightning Source LLC
Chambersburg PA
CBHW040516220526
45473CB00012B/2877